MADAME
BLAVATSKY'S
BABOON

50 YEARS OF PUBLISHING
1945-1995

MADAME BLAVATSKY'S BABOON

A History of the Mystics, Mediums, and Misfits
Who Brought Spiritualism to America

PETER WASHINGTON

276

SCHOCKEN BOOKS

NEW YORK

The following have given pemission for reproduction of copyright material:
Chatto & Windus and Mrs Lura Huxley for *Ape and Essence* by Aldous Huxley and
The Letters of Aldous Huxley, ed. D. Grover-Smith; Penguin Books Ltd for *Ecce
Homo* by F. Nietzsche; the Society of Authors on behalf of the Bernard Shaw Estate
fot *St Joan*. The author and publishers are grateful to the following for permission
to reproduce photographs: Rahda R. Sloss (1, 7, 9, 29), University of California
Press (2), Mary Evans Picture Library (3), Sotheby's (5), the Hulton-Deutsch
Collection Ltd (8, 13, 16, 27, 28), Philosophisch-Anthroposophischer Verlag (10,
11, 12), the Theosophical Society University Press (14, 25), the Liberal Catholic
Church (26), Commerce Graphics Ltd., Inc. (22), Popperfoto (33).

Library of Congress Cataloging-in-Publication Data

Washington, Peter.
    Madame Blavatsky's baboon: a history of the mystics, mediums, and misfits
who brought spiritualism to America / Peter Washington.
        p. cm.
    Includes bibliographical references and index .
    ISBN 0-8052-4125-6
    1. Theosophy—History.   2. Blavatsky, H. P. (Helena Petrovna), 1831-
1891.   3. Occultism—History—20th century.   4. Spiritualism—History—20th
century.   I. Title
    BP530.W34   1995
    299'.934 '09—dc20   94-28782
                                                             CIP

Manufactured in the United States of America

First American Edition

2   4   6   8   9   7   5   3   1

In nomine Babuine

Huxley, *Ape and Essence*

I do not wish to be a saint;
I would much rather be a clown . . .

Nietzsche, *Ecce Homo*

The Archbishop: Frauds deceive.
An event which creates faith does
not deceive; therefore it is not
a fraud, but a miracle . . .

Shaw, *St Joan*

His glassy essence – like an angry ape,
Plays such fantastic tricks before high heaven
As make the angels weep.

Shakespeare, *Measure for Measure*

for Lucy and Dan

CONTENTS

ACKNOWLEDGEMENTS

I have incurred debts of gratitude to many individuals while writing this book. Some have asked to remain anonymous. Among those who have not, I am grateful to the late Elizabeth Bennett, Charles Clasen, the late Michael Franklin, Seymour Ginsburg, Sir Lees and the Hon. Lady Mayall, Bill Thomson and Lesley Wilson.

My special thanks are due to James Moore, who has unstintingly shared with me his profound knowledge of Gurdjieff and the Work; and to Andrew Rawlinson, who generously showed me drafts of his unpublished work on spiritual teachers. Among many other things, I owe the phrase 'western guru' to him.

I have also received help and information from the Aetherius Society, the Anthroposophical Society, the Church Universal and Triumphant, the Emissary Foundation International, the Eternal Flame, the Great White Brotherhood, the Krishnamurti Centre at Brockwood Park and the Theosophical Society.

Miss Lilian Storey, Librarian of the Theosophical Society, has been especially kind, as have the staff of the London Library, the British Museum and the Public Record Office. I am also obliged to the Warburg Institute, the Williams Library of London University and Middlesex University Library.

My copy editor, Vicki Harris, whose skill and charm make editing a long text that much less onerous, is responsible only for its felicities. The superb index has been prepared by that doyen of indexers, Douglas Matthews of the London Library. Dan Franklin, who commissioned this book, patiently laboured over its various versions and encouraged me at every stage of the work, is acknowledged in the dedication.

MADAME
BLAVATSKY'S
BABOON

INTRODUCTION

The Colour Turquoise

On March 27, 1991, the British football player and ecologist David Icke gave a press conference in London to launch his new book, *The Truth Vibrations*.[1] Mr Icke (whose name rhymes with 'like') was flanked by his wife and daughter and a female colleague. All four were dressed in identical turquoise tracksuits.

Asked to explain the clothes to a group of journalists expecting a sermon on the energy crisis, Mr Icke said that love and wisdom 'resonate to the same frequency as the colour turquoise'. He went on to reveal the existence of a group of 'cosmic parents' appointed over the centuries by God to supervise the evolution of the planet. These parents, also known as Masters of Wisdom, include the prophet Samuel, the wizard Merlin, Christopher Columbus, the Lord of the Seventh Ray, the High Priest of Atlantis, and now David Icke. *The Truth Vibrations* describes their mission to save the world from material and spiritual pollution.

This news conference was a gift to the British tabloid press, especially to the *Sun*, which asked its readers the next day, 'IS DAVID ICKE OFF HIS BIKE?' and '*Do you think David Icke has gone bonkers?*'[2]—a question to which seventy-five per cent of respondents replied Yes. Furthermore, having said that in order to carry out his spiritual task he had been infused with something called 'the Christ Spirit', Icke was accused by reporters of claiming to be the new Jesus, prompting comments from his mother that were later headlined as ICKE IS MY SON NOT THE LORD'S, SAYS MUM.

But although the press had a field day with Mr Icke, he took their jibes in good part, perhaps because he knew something they hadn't thought of. For if three-quarters of interested *Sun* readers thought David Icke deluded, it follows that a quarter did not, which means that a large number of people either share David Icke's beliefs or regard them as perfectly normal. This confirms recent surveys showing that nearly twenty per cent of the British public have experience of unorthodox spiritual doctrines—far more than now attend regular Christian worship—and that many are committed to independent religious groups.

Among Americans, who are both more devout and more spiritually adventurous than Europeans, the corresponding proportion of the population is certainly higher. America is notoriously the land of spiritual opportunity, which is hardly surprising since the nation was founded partly on a rebellion against religious orthodoxy. That rebellion is still fermenting, especially on the West Coast, where David Icke would hardly be noticed among the channellers, astrologers, and rebirthers.

Indeed, one might plausibly argue that the revolt against all forms of religious orthodoxy is now stronger than ever. For the continuing decline of authority among established Christian churches, which began in the eighteenth century and accelerated in the nineteenth, has combined in our own time with powerful cultural and social movements that encourage the emergence of alternative religions and religious teachers.

The most important new forces to affect the spiritual revolution of the twentieth century are ecologism and feminism. The rediscovery of the planet as an organism and the attempt to see it in a wider cosmic context have prompted many thinkers to take the further step of identifying the ecological with the spiritual, a tendency encouraged by the popular enthusiasm for Buddhist and Hindu theology among followers of the New Age.

Many of these followers are women. More significantly, so are many of their leaders. Perhaps this was inevitable in the nineteenth century when spirituality was one of the few domains of life outside literature in which Western women could shine, but it has continued to be the case in our own time. Bypassing established institutions, the New Age has proved a popular route to female empowerment, which may be one reason for its continuing growth, even among the respectable bourgeoisie. Only recently, for example, Arianna Stassinopoulos, wife of millionaire Congressman and would-be Senator, Michael Huffington, argued in her book *The Fourth Instinct*[3] that the world needs cleaning up, both spiritually and physically, and that the two processes are closely connected. There would be no need for a welfare state, she claimed, if we all cultivated our souls, presumably with the help of her own Movement for Inner Spiritual Awareness.

Like *The Truth Vibrations*, her book is also coloured by the tendency of ecological/spiritual synthesisers to emphasise the qualities traditionally regarded as female—empathy, fertility, imagination, instinct, etc.—at the expense of a rational, patriarchal, materialist order identified with God, orthodox religion, and middle-class values. There are other similarities besides. But where do Ms Stassinopoulos and Mr Icke find these ideas and why are they fashionable? Where do the Truth Vibrations and the Fourth Instinct come from? And why do people turn in ever-increasing numbers to such teachers rather than to the established churches?

These are some of the questions addressed by this book, which attempts to answer them by telling the curious story of how Eastern Wisdom was brought to America by a renegade Russian aristocrat with a weakness for the works of a popular British novelist. It describes the invention of the Western guru by the divorced wife of an Anglican clergyman and a pederastic bishop. It chronicles the extraordinary effect their ideas had on cultural, social, and even political life in three continents. It records the transformation of these ideas in the works of an Armenian carpet dealer and a German philosopher. And it traces down to the present a saga that began in a New York apartment on September 7, 1875, when the Tibetan Masters of Wisdom began their spectacular career in the West.

ONE

The Source and the Key

The nineteenth century was a great age of independent spiritual teachers, though most remained at least nominally Christian. Indeed, the restoration of true faith was usually the reason given for breaking away from established churches in the first place. But the habit of authority ran deep, and rebels invariably involved themselves in a paradox by imposing strict obedience and conformity on their followers.

This paradox is beautifully exemplified in the career of the Reverend H. J. Prince.[1] In 1841 Mr Prince, who was Curate to the Rector of Charlinch in Somerset, inaugurated a religious revival within the Anglican Church. An Evangelical clergyman so committed to the principle of divine guidance that he consulted God about taking his umbrella when he went for a walk, Prince was also a considerable orator, gifted with personal charisma and managerial skill. Easily gaining ascendancy over Mr Starkey, the rector, who became his devoted disciple, the new curate went about his mission by preaching with such passion each Sunday that the normally stolid rural congregation of farmers, farm-labourers and their families were driven to a frenzy of religious ecstasy of the sort normally found at that time only in extreme Protestant sects.

Prince's sermons regularly left men quaking, women screaming and even small children in fits. The church at Charlinch was soon notorious and Prince came to the attention of his superior, the Bishop of Bath and Wells, who was not pleased with the behaviour of his curate. Prince's activities were clearly subversive of established order in general and the clerical hierarchy in particular. The rector's submission to his own curate set a bad precedent for the maintenance of authority within the Church, and Prince's inflammatory preaching reeked of Methodism – a creed associated in the minds of most Anglicans with revolutionary politics.

Repeatedly admonished for their excesses by the Bishop, Starkey and Prince left Charlinch and then the Church of England itself. They eventually settled in the nearby village of Spaxton and established an independent religious community known as the Agapemone or Abode of Love. This was financed by rich supporters, mainly women, including the four Nottidge sisters, three of whom Prince married to male disciples. Though her family managed to commit the fourth sister to an asylum before she followed their example, such was Prince's power of persuasion that she eventually escaped to join the others.

Money poured in to the community and Prince was soon in possession of a fortune worth over £1,000,000 in modern values. He built a grand country house at Spaxton for the Brothers and Sisters of his community, and lived in great style there, with a billiard-room, carriages and several footmen. Announcing that he was united with the Holy Ghost and therefore immortal, Prince instructed his followers to address him as 'Beloved' and received without surprise letters addressed to 'Our Lord God'.

The founding doctrine of the Agapemone was the redemption of the body through love. According to Prince this possibility was not catered to in conventional Christianity, which mortified the flesh while attending to the welfare of the soul on the pattern of Christ's sacrifice. But God had revealed to Prince that Jesus, far from being His last word on the subject of redeemers, was only one in a long line of avatars, beginning with Adam and Noah – and culminating in Prince himself. Each of these avatars had been chosen to achieve a decisive stage in the evolution of the divine plan. Christ's task had ended in the agony of crucifixion, but the Beloved had been assigned a more congenial fate. For just as the Holy Ghost had entered into union with Prince, bestowing physical immortality on *him*, so Prince was charged to extend that blessing to others.

He extended it first of all to Sister Zoë Paterson, with whom he publically consummated his divine union on a sofa in the billiard-room at Spaxton before an audience of Brothers and Sisters. Though Beloved had announced an unspecified ceremony in advance, he had not revealed its nature or the name of the lucky girl, and there was some surprise in the community at the outcome. Prince calmed his disciples by announcing that, under the new dispensation, immortality was to be accompanied by sterility, sexual intercourse having become a holy sacrament; but unfortunately Sister Zoë subsequently became pregnant. It was then revealed to Beloved that her baby was a child of Satan, sent to undermine his good work – an explanation which apparently satisfied the disciples. All the same, support for the Abode of Love began to wane after that, and financial contributions from outsiders declined steeply. Prince lived on until 1899, when he was succeeded as Beloved the Second by the Reverend T. H. Smyth Pigott, who announced his own godhead in 1902, subsequently siring two children called Glory and Power.

Prince's success in attracting respectable middle-class followers, despite his strange doctrines and exotic behaviour, is a vivid example of the quandary in which established European religions found themselves in the mid-nineteenth century – for Prince's story was being repeated all over Europe.[2] Churches were in decline. Atheists and materialists attacked them from without. The abuse of clerical privilege and collusion between Church and State exposed them to the criticism of liberals and radicals. Internal squabbles about doctrine and battles between reformers and reactionaries weakened them within. The antiquity, hierarchy and secular power which had for so long been the sources of their authority were now the cause of internal revolt and public disaffection. Putting it simply, the churches seemed to have lost their way and this was reflected in their spiritual lethargy. Even the major independent denominations had rebels within their ranks.

One inevitable consequence was the appearance of independent religious sects on a scale not seen since the seventeenth century. Led by rogue clergymen such as Prince, congregations declared unilateral independence. A new breed of priests and pastors sprang up, armed with radical doctrines and powerful personalities and ready to minister to the spiritual needs of those unsatisfied by the established churches. How could an ordinary clergyman possibly match Prince's exotic appeal to his disciples within the confines of Anglicanism? And how could the established Church plausibly deny Prince credibility when it was itself founded on a revelation not so different from Beloved's? If Jesus Christ possessed divinity, why not Prince? If Jesus was unique, so was Prince. And if the apostle Peter could found a church, why not Beloved?

Such problems of plausibility and authority are as old as religion itself. When revelation is incorporated, the forms created to embody it inevitably obscure the impulse which brought them into being. Parties arise and dispute the interpretation of doctrine. This is invariably complicated by splits between corporatists like the Bishop of Bath and Wells, who demand submission to institutional authority, and charismatics like Prince, who proclaim the validity of their revelation, meeting objections with the point that Jesus too was persecuted. Such disputes are aggravated further by quarrels between universalists in search of a common doctrine, and those who insist on the priority of each individual's relationship to God.

But the nineteenth century brought serious new difficulties. Long-standing doubts about Christian doctrine and arguments about institutional status were intensified by the growing prestige and authority of natural science and the increasing sophistication of biblical exegesis. While technology encroached further on the sacramental sense of a world created and sustained by divine power, advanced textual and historical scholars, drawing on the disciplines of philology and etymology, were demythologising the Bible and humanising the figure of Christ himself. Christianity was reduced in consequence to little more than an interesting tribal story with an influential moral, more or less embodied in Christian legal and political institutions. In such a context Jesus appeared not as the unique Christ, but as one influential teacher among many, together with Buddha, Socrates, Confucius, Manu and Lao Tzu. Some of these teachers were mythical, others historical figures wrapped in a carapace of myth which contemporary scholarship gradually stripped away – a process which suggested that Christianity itself might be a kind of fiction, a transcendent narrative that could still give meaning to each individual's own 'story', without being in any objective sense true. This weakening of Christ's exclusive divine authority made a large enough crack of doubt to let in any number of Princes.

No one of these developments necessarily denies the validity of Christian experience, excludes the possibility of spiritual life or militates against the existence of established churches as such – but together they do unsettle all three. Thus the religious revivals of the nineteenth century were frequently characterised by a tendency to identify 'true' spirituality with mysticism or occultism: the knowledge of ultimate reality experienced as something outside common expressive forms. This was one way of saving the spiritual from the corrupting effects of religious institutions. And while the established churches declined, interest in religion itself was never stronger. The process of unsettling beliefs aroused strong passions; as certainties became doubts, doubts gave rise to new needs. Spirituality itself was not in question, so much as a secure source of spiritual authority. It was this need for authority that made disciples so very vulnerable to charismatic teachers.

The problem of the source was intimately entwined with another nineteenth-century preoccupation, the search for a single key that would solve the mysteries of the universe. A key, it was thought, might unlock the source – while, conversely, the source would provide a key. The idea was not new. On the contrary, explaining apparent diversity in terms of actual unity is the formative principle of most ancient philosophies and religions. But this desire to find unity in diversity became a nineteenth-century obsession in direct proportion to the confusing multiplication of new ideologies. It was proposed, for example, that all human tongues derive from one common language, all races from one mother-race, all philosophies and religions from one original doctrine. Though the two greatest philosophers of the mid-century – Søren Kierkegaard and Friedrich Nietzsche – pointed out that a key and a source were the very things not to be had in a subjective age such as the nineteenth century, they went unheard. The need for belief in primal unity and ultimate authority ran too deep, even among sceptics. Though George Eliot satirises Mr Casaubon's search for a Key to All Mythologies in

Middlemarch, it is clear that she sympathises with the attempt. It is Casaubon's methods that are at fault, not his objective.

One powerful source promised for a while to provide a key to the deepest mystery of all. A major focus of the unsatisfied spiritual hunger which afflicted so many Victorians was an obsession with the rituals and protocols of death, fuelled by uncertainty about the nature – and even the existence – of the afterlife. This appetite was suddenly and startlingly satisfied in 1848 by the Fox family of Hydesville, Rochester, New York, when the two daughters of the house – Katherine (twelve) and Margaret (thirteen) – began receiving what they claimed were spirit messages in the form of rapping and knocking sounds.[3]

The Fox sisters interpreted these messages and replied to them in the same way by means of a simple code, summoning up their communicants with the command 'Hear, Mr Splitfoot, do as I do.' The melodramatic phrasing and the allusion to the Devil in these words might have alerted observers to the possibility of fraud, but Katherine and Margaret soon had a large and enraptured audience. The sisters communicated regularly with their spirit friends, who rapped out apocalyptic news about the dawning of a new era – the sort of news that found a ready audience in millenarian America, susceptible to every kind of new eschatology. There were sceptics who unkindly suggested that the spirit messages amounted to no more than Margaret and Katherine surreptitiously cracking their toes and fingers, but such critics were outnumbered or outshouted by the majority who wanted to believe in the supernatural origin of the Hydesville phenomena. The two girls were soon national celebrities. P. T. Barnum hired them to give public demonstrations; Horace Greeley, Editor of the *New York Tribune*, invited them to stay; and the fashion for seances began.

The seance offers a new version of holy communion, in which faith is replaced by evidence, blood and wine by manifested spirits. It was therefore especially popular among the Protestant sects of the east coast of the United States, deprived as they usually were of any sensuous fulfilment in their religion and susceptible to any sign of the workings of divine grace, however bizarre. It is no coincidence that Hydesville is in the middle of the notorious 'burned-over' district of New York State, so called because of the extraordinary number of religious fashions that swept through it in the early nineteenth century. Spiritualism blends easily with millenarian Christianity: though most of its messages were trivial, the expectation remained that these were merely a prelude to news of real import from the Other World. Having confirmed its own existence through the Fox girls, that world was now expected to come through with the facts about life after death, immortality, and even the future of mankind.

Isolated encounters with ghosts and poltergeists were already common. Their spirit friends told the Fox sisters that they had been trying to 'come through' for over half a century. The novelty of the Hydesville movement was the way in which it became a craze and rapidly took on social, moral and even political overtones. Phenomena hitherto regarded as both random and sinister now appeared to be organised prophetic tidings of a radiant future in which the living would eventually share in the joys of Summerland, the spiritualist heaven. Typically, hell played a very small role in the proceedings. Ghosts were no longer seen as discontented or displaced spirits, but as natural messengers or harbingers. Spiritualism therefore promoted belief in a spiritual brotherhood which watched over human destiny.

Having taken root in America, spiritualism rapidly colonised Europe. In the wake of failing political revolutions in 1848 – the very year of the Hydesville phenomena – it rapidly became part of an 'alternative' synthesis which included vegetarianism, feminism, dress reform, homoeopathy and every variety of social and religious dissent. Many English radicals were favourable, most famously Robert Owen, the utopian socialist, industrialist and founder of New Harmony, and several members of his family. Owen was by now well over eighty, and attracted considerable satire in the press. But spiritualism was also popular in literary circles, always open to experiment, and it had a lasting influence on Bulwer Lytton in England, Elizabeth Barrett Browning in Italy and Victor Hugo in

France. By the time Harriet Beecher Stowe visited Europe in 1853 seances were already all the rage.

If the seance took the place of communion, the spirit medium stood in for the priest, and would-be mediums abounded. It was thought that women were naturally more sensitive to spirit communications, especially if they were uneducated or even slightly subnormal. It was also said that lack of intellectual power cleared the channel for messages to 'come through' at a deeper level. International success, however, was reserved for a man: Daniel Dunglas Home (1833–86), who liked to call himself – with some justice – Medium to the Crowned Heads of Europe.[4] Though Home claimed to be the illegitimate grandson of the Tenth Earl of Home, he spent his childhood in America where he became a celebrated boy medium during the Hydesville craze. A personable, eloquent, slightly effeminate man (his enemies hinted at something worse than effeminacy), he attracted supporters and detractors in equal numbers and with equal passion. One patron, the enthusiastic psychic researcher and pederast Lord Adare, swore that he had seen Home float horizontally out of a first-floor window, pluck a flower from the nearby rhododendron bush and then drift back into the room via another window. Others put the vision down to Adare's credulity and Home's persuasiveness.

Visiting Europe in 1855, Home performed before Thackeray, the Brownings, Charles Dickens and Bulwer Lytton. Robert Browning, like Dickens, took a passionate dislike to him, perhaps because of Elizabeth's enthusiasm, and caricatured Home as the fraudulent 'Mr Sludge, The Medium'. Despite this, Home made a good deal of money. He was taken up by aristocratic society in England, France and Germany, where he impressed even the King of Prussia. His sinister ascendancy over the Empress Eugénie while she was pregnant with the Prince Imperial eventually became so great that Napoleon III's foreign minister threatened to banish him from Paris.

Though most seances were little more than popular entertainment, serious spiritualists hoped that the meaning of their experiences would soon be established on solid scientific grounds – 'science' being shorthand for 'undeniable truth' in the mid-nineteenth century. Indeed, the more fraudulent mediums were exposed, the more their clients pined for hard evidence. As Robert Dale Owen, son of the more famous Robert, breathlessly put it:

> how heart sinking, how utterly unworthy the conception that, under the Divine Economy, that grand privilege of progress to which man owes all he ever was, or will be, is denied to the Science of the Soul inhering in every other.[5]

The quest for scientific proof affected not only convinced spiritualists. Groups such as the London Dialectical Society, the National Secular Society and the more celebrated Society for Psychical Research took a close and often sympathetic interest in the progress of spiritualism. These organisations devoted much energy to collecting evidence and mounting controlled experiments in order to monitor spirit manifestations. But for those in earnest about a serious theory of spiritual science – as opposed to the practical activities of mediums and would-be learned societies – there was already plenty of material available in the work of two early western gurus, Emmanuel Swedenborg (1688–1772) and Franz Anton Mesmer (1735–1815), both candidates in the race to find a Key to Everything.

The child of a Swedish royal chaplain, Swedenborg[6] spent the thirty years of his professional career in the mining industry, but his private passions were science, mathematics, philosophy and religion. A hugely industrious man, he established Sweden's first scientific journal, anticipating a number of modern inventions, including prototype submarines and aeroplanes. He also published treatises on cosmology, lunar measurement, chemistry, physics, the circulation of the blood and sensory perception, and developed a theory of atomic structure which anticipates our own by describing matter as a system of indefinitely divisible particles grouped in swirling vortices.

This theory arose incidentally out of the project to which Swedenborg devoted most of his spare time in later life: an attempt to locate the human soul and to prove its immortality. Concluding that the soul is identical with a life-force which originates from the cortex and circulates in the blood, he embarked on a long course of detailed anatomical experiments to demonstrate his theory, but these were interrupted by a major religious crisis which began in 1743 with a series of dreams – many of them surprisingly carnal – and a vision of Jesus Christ.

Brought up in the devoutest Protestant atmosphere, Swedenborg had a strong sense of sin, exacerbated by guilt about his own ambition to be the greatest scientist of the age and the overwork necessary to realise that ambition. But whatever the causes, the long-drawn-out crisis changed his life. In the following year Jesus appeared once more, instructing Swedenborg to abandon his scientific work in favour of biblical exegesis. This he did, producing more than thirty volumes of commentary and theological argument during the remainder of his long life. His visions were now frequent. He visited heaven and hell, talking with spirits and angels and even with God Himself. He moved easily between material and spiritual worlds, inhabiting the latter through spiritual organs of perception which he equated with intuition and imagination (hence his later popularity with Romantic writers).

This visionary experience gave rise to the theory of correspond-ences outlined in the *Clavis Hieroglyphica*, translated as *A Spiritual Key* and published in London in 1784. Reflecting on contemporary controversies about the significance of Egyptian hieroglyphics and the possibility of a universal philosophical language, Swedenborg suggests that there are three different levels of meaning in any symbol: the natural, the spiritual and the divine. Natural meaning is the discourse of material things, including science and human history. Spiritual meaning refers to the intangible world of ideas and imaginings; while divine meaning leads us to the ultimate reality of God Himself. Each material thing is therefore the sign of corres-ponding spiritual and divine meanings.

The theory of correspondences has important theological and political consequences, notably Swedenborg's conviction that the universe is ultimately a harmonious whole, only temporarily dis-turbed by sin. Rejecting Protestant notions of judgement and damnation, he equated sin with error – an approach which gave his thinking a strongly utopian flavour. His visions had persuaded him that heaven and hell are not future states but permanent realities which we can enter as we choose, and Swedenborg concluded from this that it would be possible to reverse the Fall of Man if only human beings would develop intuition and imagination – their spiritual organs of perception – at the expense of reason. For reason, he believed, is only one of the paths to truth and understanding. He thus weakens the links between science and rationality, returning to an older and broader notion of spiritual science as a complete account of the cosmos achieved through all human faculties and taking into account different orders of reality.

Shortly after his death a number of Swedenborgian churches and societies were established and several still flourish, though Swedenborgianism never became a popular movement. His influence was more directly felt in the work of writers from Blake and Balzac to Baudelaire, Strindberg, Emerson and Yeats. But it had its most potent influence in the many branches of the alternative religious tradition, to which it contributed at least four vital features: the theory of correspondences; belief in the accessibility of the spirit world; trust in the reality of an imminent new political and religious dispensation; and a rapprochement between the various orders of science and religion, imagination and reason.

All four play a part in the work of Franz Anton Mesmer, who developed the theory of mesmerism under the influence of contemporary experiments in electricity and magnetism by Galvani and Volta.[7] Indeed, mesmerism was often known as animal magnetism or electro-biology. Fashionable in Paris during the 1780s, it was swept aside by the Revolution, to be revived in the 1820s, reaching Britain in 1837. With other roots in Swedenborgian notions of 'affinity', mesmerism is based on the claim that bodies are surrounded and suffused with a magnetic force or fluid (the two words are used interchangeably) which the healer (often known as a 'sensitive') can detect and direct at will for therapeutic purposes.

According to Mesmer, illness is caused by obstacles to the free flow of the fluid – obstacles which can be removed by the sensitive making passes with an iron magnet or (in the case of accomplished practitioners) with the hands and even the nose. Cures often involved putting the patient into a trance, during which he would obey orders and even prophesy the future – although it was observed by critics that on other occasions hysterical convulsions accompanied healing sessions, which collapsed in chaos. Claims about prophecies made in the trance state inevitably led to speculations concerning the relationship between mesmerism and clairvoyance. After the master's death many of Mesmer's pupils also claimed to be in psychic communion with him.

Whatever the plausibility of such claims, many otherwise sceptical patients testified to the therapeutic value of mesmerism – including Charles Dickens and the popular writer Harriet Martineau, who took a successful mesmerist cure on Bulwer Lytton's recommendation. The significance of the mesmeric force or fluid in the religious context is its uncertain location between the physical and spiritual worlds, and the particular powers and ethical demands it requires from those who manipulate it. Sensitives must not only possess a powerful magnetic gaze, refined by concentration and self-control: they must also have the good moral character and steadfastness of purpose that provide the practitioner with necessary support for his exhausting work.

Mesmerism also sat well with the craze for phrenology – or 'cerebral physiology', to give it its loftier name – which attempts the analysis of mental faculties and disorders by feeling the skull. Dr John Elliotson, who led the mesmerist revival in England, founded the British Phrenological Society in 1824 and contributed regularly to the magazine which united the two in its title: *The Zoist*, 'A journal of Cerebral Physiology and Mesmerism', founded in 1843. Together with clairvoyance, phrenology and mesmerism formed a powerful trio which prepared the way for psychoanalysis, a twentieth-century 'science' in which the analyst plays the role of sensitive.

The synthesis of Swedenborgianism, mesmerism and spiritualism seemed to pave the way to a spiritual science that would in time provide a key not only to the mysteries of life after death but to the meaning of everything. It was this expectation that provided an impetus for new brands of 'scientific' Christianity, especially in the United States. In America there was already a strong tradition of self-governing religious communities dating back to the nation's Puritan origins and enshrined in the Constitution. As the country's boundaries expanded and immigrants poured in, this tradition was enormously enriched and complicated by the influence of diverse European ideologies.

These new sects tended to fall into two types, one devoted to restoring the purity of Christian doctrine, the other to embodying the will of a charismatic individual whose personal revelation constituted the 'science' on which the sect was based. Sometimes – as in Mormonism – the two factors coincided and a powerful teacher managed to create a new church out of a personality cult embodied in a doctrine. Whatever the outcome, the two things requisite were a man (or woman) and a vision.

Christian Science belongs to the first type.[8] Having suffered a good deal in early life from personal unhappiness and persistent ill-health, largely psychosomatic in origin, Mary Baker Eddy (1821–1910) experimented unsuccessfully with homoeopathy. She was then treated by Phineas Quimby, a healer whose methods were based on mesmerism. Though Quimby effected some sort of cure, it was only a partial success, and when Eddy fell ill again after Quimby's death, she cured herself by reading about the healing miracles of Jesus in Matthew's Gospel. This experience heralded the discovery of Christian Science, described in Eddy's 1875 book *Science and Health* – significantly retitled *Science and Health and A Key to the Scriptures* in later editions. The First Church of Christ Scientist was founded to teach the doctrines of *Science and Health* in 1879.

Eddy, whose teaching follows Swedenborg at many points, rejected the Calvinism of her upbringing in favour of belief in a benevolent god. She taught that illness is error, arising from the mind's radical misunderstanding of reality, and that evil is unreal because God neither creates nor recognises it. The universe is a harmony of forces, and within that harmony only spirit has full existence. The apparent reality of the material world is simply an illusion induced in us by the strength of our carnal desires. Healing therefore requires the renunciation of these desires and submission to divine grace. Salvation requires constant vigilance against the encroachments of our mortal state if we are to make ourselves worthy of Christ. This we can do at any time, if we have the will. Like Swedenborg, Eddy believed that the kingdom of heaven is not a destination in the hereafter but an immediate spiritual possibility for all individuals who can overcome their tendency to identify the real with the material.

Mary Baker Eddy was an ascetic: a reformer for whom purity of doctrine was so important that she was forced to set up her own church in order to preserve it. That church still survives with almost 350,000 members. Although its founder is venerated, the Church of Christ Scientist owes its success almost entirely to its teaching. If forceful and independent, Eddy was no charismatic. At the other end of the spectrum is Mary Baker Eddy's near contemporary Thomas Lake Harris (1823–1906), whose teaching and style of life are strongly reminiscent of H. J. Prince. Harris's personality cult was so strong that the community he founded could not survive his death.

Born in England, Harris[9] grew up in America, where he became an independent preacher in the Universalist Church (which taught the salvation of all believers) and then a disciple of the medium Andrew Jackson Davis. Davis was a Swedenborgian, but he was less interested in that austere master's mysticism than in his theory of divine bisexuality. According to Davis's version of this theory, the male attributes of God the Father and the female attributes of Mother Nature can both be found in the spiritual constitution of all human beings. Harris, who had been left desolate by the early deaths of both his mother and his wife, found consolation in a doctrine that allowed him to locate within himself the female love for which he longed, but he soon repudiated Davis when it turned out that his teacher was preaching bisexual theory as a cover for all-too-heterosexual practice.

Abandoning both Davis and the Universalist Church, Harris tried an experiment in communal living. In 1850 he and a colleague led a hundred followers into retreat on a ten-thousand-acre estate in

Virginia. There they awaited the Day of Judgement as predicted by the twelve apostles, with whom all the members of the group claimed to be in direct communion. A man of imperious temper who reckoned without the sturdy independence of his flock, Harris decided to reinforce his own authority by insisting that in future he alone would mediate between the settlers and the apostles, but his followers revolted against this undemocratic usurpation of their spiritual rights and the community collapsed.

By the mid-1850s Harris had married again and established his own Swedenborgian church in New York, where the congregation included Henry James, father of William and Henry Junior, and Horace Greeley, utopian socialist and patron of the Fox sisters. Here Harris elaborated a new theology which was legitimated, he claimed, by direct revelation from God on the model of Swedenborg's visions in the 1740s. Harris explained to his followers that, although it was given to Swedenborg to open the gates of heaven in his *Arcana Coelestia* of 1757, it had been left to Harris to explain the meaning of that seminal work, which he proceeded to do at enormous length in his own *Arcana of Christianity*, written exactly one hundred years after Swedenborg's book and published in 1858. Varying the tripartite distinction between material, spiritual and divine, Harris explained that Swedenborg had given only the 'celestial' meaning of the scriptures: Harris would now provide their deeper 'spiritual' interpretation.

Spiritual interpretation entailed a number of curious consequences, including the description of life on other planets; the assertion that Harris was the 'pivotal' man on whom the salvation of the human race depended; the belief that synchronised breathing is the key to grace (which may derive from the cabbalistic notion that Creation is a process of divine inhalation and exhalation); a bisexual God; and the analysis of history in terms of three great crises or turning-points – the Flood, the Incarnation, and the appearance of Harris himself. The seeds of all these ideas can be found in Swedenborg, though Harris gives them a Princian twist by boldly placing himself at the centre of the cosmic drama.

But it was the doctrine of counterparts which was to make Harris notorious. This doctrine, which was Harris's version of the Key, derives from Davis's Swedenborgian notion of male and female principles uniting in Man. By the time he produced the *Arcana* Harris's grief over the loss of his mother and first wife had been dispelled by an encounter with what he called his Lily Queen or Queen Lily of the Conjugial (*sic*), an immortal spiritual bride with whom he lived in his sleep at night, no doubt to the surprise of his second worldly bride, Emily Waters. Having found his own counterpart, Harris (like Prince) was eager to help his followers to a similar discovery. This required them to be taken into Harris's close embrace. The force which then flowed out of him produced in them a vision of Christ's love from which emerged their own Lily Queen – or rather, Lily King: for the followers Harris embraced were always female.

In 1861 Harris founded another community, the Brotherhood of the New Life, known to its inmates as 'The Use'. After trying other sites, Harris established the Use at Brocton, on the shores of Lake Erie, and this time he made sure of sole and absolute control. Setting himself up in a mansion called Vinecliff on the shores of the lake, he led the life of a country gentleman together with a few selected women – including Jane Waring, whose money was used to finance the operation, and a Mrs Requa, whom Harris favoured as the nearest earthly equivalent to his celestial counterpart. Everyone at Brocton was given a new name. Harris now called himself Faithful, though members of the community addressed him as Father. Mrs Requa's sobriquet was Golden Rose, presumably in respectful tribute to the Lily Queen. The second Mrs Harris lived apart from her husband, under close supervision; not surprisingly, she was said to be easily upset. The rest of the community – including Mr Requa, a bankrupt millionaire who soon died – slept in sheds and barns, and everybody but Harris, Miss Waring and Golden Rose joined in the hard physical labour necessary to running the place. Even Mrs Harris was deputed to weed the larch plantations.

The community was in reality a badly run farm whose workers were given religious instruction when Harris was in the mood, and their spiritual progress was made dependent on the performance of unpleasant tasks, which conveniently took the form of agricultural labour. Harris believed that pride must be humbled and old habits cast off before the essential self and its true counterpart could be discovered, and he preached the familiar Victorian doctrine of breaking the will and subduing the body in order to renew the spirit. He did not work on the land himself.

Far from resisting such treatment, the inmates welcomed it. As one wrote to his wife many years later:

> [Harris] was better able to bully me than any man I had ever met, and as I needed to be bullied I remained with him until his tyrannies had had the desired effect . . . I had to be broken in, and Harris was chosen as an effective instrument, for a worse, a more unreasonable tyrant than he came to be I never encountered.[10]

Harris was a shrewd psychologist who never touted for pupils and refused to allow rich applicants into the Use until they were ready to beg for admittance and submit absolutely to his will. He also insisted that husbands and wives should share a bed without ever making love, in order to facilitate the arrival of their celestial counterparts. Yet so strong was this tyrant's grip that when he died in 1906 his few remaining disciples refused to believe that their Father could ever leave them, and watched over the body until it began to decompose. The watchers included Miss Waring, who had married Harris, to a great outcry, after his second wife's death in 1895 and spent the rest of her fortune on setting him up in style in California.

Harris and Prince have many features in common. Autocrats who founded communes where they indulged their desires in the name of religion, they nevertheless seem to have believed quite genuinely that they had found the key to the cosmic mystery in the achievement of immortality and enlightenment through mystical union with the beloved. Though taking a gross physical form as they practised it, this doctrine has strong affinities with the teachings of Hinduism and Buddhism, which were slowly becoming more diffused in nineteenth-century Europe, and it is characteristic of the turn eastwards which was affecting many branches of Western enquiry, from philology to the study of religion. Transcendentalism and Unitarianism, for example, are major Christian sects influenced by Vedic doctrines in the unity of all created things and the sole reality of spirit. Both creeds influenced Prince and Harris. Seeking to renew Christianity, the two men thereby stretched its doctrines about as far as they could go while remaining nominally within the faith.

It remained for others to take the process a stage further and release the western guru altogether from the constraints of Christian doctrine by founding his or her teaching primarily on other religious traditions. As we shall see, the most important of these was Helena Blavatsky, considered in the following chapters. But another significant teacher who pointed the way in this direction was Harris's disciple Laurence Oliphant.[11] From conventional beginnings Oliphant moulded under Harris's influence an extraordinary synthesis of Christianity and Islam which appealed even to Queen Victoria. His relationship with Harris was also a model for the intercourse of twentieth-century western gurus and their acolytes.

An upper-class Scot born to evangelical parents in 1829, Oliphant was a brilliant figure in London society and numbered the Prince of Wales among his close friends. Before becoming a Member of Parliament in 1865 he pursued an extraordinary career in business, literature, diplomacy and international intrigue, in the process becoming adviser to several prime ministers, including Lord Palmerston and Lord John Russell.[12]

In 1860 Oliphant met Harris. As he was to record in *Masollam*, his novel about the encounter, published in 1886, long after their estrangement, Oliphant's new acquaintance made an immediate impact on him. At first, he tried to follow Harris's teachings while living his normal life, but it soon became clear that this was not possible. Harris demanded absolute and unconditional commitment; what he had to offer in return was discipline, self-discovery and – at least as far as Oliphant was concerned – a genuinely 'New' life. After visiting the commune, Oliphant decided to abandon his brilliant career and join Harris in the Use, where he settled in 1867.

What provoked such a change of heart? The official reasons are given in another of Oliphant's novels, *Piccadilly*, published in 1865 while he was deciding what to do about Harris. Apparently a satire on fashionable society, it is in fact a story of worldly repentance in which the hero, Lord Frank Vanecourt, closely modelled on the author, emerges from a strange illness to renounce his beloved and forsake society for a new life in America, under the guidance of a mysterious healer: 'one whose name cannot be divulged'. In *Masollam*, published in 1886 after Oliphant's bitter parting with his master, the writer paints a portrait of Harris in the guise of an evil Armenian with extraordinary powers. Both figures are clearly non-Christian, resembling the masters of the Sufis, Islamic mystics who combine the roles of priest, magician and healer.

About the darker reasons for Oliphant's conversion rumoured at the time – Harris's occult powers and his pupil's sexual susceptibility – we can only speculate. Both men were emotionally unstable, both had led wandering, restless lives, and both were unusually close to their mothers – so close in Oliphant's case that Lady Oliphant became an even more enthusiastic convert to the Use than her son, exchanging a comfortable, conventional life in London for the hardships of Harris's American commune. But the deepest reason for Oliphant's conversion seems to have been his belief that the life Harris offered, however hard, would bring him nearer to that elusive source of authority. He also offered a key to the mysteries of existence: when the hero of *Piccadilly* finds his life to be futile, the 'healer' promises to give it meaning.

The life at Brocton was hard indeed, and mother and son became virtual slaves, turning over their considerable wealth to Harris and obeying his every command. Though Lady Oliphant was privileged to live at Vinecliff, she washed and cooked and cleaned for her keep, while her sophisticated son (now known as Woodbine) found himself mucking out stables, heaving barrels, fetching water and unloading bricks, often in a howling winter gale at four in the morning. His nose and fingers were frostbitten and he lived on whatever scraps he could find.

Oliphant left the commune to return to his old life after two years, but Lady Oliphant stayed with Harris; her son remained under his influence, at first combining a social and literary career with attempts to proselytise for his teacher among the English upper classes. The two men began to drift apart in the mid-1870s, but were only finally estranged in 1881. Visiting America to retrieve his fortune from the commune in order to finance other projects, Oliphant found that Harris and Miss Waring had moved to California, leaving the community at Brocton in the hands of a dwindling band of pupils, including Lady Oliphant, now seriously ill with cancer. Despite her feeble state, she accompanied her son to California where they confronted Harris. There was a terrible scene, Father refusing to return the money. Lady Oliphant collapsed shortly afterwards and died six days later.

At this point, Oliphant made a move which was to become archetypal among the disciples of western gurus. Instead of abandoning the religious life in disgust at his teacher's behaviour – and other damning evidence was beginning to accumulate about *that* – he embarked on the separation of Harris's doctrine from Harris's person. Arguing that though the man had become corrupt and arrogant there was nothing intrinsically wrong with his teaching, Oliphant continued to espouse it. In order to do so he set up as a teacher himself. He had long supported the cause of Zionism, so it seemed logical to found a community in Palestine, where he spent the rest of his life, taking a close interest in local varieties of Christian and Islamic mysticism which focus on the notion of union with the beloved, i.e. God.

Here, under the inspiration of the beautiful Alice le Strange, whom he had married in 1872, Oliphant taught the doctrine of sympneuma as described in *Sympneumata, or The Evolutionary Forces Now Active in Man* (1884). Though Laurence put his name to the text, it is probably by Alice, who had become an even more passionate convert to Harris's ideas than her husband. Their book elaborates the doctrine of counterparts and the ideal of an entirely androgynous society in which children will be generated by (unspecified) non-sexual means. *Sympneumata* caused a sensation. The Oliphants' friend General Gordon took a close interest in its composition; and when Oliphant dined with Queen Victoria at Balmoral on a visit to Britain in 1886, the Queen was so interested by what he told her about the book that she asked to be sent a copy.

Alice died soon after the publication of *Sympneumata* and in 1888 Oliphant married Rosamund Dale Owen, the granddaughter of Robert Owen. Rosamund had hitherto devoted her life to lecturing on the importance of purity in marriage, and the couple were less husband and wife than celestial counterparts. The marriage was short-lived. Oliphant died within a few months of the ceremony, whereupon Rosmund retired to the Palestinian commune, where she married a much younger man. When he sank into a depression and killed himself two years later by jumping overboard from a ship, she adopted an even younger man – almost a boy – and lived happily with him amid continuing scandal until her death at The Laurels, Worthing, in 1937.

Towards the end of the nineteenth century it was becoming clear that an enormous and enduring public appetite existed in the West for new and exotic forms of religious belief to supplement or even replace orthodox forms of Christianity. Swedenborg had shown one possible way forward by uniting religion and science. Mesmer and the spiritualists had demonstrated another by opening doors to the spirit world. Interest in eastern cosmologies and the occult was rapidly increasing, and both often appealed especially to those who longed for radical political and social change. But it was not only new doctrines that were wanted. The age cried out for charismatic priests, and where it did not find them politicians and writers tried to take their place. There *were* powerful religious teachers outside the established churches, such as Prince, Harris and Oliphant, but they put their novel doctrines into practice only on the small scale. Christian Science and Mormonism, however, proved that there was scope for new mass religions, and that even women could become major prophets in that chauvinist age. All that remained, therefore, was for one individual to appear who combined the personal authority of Harris and Prince and the mass appeal of Eddy with a new doctrine synthesising elements from all the radical alternatives, and the era of the western guru could begin.

TWO

Maloney and Jack

Photographs are not always revealing, especially those posed nineteenth-century portraits in which the sitters are clearly expected to conform to certain models: the dashing youth, the masterful husband, the loving wife. But Helena Blavatsky's character shines through hers: a short, stout, forceful woman, with strong arms, several chins, unruly hair, a determined mouth, and large, liquid, slightly bulging eyes. In her most typical photographs she looks straight out of the picture with the air of a woman used to confronting difficulties and getting her own way. Yet there is also a strong hint of melancholy in the heavy features. This is a pugnacious face which has been through a good deal.

Heavily bearded and bespectacled like any Victorian paterfamilias, Henry Olcott is at first more inscrutable. Though some photographs show him looking rather foolish, this could easily be the fault of the picture, not the man. In one joint portrait with Blavatsky, she leans eagerly forward to stare at the camera while he holds back. His pose is awkward, his look inward and hesitant. Beside her – and possibly because of her – he is clearly unsure of himself. Though taller, he looks less robust than his companion, whose shoulders are just as broad. His finer features suggest a more ascetic life – especially when compared with her solid torso.

This picture reflects the nature of their relationship. Perhaps it also points to their contrasting backgrounds, for they reached the same point by very different routes. Each is in certain ways characteristic of sharply distinguished national and social cultures: Blavatsky the idle Russian aristocrat turned rebellious religious teacher, Olcott the earnest American bourgeois in search of spiritual truth. At least, those were the images they were both happy to present to the world. How much truth was there behind them?

Olcott was born in 1832 to a New Jersey family claiming descent from the pilgrims.[1] After a strict Presbyterian upbringing, what he calls 'financial difficulties' (a familiar feature in theosophical biographies) forced him to cut short his education and take up farming in Ohio. There he became an expert on agriculture, publishing several books on the subject, including a treatise on sorgho and imphee (two substitutes for sugar cane) which went into seven editions. Declining the Greek government's call to the chair of scientific agriculture at Athens, he set up instead the Westchester Farm School. The venture failed, and Olcott went to work in 1859 as Agricultural Editor of the *New York Tribune*, but his career was again interrupted, this time by the Civil War, which turned him into a signals officer in the Union Army.

Invalided out, he became Special Commissioner to the War Department with the rank of colonel and the task of investigating profiteers. So successful were his investigations that when Abraham Lincoln was assassinated in 1865 Olcott became a member of the three-man board appointed to look into the President's death. Resigning his commission at the end of hostilities with commendations from the Secretary for War and the Judge Advocate General, he then read for the Bar in New York, setting up his own practice there in the late 1860s.

By any standards this is an interesting and varied early career, but it was followed by disappointment. Though reasonably prosperous, his law practice was not especially distinguished and his marriage was unhappy, despite the birth of four children. Eventually divorced from his wife, Olcott found consolation and amusement in spiritualism. He had developed an interest in 'the Other World' when learning to farm in Ohio, where he joined the Freemasons and dabbled in mesmerism and spiritual healing. Now he followed the New York spiritualist press.

Bored with his work one dull day in 1874, Olcott went to buy a copy of the *Banner of Light* from the corner shop near his office. A popular spiritualist paper, the *Banner* carried a story about psychic manifestations on a farm belonging to the Eddy family at Chittenden in Vermont, where spirits were materialising in extraordinary numbers. After a relative decline in popularity during the 1860s, spiritualism was undergoing one of its periodic American revivals, and Chittenden was very much the centre of interest. An occasional contributor to spiritualist journals himself, the colonel decided to enliven the dull New York summer with a trip to Vermont, where he could exercise his old investigative skills. During August and September 1874, he visited the farm several times, contributing articles to a New York paper, the *Daily Graphic*, about what he had seen.

There was plenty to see.[2] Mary Eddy, whose Scottish great-great-great-grandmother had allegedly been hanged as a witch, possessed second sight, and all her children – William, Mary and Horatio – inherited psychic gifts, including levitation and the ability to materialise spirits. These activities, which appeared to be involuntary, could also be awkward. No sooner were the children tucked into bed at night, for example, than they tended to float up to the ceiling. At school they were constantly surrounded by spirits banging on their desks, while at home disturbing apparitions threw them into permanent hysterics.

The most remarkable of the three was William, who turned his powers to good account by staging regular public performances at the farm for audiences of up to thirty people. Hidden in a closed cabinet on a platform at one end of a large seance-room (known to clients as 'the ghost shop'), he produced a stream of phenomena amounting to a minor vaudeville. The spirit visitors included three Indian squaws – Honto, Daybreak and Bright Star – a number of recently deceased white men, and two dead children belonging to a German lady who seemed to be a permanent member of the audience. All the apparitions hovered briefly before a curtain drawn across the cabinet in which William sat. Some spoke, most did not. Others sang and danced and two fought a duel with swords.

William's place was sometimes taken by his brother Horatio, who was assisted by a spirit guide called George Dix. George was never seen but only heard, which was perhaps just as well, since he chaffed the audience and told them vulgar stories. But his full-scale performances, which took place in the dark, included the summoning of a whole band of Indians to play a popular piece of contemporary music, *The Storm At Sea* – which seems a curiously mundane choice for Indian spirits who presumably had access to their own tunes, or even to the music of the spheres. Perhaps the fact that the German lady's husband was a musician who knew this piece well had something to do with it.

Olcott was torn. On the one hand the whole business – down to the cold lips of an invisible figure who kissed his cheek in the dark – struck him as convincing. The kiss was positively clammy, as befits a spectral embrace. On the other hand, he was determined not to be taken in, and returned to the farm several times to check his first impressions. It was on one of these occasions that he met Madame Blavatsky at the farmhouse, on 14 October 1874. She had come specially to visit him, she said, attracted to Vermont by Olcott's articles in the *Graphic*, just as his original visit had been prompted by the *Banner*. It is typical of Blavatsky's energy, enterprise and strength of purpose that, after only a short time in America, she should have made the effort to visit Chittenden in order to meet and befriend Olcott. The meeting was to prove fruitful.

If Olcott's life and background were utterly mundane, Helena Petrovna Blavatsky's were anything but. Her father, Baron von Hahn, belonged to the lesser Russian-German nobility which had provided much of the administrative and military élite in nineteenth-century Russia. Her mother was a romantic novelist descended from a much grander noble house, the Dolgoroukys. Despite their aristocratic descent, the von Hahns lived an unsettled life. The baron was a soldier and often on the move with his regiment. Madame von Hahn followed with the children, whose life was disordered further when she died. Helena, born in 1831, was just eleven when she lost her mother. Though they spent much of the time after their mother's death with their grandparents, the von Hahn children had a vagrant upbringing, with more excitement than security.[3]

Helena was a wayward, imaginative child in a confusing and exotic world, as she told her later biographer:

> My childhood? Spoilt and petted on one side, punished
> and hardened on the other. Sick and ever dying til seven or
> eight, sleep-walker; possessed by the devil. Governesses
> two . . . Nurses – any number . . . One was half a Tartar.
> Father's soldiers taking care of me . . . Lived in Saratow
> when grandfather was Civil Governor, before that in
> Astrachan, where he had many thousands (some 80 or
> 100,000) Kalmuck Buddhists under him.[4]

She was a keen reader and writer and became a more than competent pianist, but she was easily bored, and her sister later remembered how

> Helena used to dream aloud, and tell us of her visions,
> evidently clear, vivid, and as palpable as life to her . . . It
> was her delight to gather around herself a party of us
> younger children, at twilight, and after taking us into the
> large dark museum, to hold us there, spellbound, with her
> weird stories. Then she narrated to us the most
> inconceivable tales about herself; the most unheard of
> adventures of which she was the heroine, every night, as
> she explained. Each of the stuffed animals had taken her in
> turn into its confidence, had divulged to her the history of
> its life in previous incarnations or existences.[5]

Her sister also remarks that Helena later lost her powers of eloquence and invention. Evidently Madame Jelihovsky was teasing, lying or being discreet. For though Helena became lazy in middle age, she was to remain a persuasive story-teller, whose power to fascinate others against formidable odds remained intact almost to the end. This power derived from her childhood urge to create a world of her own, which she then persuaded others to accept; it also made her self-absorbed and egotistical.

Hard facts about Helena von Hahn's life before her arrival in America are hard to come by. That she married Nikifor Blavatsky, Vice-Governor of Yerevan in the Caucasus, on 7 July 1848, when she was seventeen and he just over forty, is certainly a matter of record, as is her flight from him a few weeks later. But from that moment on, myth and reality begin to merge seamlessly in Bla-

vatsky's biography. Typically, as the years passed and she retold the
story of her first marriage, the age gap widened, until the general
became in fancy an antique lecher in pursuit of a barely pubescent
girl. What remains true is that the marriage was a failure, and that
by October 1848 Helena was on the run from her new husband. Her
father agreed to take her back and servants were sent to fetch the
girl, but something persuaded Helena that she wanted neither
father nor husband. Boarding a steamer on the Black Sea to return
home, she evaded her escort and sailed instead for Constantinople
and freedom, in a caprice which foreshadows her whole career.

Until she arrived in America twenty-five years later, Blavatsky's
life (as narrated to friends and would-be biographers) makes a series
of anecdotes which are tall enough to provoke disbelief without
being entirely incredible. Periodically reappearing in Russia to visit
her sister, she spent the intervening years travelling through
Europe, Asia and the Americas. Quite how she supported herself is
not clear, though she may have had an allowance from her father
and seems to have set up as an itinerant spirit medium. She also
claimed to have ridden bareback in a circus, toured Serbia as a
concert pianist, opened an ink factory in Odessa, traded as an
importer of ostrich feathers in Paris, and worked as interior
decorator to the Empress Eugénie.

She may or may not have had lovers, including the German Baron
Meyendorf, the Polish Prince Wittgenstein and a Hungarian opera
singer, Agardi Metrovitch. All these names were linked with hers,
though she sometimes denied the liaisons and sometimes hinted that
they were true – an equivocation which became important only
when her enemies taxed her with promiscuity. Their main target
was Metrovitch, whom Blavatsky claimed to have rescued from
assassins when she found him dying in an alley (in Cairo or in
Constantinople, according to which version you prefer). She may
have borne a child by this man, though the medical evidence cited
by Blavatsky herself is against it.[6]

That such matters should become controversial issues – that her
whole life and character should become occasions for bitter dispute
– is characteristic of a woman who was to court publicity without
understanding how to manage it. Blavatsky talked brilliantly and

indiscreetly about herself, but rarely said exactly the same thing twice. The speculative outline of her life as later assembled by her great-nephew and others includes meetings with Red Indians in Canada and the United States in 1850 and 1851; a covered wagon journey across the Middle West of America in 1854; fighting with Garibaldi's army in the Battle of Mentana (1867), when she was wounded by both sabre-blows and bullets; and shipwreck at Spetsai off the Greek coast in 1871, when the *Eumonia* was blown up and many passengers lost. Between these events she is said to have dealt with cabbalists in Egypt, secret agents in Central Asia, voodoo magicians in New Orleans and bandits in Mexico.

None of this is impossible, and Blavatsky's stories are backed up with convincing details and the odd date, until it becomes impossible to distinguish between truth and falsehood. In the end, perhaps the distinction hardly matters. What counts is that she could persuade enough people to accept her version of events for her purposes, even when reason was telling them not to. Several of her later followers even found themselves in the paradoxical situation of trusting the teller though they didn't believe the tale. And although few of Blavatsky's claims are verifiable, it must be said that the nineteenth century is prodigal in extraordinary lives and remarkable travels. Nor would she have been the first European woman to venture into the heart of a dark continent with only an umbrella and supreme self-confidence to support her. If the stories strike us as preposterous taken together, each narrative is just credible on its own, allowing for legitimate hyperbole. Each, that is, except the most important. For the central event of her *Wanderjahre* – and therefore of modern esoteric history – was a meeting with a dematerialising Tibetan by the name of Master Morya.

It was a favourite boast of Blavatsky's that she had travelled alone in Tibet and lived there for more than seven years. The significance of this claim rests on the traditional belief that seven years is the period of apprenticeship for candidates seeking initiation into esoteric mysteries. Blavatsky became a celebrity by claiming that, not only had she been 'chosen' to reach the highest level of initiation in the occult hierarchy permitted to human beings, but that she owed her advancement to certain 'Himalayan Masters' with whom she had studied in their mountain homes.

As it happens, two British Army officers serving in the area testified after Blavatsky's death that they had seen or heard of a white woman travelling alone in the Tibetan mountains in 1854 and 1867 respectively.[7] This is highly improbable. Even after the Younghusband expedition of 1903, Tibet remained closed to all but a very few travellers, whose movements were closely monitored by the Tibetans themselves and by Chinese, Russian and British missions patrolling the borders and alert to the presence of military spies in the region.[8] And if there was such a white female traveller, she has never been positively identified with Blavatsky. But perhaps the strongest argument against the idea is a practical one: the thought of the breathless, tactless and massively stout Blavatsky managing to climb steep mountains in brutal weather while concealing herself from trained observers is just too difficult to imagine.

Whether real or imagined, Blavatsky's trips to Tibet were to take on considerable significance as the romantic and religious symbolism of that country increased in the late nineteenth century, in direct proportion to its perceived remoteness. The process took some curious turns. In 1894 Blavatsky's fellow-countryman N. A. Notovitch claimed in *The Unknown Life of Jesus Christ* that Jesus had spent several years in Tibet acquiring the doctrines of esoteric Buddhism, which he later transmitted to his disciples in coded form. The notion that the founder of Christianity had travelled in Central Asia,[9] thus linking him with both Buddhist and Hindu traditions, was to prove attractive to all those, like Blavatsky herself, who dreamt of a syncretism of the great faiths in one world wisdom religion; and to those who, for more sinister reasons, wanted to detach Jesus from his Jewish origins. It was also symptomatic of the way in which the centre of religious gravity was shifting eastwards. Medieval European maps put Jerusalem at the spiritual heart of the world. By 1900 that honour fell to Lhasa. The near-immortal sages of Shangri-La in James Hilton's *Lost Horizon* (1933) are based on a well-established mythology.

As we shall see, the popularity of such mythology was in large part to be the work of Blavatsky herself, though her first meeting with the being she called Master Morya took place not in the Himalayan wilderness but amid the urban sprawl of London's Great Exhibition in July 1851. She had seen Morya in visions many times before 1851, she said, but this was her first encounter with him in the flesh (or whatever counts as flesh for a creature who can dematerialise at will). That, at least, is the interpretation she was to put on an entry in her diaries which reads: 'Nuit mémorable. Certaine nuit par un clair de lune qui se couchait à – Ramsgate, 12 Août,* 1851 – lorsque je rencontrai le Maître de mes Rêves.'[10] When a helper going through Blavatsky's papers thirty years later came across this passage, her mistress explained the words as a description of the meeting with Morya, accounting for the change of place as a 'blind' in case anyone hostile should chance upon the book. Ramsgate is certainly an inspired choice if it was meant to dampen interest. As for the ambiguity of the phrase 'Maître de mes Rêves', readers must make of it what they can.

But who was Master Morya? According to Blavatsky, he belonged to the Great White Brotherhood of Masters or Mahatmas. These Brothers, Masters or Mahatmas (Blavatsky uses all three terms) are Adepts or Initiates: beings whose rigorous esoteric training and absolute purity have invested them with supernatural powers. Immortal and immaterial, the Masters can inhabit material or semi-material bodies at will (this point is not quite clear) and possess powers which enable them to move about the universe exercising their thaumaturgic and clairvoyant skills. Communicating with one another by means of a sort of cosmic radio, they form a link between human beings and the chiefs of the divine hierarchy which rules the cosmos.

According to Blavatsky's later description of the Brotherhood, this hierarchy is headed by the Lord of the World, who lives at Shamballa in the Gobi desert.[11] The Lord of the World came originally from Venus with several helpers and now inhabits the body of a sixteen-year-old boy. In descending order of authority, his helpers are the Buddha, the Mahachohan, Manu and Maitreya.

---

*31 July in the old Russian calendar.

Manu and Maitreya each have an assistant, and these assistants are the two Masters who were to play a vital role in Blavatsky's life and in the foundation of the Theosophical Society.

Manu's assistant is Blavatsky's original visitor, Master Morya, often referred to as Master M or simply M. His special duty in the distribution of cosmic responsibilities is to preside over the qualities of Power and Strength, with particular regard to the guidance of nations. As befits his task, Morya assumes the dark, powerful body of a Rajput prince and lives in a secluded Tibetan valley.

Maitreya's assistant is Master Koot Hoomi – also known as Master KH or KH – whose past incarnations include Pythagoras. KH has the body of a fair Kashmiri brahmin with blue eyes. He is a cultured fellow, a linguist and musician whose work takes in the supervision of Religion, Education and Art. Having attended the University of Leipzig, he spends much time meditating and is well qualified to look after the vast Occult Museum in underground chambers near his home, which is located in the same valley as Master Morya's.

Other Masters include Jesus, a 'Syrian' who rather confusingly has responsibility for all religions, not merely Christianity; the Hungarian Prince Rakoczi – also known as the Comte de Saint-Germain – who presides over Magic and whose previous incarnations included both Roger and Francis Bacon; Hilarion, a handsome Greek in charge of Science; Serapis, an even handsomer, golden-haired, blue-eyed Greek who has Beauty in his remit; and the Venetian Master, who is the handsomest of all. Much lower down the hierarchy there is the Master Dwaj Khool, who does celestial odd jobs.

In addition, the Brotherhood of Masters includes all great religious leaders and occult teachers of the past. Buddha, Confucius, Solomon, Lao Tzu, Boehme, Roger Bacon, Francis Bacon, Cagliostro, Mesmer, Abraham, Moses and Plato are all members. Below them (descending now to the human steps in this occult ladder) are the arhats – postulants for Mastership who have reached an intermediate level of initiation – and their disciples, known as chelas.

According to Blavatsky, the Brotherhood usually remains hidden from all but a few. When its members attempt to transmit their doctrines through human agents, these agents are rarely believed and often persecuted by human beings under the influence of malign powers variously known as the Dark Forces or Lords of the Dark Face. For that reason the Brothers work in secret to direct the destiny of the cosmos, and to preserve it from the evil influence of the Dark Forces. Occasionally the war between Lords and Brothers reaches a violent public climax in events such as the crucifixion of Jesus, when the esoteric becomes exoteric and the secret struggle is briefly revealed. But for those who understand, all human history has an esoteric meaning.

This cosmology was elaborated over a period of fifteen years, from the mid-1870s to the time of Blavatsky's death in 1891. But where did she find Koot Hoomi and the rest? It seems likely that there were two main sources for the idea of a Hidden Brotherhood: the plural divinities of Eastern religions and the mythologies of Western esotericism. The study of Asian religion had been proceeding in Europe since the late eighteenth century, when the Royal Asiatic Society was formed in London and Hindu scriptures were translated into French and English. By the 1870s German scholars were producing magnificent editions and translations of the Hindu *Vedas* and major Buddhist texts.

Though by no means a scholar, Blavatsky was a considerable autodidact who read widely if erratically in Asian scriptures. In sharp contrast to the monotheism of Jews, Christians and Muslims, Hindus and Buddhists are polytheistic: they worship multiple divinities, each assigned a role in the cosmic plan. A central feature of their religious practice is the notion of Adepthood (*mahatma* is Sanskrit for adept), whereby an individual can acquire great occult powers by training and devotion. In Blavatsky's thinking, most (though not all) Masters are former Adepts who have evolved to a very high level.

Her immediate source for this idea in Western esotericism was almost certainly the English novelist Edward Bulwer Lytton (1803–73), whose work she knew well. It would not be unjust to say that her new religion was virtually manufactured from his pages. For as one of Bulwer's own characters remarks (in lines which seem to anticipate that great occultist and Blavatsky disciple W. B. Yeats): 'In dreams commences all human knowledge; in dreams hovers over measureless space the first faint bridge between spirit and spirit – this world and the worlds beyond . . .'[12] Blavatsky's dreams were to produce the major esoteric revival in modern times.

Bulwer Lytton was no mere novelist.[13] He also had a successful career in politics, entering Parliament in 1831 and becoming Colonial Secretary in 1858 (for which he was rewarded with a peerage as Lord Lytton in 1866). But he is remembered now, if at all, as a writer. His early stories belong to the aristocratic school of fashionable romances known as 'silver-fork' novels. The heroes are criminal dandies in the style of Byron or Balzac. He then turned to writing historical fiction, including *The Last Days of Pompeii* (1834), and domestic sagas of middle-class manners. Hugely successful in everything he attempted, Bulwer Lytton attracted the envy, admiration and even imitation of such major writers as Dickens and Thackeray; but the books of his own which pleased him most were the occult romances *Zanoni* (1842) and *A Strange Story* (1862).

Bulwer was widely read in alchemy and neo-Platonism and familiar with the work of Boehme, Swedenborg and Mesmer. His occult stories bring a working knowledge of contemporary science and ancient magic, a vivid imagination and a gift for narrative to bear on the Byronic formula of the hero with a dark secret. What attracted him about magic were the analogies with modern science. Both were methods for achieving power over nature, but whereas science was testable magic was not. A cautious, sceptical man who declined to believe in most of the phenomena so luridly described in his own novels (though he predicted the discovery of atomic energy with surprising accuracy), he nevertheless thought it quite possible that science might eventually validate certain occult claims to powers such as extra-sensory perception and prophecy.

Pursuing this idea, he took part in magical experiments with his friend, the unfrocked French priest Eliphas Lévi (1810–75).[14] Lévi – whose real name was Alphonse-Louis Constant – had inaugurated an occult revival in France. He taught the existence of a 'secret doctrine' which unites all magical and religious systems, and his writings draw heavily on Eastern sources, especially Hindu scriptures. The result is a blend of orientalism and occultism which excited Bulwer and then Blavatsky: both were especially struck by Lévi's theory that the transmitters of the secret doctrine are long-lived Adepts possessing magical powers.

Bulwer's novel *Zanoni* concerns a painter and his encounters with two characters who are human yet immortal, while the hero of *A Strange Story* is a young doctor whose refusal to believe in the existence of the soul is punished by terrifying involvement with a ruthless killer in search of the elixir of life. Both novels describe unusual mental powers which enable those possessed of them to control others at a distance by the force of will. Earthly immortality and the elixir were commonplaces in contemporary romantic fiction. Balzac, Charles Maturin, Eugène Sue and E. T. A. Hoffmann all explored them in sensational stories. The difference is that Bulwer weaves these themes into a dense tapestry of learned allusions to occult and philosophical traditions, providing them with an air of authority which is not entirely spurious.

Zanoni begins with a reference to the Rosicrucians, almost certainly the main Western source in modern times of Hidden Master mythology. The irony of Blavatsky's debt to Bulwer Lytton is doubled by the fact that this secret brotherhood is itself a fiction, created in early-seventeenth-century Germany by a series of pamphlets reporting the existence of a mysterious brotherhood (*fraternitatis*) of the Rosy Cross, named in honour of the fourteenth-century knight Christian Rosenkreutz.[15] Rosenkreutz, according to the pamphlets, had studied Paracelsus and worked with the sages of Damascus, and the purpose of his brotherhood was to unify the knowledge of all wise men in preparation for the Last Judgement.

The pamphlets were written by a group of Lutheran mystics led by Johann Valentin Andreae, who also composed a fourth pamphlet, *The Chemical Wedding*, an alchemical allegory of the union between Christ and the soul. They had an enormous impact throughout Europe, despite Andreae's subsequent confession that Rosenkreutz was an invention – a sort of joke or game. But the public had taken literally what was meant to be an allegory of the spiritual life, and the mythology of Rosicrucianism took a hold on occultists which it has never relinquished, despite the conclusive evidence of recent scholars that no such person as Rosenkreutz ever existed.

Even Descartes and Leibniz took a passing interest in the Rosicrucians, joining in the search for the mysterious brothers. Swedenborg, too, was excited by them, but they could never be found. Like all the ancient orders from whom they descended – the gymnosophists, the priests of Isis, the Pythagoreans, the Chaldean brotherhood, the magicians of Babylon, the guardians of the Orphic mysteries – secrecy was their essential element. When one of the original pamphleteers, Heinrich Neuhaus, mischievously suggested that the brothers could not be found because they had all retreated to India and Tibet, he neatly made their existence or non-existence impossible to prove either way, entrenching yet further popular belief in the reality of the brothers. This imaginary retreat was to be one of Blavatsky's starting-points.

Another was the Order of Masons, whose eighteenth-century lodges (a word Blavatsky later appropriated) turned a trade guild into a blend of occult fraternity and reforming political crusade which caught the fancy of intellectuals and aristocrats alike. Though Masonry was believed to have originated in Scotland, the first known Masonic lodge was founded in London in 1717. Paradoxically associated with enlightenment, this secret order spread through Europe and was soon regarded as a dangerously revolutionary force.

Behind both the real Masons and the mythical Rosicrucians stands the mythology of the Knights Templar, a military and religious order which played a major role in the Crusades before its destruction by the French monarchy in 1312. The cruel persecution of the Templars by King Philip the Fair and his ministers (almost certainly motivated by jealousy of their power and vast wealth) was supported by papal propagandists who suggested that the order had become a secret society involved in occult practices, sexual perversion, political rebellion and heretical contacts with Islam. It was implied that the knights were trying to set up a state within the state, devoted to the overthrow of the monarchy.

The Templars, who have haunted the occult imagination ever since, were also credited with access to a 'secret doctrine'. It was believed that each knight transmits a secret – or rather, part of *the* Secret – to a fellow-initiate at the time of his death. Between them, these initiates therefore possess the knowledge of an esoteric wisdom which could unlock the mysteries of the universe; but this can only be done when the opportunity comes for all the heirs to pool their knowledge. By secrecy the initiates thus preserve their power and prepare the way for their future government of the world or even the cosmos.

Taking a line from Eliphas Lévi's synthesis of oriental religion and western magic as dramatised by Bulwer Lytton, buttressing this with her own extensive reading in Asian scriptures, and drawing on Rosicrucian, Masonic and Templar mythology, Blavatsky created a Brotherhood of Himalayan Masters who had supposedly selected her to communicate their message to the world. Quite why they should have chosen her, she never knew. But in retrospect it became clear that her apparently aimless wanderings had been under fraternal direction all along: it was the Masters who made her a concert pianist in Serbia, an amazon in Italy and a spirit medium in Cairo.

And it was the Masters who directed her to leave Paris for New York in the summer of 1873, twenty-two years after they had first made direct contact. At this point the detailed records of Blavatsky's life begin again. Boarding the boat with only enough money for her passage in steerage, she was destitute by the time she arrived in New York and had to move into a hostel for working women. There she barely supported herself by sewing purses and pen-wipers until a small legacy from her father arrived. By the time she met Olcott the legacy had been frittered away on a pointless chicken farm from which Blavatsky, like a P. G. Wodehouse hopeful, expected to make a fortune, though her knowledge of animals, farming and business was non-existent and she understood nothing about money except how to spend it.

Years later, those who had known her before she became famous, including passing acquaintances in hostels and lodging-houses, recorded their impressions, and it is easy to see why they remembered her without difficulty. One compared her with Stalin for the impression of power she gave, another remembered her smoking hashish, a third called her very unprepossessing and a fourth described the '*diaki*' (little elementals or familiar spirits) which constantly played jokes on their supposed mistress, such as tying her to the bed one night while she slept.[16]

Her physical presence was hard to forget. Though not approaching the seventeen and a half stone she later achieved by eating fatty foods, including her favourite fried eggs floating in butter, she was already stout. She had light brown hair 'crinkled like a negro or a cotswold ewe',[17] and magnetic eyes, variously described as blue, grey-blue and azure. High cheekbones and a broad, massive face with a flattened nose completed the exotic appearance suggested by shabby fantastic clothes. At the first meeting with Olcott she was wearing a Garibaldi red shirt. In later life she developed a taste for loose, badly fitting robes, preferring a sort of red flannel dressing-gown. Smoking incessantly, she carried the materials for her cigarettes in a furry pouch made out of an animal head worn round her neck. Her hands were usually covered with rings, some with genuine stones, and she looked overall like a badly wrapped and glittering parcel. She talked incessantly in a guttural voice, sometimes wittily and sometimes crudely. She was indifferent to sex yet frank and open about it; fonder of animals than of people; unsnobbish, unpretentious, scandalous, capricious and rather noisy. She was also humorous, vulgar, impulsive and warm-hearted, and she didn't give a hoot for anyone or anything.

She was in short just the woman for Olcott, who had lost all sense of direction in his dreary life. Having engineered their meeting at Chittenden, she proceeded to demonstrate her powers by introducing into the seances her own cast of materialised spirits, including her uncle, two Russian servants, a Persian merchant and a Kurdish warrior. Taking apparent control of the seances in this way changed their meaning. For whereas William and Horatio Eddy were passive channels through which spirits moved from the world of the dead to the world of the living, Blavatsky claimed to be able to command spirits as she chose.

The distinction between dominant and submissive mediums was

significant for three reasons. First, it allowed Blavatsky to contrast her powers favourably with the fraudulence, inadequacy or passivity of the competition. Second, it disposed of charges that sensitives are by nature vulnerable to manipulation and auto-suggestion. And third, it constituted the medium as a power in her own right, not a mere channel of communication with the other world. Blavatsky was later to insist that contact with the spirits of the dead was anyway of no importance in itself, though easy enough to arrange as a vulgar demonstration of psychic power. What mattered was a communion with the Masters, who, though their life existed on a higher plane, were anything but dead.

Nevertheless, the events at Chittenden soon provoked accusations of cheating. Daniel Dunglas Home accused her of fraud when she claimed to recognise during the seances a silver buckle supposedly buried with her father in Russia and materialised in Vermont for the occasion. Careful for his own credibility, Home based his charge not on the impossibility of materialising objects (known as 'apports') over distance, but on the assertion that the Russians do not bury decorations with their dead, adding that Blavatsky had already tried the same trick in Paris in 1858.

Undaunted by charges of fraud, Blavatsky and Olcott moved on from their inconclusive investigations at Chittenden to Philadelphia, where a Mr and Mrs Nelson Holmes had been holding seances of their own.[18] Their main apparition was an attractive, flirtatious young 'spook' (Blavatsky's word) called Katie King. Katie and her family were already familiar figures in spiritualist circles. She was said to be the daughter of 'John King', the spirit name of a former buccaneer, Sir Henry Owen Morgan. Both John and Katie figured largely in seances throughout the middle years of the century and John King was used as a spirit guide by many popular mediums.

Young Katie had made such a strong impression on one of the Holmeses' clients, the seventy-three-year-old Robert Dale Owen,[19] that he had given her a number of valuable jewels in return for a lock of golden hair. When she vanished at the end of the seance the jewels went with her, though the hair remained intact. Scandal broke a few days later when W. C. Leslie, a spiritualist railway contractor, called on Owen. He accused the Holmeses of fraud and produced some of the jewels in evidence, claiming that Katie King the wraith was really Eliza White, a well-built housewife formerly in league with Mr and Mrs Holmes but now ready to confess all and sell her embarrassing story to the press.

Leslie's motives in the affair are unclear but the notoriety of Katie's elderly admirer made the story local front-page news. Robert Dale Owen was the son of Robert Owen, who had himself been converted to spiritualism by an American medium in the 1850s when well over eighty. After Leslie's revelations Owen first tried to preserve his faith in spiritualism by arguing that the evidently fraudulent Holmeses were unfortunate exceptions to the usual run of honourable spirit mediums. Then he changed tack and claimed to be delighted when Olcott offered to investigate the affair with a view to vindicating the Holmeses.

Ignoring Eliza White and the tiresome W. C. Leslie, Olcott began his investigation towards the end of 1874 by insisting on the most rigorous conditions in the seance-room. To prevent trickery Mrs Holmes, the medium, was tied up and sewn into bags sealed with wax. This was all done in public, after which she was put in a cupboard, with the colonel banging each panel to demonstrate their solidity. Yet she still continued to produce phenomena, or so the colonel claimed. Though Olcott tried every kind of test, Mrs Holmes appeared to pass them all and he was soon convinced of her good faith. Alas, this was too late for Owen, who had given way under the strain of the whole affair and died not long afterwards in a lunatic asylum.

By the time they had returned from Philadelphia to New York Blavatsky and Olcott were on the closest terms, calling each other Maloney (Olcott) and Jack (Blavatsky). Fond of nicknames, the colonel also referred to his new friend as Mulligan, Latchkey, Old Horse and HPB – a sobriquet taken up by others. As these names suggest, the relationship was asexual. Olcott and Blavatsky were never lovers but what the colonel quaintly but aptly calls 'chums', and their chumship (his own word) was based on the instinctive recognition of mutual need. The colonel craved excitement and a mission in life; Madame wanted admiration and a source of income. Olcott needed someone to convince him of the spirit world's existence, Blavatsky someone to convince. Whether Olcott was Blavatsky's fellow-conspirator or her dupe, it is hard to say. The colonel was a classic case of someone whose desire to believe is hard to distinguish from belief itself.

Though living at first in separate apartments, Olcott and his new friend shared their daily life in New York, where Blavatsky's drawing-room became the centre of the colonel's life. The room was littered with manuscripts. During the day the colonel attended to his law practice; in the evenings they worked at adjacent desks, Olcott on his books, Blavatsky on letters and articles for the press. There were occasional parties in the apartment, usually for the purpose of discussing occult matters, but the chums were resolutely undomesticated. Casual visitors, though welcome, were bidden to make their own tea or coffee and to find themselves a corner among the piles of books and papers. For amusement the colonel liked to sing comic songs in the evening after his work was done, and in good weather he and Blavatsky made trips to the Hamptons on Long Island, where she paddled in the sea.

Her rooms were furnished in the usual late-Victorian manner with plush chairs and palms, but the heavy upholstery was relieved by a collection of oriental knick-knacks which prompted visiting journalists (of whom there were many) to christen Blavatsky's home the Lamasery. There were Chinese and Japanese cabinets, a mechanical bird, fans, rugs, the figure of a Siamese monk, lacquer boxes and a golden Buddha who sat on the chimney-piece. Though this kind of decoration had become favoured decorator's tat in many homes, it was meant to stand for something more in Blavatsky's case, signifying her links with a generalised 'Orient', which in turn symbolised the mysteries of living religion: the spiritual wisdom still alive in Asia but increasingly inaccessible to Westerners.

Even more striking was the collection of stuffed animals: a lioness's head over the door, monkeys peeping out of nooks, birds in every corner, lizards on shelves, a grey owl and a snake. The star of the collection was undoubtedly a large bespectacled baboon, standing upright, dressed in wing-collar, morning-coat and tie, and carrying under its arm the manuscript of a lecture on *The Origin of Species*. The appearance of Darwin's book in 1859 had prompted a spate of monkey cartoons in the press, and the ape was still a potent symbol in the continuing debate about evolution. Labelled Professor Fiske after a prominent Darwinian academic, Madame Blavatsky's baboon signalled her own posture in this debate as an adamant anti-Darwinian.

It was a bold icon to choose, but in retrospect also a risky one. The baboon obviously stands for the Folly of Science as opposed to the Wisdom of Religion; for the one who merely Knows (or thinks he does) as opposed to the one who Is; for Darwin versus Blavatsky. But involved with this lofty dismissal of Darwinism (and what Blavatsky called 'materialist science' in general) is the further message that anyone who thinks as Darwin does must be no better than a baboon, i.e. crude and crafty, foolish, vulgar, greedy, gross and deceitful. Yet these were just the charges already being brought against Blavatsky herself. And whereas the century since his death has seen the canonisation of Darwin as a secular saint, the same period has relegated Blavatsky to virtual oblivion. If she is remembered at all it is usually as the type of the fraudulent guru. In the modern allegory of Wisdom and Folly, she plays the role of the Fool.

In her own time she had powerful supporters. And there are those who argue still that if Helena Blavatsky is a figure of scandal, it is only because the slanders on her reputation are the signs of grace: the stigmata that all great marytrs must bear. This interpretation of events, which envisages Blavatsky as a latter-day saint and heroine, depends on a very familiar historical scheme. According to this scheme, western humanity turned away from religion during the eighteenth and nineteenth centuries, under the influence of science, which promised to create heaven on earth. But this was a false promise, for science can never answer completely to human needs. Given the inadequacies of Christianity, which proved unequal to the battle with materialism, it was necessary for someone to show the way forward by denouncing the delusions of both the Darwinians, who stand for false ideals of progress, and the Christians, who believe in false myths of salvation. Blavatsky's supporters argue that attacking both parties with their huge vested interests was bound to provoke a bitter response: hence the personal attacks on their idol.

Spiritualism had been meant to offer a way between the frustrating alternatives of pseudo-science and pseudo-religion, providing a true spiritual science. But by 1875, when Olcott published his account of events at Chittenden and Philadelphia, the spiritualist revival in America was faltering and it was becoming clear that the movement's original promise would never be fulfilled. Its limitations were apparent to all but the most committed. While musical dancing ghosts might be an amusement, they didn't have much light to throw on the life after death. Seances provided spectacle, mystery, and consolation for the bereaved, but they lacked clear objectives, positive doctrines, proper rituals and coherent organisation. Something more was needed. That 'something' Helena Blavatsky intended to provide.

THREE

News From Nowhere

On 3 March 1875, Colonel Olcott received a letter. Written in gold ink on green paper and folded into a black envelope, it came from a certain Tuitit Bey who lived at Luxor in Egypt – Luxor being the African base of a Great White Brotherhood of Masters to which Tuitit Bey belonged. The colonel was invited to become his pupil, supervised by Madame Blavatsky, who already knew about the offer because she had been ordered to forward Tuitit Bey's letter to Olcott under cover of her own explanatory note. Furthermore, it seemed that the colonel's correspondent had not posted his message from Egypt in the normal way, but 'precipitated' it into HPB's room.

Precipitation is a form of automatic writing by means of which a Master may transmit his thoughts, either through an amanuensis or – *in extremis* – directly on to paper. Olcott's message was the first of many addressed to all sorts of people involved with his chum at one time or another, and these letters were to play a major role in making her notorious. At first they were cited as proof that the Masters existed, but there were those who said that Blavatsky had simply written the letters herself, or caused others to write them. Sometimes they were handed on to their addressee by HPB acting as spirit postman. Others suddenly appeared on a desk, fell from the ceiling or even manifested on moving trains, apparently without the help of human agency. Especially large numbers were written during moments of crisis, usually urging the recipients to do whatever Blavatsky suggested.

In her covering letter to Olcott (written despite the fact that they saw one another every day) his chum said she had tried to persuade Tuitit Bey that he should convince the colonel of the Brotherhood's existence by a display of occult powers. She had even suggested using a novel kind of parchment 'on which the contents appear whenever you cast your eyes on it to read it, and disappear every time as soon as you have done so'. But the Brotherhood was above such cheap tricks, she said, and Olcott had to be content with ordinary paper. Nevertheless, she was sure that her chum would understand the significance of the message, warning him that he should 'Beware, Henry, before you pitch headlong into it . . . There is still time to decline the connection. But if you keep the letter I send you and agree to the word Neophyte, you are cooked, my boy.'[1] She also reminded him of her own seven arduous years of preliminary initiation. But the colonel was all too keen to be cooked, not to say roasted, and he accepted the offer without hesitation.

Olcott then began to receive a whole stream of letters from another Brother, Serapis Bey, who didn't have much to say on the subject of esoteric initiation but was full of advice about how to deal with Blavatsky and her problems. Everyone knew that the woman could be difficult, Serapis explained, and that she took no heed for her own security and safety; but she was quite unique, had a special mission in the world, and must be cared for at all costs, even if caring for her meant sacrificing the colonel's other interests, such as his wife and children. Anyway, he need not fear for them, Serapis told him: they would be looked after. And in due course they were. The boys found jobs and Mrs Olcott secured substantial alimony and later married again. So everything turned out for the best.

Blavatsky certainly needed someone to look after her. Having returned to New York from their investigations of Katie King, the chums were living in adjacent apartments, though that did not prevent HPB from contracting a brief marriage to another man. The motives for this marriage are as obscure as everything else in Blavatsky's middle years. Her new husband may have been a partner in business schemes, or Blavatsky may have been genuinely if fleetingly attracted to him. Most likely she was looking for some form of security. If so, the marriage was a disaster from the start. The Georgian Michael Betanelly was a fellow-exile but an unsuitable husband on several counts, being many years younger than his wife, near to insolvency and probably a crook. The new Madame Betanelly's marriage was also bigamous, as General Blavatsky was still alive.

She soon regretted the liaison and letters from Serapis began imploring the colonel to save his chum from her new husband. To make things worse, she had also injured her leg, which swelled and 'mortified'. A Dr Pancoast recommended amputation, but instead she cured the limb herself, by applying a white puppy poultice for two days, as recommended by Francis Bacon in his *Historia Vitae et Mortis*, on the grounds that dogs give off great therapeutic heat. Her leg recovered and during convalescence she somehow succeeded in extricating herself from the relationship with Betanelly.

Re-established in her friendship with Olcott, Blavatsky now devoted herself to a career in spiritualism. This was not a success. First she entered into an arrangement with Eldridge Gerry Brown, Editor of the *Spiritual Scientist*. In return for financial support he agreed to publicise Olcott's communications from Serapis and Tuitit Bey. But the chums ran out of money and Brown promptly lost interest in them. His magazine closed soon afterwards and he went bankrupt in 1878.

After that Blavatsky established a Miracle Club, devoted to investigating occult phenomena. This, too, was a failure. Only then did she hit on the ideas that were to make her an international celebrity. Her problem was that she had to find a way of publicising the communications from her Brotherhood of Masters and thereby establish herself on an altogether higher occult level than mere spirit mediums. This was not easy when she was in competition with other people pursuing the same goal. For the 1870s had produced a number of former spiritualists who now claimed to be in communion with hidden powers superior to ordinary ghosts.

The solution to the problem was to embody the secrets she was being taught by the Masters, in forms that would make them accessible to a wider public while making it clear that those who subscribed to the doctrine were an élite. This is the traditional esoteric approach and the best ways to achieve it are to write a bible and to found a church. In 1875 Blavatsky proceeded to do both.

*

One of Blavatsky's rivals was her friend Emma Hardinge Britten, a popular New York medium who published a book entitled *Art Magic* in the same year. Britten explains in her preface that she is not really the author of this book, only a stenographer for the Chevalier Louis, an Adept or spiritual being resembling Blavatsky's Masters. The chevalier's purpose is to communicate with the few who will understand his message. His exclusiveness was underlined by Britten's announcement that she was restricting distribution of the book to serious students, and the *Banner of Light* recorded that Mrs Britten had refused to sell copies to 'little pugs' whom she found unworthy.[2]

At all events, Olcott was not a little pug. Allowed to buy two copies of *Art Magic*, price $5 each, he was nevertheless disappointed with the text and with the portrait of the author, which Mrs Britten showed him in strict confidence, commenting in his memoirs that:

> One who has been face to face with a real Adept would be forced by this effeminate dawdler's countenance to suspect either that Mrs Britten had, faute de mieux, shown a bogus portrait of the real author, or that the book was written by no 'Chevalier Louis' at all . . .[3]

a conclusion with which no one will be able to disagree.

Art Magic was a product of the astral light, a term probably coined by Eliphas Lévi and used by spiritualists to describe the source of their power and knowledge. Divine dictation was a popular method among American occultists, prompted by spiritualism and encouraged by an interest in the prophetic books of the Bible. Its most celebrated nineteenth-century practitioner was Joseph Smith, a teenage farm labourer from New England.[4]

Given to visions of God the Father and God the Son while wandering through the fields, Smith was cautioned by both against joining any of the existing churches on the grounds that 'all their creeds are abominations'. He responded by founding his own church, inspired by an angel called Moroni, who appeared in

September 1823 and told Smith that he would find buried in a nearby hill some 'Golden Plates' containing a new gospel in a strange language. The plates were accompanied by two magic stones, Thummim and Urim, fastened to a magic breastplate which Joseph should wear when he wanted to translate the gospel. He recovered the plates, which he hid under his bed and eventually transcribed as the *Book of Mormon*, sometimes with the help of Urim and Thummim and sometimes simply by hiding his face in his hat and consulting a magic stone he had earlier used (unsuccessfully) for finding buried treasure. Though the semi-literate Smith dictated his translation to a scribe, he consulted the plates in secret, sitting behind a blanket strung over a rope while his scribe took down his words from the other side of the room.

Smith soon acquired followers whom he attempted to lead to the Promised Land. This was located at Carthage, a pleasant small town on the banks of the Mississippi, where the prophet was soon attracting thousands of converts. But his subsequent career, including adultery, polygamy, polyandry and financial fraud, was brought to an abrupt close in 1844 when he and his faithful brother Hyrum were lynched by an angry mob in Carthage Prison, where they had been lodged on charges of treason. Their followers were driven out and the Trek to Utah followed under the direction of Smith's successor, Brigham Young. By 1875 the Mormons were flourishing in Salt Lake City.

Like *Art Magic* and the *Book of Mormon* (which Mark Twain called 'chloroform in print'), large sections of Blavatsky's bible, *Isis Unveiled*, simply appeared. After a good night's sleep, the 'author' would come down to her desk in the morning to find a pile of perhaps thirty pages, written – or should one say precipitated? – by invisible hands while she slept. At other times, a Master would take over her body and write for her, unquestionably a help with a book running to half a million words. On these occasions Olcott observed striking changes in her handwriting. His chum also had recourse to a sort of astral public library which supplied her with material, and Olcott would often arrive in her study to find her gazing into space as if searching her memory for quotations. These were duly supplied by psychic means, and proved on inspection to be impressively close to the printed versions, many of which were later found on a shelf in Blavatsky's study. Where there were divergences, HPB hinted that the fault was in the printed version and not in the 'original' transmitted direct to her by the Masters, with whom her relationship was becoming ever more intimate. Olcott even noticed that there were moments during astral dictation when her voice deepened and her brown crinkled hair went straight and black, as though she were turning into an Indian, while the room filled with strange presences and the chiming of celestial music.

Isis Unveiled is an exposition of Egyptian occultism and the cult of the Great Mother. The book is divided into two sections headed 'Science' and 'Theology'. Part One begins with criticism of Hume, Darwin and Huxley, who are said to have narrowed the notion of science so that it applies only to the demonstrable laws governing the material universe. Blavatsky then argues that there are other laws of nature, as yet unknown to men but accessible to occult wisdom, and that these too deserve the name of science. Part Two is an essay in comparative religion, and an exposition of Buddhism as the wisdom doctrine within which science and religion can be united.

Olcott compared Blavatsky with Darwin, and her book is a deliberate challenge to that master, whose evolutionary theory she trumps by asserting that the evolution of monkeys into men is merely one stage in a long chain which allows men to evolve into higher beings. Blavatsky thereby transforms evolution from a limited socio-biological theory into an explanation of everything from atoms to angels. Instead of opposing religion with the facts as presented by Victorian science, she attempts to subsume those facts into a grand synthesis that makes religious wisdom not the enemy of scientific knowledge but its final goal.

The first printing of a thousand copies sold out immediately, despite the attacks of scholars, and reviewers who dismissed it as 'discarded rubbish' (*New York Sun*) and 'a large dish of hash' (*Springfield Republican*). The *New York Times* ignored the book completely. Max Muller, Professor of Sanskrit at Oxford University, accused the author of scholarly incompetence, and another critic identified over two thousand unacknowledged quotations.

The author and her chum calmly cited such quotations as evidence of her occult power.

But the point of *Isis Unveiled* was not to please reviewers and scholars. It appeals instead to passionate amateurs and spiritual autodidacts: readers too concerned with answers to important questions to be bothered with academic quibbles about authenticity and internal coherence. Blavatsky's book answered to deep needs at a time when religious doubt was fuelled by the first great age of mass education. The late nineteenth century produced a large, semi-educated readership with the appetite, the aspirations and the lack of intellectual sophistication necessary to consume such texts. It was the milieu portrayed so vividly in England by Bernard Shaw, H. G. Wells, George Gissing and Hale White: the world of autodidacts, penny newspapers, weekly encyclopaedias, evening classes, public lectures, workers' educational institutes, debating unions, libraries of popular classics, socialist societies and art clubs – that bustling, earnest world where the readers of Ruskin and Edward Carpenter could improve themselves, where middle-class idealists could help them to do so, and where nudism and dietary reform linked arms with universal brotherhood and occult wisdom.

It was to this world of secular temples and improving institutes that Blavatsky turned her attention when, having written her bible, she set about the establishment of her church. The Theosophical Society's foundation came about almost by accident when a lecture was given in her apartment on 7 September 1875 by a Mr J. G. Felt. At least, that is how Olcott presents the occasion. Mr Felt's title was 'The Lost Canon of Proportion of the Egyptians', his subject a mathematical formula used by the ancients to plan many of their buildings, including the Pyramids and the Acropolis. According to Mr Felt this formula was known only to initiates, who made it the basis of an esoteric spiritual science. Mr Felt wanted to find the formula and revive the science.

The audience included Mrs Britten and her husband; a judge and his poetess wife; an attorney; a progressive clergyman; an English barrister with a passion for spiritualism and mesmerism; a Rosicrucian; the President of the New York Society of Spiritualists; a retired manufacturer; a doctor interested in cabbalism; two journalists, described in mitigation of their trade as 'gentlemen'; a Freemason; Mazzini's former Secretary, Signor Bruzzesi, to add glamour; a clerk from a law firm; and the tenants of the apartment. No doubt they listened quietly to Mr Felt, but the meeting only came to life when the cabbalist (the same Dr Pancoast who had failed to treat HPB's leg) asked whether the formula could be used to summon spirits from the deep.

This woke everyone up. To great excitement Mr Felt said that indeed it could, offering to produce a few apparitions in support of his claim and provoking a vigorous discussion about the bidding of spirits; but before the speaker could make good his word Colonel Olcott, after exchanging notes with Madame Blavatsky, got to his feet and made a speech. The theme of his speech was that all these ideas were so interesting a society should be formed to study them, and those present voted themselves into one as soon as the speaker sat down – which took quite a while, Olcott being notoriously fond of the sound of his own voice.

Determined to establish their society on strictly rational and democratic lines, the members immediately proceeded to appoint a committee and officers. William Judge, the lawyer's clerk, proposed the colonel for President. Olcott reciprocated by proposing Judge as Secretary. Both suggestions were accepted *nem. con.* The committee meeting was then adjourned, the members resolving to continue business on the following evening, when Mr Felt was billed to give another lecture. This failed to materialise, and after extracting $100 from the society for 'expenses' Felt soon abandoned his friends and left New York for London, where he tried to set up his own Society for Occult Research, though nothing came of it.

Undaunted, they continued with their own new venture. At first the new society had no name. Egyptian, Hermetic, Rosicrucian were all suggested at subsequent meetings, but it wasn't until one of the members, flipping through a dictionary, found the word 'theosophy' that the name was established. The Theosophical Society proper thus came into being on 13 September, though it didn't hold its first official meeting until the 17th, when the members were ambitiously charged with the duty of collecting and diffusing 'knowledge of the laws which govern the universe', and the history of organised occultism in the West could begin.

The early uncertainty about a name is symptomatic of a deeper muddle about the new society's purpose. The clear distinction between occult practices and objective study of occult phenomena is hard to maintain when you are already committed to the belief in the *de facto* existence of another world and its manifestations in this one. Olcott frequently repeated that Theosophy was not intended to be a new religion but a science. Yet he continued to argue in favour of the existence of psychic phenomena, just as HPB continued to produce them.

Theosophy also assumed the existence of the secret universal doctrine it was meant to investigate. It started from the premise that fundamental truths and values are universal and that all religions are essentially the same religion. Furthermore, the Society confused the issue by proclaiming humanitarian social ideals: studying spiritual science went with promoting the Brotherhood of Man. In the early days such a muddle hardly mattered – indeed, the broad appeal might have helped to attract members. But the attempt to reconcile conflicting religious, scientific and political aims was bound to become a serious difficulty in the end.

Perhaps the word 'theosophy' itself – meaning sacred science or divine truth or wisdom – was part of the problem. The first Theosophists were supposedly the Philalethians, third-century Alexandrian philosophers (or 'lovers of truth') who were in turn descended from Pythagoras, Plato and the neo-Platonists, and influenced by the lost Orphic and Egyptian mysteries. Theosophy's last major revival had occurred in the Renaissance, when writers including the mystical cobbler Jacob Boehme used the word to describe their own blend of mysticism, esotericism and cosmology.[5] But the notions of 'truth' and 'science' understood by these earlier theosophists were quite different from the rational and pseudo-scientific standards of objectivity, precision, detachment and neutrality thought to characterise truth and science in the late nineteenth century. On the one hand Olcott and Blavatsky were attempting to operate with these standards; on the other they were trying to restore just the sense of mystery that the insistence on such standards had allegedly banished from the modern world.

While puzzling over the new society's purposes, Olcott's desire to introduce eastern wisdom into the West found practical expression in another new fad. One of the early members of the Theosophical Society was a Baron de Palm, like Blavatsky a European aristocrat fallen on hard times, and living in a boarding-house until the colonel and his companion offered him a room in their apartment. Already in bad health, the baron soon died, leaving all his assets to Olcott with the request that the colonel arrange for his cremation.

Though common in Asia, cremation was almost unknown in Europe and America. Cremation Societies had been formed in New York in 1873, and in Britain the following year, but neither had yet burnt anyone. The colonel joined the New York society on its formation, and saw that he could kill two birds with one stone by preceding the incineration with his own theosophical burial service. The combination was bound to stimulate enormous public interest and give both societies a flying start.

There were many difficulties in the way, not least finding a suitable method of burning the body. There were no crematoria in existence and the baron could hardly be disposed of on a public pyre in the Indian style. Besides, the New York City Council was suspicious of the whole business, and while they wrangled over it with Olcott, the baron's embalmed body lay unshriven. In the end the members of the Cremation Society also took fright, deciding that they did not wish to compromise their own cause by association with the dubious Madame Blavatsky and her new religion. When they refused to take part in the proceedings Olcott was forced to construct his own clay oven. This was a surprising success: the baron's embalmed body burnt easily and played its part in popularising the new custom.

The burial rites caused more problems than disposing of the corpse. A church service was obviously out of the question, so the colonel hired a hall and devised an ecumenical liturgy and suitable prayers, but on the day the ceremony turned into farce. Members of the public who had come to see the show laughed openly at the ritual, and uproar followed when a Methodist preacher jumped up shouting, 'That's a lie!' during one of the prayers, which described God as 'one first cause uncreated'. Nevertheless – or in consequence – the affair attracted attention in the press, and Olcott probably knew well enough that even the comic parody of his ceremony published in a New York newspaper, *The World*, was useful publicity in its own way. It was just as well that it should be. The baron's will leaving Olcott land and castles in Europe proved to be worthless, and there wasn't even enough money to pay for the cremation. The only things of any value in the trunk which contained de Palm's few possessions were some of the colonel's own shirts with his embroidered name carefully unpicked.

Despite the popularity of *Isis Unveiled* and the sensation of the burning baron, the Theosophical Society did not prosper. During the two years following its foundation most of the original members drifted away and few joined. By the end of 1878 the two Founders were almost alone. Combined with the failure of Olcott's book about his spiritual investigations, *People From the Other World*, shortage of money, perennial restlessness and the feeling that New York had little more to offer prompted them to set out for India.

If risky, the move was a logical one on two grounds. First, the Founders already had contacts in the East with a Vedic society, the Arya Samaj, which appeared to have similar doctrines. And second, the Theosophical Society's appeal derived in large part from its vaguely conceived orientalism – which meant in practice Hinduism and Buddhism. For despite the Society's avowed project to extract the universal elements from all religions, Theosophy was biased against Christianity and took little account of Islam or Judaism. Hinduism inevitably meant India, where there were also several hundred million people waiting to be converted to Theosophy.

But logic had little to do with their immediate reasons for moving. For one thing, logic might have sent them to Egypt, home of Tuitit Bey, Serapis and the Luxor Brotherhood. This change of destination may be symptomatic of a general shift of interest in occult circles from Egypt to the Himalayas, and after 1878 we hear little from Blavatsky about Egyptian Masters. But it also suggests comic uncertainty about where to place the best bets. Was India the only place she hadn't tried already? Or, now that the Middle East was becoming comparatively familiar to Europeans (who had begun to travel extensively in Egypt, courtesy of Thomas Cook), was it desirable to locate the Mysteries somewhere more exotic and less accessible? Or was this just another caprice, like Blavatsky's flight from her father's servants in 1848? However familiar she may have been with cosmic orientation, her sense of mundane geography had always been shaky. Her own fanciful travel stories had often taken her to different remote parts of the world simultaneously. India, Egypt – it was all the same.

More concerned with practicalities, Olcott saw financial possibilities in the move. His ambitious schemes to raise cash, which included investing in Venezuelan silver mines, extended to forming Indian business syndicates, though none of them came to anything. He then put his trust in a diplomatic passport and a vague licence to promote Indian–American cultural and commercial relations, which he extracted from the administration of President Hayes, prompting the sceptical HPB to write to a friend that her chum 'has got hopes of making his entrée into Bombay with the Govt. seal stamped on his backside'.[6] Ever confident, the colonel was sure that he had the spirit world on his side – a belief confirmed when, as he reported, $1,000 simply 'appeared' in his bank account, much as Serapis Bey's letters were precipitated into his rooms.[7]

Whatever the practical reasons, however, both the chums insisted that they had been told to move to India by the Masters; and furthermore that they had been ordered to leave New York by 17 December 1878, on pain of imminent occult disaster if they failed to do so. Disaster certainly loomed, in the material form of pressing creditors, but for those who take worldly events as signs of celestial meanings that was enough. One autumn evening, as he was reading in his room, Olcott was visited by a tall dark stranger who turned out to be one of the Hidden Masters or Brothers, not this time from Luxor but the Himalayas. Olcott was already in familiar contact with the Master Morya, whom he refers to in his diary as 'Dad'. This stranger, dressed in an amber turban and white robes, laid a hand on the colonel's head and told him that he was about to reach a critical point in his life when there was great work for him and HPB to do for humanity. Leaving the turban behind as a keepsake – its photograph appears in Olcott's memoirs – the stranger vanished as abruptly as he had appeared.

On 9 December – just five months after Madame Blavatsky had been granted American citizenship – the contents of the Lamasery were auctioned, the creditors were paid off, and on the 17th Olcott and HPB left for India. Whatever the reasons, it was a brave move to make. They were reversing the usual flow of emigration from east to west, they were not young, and they had no capital to speak of. Their only contacts in the subcontinent depended on correspondents they had never met, and an official letter commending Olcott to American consulates in the vaguest terms – hardly of much use in a country where the colonial power was a major commercial and political rival of the United States. The virtually moribund New York Society was left to the direction of General Abner Doubleday, later more celebrated as the inventor of baseball.

They arrived in Bombay in the middle of February 1879, after stopping briefly in London, where they stayed with the novelist Mabel Collins and Olcott encountered his Himalayan visitor once again – which would have been strange enough in itself, had HPB not come across the same figure at the same time in a completely different place. That a being could cross the Atlantic without, apparently, travelling by boat, and then appear simultaneously in the suburbs and the City, was as clear a demonstration of the Master's occult power as could be asked for. It was certainly more stimulating than anything offered by the tiny British Theosophical Society.

In India itself they immediately felt at home and the colonel went so far as to kiss the quayside on arrival in Bombay. This was certainly the right attitude to take if Olcott and HPB wanted to make friends among the native population, though it didn't help him with their first host, Hurrychund Chintamon, a member of the Arya Samaj. Having urged them to visit India, he provided lavish hospitality, including a grand reception, and then presented them with a huge bill for everything, including his own telegram of welcome. It also seemed that he was still in possession of the money they had earlier sent to the Arya Samaj as a contribution and token of good will. Retrieving the cash amid acrimony and threats of revenge, they moved out of Chintamon's house and found a place of their own in Girgaum Back Road, a native quarter of the town.

Despite this embarrassment, and despite the suspicions of the imperial government, which had them followed by a comically visible spy called Major Henderson until Olcott protested, things began to look up. In April 1879 they started a magazine, *The Theosophist*, which soon moved into profit. Within three months the circulation had risen to over six hundred. They also began to travel about the country visiting sacred sites and teachers. Their new acquaintances included Swami Dayananda Sarasvati of the Arya Samaj, who expounded the practice of yoga and the powers it can produce. These include levitation, the occupation of other bodies, prolongation of life and the transformation of matter. The swami, however, was careful to distinguish between such important matters and the tricks that so amused Europeans. Making things appear and disappear, for example, depended not on profound religious practices but on sleight of hand: a skill, not a science. The powers of yoga were not to be abused in such a fashion, though any yogi could easily perform these tricks if they wished to for a particular purpose.

HPB, however, was ready to set up as a teacher in her own right, and she laid public claim to this status by a series of just such demonstrations of sleight of hand. By the time the chums had returned from their travels at the end of December 1880 and settled in a new house, Crow's Nest, in a more salubrious part of Bombay, these demonstrations were under way. They included making a brooch appear in a flowerbed, finding a teacup and summoning music out of thin air. There was constant demand for such 'phenomena' in the Anglo-Indian circles to which HPB gradually gained access. They were said by many, however, to be precisely what Swami Dayananda had denounced as *tamasha*, i.e. deception or tricks. Perhaps the swami's distinction – between phenomena produced by genuine occult means and trivial conjuring – proved too difficult for Europeans to sustain.

In time, phenomena, like precipitated letters, were to become a subject of painful debate within the Theosophical Society, with most of Blavatsky's supporters admitting that some of her tricks were indeed just that, but insisting that others were genuine occult events, and that it is simply impossible to draw a line between the two. The question, they maintain, is not whether HPB was a charlatan; but whether she was sometimes foolish enough to compromise her real powers with displays of cheap conjuring to please the public. Her own line in later life was to suggest either that there was indeed a distinction in her work between the false and the true, attributing the false to her own base nature and the true to the guidance of the Masters; or that the very dubiousness of some of her own tricks was part of a larger plan. What that plan is she does not specify, and her claims are invariably undermined by embarrassing evidence. The brooch in the flowerbed, for example, turned out to have been pawned by its owner in Bombay whence HPB had redeemed it.

Though usually excluded from all but the largest official gatherings by an establishment which never shook off the suspicion that she was a spy, Blavatsky gradually acquired a wide circle of acquaintances including influential figures in the Raj (among them the Major Henderson deputed to spy on her and Olcott during their first weeks in India). She also became a minor celebrity among Britons and natives alike. Much of her fame among the Anglo-Indians she owed to Alfred Percy Sinnett (1840–1921) and Allan Octavian Hume (1829–1912).

Alfred Sinnett had worked as a journalist in London and Hong Kong and was now the Editor of a major Indian newspaper, the Allahabad *Pioneer*. He and his wife Patience maintained an intellectual salon of sorts in Allahabad, numbering Rudyard Kipling's father among their friends. The Sinnetts were eager spiritualists, avid for seances and manifestations. They were also rather snobbish, and Sinnett, who liked to introduce HPB as 'the Countess', readily provided her with valuable space in his newspaper – rather too much space, in the opinion of his employers, who eventually dismissed him for letting his cranky opinions invade their journal. In December 1879 Olcott and Blavatsky visited the Sinnetts at

Brightlands, their house in Simla, and though Olcott was merely cordial, HPB became close friends with both her hosts. Over the next decade she was to confide in them frequently by letter and to provide Alfred with materials for a memoir of her life.

A. O. Hume also had a large house in Simla, the imposing 'Rothney Castle', where he became an expert on Indian ornithology. He had served with distinction in the East India Company, the Indian Army (reaching the rank of colonel) and the imperial civil service, in which he achieved high office, becoming Secretary to the Government of India. But Hume, who was the son of the British Liberal MP Joseph Hume, inherited his father's intractable disposition. He had quarrelled bitterly with his superiors at about the time of Blavatsky's arrival in India, and although the resulting demotion was officially put down to personal conflicts and Hume's inability to take orders, there may have been deeper reasons. Hume was too sympathetic to the Indian people for the government's taste. He was deeply embroiled in nationalist politics, and a moving force behind the formation of the Indian National Congress, which first met in 1885. Less credulous than Sinnett, with whom he shared an interest in Buddhism, Hume was touchy and at times impetuous. He was also intrigued by Blavatsky and her Masters.

Hume and the Sinnetts wanted very much to trust their new friend, but they soon became aware of the difficulties involved. 'Tho' I am desperately inclined to believe at times that you are an impostor,' Hume wrote to her in 1881, 'I believe I love you more than any of them.'[8] It was a common reaction, and it gave rise to a nickname – the Old Lady – which HPB immediately appropriated, referring to herself in correspondence as 'the OL' and gleefully playing up to the role of an unreasonable, crotchety and improvident yet fascinating old crone, inclined to get other people into unnecessary scrapes.

She also enjoyed tormenting these two correct Englishmen, whom she freely criticised behind their backs and – somewhat unwisely – to one another, describing Hume in a letter to Sinnett as 'A Jupiter offering himself as a goat-herd to the God Hermes, to teach the latter manners . . . A poor dry weed rolling down the Cheops Pyramid.'[9] Sinnett was more trenchantly dismissed as a ninny. Endlessly satirical about the pretensions of India's British rulers, Blavatsky alternated humorously between proclaiming the superiority of her own aristocratic birth to Queen Victoria's, and toying with the idea of taking British citizenship and calling herself 'Mrs Snookes or Tufmutton'.[10] She also relished the challenge her friends presented. The commonsensical English, she noted, 'believe more in the Russians than in the Brothers',[11] yet they have an 'insatiable' appetite for proof of psychic phenomena. Though priding themselves on their scepticism, they are limitlessly credulous about anything once convinced of its existence by 'evidence'.

Judging from their letters, it is clear that Sinnett and Hume also enjoyed Blavatsky's taste for intrigue: the complex correspondence between the three of them (and between HPB and Patience Sinnett) is studded with gossip and a perpetual flirtation with the idea that HPB might be a fraud after all. She is constantly denying charges of dishonesty from various quarters, they as constantly bringing them up. Her new friends also adopted her own irreverent tone. 'If they *don't* exist,' Hume wrote to her about the Masters, '*what a novel writer you would make*! You certainly make your characters very consistent. When is our dear old Christ – I mean K.H., again to appear on the scene – he is quite our favourite actor . . .'[12]

She was right about their credulity. Though Hume proved resistant in the end, Sinnett surrendered completely to Blavatsky. To assuage any lingering doubts, she decided to admit them to communion with the Master. They were both eager for the privilege, hoping to become chelas of the Brotherhood; but because all messages to Morya and Koot Hoomi had to go through her hands, that involved the would-be chelas in a complicated minuet with HPB herself. She forwarded letters and arranged replies, either directly or by precipitation. Sometimes the original letter was returned with superscriptions in the Master's hand, often in HPB's own lively style.[13]

Controlling communication with the Brotherhood was the source of Blavatsky's authority, but it was not a secure one: as so often in the Theosophical Society, it was a letter which brought about the rupture between Hume and HPB. He and Sinnett soon became dissatisfied with the replies they were receiving from Koot Hoomi.

In the place of answers to their metaphysical questions they received constant injunctions to be kind and understanding to HPB. 'You can hardly be too indulgent with her,' Koot Hoomi told them,[14] and for a while they obeyed him. But in 1882, perhaps suspecting fraud, they decided to bypass their postman and write directly to the Mahachohan, suggesting that in future they should correspond without intermediaries. Unfortunately, there was then no option but to give the sealed letter to the Old Lady for forwarding as usual. She retired to her room with it, supposedly intending to play the piano while precipitating the envelope to its destination, but a very different kind of music was heard from the room a few minutes later, when she emerged screaming betrayal and treason, having opened the letter and read it.

From that moment Hume's wavering faith in Blavatsky collapsed. She was clearly supplementing whatever real psychic powers she might have with fraud, replying to letters herself and passing off the replies as occult communications. Yet, still pining to believe in the Masters, at first he rejected only their self-appointed messenger, calling her a liar, a sham, a mediocrity and a chronic humbug. But within a few months he had abandoned the Theosophical Society altogether, dismissing even the Masters as 'selfish Asiatics'.[15] This pattern of initial enthusiasm and friendship for HPB followed by rapid disillusion was to be repeated many times in the years ahead. Sinnett continued to believe in her, eventually rising to be Vice-President of the Society after her death. His wife remained a confidante, but their relations were never easy after Hume's defection, and HPB's later letters contain many withering critiques of Sinnett's idiocy and feebleness.

The trouble was that, however much Blavatsky might defend herself, and however much she wanted to be accepted by Anglo-Indian society, she could never resist the opportunity of poking fun at the solemn prudery of English officialdom. 'My graceful, stately person, clad in half-Tibetan, half-night-dress fashion,' she wrote from Ootacamund in 1883,

> sitting in all the glory of her Calmuck beauty at the
> Governor's and Carmichael's dinner-parties; HPB

positively courted by the aide-de-camps! Old 'Upasika'*
hanging like a gigantic nightmare on the gracefully
rounded elbows of members of the Council, in pumps and
swallow-tailed evening dress and silk stockings, smelling
brandy and soda enough to kill a Tibetan yak.[16]

Perhaps Blavatsky knew that scandal is as good a way as any to make a mark on the public mind. It certainly seems to have worked in her case, in so far as the Theosophical Society prospered, despite the disillusionment of individuals such as Hume. She was also to discover that upsetting Anglo-Indians did her no harm with the native population: for every European who gave her up in disgust, ten Indians joined her cause. And perhaps she also sensed that scandal was an important part of her armoury as a teacher and public figure. To fit in with things would be to pass unnoticed: rightly used, controversy could be fruitful, creating around her a permanently electric atmosphere of expectation. Unfortunately, she knew how to make controversy but not how to manage it.

The continuing commotion eventually prompted Olcott to pull away from his old chum and follow a line of his own. He was, after all, President of the Theosophical Society, whereas HPB was only Corresponding Secretary – a point about which he reminded her from time to time. Olcott was all the more conscious of his position because of Blavatsky's increasing tendency to give herself airs, implying that she was the chosen vessel, the gifted seer selected by the Masters, whereas the colonel was just her assistant. When he stood on his dignity, HPB responded by telling her correspondents that Olcott was a windbag, a bore and a pumpkin-head blown up with vanity. Apprised of these comments, Olcott snapped back with criticism of her indiscreet letters and her fondness for causing rows.

The two had always been incompatible characters, united only by their mutual need and by the colonel's belief in Blavatsky's powers.

---

*Yet another HPB nickname.

Thrown together with Olcott in a strange land, the quick-witted and quick-tempered Blavatsky became more and more intolerant of his slow, prosing ponderousness, while he dreaded the problems each new day's intemperate outburst would bring. Growing older, Blavatsky was more reckless. When her tricks were exposed she would sometimes bluster, and sometimes cheerfully confess the deceit with a wink and a chuckle. The evidence of her fraud increased almost daily, and although he found it as hard as Hume and Sinnett to believe her altogether an impostor – where would that leave his own claims to occult wisdom? – Olcott was increasingly coming round to the view that his old chum was at best a complex and unpredictable character, and at worst a serious liability who interfered with his own patently valuable work. He therefore had every reason for staying away from home, not least the stream of domestic rows in which leading Theosophists seemed to be forever involved.

By December 1882 the Society's income from subscriptions and *The Theosophist* had made it possible for Blavatsky and Olcott to move from Crow's Nest to a small estate at Adyar near Madras, where Theosophical headquarters remains to this day. The site is a beautiful one at the mouth of the Adyar River, and the chums made themselves comfortable in the house. But by the time they moved to Adyar, they were already drifting apart. Olcott began to spend increasing amounts of his time on missionary travels in Burma, northern India and Ceylon – especially Ceylon, where Theosophy was proving popular, not least because of the colonel's own enthusiasm for Buddhism.

The chums had visited the island for two months in May 1880. Almost as soon as they arrived Olcott went native, dressing like a brahmin in sandals and dhoti and adopting local ways. They opened seven Singhalese branches of the Society, and Olcott began to espouse the Buddhist cause against the Christian missions which dominated the island by imposing religious conformity. Only Christian marriages were legal in Ceylon. All education was Christian-dominated – 805 Christian schools as against four Buddhist – and school grants depended on teaching the Bible. Because it was necessary to have recognised qualifications to get a civil service job, all government employment was therefore closed to non-Christians.

Singhalese Buddhists had been protesting about this situation for some time. In the 1860s the protests became militant, and when Olcott and Blavatsky arrived in Ceylon and 'took pansil' – a form of Buddhist confirmation – it signalled their identification with the forces of revolt. At Kandy they were shown a most sacred relic: the Buddha's tooth, mounted on gold wire. HPB tactlessly described it as being the size of an alligator's. Olcott, pointing out that the tooth obviously dated from the period of Buddha's incarnation as a tiger, was more diplomatic. He also addressed public meetings in favour of Buddhist/Christian equality, promoted the development of a Buddhist school system on equal terms with the official education service, and when in London made representations to the Foreign Office on behalf of the Singhalese priesthood. Using his considerable managerial skills, he set up a Buddhist Defence Committee, teaching the monks how to be politically effective in pursuit of their rights. And perhaps most remarkable of all, he even produced in July 1881 an English *Buddhist Catechism*, which went into many editions and is still in print.

The results were impressive. By the 1960s, when Ceylon's education service was nationalised, the Buddhist Theosophical Society had over four hundred schools, with many former pupils in important positions. Olcott's efforts produced one of the Society's earliest and most remarkable social triumphs; in the process they had a formative influence on Singhalese nationalism.

These were real and lasting achievements, and they may turn out to be Theosophy's most enduring monument. Olcott's name is certainly remembered in the island, where there is a street named after him. In 1967, on the sixtieth anniversary of his death, the authorities issued a commemorative postage stamp and the Singhalese Prime Minister remarked that 'Colonel Olcott's visit to this country is a landmark in the history of Buddhism in Ceylon.'[17]

FOUR

Troubles

Throughout the 1880s the Theosophical Society steadily recruited members.[1] By 1885, 121 lodges had been chartered – 106 of them in India, Burma and Ceylon, where the Society had the bulk of its membership. Within a decade of Theosophy's foundation that membership was running into thousands, and distinguished converts included the poet Ella Wheeler Wilcox, Darwin's collaborator Alfred Russel Wallace and the inventor Thomas Edison. But, however welcome, increasing numbers put growing strains on the direction and administration of the Society, aggravated by personal conflicts between Blavatsky and Olcott, their remoteness from Europe and America and the ambitions of local leaders.

The problem was made worse still by the Society's structure. It was composed of lodges on the Masonic model. To begin with, each lodge was chartered directly by the parent body at Adyar and the members took democratic decisions by vote. But as the membership rose lodges were organised into national units with ruling councils. America was the first independent national 'section', constituted under Judge's leadership in 1886, followed by England (1888), India (1891), Australia and Sweden (1895), New Zealand (1896), The Netherlands (1897) and France (1899). The rest of the world was gradually colonised over the next thirty years. Although the councils were elected by the lodge members, they soon tried to assert their authority over the lodges and against the centre. The result was a three-way power struggle between Adyar, local lodges and national section councils, producing severe internal strains which erupted with increasing frequency into major scandals.

The situation was made worse by the uncertainty about Theosophy's purpose and identity. From its earliest days the Society had three basic goals, defined in 1896 as

1 the formation of a universal human brotherhood without distinction of race, creed, sex, caste or colour,
2 the encouragement of studies in comparative religion, philosophy and science, and
3 the investigation of unexplained laws of nature and the powers latent in man.

These goals are less straightforward and mutually compatible than they seem. There is, for example, debate about the exact meaning of the first. To what extent is this a political programme, to what extent merely a declaration of universal tolerance? And is such tolerance as universal as it at first appears to be? It is hard to imagine belonging to the Society, for example, if one does not believe in *some* sort of divine power.

Even the wording of the second goal is ambiguous. Does it mean comparative religion, comparative philosophy and comparative science? Or philosophy, science and comparative religion? The third goal embodies the founding impulse of the Society, but its bland formulation was to provide cover for the most outrageous impostures. Finally, the statement of all three implies that the Society is objective and non-partisan. This is of course nonsense. There is nothing objective about the study of occult phenomena by a society that has already decided that they exist and merely remain to be located and explained.

But if the three goals are individually ambiguous, they are even more confusing taken together. The ideal outcome of theosophical work is presumably that discovery of the powers latent in man through the occult study of science, philosophy and religion shall be the preferred route to the social harmony and equality which will prefigure – and perhaps become – the divine harmony. But the three goals are not necessarily compatible. They are not even couched in comparable terms, (1) being prescriptive while (2) and

(3) are supposedly neutral and 'scientific'. What they actually reflect are not universal needs and laws but the political prejudices of the well-meaning bourgeoisie.

The Society's lack of administrative and doctrinal coherence was at first its strength: the larger the goals and the vaguer their formulation, the wider the membership could be. But as we have seen, it was precisely the increase in membership that led inevitably to conflict. The rules of the Society were careful to specify that members should believe whatever their consciences told them to, on the grounds that Theosophy's objective was not the teaching of doctrine but 'scientific' research into all doctrines. It was difficult to sustain such a high-minded stance when it became clear that much of Theosophy's drawing-power rested on the sensational induce-ment of Blavatsky's claims to occult communion with the Great White Brotherhood of Masters. And although it was later decreed that belief in the Masters was *not* a condition of membership, such casuistry meant little to the ordinary member, who was less interested in bloodless discussions of theology than in contact with the Rulers of the Universe.

The situation was made worse still by the Society's tendency to attract the neurotic, the hysterical, the destructive and the down-right mad. All organisations which depend on enthusiasm and opposition to conventional opinion suffer from this problem to some degree; Theosophy appears to have been especially prone to it. The permanent residents at Adyar during the 1880s and '90s were typical. A quarrelsome collection of minor English aristocrats, rich American widows, German professors, Indian mystics and hangers-on of every description, they were all eager to have their say, especially during Olcott's prolonged absences, and all ready to quarrel with one another.

The first signs of serious trouble appeared not at Adyar, however, but in London, where Anna Kingsford and Edward Maitland were elected respectively President and Vice-President of the London Lodge on 7 January 1883. Mrs Kingsford was already a celebrated figure in esoteric Christian circles.[2] She was a strong and even charismatic woman and her relationship with Theosophy – and more particularly with Blavatsky – was uneasy from the start. Her career as a theosophist was therefore inevitably short-lived – about eighteen months – and it shows what difficulties the Society faced.

Maitland, who survived to write the life of his friend and colleague, records that Annie Bonus was born in 1846, the daughter of a rich City merchant of French descent. A talented child, who published poetry and stories in adolescence, she became financially independent at twenty-one, inheriting an annual income of £700 on the death of her father in 1867. In the same year she married a Shropshire clergyman, William Kingsford. She was a high-spirited, wilful girl, fond of hunting and other sports, and indulged by her parents and her husband. She also knew her own business, and it was a chance encounter in the execution of that business which changed her life, when she met a spiritualist while campaigning on behalf of married women's property rights. The woman gave her a copy of *Human Nature*, a spiritualist periodical which – very typically – also contained articles on Dress Reform, the campaign to do away with the corsets, crinolines and tight shoes of the mid-Victorian era in favour of healthier and more comfortable clothing. Mrs Kingsford was immediately converted to both movements, becoming a keen spiritualist and dress reformer, and this was the beginning of her lifelong involvement in alternative religion and the good causes which so often went with it.

Physically fragile and exquisitely pretty, Annie was beset by organic and psychosomatic illnesses. Despite the birth of a daughter, she seems to have lived with her husband largely on terms of friendship. He allowed her an unusual degree of personal freedom: she underwent conversion to Catholicism, and owned and edited a London journal, the *Lady's Own Paper*. This journal, which campaigned for the radical causes favoured by its owner, soon went bankrupt for lack of suitable advertising (most advertisers being excluded on ideological grounds), leaving Mrs Kingsford free to work for her ideals in other ways.

Female suffrage and women's property rights were soon outstripped, though never entirely displaced, by new passions for the animal and spiritual kingdoms, and Anna (as she was now called) devoted the rest of her short life to religion and the anti-vivisection movement, in which she took a violent and even murderous part.

To further the interest of animal welfare she decided to qualify as a doctor. For a woman this meant taking preliminary qualifications at London University and then studying for finals in the Paris medical faculty, the only place in Europe where female students were accepted.

In the mean time she had met and begun to correspond with the much older Edward Maitland, who found in her a muse and (apparently platonic) mistress combined. Though he looks from his photographs like a tired fish, Maitland was highly susceptible: in his *Life* of Anna he coyly alludes to his earlier relationships with several other 'noble women'. But even without his descriptions of her golden hair, long lashes and hazel eyes – he called her a 'blonde goddess'[3] – it is clear from every page of the biography that Maitland was infatuated with Anna, and for the rest of her life they collaborated in a religious quest.

An upper-middle-class drop-out and veteran of the 1849 California Gold Rush, Maitland had returned to England in 1857 after a hard and adventurous life in Melanesia and a slightly easier one in Australia, where his cousin was Governor General. Originally driven to the Antipodes by personal and spiritual troubles (he describes himself as a spoilt ordinand), he returned to Europe still in quest of a satisfying romantic relationship and a rational religion. His spiritual ideal was a Christian doctrine so logically sound as to be irrefutable and therefore undeniable; but such a doctrine, he believed, would also turn out to be a demonstration of the fundamental unity of all the great religions, deriving ultimate strength from its universality. At the same time, he saw this doctrine in terms of personal revelation and the individual's relationship to God. Like so many of his contemporaries, Maitland craved intellectual and spiritual certainty while detesting what he calls the sacerdotalist materialism of the times: the rule of a priestly hierarchy, whether Catholic or Protestant, who encourage their flocks to worship idols instead of getting to know inner spiritual realities.

Anna enthusiastically agreed with her friend that the great religious failing of the moderns was to take signs for realities. But the whole visible, tangible universe was in her view only the image of a higher spiritual order, accessible to a few extraordinary beings, of whom she turned out to be one. Spiritual enlightenment could never be communicated by or through orthodox religious institutions for the simple reason that 'Truth is never phenomenal; it is always noumenal.'[4] The soul can only perceive wisdom subjectively. But this is not a matter for the vulgarities of the seance-room. Though she heard voices and saw visions, Kingsford was just as careful as Blavatsky to distinguish herself from the common run of mediums and clairvoyants. Constantly in communion with the spirit world, she was assured by its denizens that she was herself a prophet, not a medium; her body, they told her, was the vehicle for an ancient spirit to which she referred as her genius. Her inspiration therefore came not from without (as with mediums) but from within. She had risen far above the vulgarities of spiritualism and clairvoyance to the higher level of illumination or gnosis: the direct intuition of spiritual truth.

This view was supported by other spirits who told Edward – speaking, of course, through Anna – that he must never offend her or question anything she said or wrote 'under illumination' because such communications were sacred. The instruction was hardly necessary. Edward venerated his partner's powers as much as he adored her person, regarding her revelations as far superior to what he calls the obscure hints of divine truth given in Plato and the Bible. Even if her gifts had not commanded his respect and obedience, Anna would have dominated her friend with ease. She was by far the stronger character: a bossy and capricious woman who ruled over Maitland with his glad consent – which is just as well, given her strength of mind. In the course of her campaign against animal experiments, Mrs Kingsford claimed to have *willed* to death several famous French vivisectors, writing after one expired of fever: 'The will *can* and *does* kill . . . I *have* killed Paul Bert, as I killed Claude Bernard; as I will kill Louis Pasteur . . .'[5]

Edward and Anna were soon working closely together with the blessing of Mr Kingsford, who requested Maitland to accompany his wife to Paris as her chaperon, he himself being tied to his Shropshire parish by pastoral duties. When not in Paris the friends lived partly in Shropshire with the rector and partly in London, where Anna rented a succession of houses in Mayfair. Spirituality did not exclude fashionable life and Mrs Kingsford was part of a distinguished circle which included the Hon. Roden Noel, Lord and Lady Mount Temple (the closest friends of Laurence Oliphant, who crassly attempted to recruit Mrs Kingsford to his cause), Lady Ribblesdale, Lady Tennant, Lady Archibald Campbell and the Hon. Mr and Mrs Percy Wyndham. There was also the Cuban-born Countess of Caithness, who lived in a palace in Nice and dressed like Mary, Queen of Scots, of whom she claimed to be the reincarnation.[6] A friend of all the leading theosophists and occultists, Lady Caithness spent her time writing them passionately spiritual letters or giving grand parties (to which they were not invited) at her houses in Paris and the south of France.

Though less flamboyant, Anna was equally energetic. When she wasn't studying medicine or expounding visions she was often to be found putting on plays about Buddha in Belgravia drawing-rooms. Before long Edward, too, developed his modest psychic powers under her influence. He saw into the insides of trees and encountered the spirit of his long-dead father, who now confessed to the error of quarrelling with his son in life.

Thinking of themselves as two halves of a psychic unity, the pair co-operated, though Anna was very much the dominant partner. Maitland transcribed what Mrs Kingsford dictated, adding occasional picturesque details of his own. Anna's visions came to her in trances or in dreams which revealed all manner of strange things. Sometimes she saw her own inner organs, thus diagnosing illnesses. She was visited by Joan of Arc, the Virgin Mary and Anne Boleyn; by Swedenborg's wraith, who mentioned in passing that Jesus had revived Confucianism; and by an American spirit who told her that, in their working relationship at least, she took the masculine role and Edward the feminine. No doubt this was reassuring for Mrs Kingsford.

More importantly, she was vouchsafed the revelation of a whole new doctrine, which appeared in serial parts like a cosmic soap opera. This doctrine was founded on the Swedenborgian notion that the universe available to our senses is composed of symbols and that religion is therefore a form of hermeneutics, the science of interpretation. Anna accordingly gave Hermes – the tutelary god of interpreters – a higher place than Jesus in her ecumenical pantheon, and wrote extensively about the true interpretation of mythology, and scriptural and liturgical texts, expounding doctrines of karma and reincarnation.

Given the complexity and completeness of her own theology, it is hard to see what Kingsford found in Theosophy. She later claimed to have mistrusted the Society and its Founders from the start, having joined only in the vain hope of reforming it from within. It seems likely that she expected to take over Theosophy, in England if not elsewhere, and to use the organisation to propagate her own views. Introduced through the good offices of an idealistic early member, the barrister C. C. Massey, who was looking Maitland-like for noble women to counter HPB's tendency to mischief, Anna was soon prominent in the London Lodge, and her urge to dominate any enterprise she undertook propelled her to its presidency in record time.

Before long Mrs Kingsford was beginning to regret her association with the Society, though it was not Blavatsky who caused the trouble this time but A. P. Sinnett, who had recently published two books about Theosophy, both of which stirred up scandal. This was hard on Sinnett, who was only trying to help his new friends. In his first book, *The Occult World* (1881), he had printed (at the Master's own suggestion) letters received from Koot Hoomi via Madame Blavatsky. The book circulated widely in spiritualist circles and came to the attention of the American medium Henry Kiddle, who wrote to Sinnett pointing out that Koot Hoomi appeared to have reproduced, almost verbatim, a passage from one of his own speeches. When Sinnett failed to reply to his letter, Kiddle published the charges of plagiarism in the spiritualist journal *Light* and there was a row. HPB was contemptuous: 'Koot Hoomi *plagiarized* from Kiddle! Ye gods and little fishes . . . Plagiarize from the BANNER OF LIGHT!! – that sweet spirits' slop-basin!'[7] Admitting the resemblance between the two passages – and perhaps fearing further research into other parts of the book – she suggested that Koot Hoomi had somehow picked up Kiddle's speech on the astral radio waves and then forgotten about it, in the way that one reproduces phrases without thinking. This cast a curious light on the allegedly powerful Master's fallibility, and few people believed her.

By the time the Kiddle scandal broke in 1883, Kingsford and Maitland were already having serious doubts about Theosophy, but it was Sinnett's second book *Esoteric Buddhism*, published later that year, which enraged them by equating Theosophy with the author's highly selective interpretation of Buddhist scriptures. This was bad enough for the christocentric[8] Anna, already alarmed by the Society's tendency to jettison Christianity in favour of eastern occultism. What made it far worse was that Sinnett had concerned himself with what she regarded as the frippery side of Buddhism: psychic phenomena, bodisattvas (little buddhas) and the manifestation of spirits. He had thereby committed the cardinal sin of taking symbols for realities. Far from being esoteric, in her view the book was thoroughly meretricious and materialistic: sensational in every sense. If this was the official theosophical line – and HPB herself appeared to be a Sinnett supporter – she wanted nothing to do with it. Now living in England – he had returned from India in 1883 after his dismissal from the Allahabad *Pioneer* – Sinnett was a member of the London Lodge, which promptly split into two parties, some members for Sinnett, others for Kingsford.

In February 1884 HPB and Olcott sailed for England to sort out the row. Having described Anna's followers as 'a lot of weak cowardly Grundyists, a flock of *moutons de Panurge* following [their] Jockey-club scented leaders',[9] Blavatsky was not inclined to put up with rebellion. Sweeping into a meeting, where some of the more theatrical members sank to their knees before her, she attempted to subdue Maitland and Kingsford by staring them down, but they were not to be cowed, and accused her of trying to put a spell on them. The colonel, fearful that the simmering row might precipitate something worse, defused the tension by humorously instructing HPB not to 'magnetise' her opponents.

The rebels were briefly placated by the creation of a new Hermetic Lodge under Anna's direction, founded on 9 April 1884. Members of the London Lodge were then left free to choose between the orthodox group and the new one. But even this concession wasn't good enough for Anna. Within a matter of days, convinced of Theosophy's thorough corruption, she felt the need to assert her purity, authority and independence by breaking away to found her own Hermetic Society on 22 April. The new society's declared objectives – the comparison of eastern and western mythologies and the interpretation of scriptures – were close to Theosophy's, but, as Anna remarked, there was no nonsense about Masters in Tibet to cloud the issue.

The conflict between Blavatsky and Kingsford was both personal and doctrinal. Two strong women, each with a mild and credulous male follower, were bound to clash. Characterising Maitland and Kingsford as 'the irrepressible *Perfect Way* twins', HPB reacted violently to her rival, describing her as 'an unbearable female snob', a 'divine whistle-breeches' and 'a snake, a horned aspic among roses, a selfish, vain and *mediumistic* creature'.[10] Conscious of the younger woman's pretensions and her attractiveness to men, she poked fun at Anna's fashion sense and her literary style, satirising the 'scientific gibberish' and 'flapdooble interpretations'[11] of the 'zebra-clad Kingsford'.[12] Though less colourful, Anna was equally scathing.

This was an opportunity missed. The two women had different strengths which might have been complementary. If Anna had the edge over HPB in looks, wealth and social position, HPB had control of an international organisation. But the differences went too deep. They were described by Anna herself in terms of oriental occultists versus occidental mystics, and this conflict was to cause frequent schisms within the Society in the years ahead. While HPB dismissed Kingsford as a mere medium, in Anna's book her rival was an occultist – and occultists were well down the religious ladder, in contact with the spirit world only at second hand.

Shortly before her own death Anna Kingsford claimed to have dreamt that she met HPB in the Buddhist heaven. Blavatsky was still smoking her foul cigarettes, but she did so only after humbly asking permission of Anna's own patron, Hermes (whose presence in the Buddhist heaven remains unexplained). The scene is aptly symbolic. The split between western and eastern faiths – a split that curiously echoes the dividing of the Christian churches many centuries before – was the first but by no means the last rebellion by those who felt that Theosophy was turning too far towards the East and abandoning the traditional Christian faith. This was not, according to its critics, a sign of religious universalism but the whole-hearted embracing of an alien creed.

At this stage, the Theosophical Society was strong enough and small enough to withstand the crisis, and Anna's early death in 1885 removed the danger of a major rival. But the serious doctrinal disputes in London were as nothing compared to the farcical drama brewing back at Adyar, where the uneducated housekeeper left in charge by Blavatsky turned out to be another strong woman and a far more formidable enemy than the cultivated and brilliant Anna Kingsford.

Emma Cutting had met HPB in Cairo in 1872 when Blavatsky was trying to set up a seance centre staffed by local mediums. The business collapsed in a matter of weeks with accusations of fraud all round, and Miss Cutting later claimed that she had lent her new acquaintance money to help her out of the scrape. Emma subsequently fell on hard times herself, despite marriage to a Frenchman, Alexis Coulomb, and several stabs at the hotel business in various parts of the world. None of their ventures was successful, and by the 1880s the Coulombs found themselves virtually destitute in Ceylon. When they saw a newspaper announcement of Blavatsky's arrival in India they clutched at this straw. Madame Coulomb immediately wrote to HPB, who invited them to join her, which they did, their tickets to Bombay paid for by the French Consul, who must have been glad to see the back of them.

Emma was later described in an angry pamphlet by one of Blavatsky's henchmen, Dr Franz Hartmann, as 'a weird witch-like creature with wrinkled features, a stinging look, and an uncouth form . . . She seemed to consider it her special purpose in life to pry into everybody's private affairs . . .'[13] while her husband was

> a ghostly-looking Frenchman with the complexion of an
> ash-barrel to which is attached a beard. While he speaks
> with you, his one glass eye stares you out of countenance,

and his other eye with characteristic politeness wanders out
of your way.[14]

The Coulombs settled in at Theosophical Society headquarters as
unpaid housekeeper and handyman and the fur soon began to fly.
Emma and Alexis were of no importance in themselves, being
excluded from the Society's management, but that was part of the
trouble: Madame Coulomb saw herself belittled by her lowly job
and by her old friend's patronage. She was a haughty, vengeful and
quarrelsome bitch, and a petty thief who was not above siphoning
off the housekeeping money. As for Alexis, he lived completely
under the thumb of his sharp-tongued and ambitious wife, who
made up for her inferior station by hinting to everyone within
earshot that, but for her loyalty to Blavatsky, she could open their
eyes to extraordinary goings-on. For once she was telling the truth;
finding her an invaluable help when it came to staging complicated
'phenomena', HPB had foolishly taken Madame Coulomb into her
confidence.

The matter might have blown over, had not Emma's growing
spite been stimulated by powerful attacks from two other sources.
The Christian missionary societies in Madras and Ceylon were
incensed by the Theosophists' activities, and more especially by
Blavatsky's open contempt for Christianity. Though it was certainly
not excluded from the synthesis of the theosophical wisdom
religion, there was a clear move against it apparent in the colonel's
drift towards Buddhism, HPB's indifference to all religions except
her own personality cult, and their joint cultivation of everything
native. Christianity was the official faith of the ruling power in
India, though the British government had been careful not to
impose its own creed on the native population. This made Christian
missionaries all the more aggressive. After comparatively little
progress in the subcontinent in over a century – nothing to compare
with their African successes – they were not inclined to tolerate
rivals such as the Theosophical Society. The Principal of the
Christian College in Madras, many of whose students provokingly
supported HPB and Olcott because of their nationalist stance, was
especially keen to see Theosophy discredited.

At the same time, the Society for Psychical Research decided to investigate Theosophy.[15] Founded in London in 1882, the SPR rapidly became an influential body, including John Ruskin, Lord Tennyson, W. E. Gladstone and William James among its members. Though more limited in scope, it had affinities with Theosophy's scientific project, and several Theosophists – notably Edward Maitland and Alfred Russel Wallace – had joined. Both organisations claimed to be devoted to the objective study of the spirit world, the SPR rather more convincingly than the TS.

Before leaving for London, HPB had put light to the tinder by quarrelling with her housekeeper. As so often with Blavatsky, the problem involved money. It appeared from his complaint to the Founders that Emma had tried to extract a loan from one of Theosophy's most promising upper-class neophytes, Prince Ranjit-sinji. This was not the first time she had approached members for money, and she was sternly forbidden to do it again. Hearing in London that Emma was still agitating for a loan, both Olcott and HPB wrote telling her to desist on pain of their displeasure. Their letters only fuelled the housekeeper's bitter hostility. Well treated by her patrons, she resented their patronage while wanting to profit from it even more than she already had.

She saw her way to advancement by stirring up trouble in Blavatsky's absence. The situation at Adyar was already tense. The Theosophical Society headquarters had been left in the charge of a board of trustees including St George Lane Fox, a wealthy and excitable former electrical engineer and the scion of an English upper-class family, and Franz Hartmann, a sharp-tongued German physician previously settled in America. Although the board included Indian members the Europeans were dominant, and this caused bad feeling between the races which Madame Coulomb was ready to exploit. In possession of the keys to her patroness's rooms, she saw her opportunity to blackmail Hartmann and Lane Fox, who both dreaded scandal.

First she claimed to have compromising letters from HPB in her possession – many of them signed 'Luna Melancholica', yet another of Blavatsky's nicknames. Addressed to Emma, these letters made it clear that HPB had deliberately set up phenomena to defraud the public by arranging for her housekeeper to stage them in Blavatsky's absence. She had used Emma as an accomplice to precipitate letters, materialise saucers and provide visions of the Masters.

Madame Coulomb presented Hartmann and Lane Fox with a simple ultimatum: pay up or have the frauds revealed by publication of the letters. When they hesitated, Emma went into convincing detail. She showed them how she and HPB had made a doll together, which they nicknamed Christofolo and manipulated on a long bamboo pole in semi-darkness to provide the Master's alleged apparitions. Emma had also dropped 'precipitated' letters on to Theosophical heads from holes in the ceiling, while her husband had made sliding panels and hidden entrances into the shrine-room to facilitate Blavatsky's comings and goings and make possible the substitution of all the brooches, dishes and other objects that she used in her demonstrations.

Embarrassingly enough, the shrine-room – the scene of many theosophical miracles – adjoined HPB's bedroom. The shrine itself was a sort of glorified wardrobe with a lock, and only HPB and Emma had access to it. According to Emma, it also had a secret entrance from the bedroom. The tricks they had played there were crude. One of the compromising letters seemed to show quite clearly that Blavatsky had set out to fool a visiting general into believing that a broken saucer was reconstituted in the shrine, simply by arranging for Emma to substitute an identical whole dish for the broken one by sleight of hand.

The Board of Trustees resisted at first, threatening the Coulombs with instant eviction for gross libel and dereliction of duty, but their faith was shattered into as many pieces as the general's saucer when they visited the shrine-room to investigate. One of them struck the shrine saying, 'You see, it is quite solid,'[16] and the middle panel flew up in his face, revealing the truth of Emma's charges. The following night the board members burnt the incriminating cupboard and entered into negotiations with the Coulombs.

First Hartmann offered them shares he happened to own in a Colorado silver mine, with the hint that they might like to visit America in order to stake their claim personally. These shares they wisely refused in favour of cash, but then they overplayed their hand by holding out for too much. The members of the board called their bluff – what were a few more allegtions of fraud against HPB, after all? – and eventually Emma and her husband were forced out of Adyar empty-handed in the summer of 1884, though not before Lane Fox had punched Coulomb in front of a policeman called in to arbitrate between the disputing parties, for which he was fined £10.

Meanwhile letters from the Masters and their human agents were flying in every direction. At this point HPB lost control of correspondence between the Brotherhood and the world. First, Master KH wrote to Hartmann telling him not to expel the Coulombs. Then Master Morya told him the opposite. Olcott received anonymously a letter which at first appeared to be from Hartmann to Madame Coulomb, accusing Blavatsky of trickery, and then turned out to be a forgery – but by whom and for what purpose? HPB herself wrote to everyone or was alleged by them to have done so, supporting whatever position they took and exculpating herself from all present, past or future charges. It seemed that her creations, both divine and mundane, had got thoroughly out of hand.

But worse was to come, and once again letters were the source of the trouble. So far, scandal had remained within the walls of the Adyar compound. All this changed when Emma, expelled from that paradise, sold the collection of letters, supposedly written to her by HPB, to Blavatsky's bitter enemy, the Reverend Patterson, Principal of the Madras Christian College and publisher of the *Christian College Magazine*. Fiercely hostile to Theosophy and its frankly anti-Christian stance, Patterson was on the look-out for anything to discredit the Society. With perfect timing he issued the first batch of letters in September 1884 – just as Richard Hodgson, the investigator appointed by the SPR, embarked on his enquiry into the charges against Theosophy.

Blavatsky and Olcott were still in London sorting out the Kingsford affair. They were interviewed there by the SPR and did not return to Adyar until December 1884. Hodgson thus had a clear run to interview whom he chose in India. He was not concerned with the existence or otherwise of the Masters. His brief was simply to investigate the phenomena reported by Blavatsky and her followers: astral bells, music, moving bodies, precipitated letters and the rest. His preliminary report, published at the end of the year and relying heavily on the evidence of Madame Coulomb, was inevitably damning. All the phenomena were dismissed, either as HPB's deliberate forgeries and deceptions or as hallucinations and misunderstandings on the part of witnesses, especially Olcott, who is branded (in politer language) as a credulous old fool. Inclined to accept Blavatsky's own opinion of Olcott as 'a wind-bag full of vanity',[17] Hodgson described HPB herself as 'neither the mouth-piece of hidden seers, nor as a mere vulgar adventuress; we think that she has achieved a title to permanent remembrance as one of the most accomplished, ingenious, and interesting impostors of history'.[18]

But the criticism which enraged her most was his hint that she might be working in the pay of 'Russian interests'.[19] This was a common suspicion among officials of the Raj, reinforced by reports of HPB's mild but unwise criticisms of their regime, her apparent support for Indian Home Rule and her reiterated insistence that, despite its harsh treatment of political prisoners, the Russian government was more liberal in social matters than its British counterpart. When Olcott begged her to make her loyalty plain, she wrote to Sinnett and others protesting that she had no quarrel with the British, but the suspicions remained. They reached a ludicrous climax when a page from one of her manuscripts written in some strange language was stolen by Emma Coulomb and sold by her to the Madras Christian College, who passed it on to the Calcutta police as a probable spy cipher. After studying the page for several months, the police could make nothing of it: hardly surprising, as it was written in Senzar, a language supposedly dictated to Blavatsky by the Masters.

Eventually Hodgson withdrew his claim that HPB was a Russian spy, but the upshot of his report was uproar inside the Theosophical Society. Everyone accused everyone else. HPB claimed that Emma Coulomb had doctored her letters. She also accused Hartmann of lying and intriguing and told Sinnett that she didn't trust Olcott. Olcott reproached his chum for her indiscretions. Lane Fox and

Hartmann both blamed the incompetence of Indian members of the Board of Trustees for the scandal, and the Indians blamed the Europeans for lack of trust.

Hodgson's judgement of HPB has been angrily disputed by Theosophists ever since. They point out that Hodgson compiled most of the report alone, that his methods of taking evidence were dubious in the extreme, and that he simply chose to believe one highly unreliable testimony (Madame Coulomb's) rather than another. They also insist that the SPR is, *de facto*, hostile to spiritualism and the manifestation of phenomena. But as Hodgson says in the introduction to his report: 'whatever prepossessions I may have had were distinctly in favour of Occultism and Madame Blavatsky'.[20]

However, though Theosophists were wrong about Hodgson's own attitude, they were right to point out antagonism to their activities within the hierarchy of the Society for Psychical Research. The SPR tended to polarise into three parties, one sympathetic to spiritualism, the second hostile, the third (and smallest) genuinely committed to dispassionate scientific investigation. The governing body was dominated by the hostile party, led by a group of Cambridge intellectuals including the President of the SPR, Henry Sidgwick (Professor of Philosophy at Cambridge), and Frank Podmore, a founder of the Fabian Society. Though a serious investigator committed to scientific neutrality, Hodgson belonged to the SPR's pro-spiritualism party and he was disappointed by the exposure of HPB's frauds. In later life, under the influence of the American medium Lenore Piper, he began to receive his own spirit messages from a childhood sweetheart. After his early death in 1905 he became the first psychic investigator to have a university appointment named after him: the Hodgson Fellowship in Psychical Research at Harvard. He has not been heard from since.

HPB's reputation in Anglo-Indian circles never recovered from the double blow inflicted by the SPR and the *Christian College Magazine*. But the adverse publicity actually enhanced her standing with many Indians, because of the way in which it polarised the antagonism between Hindu nationalists and Christian missionaries, which was in turn part of the larger conflict between the colonisers and the colonised. Blavatsky appeared to be firmly pro-Hindu in India, just as Olcott was pro-Buddhist in Ceylon. Any attack by the missionary societies or western organisations such as the SPR therefore simply obscured issues of occult truth and falsehood by identifying Blavatsky with the cause of Home Rule in the eyes of her Indian supporters.

On her return to Madras from England in December 1884, HPB was consequently fêted by native well-wishers – including many students from the Christian College in rebellion against their own Principal. Elated by her reception, she wanted to sue her enemies for libel, but Olcott knew better. He was well aware that any lawsuit she brought would simply turn into a trial of Theosophy and its leaders, who would not find imperial justice quite as sympathetic as nationalist crowds. Convoking a council of the Society to give him the advice he wanted to hear, he announced their decision that Blavatsky would be unwise to prosecute, and her popular victory turned into a personal defeat. Recognising that the game was finally up, and that there was no way she could live down the exposure of her trickery among her own closest associates, she resigned her office as Corresponding Secretary and left for Europe in March 1885, under considerable pressure from Olcott to do so. Their friendship was effectively over.

Perhaps it was just as well. HPB had been ill for some time, writing to Mrs Sinnett in 1882 that

> I am afraid you will soon have to bid me goodbye –
> whether to Heaven or to Hell – connais pas. This time I
> have it well and good – bright's disease of the kidneys; and
> the whole blood turned into water with ulcers breaking out
> in the most unexpected and the less explored spots, blood
> or whatever it may be forming into bags *à la kangaroo* and
> other pretty extras and et ceteras . . . I can last a year or
> two . . . but . . . can kick the bucket at any time . . .[21]

By 1884 she was 'an old, squeezed-out lemon, morally and physically, good only for cleaning Old Nick's nails with . . .'[22] and

> falling to pieces; crumbling away like an old sea biscuit,
> and the most I will be able to do, will be to pick up and
> join together my voluminous fragments and gluing them
> together carry the ruin to Paris . . .[23]

Her illness was made worse by such grotesque obesity that at times she could hardly move, and the combination of illness and fat meant that when she took ship at Madras she had to be hauled on board in a chair attached to a rope and pulley.

Like this last Indian episode, much of HPB's life is a glorious comedy, as the tone of her letters often tacitly recognises, but it could have tragic consequences for those who trusted her. In 1886, while Blavatsky was enjoying comparative luxury in Germany, Olcott received a letter from Koot Hoomi about one of her most faithful followers, Damodar K. Mavalankar, a young brahmin who had left his wife to become a fervent supporter of the Society. It seems that his passion for Theosophy had involved Damodar unwittingly in Blavatsky's frauds, when she used him to precipitate letters.

Ashamed of his role in the scandal, Damodar set out on a journey to find the Masters for himself in the high mountains of Sikkim. On the final stages of his journey he travelled alone. According to Koot Hoomi's letter Damodar had reached his goal despite appalling sufferings, and was ready to undergo initiation as an Adept. He was certainly never seen alive again by human eyes, and when a corpse was found Olcott suggested that it was 'a Maya', or illusion, 'to make it appear as if the pilgrim had succumbed'.[24] But there were those who pointed out that the frozen body discovered on the mountain path not far from where Damodar was last seen had been dressed in his clothes. Blavatsky's most recent biographer responds to this evidence with the interesting suggestion that Damodar had obviously changed into something warmer to accommodate the climate of the mountains.

FIVE

Apostolic Succession

After the publication of the full SPR report in December 1885, resignations poured in to the Adyar HQ and Blavatsky was savaged in the press. Scandal followed her as she travelled through Europe, trying to decide where to settle. In Germany she stayed with Frau Gephardt, distinguished as a former pupil of Eliphas Lévi, but there was trouble when one of the theosophical party went mad and threatened to tear HPB limb from limb.[1] For a while she shared lodgings in Ostend with her sister Vera and Countess Constance Wachtmeister. Falling seriously ill, she was visited there on an unsuccessful peace mission by Anna Kingsford and Edward Maitland, and by Master Morya, who told HPB she could choose between the peace of death and the struggle of life. He was right about the struggle. Choosing life, she wrestled with a vast new book and found herself permanently short of money.

Her constant demands for more from Adyar were carefully monitored by Olcott, who knew all too well that his chum would fritter their entire resources if allowed to do so. He warned Blavatsky to 'keep your cash for bread',[2] explaining that the Society could no longer afford to tolerate her expensive whims. Olcott also told his colleague bluntly that Theosophists had a 'grim determination' to have nothing more to do with phenomena or with attacks on individuals – a scarcely veiled reference to HPB's habit of stirring up trouble with anyone who offended her. Though he knew that it was 'equivalent to asking you to give up the breath out of your body', he wanted to 'keep things quiet and go on steadily with useful work', fearing that any more scandals would ruin Theosophy irretrievably. Insisting that HPB was welcome to return to Adyar whenever she chose, Olcott nevertheless warned her that 'the proverb says "It's an ill bird that fouls its own nest." Don't make yours uninhabitable.'

She was not an easy guest, and many of her stays ended in tears. The entourage she travelled with didn't help. They included a half-witted Irish girl who had daily visions of the Masters, and the tiny Hindu who eventually went mad in Germany. But it was the third member of her suite, a handsome brahmin called Mohini Mohandas Chatterjee (1858–1936), who caused the worst trouble when he became entangled with a Miss Leonard who bared her breasts at him as they walked together through a wood near Paris.

Miss Leonard was not the only one to become infatuated with Mohini. Blavatsky, who hated sex with her own sort of passion, wrote to Mrs Sinnett that

> There *are others in the group*, and not one but *four in number*, who burn with a scandalous, ferocious passion for Mohini – with that craving of old *gourmands* for *unnatural* food, for rotten Limburg cheese with worms in it to tickle their satiated palates – or of the 'Pall Mall' iniquitous old men for forbidden fruit – ten year old virgins! Oh, the filthy beasts!! the sacrilegious, hypocritical harlots.[3]

Indians were to prove sexually fascinating for many a theosophically inclined European woman. It appeared that one girl had even learnt a trick or two from her elders, sending Mohini letters as though from a Master, inviting him to use her body as he thought fit. HPB also fired off foolish letters, calling Miss Leonard Messalina and Potiphar's wife, until the lady's solicitors threatened to sue for libel. It turned out that Mohini himself had written some more than compromising letters to Miss Leonard, and HPB was forced to offer her an apology under threat of legal proceedings. Raving against the libel laws of England and the stupidity of her followers, she complained to Sinnett that 'A too erotic spinster falls in love with a nut-meg Hindu with buck eyes, and one of the results is that . . . a third party innocent of the squabble from beginning to end – myself – is *smashed* in the affray.'[4]

Mohini ended by causing her as much trouble as the equally delectable Anna Kingsford, prompting HPB to lump them together as Don Juan and St Teresa. She evidently knew more about his ways than she admitted to most of her correspondents. Hearing of her letter to Miss Leonard and not apprised of the impending lawsuit, Olcott wrote praising his old chum for once: 'I know the scandal about Mohini . . . Your "Mrs Potiphar" theory is capital. If he has not really played the goose and – manufactured a Eurasian.'[5] But the colonel changed his tune when the scandal erupted, lamenting yet another outbreak of Theosophical correspondence:

> Such a showering around of private letters that were meant to be kept secret, I never heard of in my life before! Mine to Hubbe and the Gebhardts, to Hoffman, and others; my letter to the L.L. intended to brace up our branches at a crisis and sent by Mrs Cavell to an N.Y. paper! Leadbeater's to Sinnett or Miss A.; and now yours to Madame de Morsier . . .[6]

Mohini survived the scandal, but his relations with Madame Blavatsky did not, and they went their separate ways. He left the Society, setting up as a spiritual teacher in his own right. After spending several years in London he returned to India, where he ended his days in charge of a home for fallen women.

If she had little taste for men or they for her, HPB was attractive to her own sex, whose psychic powers were awakened by her influence. Under Blavatsky's guidance one woman had a nocturnal visit from Master Morya after gazing at his portrait for more than an hour earlier that day. Several heard astral bells in Madame's presence. Some even received personal communications from the Masters. Constance Wachtmeister, an Anglo-Italian married to a Swede, was especially receptive to the other world, being not only clairvoyant but also clairaudient. When she saw streams of astral light coming from HPB's cuckoo clock, the clock's owner attributed them to a 'spiritual telegraph' whereby the Masters charged her with energy for the following day's work on her writing. Her output continued unabated by discomfort or ill-health as she laboured on another huge book, *The Secret Doctrine*.[7]

Others were more sceptical. The Russian journalist V. S. Solovieff claimed to have caught her red-handed with the silver bells which produced astral music. He also found in her desk drawer a pile of the (unused) envelopes in which the Masters delivered their letters.[8] This was not in itself evidence of fraud, since it is supposedly only the text of letters which is precipitated, not the paper. But evidence was hardly necessary: as she so often did when carried away by the need to confide or to boast, Blavatsky confessed to Solovieff quite bluntly that the phenomena were fraudulent, adding that one must deceive men in order to rule them. He professed to admire her Machiavellian doctrine. HPB responded by dubbing him 'the Iago of Theosophy'.[9] Such admissions probably made little difference to her reputation and one can hardly blame her for indulging in a bit of fun. Life on the road was hard. She was suffering from dropsy, among other ailments, her breathing was often difficult, and getting in and out of carriages or up and down stairs was positive torture. But she was not finished yet.

After her prolonged travels in Europe, she finally settled in London in the spring of 1887, supported by the rich and aristocratic friends who helped to sustain her last years, including Lady Caithness, Countess Wachtmeister, Miss Francesca Arundale and the Keightleys, uncle and nephew. They helped to set up her journal, *Lucifer*, and to found an exclusive arm of the Society in London, the Blavatsky Lodge. HPB enjoyed the attentions of her new admirers, but she had more in view than satisfied vanity. Olcott was not forgiven for driving her out of India and she wanted revenge. This she determined to take by establishing her own European power base as a challenge to Adyar.

She did not look forward to life in England. 'What's the use asking me to go to London?' she enquired of one of her British supporters. 'What shall I, what *can* I do amidst your eternal fogs and the emanations of the highest civilization?'[10] And although she was duly grateful to Miss Arundale for an offer of hospitality, she predicted that she would 'become obnoxious to them in 7 minutes and a quarter, were I to accept it and land my disagreeable bulky self in England'.[11] The prediction seems to have been justified, for HPB later referred to Miss Arundale and two of her male friends as 'the theosophica-Ethical Urn with the two chela handles'.[12]

She lodged first in a south London suburb with the popular novelist Mabel Collins, and continued to tinker with her new book. The manuscript was in chaos. Bertram Keightley, Secretary to the London Lodge, and his uncle Archibald (the two 'chela handles') had agreed to act as editors, but despaired when confronted with a pile of scribbled papers three feet high and in no discernible order. They began their task by moving Blavatsky to their own house at 17 Lansdowne Road, Holland Park, where they could keep an eye on her.

She received a stream of distinguished guests in Lansdowne Road, including W. B. Yeats, who later compared his hostess to an old Irish peasant woman, at once holy, sad and sly. Yeats took the revival of eastern wisdom very seriously and dabbled in a wide range of esoteric 'sciences' including cheirosophy (palmistry), celestial dynamics (astrology), chromopathy (healing by colours) and polygraphics (a form of automatic writing). Alerted to Theosophy by Sinnett's *Esoteric Buddhism*, but doubting the objective existence of the Masters, he was converted to membership by Mohini Chatterjee, who arrived in Dublin in 1885 'with a little bag in his hand and *Marius The Epicurean* in his pocket'.[13] Mohini, who returned to Ireland in the following year to address Yeats's recently formed Hermetic Society,[14] told the poet that 'Easterns' had a quite different sense of what constitutes truthfulness from Europeans, a claim in which Yeats heard no irony, perhaps because he found 'the young Brahmin' seductive.[15]

Yeats later described the difficulty of trying to awaken from the spell Mohini cast over all who met him. Always susceptible to charm and beauty, the poet preferred both Mohini and Kingsford to HPB, whom he found less intuitive if more humorous than either, though he did use her as a model for the character of Mrs Allingham in his novel *The Speckled Bird*, in which Anna Kingsford also appears. Anna was equally charmed by Mohini. A man who could so beguile Yeats, Kingsford *and* the vulgar Miss Leonard was clearly a force to be reckoned with.

Though he never quite trusted her, Yeats was fascinated by HPB, feeling that here at last was someone who could cut through the tedious vagueness of most occult writing and produce hard evidence for psychic phenomena.[16] In search of such evidence he joined the recently formed Esoteric Section of the Theosophical Society at Christmas 1888. He also engaged in occult experiments with a group of friends. First this group tried to raise the ghost of a flower from its ashes. Then each put some of the ashes under his pillow and recorded his dreams. Though the results were disappointing Yeats was not discouraged. However, his experiments had to continue outside the Society, from which he was expelled by Blavatsky in 1890 for reasons which are obscure.[17] Transferring his loyalty to the Golden Dawn, a magical fraternity based on Rosicrucianism, Yeats found himself better suited. He had come to understand the difference between rational scientific organisations, such as the SPR, and secret magical orders in which the members constitute an exclusive mystical whole, and believed that the TS had disastrously confused the issue by trying to be both at once.[18]

While Yeats was visiting HPB at Lansdowne Road, her hosts were struggling with the new book. The Keightleys divided the chaotic manuscript into four sections. Of these, only the first two – *Cosmogenesis* and *Anthropogenesis* – were issued, in the autumn of 1888, by a publishing house they set up to produce the book at their own expense. *The Secret Doctrine* is a difficult read. Supposedly based on stanzas from *The Book of Dzyan*, which was written in Senzar (a language unknown to any linguist), HPB's text explicates these stanzas and their commentaries. *Cosmogenesis* explains how and why the universe came into being. *Anthropogenesis* covers the history of Man – though HPB is as ready as Darwin to concede that the ancestors of humanity are not themselves human. In fact the whole of the second volume is a commentary on Darwin. Mankind is shown to be descended from spiritual beings from another planet (the moon) who gradually took physical form through a series of what HPB calls 'root races'. Human history is one phase in spirit's attempt to rise up again through a vast series of rebirths moving through the cosmos from planet to planet.

The first of the root races consisted of little more than multiplying cells: sexless, ethereal and eternal. Gradually but very slowly the cells evolved into physical forms until a group of characters variously called the Sons of Wisdom and the Lords of the Flame arrived from Venus to give earth's primitive beings a leg-up into a higher stage. Different continents and civilisations – such as Lemuria, where Adam and Eve lived, and Atlantis, which survived in collective memory as the Golden Age – then came into being and were destroyed by folly or cataclysm. For each stage of cosmic evolution has its own cyclical development modelled on the alternation of day and night. At present, for example, we are still in the Kali Yuga (dark age) of the Fifth Root Race, which started with the death of Krishna, killed by an arrow on 16 February 3102 BC.

Though *The Secret Doctrine* sold quite well, reviewers and scholars were hostile, dismissing it as the usual farrago of Buddhism and occultism. By far the most enthusiastic notice appeared in the *Review of Reviews*, a magazine edited by W. T. Stead.[19] A popular journalist who took up many good causes including socialism and social reform, Stead was an aggressive and emotional man, painfully obsessed with sin. He had dabbled in automatic writing and spirit photography, but it was only after the death of an American girl he met in Switzerland at the Oberammergau Passion Play that Stead's interest in spiritualism turned to passion. When the dead girl, Julia Ames, began sending back messages from the Borderland (the spiritualist limbo) to her friend in Illinois, the friend contacted Stead, and he immediately tried to get in touch with Julia himself. The result was his *Letters from Julia*, published in 1897. When Stead's son Willie died in 1908, he too began to communicate with his father; and when Stead went down on the *Titanic* in 1912, he in turn sent messages to his fervently spiritualist daughter Estelle.

Stead numbered H. G. Wells, George Bernard Shaw and most of the early Fabians among his friends in a group of intellectuals and reformers which included Annie Besant, whom he commissioned to review *The Secret Doctrine* for the *Review of Reviews*. The results were dramatic. After describing the book in glowing terms, Mrs Besant was taken to meet the author, and the meeting resulted in her own conversion to Theosophy.

Already a public figure, well known beyond radical circles, Mrs Besant[20] was a self-conscious heroine in the mould of that other Theosophical Annie, Mrs Kingsford. There were many parallels between them. Like Kingsford, Annie Besant, née Wood, was of mixed blood, being more Irish than English. An idealistic, attractive and strong-willed woman born in 1847, Annie Wood also came from a distinguished City family, though her father belonged to an impoverished junior branch. Mr Wood died early, leaving the family in straitened circumstances and Annie with a permanent hankering after strong male guidance; but she was fortunate enough to be taken up by a wealthy and cultured spinster who befriended her widowed mother. This lady persuaded Mrs Wood to allow Annie to live with her, and the consequence was an excellent if idiosyncratic education.

Annie's youth was filled with the longing to serve humanity by some sort of glorious martyrdom which also haunted Anna Kingsford. She was deeply religious as a child, but after the failure of her marriage to the unsympathetic Mr Besant, a dour Anglican clergyman, growing religious doubts and domestic unhappiness drove Mrs Besant out of her faith and her husband's Lincolnshire rectory at the age of twenty-seven.

With an allowance from the vicar of £110 per annum – comparatively good fortune for an erring nineteenth-century wife – Annie drifted into London radical circles, where she soon met and became the close friend and collaborator of Charles Bradlaugh, leader of the National Secular Society.[21] Bradlaugh was famous as a campaigner for causes of every sort, and it was soon popularly assumed that Annie Besant had become his mistress, on the grounds that free-thinkers must be free-livers. This seems not to have been the case. Intellectually radical, a republican and an atheist, Bradlaugh was morally and socially conservative, even prudish. He accepted contemporary social distinctions and struggled to make his own provincial accent conform to middle-class standards. Upholding the highest ethical principles, he believed firmly in parliamentary institutions, and was equally contemptuous of established injustice and violent revolution. In private life he was a polite and kindly man, who cared at length for his drunken wife and then for his drunken brother (who nevertheless converted to evangelical Christianity, as if to spite him).

Bradlaugh was a brilliant, ruthless and untiring public speaker, able to pack every hall he addressed. All his opponents conceded his outstanding skill in debate. Under his tutelage the diminutive Annie Besant developed her powers of oratory and learnt to revel in managing huge crowds. Bradlaugh and Besant pursued a number of joint reforming campaigns, but their *cause célèbre* managed to involve all their interests – press freedom, censorship, women's rights and atheism – in a case which riveted the attention of Victorian England. In 1876 a Bristol bookseller was arrested for selling obscene literature in the shape of *The Fruits of Philosophy*, a misleadingly entitled tract about birth control. The book had been reprinted several times in Britain and America since its first appearance in 1833, but the bookseller had since inserted some helpful diagrams which were thought to push a dubious text over the border of decency into illegality. The original publisher of the stock was prosecuted and fined.

Bradlaugh and Besant became involved in the case when they republished *The Fruits of Philosophy* after the original trial. They soon found themselves in the dock, where they made gargantuan speeches in their own defence, to no avail. Though their conviction was set aside on appeal – both of them having the taste and talent for litigation – Annie's initial conviction gave Mr Besant the chance he wanted to secure complete control over his two children and Annie lost her allowance.

In the following years she drifted away from secularism to socialism, just as she drifted away from Bradlaugh towards Shaw and Edward Aveling. Annie was an attractive, feminine woman, whose beauty and soft-spoken charm in private belied her fiery public presence. She was also highly susceptible to male influence, and it is impossible to separate her changing convictions from her changing affections. Aveling was a monster of selfishness and wickedness; fortunately for Mrs Besant he transferred his affections to Karl Marx's daughter Eleanor, who later committed suicide as a direct result of his cruelty. Shaw was kinder, but no less elusive.

The question of their marriage was briefly mooted, then put aside. With Stead, too, she seems to have fallen in love.

It was GBS who described Annie Besant's life in theatrical terms.[22] She saw herself, he thought, in a series of glorious roles, each new one coming along opportunely just as she tired of the last. This is cruel but accurate, though one might add that Shaw himself never wearied of playing to the gallery even when there was only one person in it, such as Annie herself. It was also Shaw who gave the most vivid and touching portrait of Annie, as Raina in his play *Arms and the Man*. By turns disarmingly frank and absurdly self-dramatising, Raina admits to doubts about her romantic ideals even as she proclaims them – an unlikely admission from Annie. But the 'thrilling voice' Raina uses to get her way is certainly taken from Annie who, modest enough off-stage, took on a larger, surer and perhaps more suspect persona when she stepped on to the public platform and carried away both herself and her audience. Yet Shaw saw both women as at heart sincere, passionate and loving.

There is, however, a crucial difference between Annie and her fictional counterpart. Whereas Raina in her more realistic moments can distinguish between flights of romantic fancy and her true self, there is considerable evidence that Annie could not. When she took up a cause she identified with it completely – which helps to explain her ability to move from one to another with such ease, even when they seemed complete opposites.

Not that the ideals of Theosophy and Fabian socialism were that far apart. We have already seen how often radical politics went with a strong religious bent in this period. Robert Owen and his son were political radicals and spirituals. Laurence Oliphant's second wife, Rosamund Dale Owen, was a founder member of the group which gave birth to the Fabians. In later life Shaw, too, enjoyed describing himself as a religious man. Certainly he had no time for the paraphernalia of Christianity, which he regarded as primitive superstition. But if he thought conventional religion barbarous, no religion at all was far worse: a mere grovelling in the cosmic gutter. In Shaw's view, Man cannot and should not live without a sense of purpose. This was not merely a personal preference: never given to understatement, Shaw thought that 'civilization needs a religion as a matter of life or death'.[23] He agreed with Blavatsky that the purpose once provided by belief in God had been destroyed by a combination of materialism and Darwinism. But that destruction, he believed, was only a prelude to the emergence of a new and rational faith.

Announcing that this new faith would also be a science of metabiology and christening it Creative Evolution – the religion of the twentieth century – Shaw described something strangely like Theosophy. He does not demand that we *worship* the life force which drives Creative Evolution or the near-immortals he expected it to produce – far from it; but he does want us to understand them. He wants us, in other words, to experience the 'revival of religion on a scientific basis'. The test of a dogma, he tells us in the preface to *Back to Methuselah*, is its universality. We should pool our international religious legends to make one common stock of fictionalised wisdom. Science, art and religion are not enemies but expressions of the same thing. A religion must be both serious and popular. He even accepts the (scientific) possibility of clairvoyance. In fact, if one strips away Blavatskian phenomena and tricks with broken saucers there is not so much in theosophical doctrine for Shaw to disagree with. Perhaps that encouraged him to treat Annie Besant's conversion – otherwise a subject for the broadest comedy – with comparative circumspection.

One commentator has invoked Jung's notion of enantiodromia – a passing-over into the opposite – to explain Annie Besant's apparently Pauline conversion from atheism, republicanism and socialism to the theocratic, hierarchical, élitist world of the Theosophical Society; but less dramatic explanations are in order.[24] On her own account, Mrs Besant was ripe for Theosophy by 1889. She had already studied works by Sinnett and others and she later claimed to have been convinced of the reality of spiritualism, clairvoyance and clairaudience before she ever encountered *The Secret Doctrine*, which had merely confirmed her growing convictions and provided them with an intelligible basis.

It is also the case that Annie Besant always needed something and someone to believe in. She wanted a cause to fight against the world, but she also craved moral and emotional support. Madame Blavatsky provided both. Losing her father when she was only five, Annie was parted from her adored mother for much of her childhood. Mrs Wood died not long after her daughter separated from Mr Besant, and within a few years Annie had also lost her children to her husband's custody. There had followed a series of frustrating liaisons with difficult men. And here, in the person of Madame Blavatsky, was an older woman at once heroic and maternal; a woman who, like Annie herself, had sacrificed all for the truth; a woman who would take the emotional place of mother and father, husband and children in her new convert's unhappy life.

When they finally met at Lansdowne Road in the spring of 1889 Mrs Besant was profoundly affected. She visited HPB with her friend Herbert Burrows, who was for a while the dominant male influence in Annie's life. An erstwhile collaborator with Besant and Bradlaugh in various reforming causes, Burrows had been driven to religion, like so many contemporaries, by the death of a loved one – in this case his wife. He had joined the Theosophical Society in 1888, encouraging Annie to follow him, and it may well be that he played a more significant role in her conversion than any amount of reading in *Esoteric Buddhism*.

Mrs Besant records in her *Autobiography* that although Madame Blavatsky talked to them with energy and brilliance, she said 'no word of Occultism, nothing mysterious' until the moment when her visitors rose to leave. Then she stared into Annie's eyes and said with a 'yearning throb' in her voice: 'Oh my dear Mrs Besant if you would only come among us.'[25] It was a psychological masterstroke.

So strong was the impression Blavatsky made that when she showed Annie the Hodgson report, inviting her to make her own judgement, her visitor not only applauded Blavatsky's frankness but rejected the report out of hand, so convinced was she of her hostess's absolute honesty. Nevertheless, owning up to her conversion took great courage. The press, who had long since scented Annie's appetite for publicity and a certain flightiness in the espousal of one cause after another, had a field day. For one thing, her new faith involved public recantation of her most famous cause: contraception. Koot Hoomi had spoken out against it, and the Society's official doctrine was that birth control simply encouraged the indulgence of those animal passions which prevented men from rising to their higher selves.

More worrying were the susceptibilities of her friends, especially Bradlaugh and Shaw.[26] At first she remained a member of the Fabian Society Executive and attended the International Workers' Congress held in Paris in 1889, leaving the meetings only to stay with Blavatsky who was holidaying near Fontainebleau. As usual with women, GBS reacted equivocally, laughing at Annie and sympathising with her at the same time. His equivocation may be explicable in terms of the peculiar spiritual views he himself eventually developed, though these don't explain why he later insisted that he, and not Stead, had sent Annie the copy of *The Secret Doctrine* which changed her life. He also continued for some time to attend lectures on Theosophy held in Annie's house. Perhaps he was more possessive than he liked to think; or perhaps he enjoyed the idea of shaping the future of the Society with a casual gesture. Bradlaugh was less detached. He was shocked by Annie's surrender to Blavatsky, and although his old comrade wrote movingly about him when he died in 1891, she was writing about the past.

If Bradlaugh disliked Blavatsky's ascendancy over Annie, HPB's disciples resented the upstart's influence over their leader, who turned increasingly to Mrs Besant for advice and support.[27] The notorious newcomer soon became a daily visitor to Lansdowne Road, and HPB's closest confidante. Rumours of lesbianism are unfounded – both women mistrusted sex – but they were certainly intimate. Annie threw herself into theosophical work with all the energy and enthusiasm she had brought to earlier causes, and was soon made Co-Editor of *Lucifer* and President of the Blavatsky Lodge. It was not long before she had her own vision of a Master, while staying with her new friend at Fontainebleau, though like Yeats she was inclined at this stage of her theosophical career to think of the Masters as products of the individual's psychic power and not as living beings. She also made her house in St John's Wood available to the Society for its London base, building on to it a large and appropriately decorated Occult Room. When HPB left Lansdowne Road in July 1890 she moved in with Annie and the house at 19 Avenue Road rapidly became the centre of theosophical work in London.

Meanwhile, Blavatsky continued her war with Olcott. She was determined to have control of Theosophy in the West, and there were two ways to get it. First, she persuaded the colonel to agree to the establishment of the Esoteric Section in 1889. The ES was to be an exclusive group within the Society, open only to advanced esoteric students and under the direct control of HPB. Olcott might be President of the Society and a better manager, but his old chum still had prior claim to psychic authority. Olcott could live with the Esoteric Section, which posed no threat to his administrative authority, but then the British Section of the Society appointed HPB to be European President in July 1890. This was too much, and Olcott cancelled the appointment by presidential directive. When Blavatsky responded by threatening resignation and secession, Olcott himself offered to resign – a move which would split the Society from top to bottom, as HPB well knew. Olcott's high-risk strategy was successful for the time being. The chums compromised and Olcott stayed in place with full authority, while conceding greater autonomy to national sections and to the ES. But peace was to be short-lived. Within a few months, while Annie was on a lecture tour of America, HPB died in London on 8 May 1891. Her death was followed by a fierce struggle for power between Olcott and his former lieutenant William Quan Judge.[28]

One of the Society's founding members, Judge had stayed in America when Blavatsky and Olcott moved to India. He had built up the American Section into a thriving concern through sheer hard work. With his membership steadily rising – it had reached six thousand by the time he died in 1896 – Judge was now weary of his subordinate role and ready to wage war on Olcott. As we have seen, the Society's organisation made such conflict likely: once Olcott conceded greater power to national sections it became inevitable. Theosophy was still theoretically ruled by a presidential council, with Olcott in charge. In fact, affairs were increasingly under the control of national leaders, who now had more or less power according to the strength of their membership and the consequent size of their subscription income. Olcott might reign at Adyar, but the English, American and Asian Sections went their own ways, with the President running India and Ceylon, Blavatsky all-powerful in London and Judge in charge of America. Olcott's position was also weakened by Judge's appointment as Vice-President of the whole Society in 1888. Should anything happen to the colonel, Judge could hope to step into his shoes.

After Blavatsky's death Judge was in a strong financial and political position. The American Section was the richest and he also had the advantage of publicity in *The Path*, the American Section's own magazine. In *The Path* Judge presented himself as the spontaneous guardian of Blavatsky's spirit, in contrast to the colonel's pedestrian preoccupation with organisations and institutions. He intimated that Blavatsky herself had rebelled against such corporatism, which, he claimed, was stifling the Society's spiritual mission and diverging from her own original purposes. Thus Judge made a clear distinction between HPB's role as the Society's guiding spirit and Olcott's inferior place as administrator. This comparison, which underestimates Olcott's crucial part in the early days, was part of the process of canonisation Blavatsky underwent after her death. It was to be repeated by the leaders of many splinter groups in the years to come. With extraordinary speed her less amiable traits were replaced by the anodyne image of a maternal mystic: the inspired teacher whose existence was the entire raison d'être of the Theosophical Society. From now on, the guardianship of HPB's legacy was a vital element in rows within the Society.

Judge also had Annie's warm support; they had become great friends during her trip to America. When she returned to London at the end of May 1891 to find that HPB had died in her absence, bequeathing her the leadership of the Esoteric Section, Annie was ready to listen to Judge's criticisms of Olcott's presidency. Blavatsky had not long since created a sort of inner cabinet out of the council of the Esoteric Section, with herself as Outer Head (the Inner Heads being the Masters). The Council of the ES, selected by Blavatsky, was composed of the most powerful figures in the

Society. Therefore its *de facto* ruling body, it was often in conflict with both the national councils and the Supreme Council. Judge now proposed to Annie that they dissolve the ES Council, nominating themselves as joint Outer Heads, thereby vesting power in their own hands – and ultimately in his alone.

Olcott, who naturally opposed them, was not without his own wily resolution. Some years earlier Sinnett and Hume had persuaded Blavatsky in a moment of weakness to sign an order deposing the President an order which Olcott, returning briefly to Adyar from his travels, had compelled her to revoke. It was such embarrassments that encouraged him to get her out of India in the first place. He was not going to give up his power now that she was dead – and to Judge, of all people – even though the Masters seemed to be against him, for letters from the Brotherhood began to appear supporting Judge, who claimed to have direct communications from them in his favour. One note even cropped up among Annie's private papers saying, 'Judge's plan is right,' and all were signed with Master Morya's seal. Annie at first took Judge's side. So impressed was she by these messages and their authenticity that she lost her head. On 30 August 1891, during her farewell speech to the National Secular Society given in Bradlaugh's old stamping-ground the Hall of Science (of all places), she announced in Olcott's presence that HPB was still precipitating letters from the Other Side.

Olcott knew better. Having rushed to London to canvass Annie's support before Judge could swing her against him, he was determined to expose the head of the American Section. To begin with, Judge had always previously had to ask the colonel to intercede with the Masters. How was it that he was now in a position to communicate with them directly? More damningly, 'Master Morya's seal' was one Olcott himself had had made in the Punjab in 1883, when he presented it to Blavatsky, from among whose effects it mysteriously disappeared a few years later. In the face of palpable fraud the President ordered Judge to put a stop to his campaign. Judge responded by threatening to cut off American funds. He also hinted that if Olcott brought up the matter of Judge's letters, the members of the Society might be shocked to hear about the true origins of Master Morya's seal, which they took – with Olcott's tacit encouragement – for the genuine article.

The row dragged on, reaching a height of absurdity when Judge persuaded Annie that Olcott was plotting to poison her. Then in January 1892 Judge and Besant tried to persuade Olcott to resign – a move which would have made Judge President. When Master Morya wrote to Olcott ordering him to retain the presidency, Master Koot Hoomi wrote to Judge encouraging him to depose the colonel. Olcott, accused of an immoral liaison, finally resigned in Judge's favour and then revoked his resignation. The European Section called Judge to lead the Society – but also instructed Olcott to stay in office. Annie wavered between the two men, moving against Judge only after her arrival in India in November 1893 convinced her that Olcott was in the right after all. She then began to pursue Judge with charges of fraud and misrepresentation of the Masters in forged letters, and persuaded Olcott to convene a judicial committee of the Society to try the case against him.

Olcott returned to London once more in July 1894, to chair the committee. But the members eventually sidestepped the whole issue by accepting Judge's claim that because he had acted in a private capacity – i.e. not in his role as head of the American Section – it had no jurisdiction over him. More puzzlingly still, it asserted that there were no grounds for comment on the messages he had supposedly received from the Masters, because belief in the existence or otherwise of these beings was a matter for the individual, not a positive doctrine of the Society. Keen to make peace, Olcott agreed, announcing that Judge's suspension as Vice-President was itself suspended. The upshot of this judgement was a ludicrous situation in which the very existence of the Brotherhood of Masters on whose revelations the Theosophical Society was allegedly founded was put in doubt. As one wit put it, 'every Theosophist is in future free to circulate Mahatma messages, but no Theosophist to test their genuineness',[29] which was the exact opposite of the Society's original objective.

The whole row was a gift to the press – all the more so because the magisterial messages which Besant now accused Judge of forging were the very letters she had produced at her 1891 lecture in the

Hall of Science as evidence of Blavatsky's posthumous correspondence with her. Disgruntled TS members, some enraged by Besant,
others by Judge, fed the newspapers with juicy details, and the
Westminster Gazette published a series of articles called 'Isis Very
Much Unveiled' which amounted to a complete exposé of the whole
Society. Stead defended Annie and Judge defended himself, but
there was no stopping the tide of satirical articles, cartoons and
pantomime sketches.

The crucial weakness in the organisation was thus exposed:
barely united on the one hand by the vaguest social and spiritual
ideals, Theosophy was split on the other by bitter personal rivalry
disguised as occult research. In the years following Blavatsky's
death the Society was to split again and again, while its officers
alternated between charging one another with fraud, and then
withdrawing the charges – an absurdity summed up in Annie's
efforts to patch up her relationship with Judge by moderating her
accusations against him from forgery to 'giving a misleading
material form to messages received psychically'.[30] The concession
did little good. Besant and Judge ended by solemnly expelling one
another from the leadership of the Esoteric Section.

SIX

Second Generation

Whatever the theosophical reasons for her change of tack, there were deeper forces at work behind Annie Besant's rift with Judge and the alliance with Olcott. Having been warned against going to India by Judge, her first visit there in 1893 came as a revelation: the beginning of a love affair that was to consume the rest of her long life. Here at last, in the suffering of the people and the magnificence of their ancient religions, were causes to match her aspirations. Never one to underestimate her own powers, Annie's belief in her ability to meet the challenges India presented was enhanced by the reception she received. Reaching Colombo in mid-November, she was greeted by Olcott and an impressive tally of Buddhist and British high officials, and her subsequent journeys round the subcontinent resembled a royal progress. Following the eighteenth Theosophical Convention, held at Madras after Christmas, Olcott took her on the rounds of all the Indian lodges, where she made frequent speeches, turning both the convention and the trip into a Besant lecture tour with audiences numbering up to six thousand people – equal to the complete membership of the American Section. This rapturous welcome awakened all the missionary zeal she had once brought to the mundane details of contraception and parish school reform.

Ironically, her popularity was founded on a misunderstanding Annie shared with most of her audiences, who failed to distinguish between the Hindu religion and Hindu nationalism. Preaching spiritual liberation in the language of a native creed, Mrs Besant appeared to them to be inciting political revolt, and it was not an impression she took much trouble to correct. The imperial government and the Society were both alarmed. Theosophy had been unofficially involved with nationalist movements in the subcontinent since the arrival of the Founders, but it had produced no major political figures. Olcott's work in Ceylon was peripheral and A. O. Hume, though deeply involved in the formation of Congress, had left the Society before the Home Rule movement really got under way. But as Blavatsky's chosen heir *and* a celebrated political agitator, Annie was a very different matter.

The viceregal court was well aware of Mrs Besant's Irish descent and her radical past, which had included speeches in favour of Irish independence and – worse still – reform of the Indian Empire.[1] The last thing the government needed in the permanently volatile atmosphere of Indian politics was a white Home Rule crusader. Their nervousness was justified. Nationalist papers, familiar with Annie's politics, impressed by her record as an agitator and flattered by her pro-Hinduism, hailed Besant as their saviour, calling upon her to lead a campaign against the colonial government. At times the press even referred to her as a divinity – an avatar of the Indian mother goddess.

The situation was further complicated by the fact that, however radical she might be, Annie was also a member of the ruling élite by virtue of her status as an upper-middle-class Englishwoman in India, and her political influence on old friends who were now senior figures in the British Liberal Party, including the future Lord Chancellor, Viscount Haldane. These social and political connections were to cause serious embarrassment for the Viceroy and his staff, and she did not hesitate to exploit them.

Olcott, too, was annoyed. Quite apart from the trouble Annie was causing with the government, there was the delicate question of inter-denominational relationships to consider. Though it largely ignored Islam and Christianity, Theosophy supposedly cultivated religious neutrality. In fact, Olcott himself had found relief from his troubles with HPB and Judge in a campaign to promote ecumenical Buddhism throughout the East. The colonel dreamt of uniting northern and southern Buddhists in a common doctrine. His dream took him as far as Japan, where he met the Prime Minister and dined at the Peers Club in 1889 and again in 1891. But despite his own prejudices – and a personal campaign to help the Untouchables which was bound to alienate higher-caste Hindus – he was adamant that Theosophy was a religious and social movement, not a political party, and he warned Mrs Besant to take more care.

As usual with Annie, there was also a man in the case. Shortly before leaving for her first trip to India, she had attended the 1893 World Parliament of Religions in Chicago as Olcott's personal representative. She travelled to America with one of the other Theosophical delegates, Gyanandra Nath Chakravarti, a brahmin professor of mathematics who stayed at Avenue Road on the way from Adyar. A brilliant speaker, an ardent Hindu and an attractive man, Chakravarti captivated Annie much as Mohini had conquered Miss Leonard and Mrs Kingsford. Mrs Besant told her friends that at last she had found her own guru. She was so besotted with the professor that she proclaimed Chakravarti's daughter to be the reincarnation of the recently deceased Madame Blavatsky.[2] His presence in India was certainly a key factor in her decision to ignore Judge's advice and visit the country. Alert to Annie's susceptibility, Judge had accused Chakravarti of hypnotising her. In reality the handsome brahmin was only the latest in a line which had included Bradlaugh, Stead, Aveling, Shaw, Burrows and perhaps even Judge himself.

Having alienated Judge by her change of loyalties and Olcott by her political activities, Annie found herself isolated. Settling not at Adyar but at Benares, she bought a house with money from a friend. Annie had a genius for raising money and attracting rich benefactors which was to be crucial in her domination of the Society. She spent each winter at Benares, returning to England in the spring. In the summer and autumn she made extensive foreign tours to proselytise for the Society. Under her influence, Benares became the head-quarters of the Indian Section, with Adyar serving as international HQ. While Olcott ran the Society and worked for Buddhism, Annie built up the Esoteric Section, of which she was now the undisputed Outer Head. She also began to learn Sanskrit and founded in Benares the significantly named Central *Hindu* College, where the native curriculum was given a westernising theosophical twist by

teaching science and practical skills. The college was supported by
the Maharajahs of Kashmir and Benares and by popular subscriptions, which increased sharply whenever it was denounced by the
imperial government for encouraging Hindu nationalism.[3]

In the decade between her establishment at Benares in 1896 and
Olcott's death in 1907, Annie Besant's time was to be equally
divided between Theosophy, social reform and politics. The combination was a cause of perpetual conflict, especially among older
members of the Society. Many Theosophists, already angered by
her proprietorial attitude to HPB, were outraged when Annie took
control of her friend's literary estate, publishing further volumes of
The Secret Doctrine in her own heavily doctored edition. Furthermore, most middle-class British members were good imperialists
who wanted no truck with Hindu nationalism. The Brotherhood of
Man was all very well, but there was no reason, they thought, to
make it any less hierarchical than the Great White Brotherhood on
which their faith was founded.

As Olcott aged, tacitly resigning more and more power to Annie, the
complaints grew louder. Arguments focused on the question of
inheritance. Who was Blavatsky's rightful heir? Mrs Besant thought
she knew the answer to this question, and she had HPB's last testa-
ment appointing her Head of the ES to prove it. Others took a different view. The consequence was a number of 'Back to Blavatsky'
movements, which rumbled on in the years before Olcott's death.
These were encouraged by HPB's pre-Besant disciples such
as Alice Cleather and her friend William Kingsland, who waged lifelong campaigns against Annie in Britain.[4] Cleather and Kingsland
both argued that Blavatsky's comparatively early death had been
the ruination of the Theosophical Society, which fell prey to Mrs
Besant's whims for one cause – and one man – after another.

They were not, however, her most powerful enemies. In 1895,
Alice Cleather abandoned Mrs Besant in favour of the latter's most
effective rival, the American Katherine Tingley, who succeeded
Judge as leader of the American Section.[5] Tingley and Besant were
exact contemporaries. Similar characters in many respects, they
make a curious trio with Anna Kingsford. Born in 1847, Tingley ran
away from an early marriage to become an actress in a stock

repertory company, where she acquired a taste for finery. Disappointed by a childless second marriage to a railway inspector in the 1880s, she adopted the children of her first husband by his second wife, but this scheme was equally ill-starred. When another orphan she tried to care for ran away, Tingley turned with more success to charitable works in prisons and hospitals, and then to spiritualism.

In 1888 she made her third marriage, to Mr Philo Tingley; but the encounter that was to change her life did not occur until 1894, when she met William Quan Judge while running a soup kitchen for striking workers in New York. She became a Theosophist almost immediately. Unhappy in her private life, Tingley found in Theosophy the outlet for her powerful spiritual, maternal and philanthropic urges. She and Judge also recognised their mutual need. He provided the institutional backing she needed for her ambitious schemes, while she gave him moral support. Judge's diaries even suggest that Tingley put him in touch with HPB by means of her psychic powers – an important advantage in the war with Adyar.

By the time of their meeting the Vice-President was already in poor health and had not long to live. When he seceded from Adyar in the following year, taking nearly six thousand members with him, Tingley was his most trusted colleague, and on Judge's death in March 1896 she took immediate control of the American Society. There was strong opposition, but Tingley claimed the right of apostolic succession from HPB on the grounds that, although Tingley and Blavatsky had never even met, Blavatsky had once asked Judge in a letter, 'Has your new chela turned up yet?'[6] Who could that chela possibly be, asked Tingley, but herself? She also reported that the dead Judge was communicating with her from the Other Side, and that his message was a simple one: all his former followers should obey Tingley. Judge's words were conveyed to the faithful by August Neresheimer, a New York diamond broker who became for a while virtually Tingley's slave in a pattern which was to be repeated many times over the next thirty years.

Tingley then strengthened her position further by arranging an audience with one of the Masters while on a proselytising visit to India. The other members of her party – especially her main rival, Ernest Hargrove – wanted to share the audience, but Tingley had no intention of allowing anyone to trespass on her exclusive privileges. One morning, as they were camped near Darjeeling, Hargrove woke to find that his leader had disappeared. She had gone to a private meeting with Koot Hoomi, later described in her book *The Gods Await*.

Together with other disgruntled Judgeites, Hargrove soon left Tingley's society to form his own. This hardly mattered to the Purple Mother, as she was now known, who already had a fierce maternal grip on the affections of her other followers. These included Gottfried de Purucker, a young Swiss-American Theosophist who was to succeed her thirty-five years later. Purucker, a suave, scholarly and ascetic fellow almost thirty years younger than Tingley, soon became her surrogate son and right-hand man.[7]

During the next decade she established her complete dominance over the American Section – now renamed the Universal Brotherhood and Theosophical Society – by driving out her rivals and closing down most of the lodges, expropriating their funds for her own schemes. She also embarked on a world-wide crusade to strengthen the Universal Brotherhood abroad. Despite the use of American hard-sell techniques, the crusade was not successful. In fact it proved counter-productive, when Annie Besant began to retaliate with foreign tours of her own. Annie was a more effective speaker and soon took the battle on to Tingley's own territory in the United States, where she made a thousand converts for Adyar on her first mission. The delighted American press reported a 'Battle of the Fair Theosophists'.[8] Tingley fought back with further European missions, scoring a minor coup when she managed to buy Besant's former house in Avenue Road, but her foreign journeys produced few converts. This hardly mattered, as they were incidental to Tingley's major project, which was nothing less than the founding of a new community at home in America.

Although Tingley shared Besant's commitment to social reform, in her case this meant not the improvement of existing institutions but the founding of an alternative society that would become the basis for the transformation of American life – a 'white city' whose citizens would inaugurate a new religious and political dispensation. Alternative communities were a familiar feature of nineteenth-century American life. Indeed, it might be said that America itself was the most ambitious alternative community of all. But Tingley's utopia, established at Point Loma on the Californian coast near San Diego, was more elaborate than most, closer to Hollywood than Jerusalem.

Formally inaugurated with a vast congress in April 1899, including religious rites, lectures, exhibitions, plays and the laying of an Irish foundation stone, the community was situated on a magnificent headland overlooking the Pacific. This romantic site was soon covered with equally romantic buildings when Muslim domes, Hindu temples, Egyptian gates and Greek theatres sprang up along the hillside as Tingley's fancy dictated. The theory was that universal religion should be reflected in universal architecture.

Building work provided therapeutic activity for a growing community of residents, whose cultural and aesthetic welfare Tingley took to heart as much as their spiritual development. Wagner's theatre at Bayreuth was her model and the Purple Mother clearly had in mind the Wagnerian notion of an artistic synthesis combining music, words, movement and the plastic arts in an all-embracing spiritual experience. Theatre as sacrament was the focus of activities at Point Loma, with Katherine Tingley as director, celebrant and star performer.

Tingley was also able to gratify her old passion for nurturing and directing the young. Children were especially well provided for at Point Loma, in schools which explored Tingley's interest in new methods of education. Once again her theatrical experience came in useful. Drama, music, yoga and dance were central to a curriculum which emphasised practical skills, creativity and meditation. By 1910 the schools at Point Loma catered for up to three hundred pupils, including difficult and delinquent children from outside the community. There was nothing free and easy about these schools. Though there was no corporal punishment, the discipline was strict and children were compelled to work and eat in silence. Nevertheless, the system proved popular with parents and children alike. Helping with medical relief in Cuba after the Spanish–American war of 1898 gave Tingley the idea of taking on some Cuban orphans in her school, and then of establishing similar institutions – known as Raja Yoga schools – in Cuba itself, where they were supervised by an English Judgeite, Nan Herbert, daughter of the leading English politician Auberon Herbert. Tingley also set up homes for poor children and eventually there was even a Theosophical University, chartered in 1919.

One of the community's central features was the School of Antiquity, which mingled serious archaeological research with theosophical fantasy. At least one scholar working at Point Loma, William Gates, was a distinguished student of Mayan glyphs, who hoped to use the school as a basis for his scientific researches. Tingley encouraged him, but her interest in the matter was more fanciful. Returning to Blavatsky's original point of departure, she had decided that Egypt was a far older civilisation than India and a more important occult centre, a belief that sat well with her determination to minimise the influence of Adyar.

She also took up fashionable ideas about early American settlements and racial migration. Excavation of Mayan and other Central American sites would prove, she believed, that 'American' civilisation was the oldest in the world – and antiquity could in this case be equated with esoteric significance. Given one theosophical view, derived from Blavatsky's writings about root races, that California might become the next centre of world civilisation (and thereby of cosmic evolution), this made the siting of Point Loma all the more significant. But like everything else in Tingley's utopia, serious work at the School of Antiquity began well but eventually fizzled out, leaving it to serve only as a focal point for the elaborate rituals to which Tingley became increasingly addicted.

The comparison with Adyar, also a large and beautiful compound near the sea, is inescapable, and Tingley comes out of it well. Her schools flourished for a while, her educational methods had some influence outside Point Loma, and the community which grew up there was surprisingly large, varied and dynamic while it lasted. Besides the buildings there were extensive gardens and large fruit-orchards, watered by a remarkable irrigation system specially devised for the site. So involved did the community become in fruit-growing that they introduced new methods and varieties, setting up their own agricultural laboratories. There was nothing to compare with this at Adyar, or with the ambitious industrial programme which included the weaving and dyeing of cloth, the production of tiles, and a private printing press.

Yet the appearance was not the reality. The Purple Mother's passion for grandiose new projects outstripped her capacity to finance them; most of the activities she instigated consumed more money than they produced; and her schemes tended to last only for as long as there was someone to pay for them. Typically, for all its efforts and investment in agriculture, the community was not self-sufficient in food and even the flourishing fruit farm made a loss, compounded by the huge expenditure involved in irrigating the beautiful but useless gardens. The closing of almost all the lodges in Tingley's Society produced short-term gains but proved to be a long-term disaster by cutting off a major source of income, so that she was forced to rely on hand-outs from rich members such as Neresheimer, who became ever more reluctant to provide.

The root of the problem was to be found in Tingley's own authoritarian character. She brooked no opposition within the community, often imposing unpopular rules on a whim. Though the children at Point Loma were given excellent schooling, for example, they got it only on condition that they live apart from their parents, under Tingley's direct supervision. At the same time the inhabitants of San Diego were becoming more resentful about the influence of Point Loma over their lives. The community's financial pull was considerable. When Olcott tried to stay at the local hotel in 1901, Tingley successfully ordered the manager to revoke his booking by threatening to withdraw her favour. She also antagonised the clergy with her spiritual pretensions, and quarrelled with local newspaper owners about their hostile coverage of Point Loma, an approach which simply fuelled their dislike.

Worst of all, she tyrannised over her own intimates while making them take responsibility for her follies. In later years Tingley took to travelling abroad for what amounted to extended holidays, leaving her colleagues at home to worry about the financial and institutional problems she had created. Then she would return home and compel them to take part in frequent and elaborate rituals whose only point seemed to be the glorification of the Purple Mother. Everyone at

Point Loma was obliged to attend these ceremonies, dressed in absurd Greek clothes – everyone, that is, but Tingley herself, who made quite sure that she looked her fashionable best on such occasions.

There were frequent rebellions and many defections. One disillusioned follower summed up the feelings of many when he referred to

> this freakish Oriental Court of hers at Point Loma . . . I
> stood it myself for a while. I wore long gowns and
> ridiculous hats in her presence and tried to take part in the
> foolish ceremonies with some belief that they might have a
> meaning. But I knew that pretty soon it meant that we
> would have to crawl into Mrs Tingley's presence on all
> fours . . .[9]

By the outbreak of World War One things were already on the slide. The schools in Cuba had closed, the attempt to produce silk at Point Loma had collapsed, the gardens had to be scaled down for lack of resources, and building had slowed almost to nothing. The Purple Mother staggered on for another fifteen years, sustained by belief in herself and perhaps even more by the furious 'beauty contest' with Annie Besant, but within a very few years of her death the community had been forced to close. It was clear that although Tingley's energy and drive had built Point Loma they had also destroyed it.

Annie Besant meanwhile had found a new supporter. Her relationship with Chakravarti had been undermined by her inability to share his strident Hindu nationalism, and by the fact that he was married. Like Katherine Tingley, Mrs Besant wanted a man who would be, as it were, both husband and son and yet neither; but she was a more sensitive and vulnerable character than the Purple Mother, and her needs were accordingly more complex. Tingley either dominated men or rejected them. Besant needed to collaborate with her partner: to offer him submission in some respects while retaining the initiative in others. In particular, she liked to control events while someone else supplied the ideological framework which gave meaning to those events. In C. W. Leadbeater she found the answer to her prayer.[10]

According to his own account, Charles Webster Leadbeater was born in 1847 – the same year as Annie Besant and Katherine Tingley.[11] He came of aristocratic stock, his name deriving from the Norman family of Le Bâtre. After a conventional well-to-do childhood, he and his brother Gerald were taken to South America in 1859 by their father, the director of a railway company. The boys had an extraordinary time there, helping to capture a defaulting cashier in a high-speed locomotive, discovering Inca gold and being attacked by Indians in the interior of Brazil.

They survived the Indian attack only to be captured by rebels, who demanded that the three join their band. This Mr Leadbeater Senior declined to do, on the grounds that as an Englishman he refused to take part in such affairs, and when he escaped into the jungle the rebels killed Gerald and tortured Charles by burning his feet. In spite of this cruel treatment, young Charles was kept up to the mark by the ghost of his brother, who urged him not to give way to rebel demands. Eventually he was rescued by his father and a faithful Negro servant, and the three of them pursued the rebels, defeating their leader, General Martínez, in a sword-fight. Martínez was then executed by firing squad and the Leadbeaters decorated by a grateful government. Back in England, Charles went up to Oxford (in some accounts this is Cambridge) and had an encounter with werewolves in the Orkneys before being compelled to give up his university career when the family lost their money in the Overend Gurney bank crash of 1866. Some time later he took holy orders and became a curate in Hampshire.

Only the last sentence of this colourful account is true, though the details are repeated in various permutations in many of the Society's official publications. The facts are less exotic. Leadbeater was born on a new housing development in Stockport in 1854, the son of a railway clerk. The family moved to London, where Papa died in 1862, and the young Charles was brought up by his mother in very reduced circumstances. After a series of lowly jobs he managed to

get himself ordained in 1878, securing a curacy at Bramshott
through the rector, his uncle by marriage.

Leadbeater's supporters have a number of explanations for the
discrepancies in these accounts. Some put them down to occult
interference, while others posit the simultaneous existence of two
Charles Leadbeaters, whose lives have in some strange Borgesian
fashion become intertwined. The truth is simpler. Just as Blavatsky
told stories and Besant cast off old roles for new, so Leadbeater
decided to reinvent himself in a more pleasing image. Even his
detractors (and there were to be many) admitted his power as a
story-teller. He could hold an audience of children enthralled with
tales of ghosts or high adventure, and his talent for fiction seeped
into his life.

It was also his route to success with the boys who took up so much
of his time. At Bramshott Leadbeater was able to combine his major
interests: ritualism, spiritualism, élitism and adolescents. He joined
the Confraternity of the Blessed Sacrament, a secret society dedicated to the Real Presence[12] and forbidden by the Church of
England. He ran the local Sunday school. He read widely in occult
literature, and was especially impressed by Sinnett's *Occult
Doctrine*. And he took a special interest in two brothers who
appeared to be psychic.

All these enthusiasms increased after the death of his mother in
1882, and in the following year he was introduced into the
Theosophical Society by Sinnett. Like most of the early members,
Leadbeater was keen to get in touch with the Masters. He tried first
by attending the seances of a Mr Eglinton, whose control or spirit
guide, Ernest, agreed to take messages. Leadbeater left a letter
sealed inside several envelopes, and a few days later the envelopes
were returned with the seal intact but no letter inside, only a
message saying that Master Koot Hoomi had his correspondence
and would be replying in due course, or words to that effect.

When the promised answer failed to materialise, Leadbeater
bravely consulted HPB herself. She promptly arranged for the
Masters to post a letter in Kensington telling the young curate not to
despair. They told him that he was accepted as an Initiate and, as a
special favour, need not serve the customary seven years' probation.

Instead, he was authorised to complete his term of apprenticeship by accompanying Blavatsky to Adyar. When Leadbeater went up to London to offer his services in person, HPB obligingly precipitated another letter from Koot Hoomi, ordering him to sail for India at once. He resigned his curacy, settled his affairs and took a boat for Egypt, where he met Blavatsky at Cairo and travelled on with her to Adyar.

His probation turned out to be more difficult than he anticipated. Though Koot Hoomi was kind enough to transmit yet another message instructing HPB to 'Tell Leadbeater I am satisfied with his zeal and devotion,'[13] and the Master Dwaj Khul even materialised before him while he was sorting papers in HPB's state-room, Blavatsky was a hard taskmistress, treating him more or less as a slave and setting him difficult tests. On one occasion he had to parade the entire length of the boat-deck in front of all the passengers clutching a brimming chamber-pot.

Like Olcott before him, Leadbeater was much taken by Ceylon, where he caused a stir as the first Christian minister to become a Buddhist. He also visited Burma in the colonel's entourage. But his first weeks at Adyar were mainly spent living on boiled wheat and learning to be a clairvoyant from the Master KH, who considerately taught him the technique in a mere forty-two days. After that the Masters couldn't keep away from Leadbeater, visiting him almost daily. This caused a slight frostiness in his relations with HPB, who was determined to maintain her exclusive rights to magisterial communications.

Leadbeater later painted a rosy picture of life at Adyar. His letters tell a different story.[14] He was wretched and lonely, ignored or patronised by the other inhabitants of the compound, including even the few Europeans left after the Coulomb scandal. It must have been a relief when he was dispatched to Ceylon in 1886. He remained there for three years, living in abject poverty and editing an anti-Christian weekly paper called the *Buddhist*, in the service of Olcott's ambition to colonise Ceylon for Theosophy.

During his stay in Ceylon Leadbeater met a handsome boy called Curupumullage Jinarajadasa, with whom he became so infatuated that he tried to abduct the lad from his vigilant parents by swimming out to a waiting boat in Colombo harbour with him. The boy was retrieved at the last minute by his family, who threatened Leadbeater with a revolver and legal proceedings; but after being assured that he only had their son's best interests at heart and proposed to take him to England where he would be given the best available education, they relented and allowed the pair to go.[15]

Returning to England in 1889, Leadbeater became resident tutor to Sinnett's son and another theosophical boy, George Arundale, the nephew of HPB's former hostess Francesca Arundale. He taught the two, together with Jinarajadasa, until a row brought the arrangement to an end. The causes of this row are obscure. There were those who said that Sinnett could no longer afford a tutor, but others rumoured immorality. Whatever the reasons, the result was that Leadbeater and his Singhalese pupil retired to discreet poverty. The affair also alienated HPB. Originally his patroness, she had long taken a sceptical view of a follower whose claims to psychic powers threatened her own authority. Given Blavatsky's coarse sense of humour and her fondness for puns, it seems more than likely that her attitude to Leadbeater is summed up by a copy of *The Voice of the Silence* she gave him, carefully inscribed to *W. C. Leadbeater*.

His luck changed when he met Annie Besant in 1890. The attraction between them is hard to define. It was certainly not sexual. As one of his critics put it, his tastes ran mainly to boys and tapioca pudding. Leadbeater found women so repulsive he could hardly bear to shake their hands and refused to remain alone in the room with any female but Annie. Yet he had considerable physical charm for women, even magnetism. A tall, robust man, brimming with health and confidence, his bright blue eyes, huge beard and loud voice contributed to the general sense of glittering vitality. An admirer later described him as prancing along like a great lion. Only his long, pointed teeth, disturbingly reminiscent of a vampire, spoilt the impression of vigorous well-being.

Boundless self-confidence also played a part in his ascendancy over Annie, who was intellectually and emotionally more insecure than she appeared. The decisive factors in their relationship were probably her suggestibility and the consequent effect of Leadbeater's psychic powers, so resented by HPB. Though Mrs Besant was visited by her own dim images of the Masters, these were hazy compared with Leadbeater's technicolour visions, which were to become the staple fare of theosophical literature for the next four decades.

Rising on the coat-tails of his new sponsor, Leadbeater became the Society's star lecturer and writer. Annie's influence was not the only reason for his success. He was talented, hard-working, tough and resilient. But he reached the top of the Society, despite a series of scandals which would have ruined another man, only because of Annie's staunch support. What Olcott had been to Blavatsky, Maitland to Kingsford and Judge to Tingley, Leadbeater became to Besant. Each relationship was different, ranging from the chumship of Blavatsky and Olcott to Maitland's erotic infatuation with Kingsford, but the electricity provided by variations on the male/female, submissive/dominant combination was central to their success.

In 1895 Leadbeater and Jinarajadasa moved into the headquarters of the London Lodge, at Annie Besant's house in Avenue Road, where Leadbeater became Assistant Secretary to the European Section. He also began to write and publish prolifically. His first book, *The Astral Plane*, had appeared in the previous year under unusual circumstances. Having instructed Jinarajadasa, who was now his amanuensis, to prepare a clean text from the backs of old envelopes on which he had written his book, Leadbeater told his faithful pupil that Master Koot Hoomi had asked for the manuscript because he (the Master) wanted to deposit it in the Records of the Great White Brotherhood. According to KH *The Astral Plane* was 'a landmark for the intellectual history of humanity'.[16] So Jinarajadasa put the manuscript under a pile of books in Leadbeater's mother's old workbox, which acted as a sort of astral post office. The next morning the bundle of papers had vanished and the author told an astonished amanuensis that he had personally delivered them to the Master in his sleep.

Leadbeater's energy was phenomenal. While continuing to write and publish, he made a series of missionary trips to America, Europe and Asia, to such effect that Olcott several times singled him out for praise in presidential addresses at Theosophical congresses. He also found time for psychical weekends, retreating to a country cottage with Annie, Jinarajadasa and Jinarajadasa's cat Ji. Annie later claimed that her hitherto limited psychic gifts had expanded overnight as a result of meeting Leadbeater, and the weekends eventually resulted in a number of books jointly written under spiritual guidance.

These books cover a wide field. Leadbeater and Besant rewrote the geology and history of the world, investigating by occult means the continents of Atlantis and Lemuria and the ancient races of mankind. They expounded the true history of Christianity, revealing Christ to be an Egyptian Initiate born in AD 105. In *Occult Chemistry* they penetrated the secret of the atom, describing the structure of each molecule. It was not easy work. Though the authors made several of their chemical discoveries while sitting on a bench in the Finchley Road, as so often in scientific research the right materials were not always to hand and Leadbeater had to make several astral visits to glass cases in museums where the rarer metals and minerals were housed. But they struggled on together and Jinarajadasa gave what help he could. The cat's contribution is not recorded.

Leadbeater's most extraordinary and far-reaching psychic discoveries involved the study of past lives. HPB makes no mention of reincarnation in *Isis Unveiled*, but it plays a central role in *The Secret Doctrine*, which was Leadbeater's main starting-point for his occult work. In 1894, with the help of the ever-obliging Masters, he embarked on a momentous search for the past histories of the Society's members. He also employed psychometry, the technique of divining the properties of a thing by mere contact with it. The thing might be an object in the person's possession – an heirloom, say – or something less obviously tangible, such as a dream. There is a link here with psychoanalysis, which works with similarly tenuous material on comparably dubious grounds. The theosophical equivalent of the psyche is the Akashic (or imperishable) Record – a sort of astral library of everything that has ever happened in collective spiritual history.

To this brew of psychology and spiritualism Leadbeater added potent dashes of snobbery and family pride, calculated to appeal to class-conscious late-Victorians. For not only was everyone in the Society found to be the reincarnation of past celebrities; it also turned out that they were all related to one another in bizarre combinations. Furthermore, reincarnations ranged through both time and space, as spirits were found to move from planet to planet and even cosmos to cosmos. There was a surprising regularity in the pattern of reincarnations. Leadbeater traced sixteen past lives for each individual. Each life averaged fifty-five and a half years in length and each was separated from the next by 1,264 years. It happened that in every case the first three and the last seven existences were in male form, the intervening six female. Thus it might transpire that Leadbeater had been Annie's daughter on Mars or her mother-in-law in ancient Egypt.

But perhaps Leadbeater's greatest passion was not the past but the future, in the form of his work with young people. In 1897 he began contributing articles on the psychic education of children to the journal *Lucifer*, and in 1902 the Society gave him a charter to establish the Lotus Lodge and Journal world-wide in the service of the theosophical youth movement. He also took a personal interest in individuals and his entourage usually included one or two pubescent and pre-pubescent boys, entrusted to him by admiring parents. These boys were to be his downfall.

On 25 January 1906, when Leadbeater was at the height of his popularity within the Society, Mrs Helen Dennis of Chicago, mother of Robin Dennis, one of Leadbeater's favourite boys, wrote to Annie Besant accusing her confederate of secretly teaching boys to masturbate under cover of occult training, and insinuating that masturbation was only the prelude to the gratifying of homosexual lust.[17] Her letter was countersigned by several officials of the American TS and it suggested that Robin was not the only boy to suffer from Leadbeater's attentions. If the accusations were true it meant that Leadbeater was guilty of breach of trust, immoral practices, corruption, deceit and a perversion of the Masters' teaching which put Judge in the shade. As one lad said: 'I think that was the worst part of the whole thing, somehow he made me believe it was Theosophical.'[18]

Annie at first refused to accept any of the charges, but enemies within the Society suspected Leadbeater of sinister occult influence over Mrs Besant. Recalling her passionate advocacy of birth control in earlier days, they also wondered whether she actively supported the practice of masturbation as a means to limit population growth. In the face of mounting evidence against Leadbeater, Annie retreated from her uncompromising support for him, accepting that perhaps he had given unwise advice but refusing to condemn him for it. Challenged to explain why her occult powers had not forewarned her of Leadbeater's activities, she made an unfortunate comparison with the occasion when HPB invited Oscar Wilde to join the Society before his dealings with boys became public knowledge. If even Blavatsky's powers had failed her, Mrs Besant asked, why should hers prove more effective?[19] A disapproving public ignored the rhetorical question but noted the outcome of the Wilde affair.

Annie Besant was now in a very awkward position. For some years she and Leadbeater had been visiting the Masters regularly at night in their astral bodies. A great deal of weight was attached to these visits, for major decisions within the Society were seen to require the magisterial sanction granted in these interviews. Annie had frequently referred to them. But according to theosophical doctrine only the pure in heart, mind, spirit and body could become Initiates – and only Initiates were able to visit the Masters. Indeed, initiation was altogether a very tall order, requiring perfect physical and mental health, an absolutely pure life, complete unselfishness, charity, compassion, truthfulness, courage, and indifference to the physical world. If Leadbeater were not pure he could not be an Initiate, and if he were not an Initiate the visits to the Masters could not have taken place. What then became of Annie's vivid recollections of their joint interviews?

At this point a coded letter was discovered by a hotel cleaner, addressed by the former Curate of Bramshott to one of his charges. When the code was translated the following lines appeared:

> My own darling boy . . . Twice a week is permissible, but you will soon discover what brings the best effect . . .

Spontaneous manifestations are undesirable and should be discouraged. If it comes without help he needs rubbing more often, but not too often, or he will not come well . . . Glad sensation is so pleasant. Thousand kisses darling . . .[20]

A clamour now arose for Leadbeater's expulsion. His enemies hinted that he had given his boys more than advice. Conceding that there was a serious case to answer, Olcott and Besant convened a judicial committee of the Society to hear the case. Leadbeater appeared before the committee, but before they could reach a verdict he resigned, accusing black magicians of working against him. Throughout the proceedings he claimed that his teachings on sexual matters were intended to preserve the purity of his boys, to encourage the diversion of their erotic energies on to a higher spiritual plane and to relieve their feelings of guilt; but he also confused the issue by insisting that the admissions recorded in transcripts of his interviews with the committee were in fact the stenographer's mistakes.

Annie, well aware of her identification with Leadbeater and the embarrassing situation in which he had involved her, also offered to resign, then withdrew her offer and condemned her friend in private to Olcott, while in public trying to maintain the fiction of a distinction between unwise advice and basically sound character. Her line was that Leadbeater's teaching on masturbation was well-meant but mistaken. But although there was a brief coolness between them and Leadbeater never again held office at TS HQ, his old friend was soon coming round to him again. Annie badly needed his support and encouragement, and by August of the same year the two of them were in Germany, at work once more on their occult researches into reincarnation.

Olcott, too, was having second thoughts about Leadbeater, prompted by ill-health and the influence of a new friend, Mrs Marie Russak. A rich American widow, Mrs Russak had greeted the colonel at Southampton on his last visit to Britain with the news that she had been sent to him by a psychic message from her dead father. Finding Olcott painfully afflicted with gout, she and her maid, Miss Renda, offered to look after him. The colonel gratefully accepted the offer and took the two women back with him to Adyar, where they became enthusiastic Theosophists and Mrs Russak immediately set about improving the premises at her own expense.

Having condemned Leadbeater and expelled his supporters, including the faithful Jinarajadasa, Olcott now regretted his precipitate action, and the Brotherhood of Masters unanimously encouraged him to repent. Koot Hoomi, Morya and Serapis all came to his sickbed, both in private and in the presence of Annie, Mrs Russak and Miss Renda. The Masters instructed him to forgive Leadbeater, even dictating a letter which is a masterpiece of prevarication and vagueness. They also suggested that he appoint Annie his successor, which he proceeded to do.

Both moves caused uproar, especially the second. Annie had already made bitter enemies within the Society. It was also pointed out to Olcott that he had no business appointing anyone: the Society's constitution allowed him only to nominate a successor. He promptly issued another letter in the name of the Masters altering his appointment to a nomination. It hardly mattered. Within six weeks Olcott was dead, and an election for President was held four months later, on 28 June 1907.

Annie was the obvious candidate, though she was not favoured by A. P. Sinnett, the long-standing Vice-President, who took control of the Society during the interregnum. Sinnett, who had long resented her ascendancy and his own eclipse, virtually expelled Annie from Adyar, declaring her to be 'misled by the Dark Powers'[21] – for which read 'Leadbeater'. It was no use. Annie Besant was now by far the most powerful figure in the Society and she had Olcott's deathbed blessing. Having carefully promised not to reinstate Leadbeater before two years were up, and then only if the members requested it and he repudiated his former teaching on sexual matters, she was duly elected by a huge majority. The Society numbered thirteen thousand members world-wide (excluding, of course, the Point Loma Theosophists); Annie won almost ten thousand of their votes.

In a last spasm of rebellion the British Section refused Leadbeater readmission in November 1907, but by the end of the year his faithful friend the new President had persuaded the General Council of the Society to reinstate him on the same basis as Judge – by passing a motion affirming freedom of speech and conscience, which effectively allowed Leadbeater to say and do whatever he liked. Following his reinstatement many members, including the entire Sydney Lodge in Australia (the world's largest since the defection of the Judgeites), resigned in protest. Even A. P. Sinnett and Annie's old friend Herbert Burrows decided to go their own ways, as did Blavatsky's former secretary, G. R. S. Mead. The new President was not disturbed. She wanted to make Theosophy the world's leading ecumenical religious and social movement, and this she proceeded to do.

SEVEN

Boys and Gods

Theosophy is a spiritual science in two senses. It expounds a body of religious knowledge (or dogma) acquired by psychic means, and it teaches spiritual techniques designed to promote enlightenment, including study, prayer and meditation. Leadbeater developed both aspects of the Society's work; but while he encouraged rank-and-file members to develop their devotional skills, he reserved psychic powers largely to himself. Like Blavatsky before him, he under-stood how important it was to control access to the Masters.

At the heart of his teaching was the idea of 'the Path': the route individuals must follow to develop their spiritual life.[1] This idea had always been important in Theosophy, even under Blavatsky. But whereas she had tended to emphasise the difficulty for ordinary mortals of following the Path, Leadbeater neatly turned this formula on its head by implying that no one closely associated with him could possibly be ordinary and that all the members of his circle must therefore be *de facto* on the Path. The consequence was the appearance of a sort of spiritual honours system among the Theosophical élite in which Leadbeater's friends and disciples (they amounted to the same thing) were encouraged to be constantly on the look-out for promotion. To the dismay of his enemies within the Society – and there were many – Annie not only went along with this; she actively encouraged it.

At the same time she indulged her own passion for founding new organisations within the Society. Between her election as President in 1907 and the outbreak of war in 1914 she established or actively supported the Theosophical Order of Service, the Sons of India, the

Daughters of India, the Bureau of Theosophical Activities, the Order of the Rising Sun, the Order of the Star in the East, the Distressed Indian Students Aid Committee, the Temple of the Rosy Cross, the Order of Theosophical Sannyasis, the Preparation League of Healers, the League of St Christopher, the Servers of the Blind, the Imperial Services League of Modern Thought, the Order of World Peace, the Brotherhood of Arts, the Prayer League, the Redemption League, the Humane Research League, a dozen Buddhist schools and the Theosophical Bank of Finland.

The result of Annie's enthusiasm for starting societies, combined with Leadbeater's interest in sacraments, orders and vestments, was a huge increase in theosophical paraphernalia. Though her own early writings (like Anna Kingsford's) put great stress on inwardness and the folly of mistaking appearance for reality, Annie Besant was not a little vain of her own appearance and enjoyed dressing up in the regalia of the various theosophical orders she and Leadbeater founded together. As the years passed, both of them became more and more besotted with ceremonies and uniforms, offices and decorations.

Leadbeater was equally free with his predictions of imminent marvels. HPB, reckless with phenomena, had always been more circumspect when it came to prophesying major spiritual events, insisting that 'No Master of Wisdom from the East will himself appear or send anyone to Europe or America . . . until the year 1975',[2] by which time she herself would be safely out of the way. Her self-appointed disciple disagreed, unafraid to challenge Blavatsky's authority when it suited. He believed, he said, that Lord Maitreya – a being he confusingly identified with Christ – was about to 'manifest' for the beginning of a new era and Leadbeater was looking out for the vehicle of the manifestation: the new Messiah or World Teacher.[3] This gave him the opportunity to test a number of attractive boys for the role. One – Hubert van Hook – was groomed as the future saviour.

Suitably enough, Hubert's father, Dr van Hook of Chicago, had been Leadbeater's strongest American defender during the trials of 1906, and in November 1909 Mrs van Hook brought young Hubert to Adyar to take up his mission. This required close proximity to

Leadbeater, who was to supervise his every move. But by the time the van Hooks reached Madras with Mrs Russak in November 1909, events had already overtaken them and Hubert found himself doing lessons with a boy who had ousted him before he arrived. For Leadbeater had already encountered another vehicle who seemed even more promising.

The story of Krishnamurti's discovery was to become a central part of theosophical mythology. It goes as follows. Shortly after Leadbeater's return to Adyar from Europe in February 1909, Annie set out for a long trip to London, leaving him in charge. His two assistants, Ernest Wood and Johann van Manen, were accustomed to bathe in the sea of an evening, and Leadbeater sometimes went with them, though he stayed on the beach while they swam. His psychic powers included the ability to perceive auras, the coloured magnetic force-fields which, according to Mesmer, accompany every object, though they remain invisible to ordinary sight. One evening in the spring of 1909 Leadbeater noticed an extraordinary aura surrounding one of the Indian boys paddling in the shallows. The boy was dirty and unkempt. He also struck several witnesses, including Wood, who had already helped him with homework, as almost half-witted – so it may be possible to give Leadbeater the credit of overcoming his pederastic preferences in favour of real insight. Whatever the reasons, the boy took his fancy, and within days Leadbeater had told his followers that this child was destined to be a great teacher, even greater than Mrs Besant herself.

Jiddu Krishnamurti was the son of Jiddu Narianiah, a retired civil servant and keen Theosophist, who lived in great poverty just outside the Adyar compound. Leadbeater asked Narianiah to bring Krishna (as he was known) to see him one Saturday. The boy and his new patron sat next to one another on a sofa, and Leadbeater placed his hand on Krishna's head while he investigated the boy's past lives. These investigations continued for several Saturdays, and Leadbeater eventually wrote to Annie, then in Europe, that Krishna had 'a better set of lives even than Hubert, though I think not as sensational'.[4] Deciding that the boy was indeed the avatar of Lord Maitreya, Leadbeater immediately took charge of Krishna, who was scrubbed and cleaned and submitted to a strict educational and hygienic regime within the compound. He was also put on occult probation with the Master Koot Hoomi, whom Krishna visited every night in his astral body for fifteen minutes' instruction.

Meanwhile, Leadbeater dictated the results of the Saturday sessions to Wood and van Manen, and the dictations were then written up as a series of articles for *The Theosophist* under the title 'Rents in the Veil of Time', eventually issued as a book called *Lives of Alcyone*. These 'rents' went far beyond anything Leadbeater had previously discovered, and they were soon the talk of the Society. There were thirty lives in all, ranging in time from 22662 BC to AD 624, and each took the form of a biography of Alcyone (the name Leadbeater gave to the being supposedly now inhabiting Krishna's body), complete with a supporting cast of his relations and friends. For it turned out that in each of these previous lives everyone else known to Leadbeater also figured, but with different identities and sometimes different sexes. Some had been famous historical characters. Others had lived on the moon and Venus.

Thus in 40000 BC Leadbeater had been Annie's wife and Krishna their child, while in 12000 BC Leadbeater married Francesca Arundale in Peru and produced Bertrand Keightley and A. P. Sinnett as offspring. In other ages Mrs Besant acquired twelve husbands for whom she roasted rats, and Julius Caesar married Jesus Christ. The final charts are a triumph of cosmic soap opera, including over two hundred characters. Inevitably in such a large undertaking there were occasional contradictions or discrepancies. Whenever Leadbeater's assistants found one they would tell their master, who immediately went into a brief trance and rectified the errors.

So popular were the results that members of the Society went around asking each other anxiously, 'Are you in the Lives?' and the *Lives of Alcyone* threatened to become the Debrett of the spiritual world as Theosophists competed fiercely for places in the Band of Servers: a body of eternal spirits who always accompanied Lord Maitreya, taking material form in whatever bodies came to hand. This had its problems. Members were anxious not to appear among the villains of the piece – all of whom were easily recognisable as anti-Theosophists or Leadbeater's critics in the 1907 scandal. Some also noticed disturbing anomalies.⁵ Whenever Leadbeater became interested in a new boy, he would suddenly begin to appear in the *Lives*; indeed, Krishna's role got grander and grander as Leadbeater became more and more besotted with him, tracing his incarnations back further and further. But Wood and van Manen also found evidence of faking in their boss's rooms: careful notes and charts drawn up before the allegedly spontaneous astral revelations of the Akashic Record. So damning was this evidence that they persuaded the Theosophical Publishing House to suspend publication of the book indefinitely. (The faithful Jinarajadasa finally published the complete *Lives* in 1923, but by then everyone had lost interest.)

Leadbeater's enthusiasm for Krishnamurti was not reciprocated. He was an impatient, autocratic teacher, and Krishna was, to put it kindly, a dreamy boy. At school the masters often punished him cruelly for stupidity and lack of attention. On one occasion Leadbeater himself slapped the boy and Krishna never forgot it. He was certainly not a good scholar. After twenty years in the Society he confessed that he found it impossible to read any theosophical books from beginning to end, let alone remember the contents, though this may not surprise anyone who has struggled with *The Secret Doctrine* or *The Astral Light*.

He did, however, have a talent for occult communion with the Masters, whom he saw constantly, from his first sessions with Leadbeater until the day, years later, when he accidentally walked through one of them and they declined to appear again. On account of this talent Leadbeater was prepared to forgive him a good deal, and Krishna's visits to Koot Hoomi bore fruit with the publication in December 1910 of a short book, *At The Feet Of The Master*, in which he recounted KH's teaching. This was a stupendous effort for a backward lad of sixteen with poor English, and could only be explained by supernatural means – or by the fact that Leadbeater had written most of the text himself. As Wood sourly noted later, the book was 'very much in Mr Leadbeater's own style',⁶ though his former boss countered by claiming that this was quite natural in a boy under his own influential supervision, and in no way detracted from the volume's authenticity or authority. Readers agreed. *At The Feet Of The Master* went through five English and twenty-two foreign-language editions in a very short space of time, bringing Krishnamurti to the attention of a wider public. Eighty years later it is still in print.

Krishna's occult advancement moved with the greatest rapidity. Having been accepted for Probation, he became a full pupil in under five months – 'the shortest probation of which I have ever heard', according to Leadbeater.[7] Under his teacher's powerful influence Krishna also 'remembered' several of these visits and dictated or wrote detailed accounts of them to Mrs Besant, who was keen to return from England to Adyar and meet the new prodigy. For it seemed that once again dear Brother Leadbeater's occult instincts were unerring: here indeed was the new Messiah, the World Teacher.

When she did return, in November 1909, Annie immediately took to both Krishna and his younger brother Nitya, who shared his life at Adyar. Krishna returned her affection in full measure. She had long been deprived of her own children and he had lost his mother at ten years old. Whatever their doctrinal and political differences, they both remained faithful to this love until Annie Besant's death twenty-five years later.

But if Krishna and Nitya had found a substitute for their dead mother in Annie, Leadbeater's usurpation of the paternal role was less acceptable, especially to their living father. Their new life inevitably drew the brothers away from Narianiah. Though previously a keen Theosophist, he was also a pious Hindu, disturbed by the violation of sacred rites and customs this education entailed. In particular, European methods of washing affronted both Hindu tradition and the native sense of shame. Aware of Leadbeater's scandalous reputation, Narianiah was even more unhappy about his personal influence on the boys. To cap it all, the excessive reverence being paid to Krishna by Theosophists at Leadbeater's behest threatened to make the boy and his family a laughing-stock among ordinary Indians, who were apt to be more familiar with their huge pantheon of deities than pious westerners.

Serious trouble began in March 1910 when Annie persuaded Narianiah to cede to her the legal custody of Krishna and his brother. Almost immediately repenting the move, Narianiah began to complain about Leadbeater's influence over his children. Annie disregarded the complaints and took the boys to Shanti Kunja, her house near Benares, where they were surrounded by a select group of companions. Here they took lessons from Leadbeater; George Arundale, now Principal of the Central Hindu College; and A. E. Wodehouse, brother of P.G. and Professor of English at the college. Besides their academic work they played tennis and cricket, went for long bicycle rides and were read to from Kipling, Shakespeare and Baroness Orczy. Occult training apart, their education conformed to the English public-school pattern: plenty of games, some classics and a little light reading.

Indulging her passion for new organisations, Annie founded at Benares the exclusive Yellow Shawl Group and, within it, the even more exclusive Purple Order, with Krishna at the head of both. Each had its distinctive insignia – a yellow shawl and a purple ribbon – offering plenty of scope for ridicule. Composed of the chosen few who were intended to support Krishnamurti in his mission as the World Teacher, much as the apostles supported Jesus, these small groups were supplemented in 1911 when Annie and George Arundale went on to found the more ambitious Order of the Rising Sun – later renamed the Order of the Star in the East (usually known as the OSE). Specifically devoted to preparing the world for Krishna's mission, the OSE extended membership beyond the Society, though members of one were usually also members of the other.

In order to promote this mission, Annie proposed to take the boys to London. For this she required their father's permission. It is easy to imagine how Narianiah felt when she asked for it. First his sons had been secluded from him in Benares and educated in an alien faith and culture. Now they were going to the other side of the world on a journey which was bound to alienate them even further. On the other hand, it was a great opportunity for two poor boys, and Narianiah reluctantly gave Annie custody for two visits in 1911 and 1912, on condition they were kept away from Leadbeater's baleful influence. Annie accepted the conditions, but immediately reneged on her agreement.

Leadbeater's charge of Krishna and his brother Nitya entailed close personal supervision, regulating every detail of their lives. He dictated their diet, regulated their day and even taught them to swim. When first discovered they were suffering from malnutrition, and this regime was well suited to cure them. But while their health and looks improved generally, not all the changes were to the good. Believing in the virtues of a nourishing English diet, Besant and Leadbeater stuffed them with porridge, eggs and large quantities of milk, which produced years of painful indigestion in boys unused to such stodgy food. The omniscient Leadbeater also supervised their hygiene, which caused another sort of problem. Given the necessity of absolute purity for all Initiates, Leadbeater was naturally concerned with both their mental and physical cleanliness. He was adamant that the boys should not be polluted by too much contact with women, and even presided over their ablutions himself. It was no wonder Narianiah complained.

Events approached their climax when the boys returned from their first visit to England. At a meeting of the new OSE in Benares in December 1911 it was suggested that Krishna should preside and hand out membership certificates to those present. According to Leadbeater, an extraordinary transformation came over the hall during this ceremony, like the outpouring of the Holy Ghost at Pentecost, and the occasion was transformed from a mundane meeting to an ineffable experience of the godhead. Many members of the Society, including Nitya, prostrated themselves at Krishna's feet, recognising that something marvellous had happened – though there were those who saw simply a 'very embarrassed Indian boy handing out slips of paper to a crowd of strangely behaving people',[8] and some who observed that while Mrs Besant forced others to prostrate themselves, she and Leadbeater stayed in their seats.

In February 1912 Annie and the boys left for their second trip to England with Narianiah's ever more reluctant consent; but the farce of the OSE meeting – as Narianiah saw it – combined with clear evidence that Leadbeater still had control over his sons, prompted him to take action. He was egged on by extreme Hindu nationalists, who were now fiercely opposed to Theosophy, seeing it as little more than another means of white cultural repression. Many of them also took exception to Annie's political campaigns on their behalf, which they perceived as compromised and patronising. From their own standpoint, they were quite right. Annie's fervour for Indian autonomy was tempered by British patriotism and a fondness for managing things in her own way. Supported by the nationalist paper the *Pioneer*, Narianiah therefore decided to revoke the custody agreement and then unsuccessfully sued for repossession of his children, in a bizarre lawsuit which included charges of deification and sodomy.

Always relishing a legal battle, Annie had no hesitation in fighting the case. Knowledge and experience of the law were both on her side, and she had the Society's extensive resources to support her. Nor did she think for a moment that it was wrong or unwise to take the children away from their father, putting the cause she believed in before any natural ties. And for all her belief in universal brotherhood, her real sympathy with the native races and her support for limited Indian Home Rule, Mrs Besant was in her own way a staunch royalist and patriot, who saw London as the centre of the universe – whatever the Himalayan Brotherhood of Masters might think. Despite her occult adventures and advanced views, she was an unimaginative woman, conventional enough to want Krishna to graduate from Oxford and to be at home in good European society – curious requirements for a future messiah. In the process of preparing him for his future role, she therefore severed the boy from his roots.

Yet the severance was never complete, nor could it be. Krishnamurti was to take his place among the millions removed from one milieu but never at home in another. He had lost his mother; now he was to lose his father, his family and his country. In future he would belong to no one and to nowhere, a completely free agent without ties or obligations. This condition was to be the source of his enormous moral and spiritual authority. It was also to be the source of considerable mischief and measureless anguish.

Substitute mothers were to play a major role in Krishnamurti's life. When Annie and her charges had arrived in England in May 1911, among the large crowd waiting to meet them at Charing Cross Station was Lady Emily Lutyens, wife of the famous architect Edwin Lutyens. Lady Emily, born in 1874, already had Indian and occult connections of a sort. She was the daughter of the first Earl of Lytton, Viceroy of India, and the granddaughter of Bulwer Lytton, whose novels had supplied Madame Blavatsky with so much of her inspiration.

A shy, ugly, awkward woman who disliked her own upper-class milieu, she was also, in her aristocratic fashion, a minor Annie Besant. In childhood little Emily had been intensely devout, believing that the Second Coming would occur in her lifetime, and even entering into a correspondence about her faith with an elderly clergyman, which was published many years later. As an adult, bored and frustrated by the demands of children, housekeeping and her husband's professional life, she turned to good causes and social reform, taking an interest in sex education and the prostitution laws, and visiting VD hospitals. She was a member of the Fabian Society; and a keen supporter of women's suffrage, like her sister Lady Constance Lytton, who had been imprisoned and force-fed for throwing stones through windows in suffragette protests.

It was among the Fabians that Lady Emily first heard Annie Besant lecture, in 1910. She had joined the Theosophical Society earlier that year, but had been disappointed by the meetings, which seemed to be obsessed with the petty details of Society business when she was looking for inspiration. But Mrs Besant, dressed in flowing white robes to match her white curly hair, revived all her enthusiasm with a brilliant oration; from that moment on, Emily Lutyens devoted herself to Theosophy body and soul for almost twenty years.

Devoted as she was to Annie, it was to be Krishnamurti who really held her attention, and the day when the thirty-six-year-old woman and the sixteen-year-old boy first met on Charing Cross Station brought a kind of love at first sight. Her maternal emotions were deeply stirred by this fragile, exotic figure who bore on his shoulders the spiritual destiny of mankind – including herself. But if her love was romantic and maternal, there was also a powerful erotic element in it, though several years passed before she understood this. She was not happy with her husband, a charming, witty, worldly man, and their tastes and interests were so very different that she had been no more than a dutiful wife, and sometimes scarcely that. Krishnamurti was dark, exotic, vulnerable, beautiful, powerful, demanding and giving all at once.

There was also a kind of safety in his love. As a potential Master he was sworn to complete abstinence from sexual passion; for the future World Teacher there could be no question of love or marriage. Women could therefore give him their full devotion without risk – or so it seemed. He was to inspire this blended passion – a mixture of adoration, dependence and protectiveness – in many women over a period of sixty years. Annie Besant was the first to feel it, Emily Lutyens the second.

The feeling was reciprocal. Krishna once showed Lady Emily a page he had cut out of the *Daily Mirror*. The picture showed a small boy sitting on a park bench dreaming that he was sitting on his mother's lap. Krishnamurti felt that he was that boy. He was then nearly seventeen.

Despite Leadbeater's dislike of them, older women played a major role in Krishna's theosophical life from the start. Besides Annie and Emily, two of Lady Emily's recent converts helped to supervise his early years. Lady Muriel Brassey, yet another bossy theosophical lady, was the estranged wife of Lord De La Warr, and described by Emily as someone who was 'rather fond of managing other people's lives'.[9] Krishna was no exception. While she provided him with hospitality she also bullied him into a strict dietary and personal routine and brooked no contradiction.

Lady De La Warr's immensely rich and crippled American friend Miss Dodge, with whom she lived in St James's Place and Wimbledon, was altogether more relaxed. Miss Dodge was exceptionally generous, as she could well afford to be.[10] It was whispered that she had an income of over £1,000,000 per annum inherited from her father, a railroad and real-estate king. Even a tenth of this sum would have been vast riches at the time. Miss Dodge supported theosophical publications, contributed to the Society's building projects and made personal gifts to Krishnamurti, including an annual income, which made him independent of the Society. Other contributions, in response to an endless stream of requests, were less well judged, though even Miss Dodge drew the line at providing silk underwear for male officers in one of the Society's sister-organisations.

Though she was the most open-handed of its patrons, Theosophy attracted many rich women who made large contributions to its funds. In 1927 one supporter left Annie Besant a personal bequest of £25,000. Others were generous with hospitality and support, including Annie's old friend from Secular Society days, Esther Bright, with whom the boys often stayed in London; George Arundale's aunt Francesca, Krishna's housekeeper during World War One; and Dr Mary Rocke, a physician.

Not all of these women were strong-minded, but they were all strong-willed and often argued over Krishna's education and domestic routine. Most of them were single, widowed or divorced, and many had private means. They were looking for a purpose in life and ready to pay for it. But some expected personal and spiritual privileges in return for their largesse. Each guarded Krishna jealously when in their possession, and though their fights make comic reading now, it must have been a miserable existence for a young man plucked out of obscurity to head a world religion in a strange continent. It is hardly surprising that he often lamented, 'Why on earth did they choose me?' to anyone who would listen.

His powerful female companions were determined that he would receive the academic and social education of a European gentleman. Their reverence for eastern religious teaching never dented an unarticulated belief in the superiority of western civilisation. The social training was no problem. On their later visits to London an elderly barrister, Harold Baillie-Weaver, was produced to show the boys how to behave and to buy them the right sort of clothes from Savile Row and Jermyn Street. Their shoes came from Lobb, their suits from Meyer & Mortimer (Krishna later moved to Huntsman), their shirts from Beale & Inman, and their ties from Liberty. Inevitably, their hair was cut at Trumper's. Krishna continued to dress with the greatest care throughout the rest of his life, taking particular trouble with the shoes for his tender, narrow feet. Lady Emily noted approvingly the contrast between his aristocratic demeanour and fine clothes, and the taste for tweeds and sandals prevalent among most Theosophists.

In general the boys lived a relaxed version of the upper-middle-class life of the period. Baillie-Weaver took Krishna and his brother to the theatre, which they loved, especially the musicals and light comedies then popular. They also rode in the park and later on motor bikes; played golf, croquet and tennis; and flirted with girls, who fell for them as easily as older women did. Both Krishnamurti and his brother returned their affections, but since it was clear to everyone that there could be no question of Krishna marrying, absolute chastity being a *sine qua non* of initiation – at least until someone decided otherwise – the very prohibitions that made relationships with older women possible made his involvement with young girls both safe and unreal while giving them a curious bitter-sweet intensity.

Education was a problem. They continued to take lessons in arithmetic, algebra, Sanskrit and essay-writing, as they had begun to at Adyar. Nitya was bright and passed his examinations easily but, struggle as he might, Krishna could not pass them at all, so the idea of university had to be given up altogether. Perhaps it was just as well. As Emily's daughter Mary Lutyens later remarked, the Oxford of the 1920s was unlikely to accept a black man who had not only been proclaimed the Messiah but also accused of sodomy by his own father.[11]

Meanwhile, Leadbeater and Annie Besant continued to set up an elaborate framework of organisations to support Krishnamurti and to carry his message. The Esoteric Section of the Society had already been increased in importance, its members an élite corps pledged to answer directly to the President and so prepare for the coming of the World Teacher. The manner of this preparation had previously been unspecified. Now it was known who the World Teacher would be, the ES was devoted to his service and divided into a system of degrees, each with its own order, ribbon, medals and stages of initiation. The Order of the Star in the East increased its member-ship, as the full Society grew from thirteen thousand members in

1907 to sixteen thousand by 1911, with new applicants joining every week. It soon became clear that the World Teacher was having a dramatic effect on Theosophy's prestige. By 1920 Krishnamurti's fame had helped to push membership to thirty-six thousand, and in 1928 the numbers rose to an incredible peak of forty-five thousand.

Despite this impressive growth, many older Theosophists watched with alarm as Annie, prompted by Leadbeater, transformed the Society into an elaborate series of theatrical performances disguised as complex rituals and prettified with costly uniforms and shoddy trinkets. No doubt they heaved a sigh of relief when in 1914 Leadbeater, harried by the Hindu press and chafing against the need to defer to Annie in everything, decided to leave Adyar and settle in Australia. They were soon to discover that his malign influence reached more than half-way round the world.

In Sydney Leadbeater made friends with James Wedgwood. The two men had earlier been enemies, perhaps because Wedgwood was a ghastly parody of Leadbeater himself, with the same taste for magic, ceremonial and boys, and the same inexplicable influence over middle-aged women. A restless, well-educated Englishman born in 1883 and supported by a small private income, Wedgwood had reacted against the atheism and agnosticism of his clan, which comprised the most distinguished intellectual dynasties in England, including the Huxleys, Darwins and Arnolds. After exploring the orthodox churches with a view to ordination, he joined the Theosophical Society, whose English Secretary he became in 1911.

Like Leadbeater, Wedgwood relished the elaborate rituals of Anglo-Catholicism and found plain Theosophy insufficiently colourful. In 1912 he tried to cheer things up by founding the Temple of the Rosy Cross, an offshoot of Rosicrucianism with a complicated ritual allegedly inspired by Master the Count de Saint-Germain. He found willing helpers for this enterprise in Lady Emily Lutyens and Olcott's old friend Mrs Russak, now living in London. Members attended ceremonies in long white satin gowns, with swords and Templar headdresses, and lit candles for various deities – harmless enough activities which prompted George Arundale to suggest that the Temple's motto, Lux Veritatis, should be translated as Looks Very Silly.[12]

It is extraordinary just how absorbed in trivia the leaders of the Society could become. When Annie Besant wasn't conducting interviews with the King of the World she was fussing over the exact shade of blue ribbon required for members of the Order of the Star in the East. It was eighteen months before she found three thousand yards of just the right colour in Paris, giving Lady Emily news of this in a letter which exactly conveys the President's combination of enthusiasm, business sense, bossiness and naïvety·

> Please set a lot of people to cut it, or as much of it as is wanted, into ¼ yard lengths. Then ask Krishnamurti to magnetize it in bulk. Let each Corresponding Secretary have as many yards as he or she wants, reckoning 1 yd. to 4 members. Charge them 25% over the cost of the ribbon, which I will let you know; it is to be sold to members at 1d the quarter yard. This ribbon is only to be worn with badges of the three grades.[13]

Emily's husband Edwin, who was bemused by his wife's complete immersion in the dottier aspects of Theosophy, remarked that he didn't like 'magnetized ribbons, blue or any other colour'.[14] He was no more enthusiastic about the Temple of the Rosy Cross. Nor, for that matter, were the Theosophical elders. Although Mrs Besant gave it her guarded blessing, Leadbeater withheld his simply because the Temple had been founded without his approval. In 1914 the inevitable followed, when Master Koot Hoomi ordered the Temple's dissolution – through Leadbeater, of course.

By that time Wedgwood, too, had migrated to Australia, having transferred his allegiance from the Rosy Cross to the Co-Masonic Order, in which he had already reached high rank. Co-Masonry was another theosophical offshoot, founded in France in 1893. The Co-Masons emphasised the occult and ritualistic elements in Masonry. They also extended membership to women. As an inveterate joiner, Annie Besant became an early member, rapidly achieving the office of Very Illustrious Most Puissant Grand Commander of the British Jurisdiction; while Leadbeater rose through the Antipodean ranks to become Australian Administrator General. According to Leadbeater, Master the Count, inspirer of the Temple, also had special responsibility for the Co-Masons.

More perplexing is the Society's relationship with the Old Catholic Church – a confusing institution in itself. This tiny church, established in 1870 by Catholic dissenters from the doctrine of papal infallibility promulgated in that year, had branches in Holland and England. It claimed both autonomy and apostolic succession and engaged in a flirtation with Theosophy when the head of the church, Archbishop Mathew, agreed to consider Wedgwood for ordination. Reading the small print of the Society's rules, Mathew decided in 1915 that membership of the Society and Old Catholicism were perhaps incompatible after all, upon which Wedgwood staged a coup d'état, leading most of the clergy and congregation of the Old Catholic Church (numbering a few hundred) into a new body, the Liberal Catholic Church, while Mathew returned to the safety of Rome.

On his arrival in Australia, Leadbeater soon reached an accommodation with Wedgwood, whom he recognised as a useful ally and a dangerous enemy. In 1916 he was ordained priest in Wedgwood's newly independent LCC, being consecrated bishop with medieval alacrity just seven days later. Thereafter he preferred to be known as Bishop Leadbeater and took to wearing purple robes, a gigantic pectoral cross and an amethyst ring. As he artlessly wrote to Annie:

> My own Master . . . remarked: 'You thought you had given up all prospect of a bishopric when you left your church work thirty-two years ago to follow Upâsika [i.e. Blavatsky]; but I may tell you that it would have been in this very year that you would have reached it had you remained in your original work, so you have lost nothing except the emoluments and the social position, and have gained enormously in other ways. No one ever loses by serving us!' That struck me as curious, for I had never thought of it in that way.[15]

Wedgwood proposed the church as a suitable vehicle for the World Teacher, against the opposition of many Theosophists, who pointed out that HPB had specifically condemned apostolic succession as a 'gross and palpable fraud'.[16] Leadbeater was nevertheless enthusiastic. Under the occult direction of Master the Count, he composed a hymnbook and a new liturgy – with considerable difficulty, since the count thought and dictated in medieval Latin. The Australian congregation gradually expanded, and work was started on building the Cathedral of St Alban and a great conference centre in Sydney. Other leading Theosophists including George Arundale took an interest in the church, and branches multiplied in Europe after World War One. But Leadbeater had lost interest in Europe. Having once predicted that the world's new race would emerge in California, he now transferred his prophecy to the Antipodes.[17] Australia was to be the home of the new generation and the Liberal Catholic Church its vehicle.

The Bishop's glory was to be short-lived, however. Already under attack when he left Adyar in 1914, by 1917 he was the target of several anti-Leadbeater, Back to Blavatsky movements, instigated by Theosophists angry at his attempts to turn the Society into a church and ready to use his reputation for immorality against him. The most prominent figure in these movements was the trenchant H. N. Stokes, Editor of a leading theosophical journal, the *OE Library Critic*. Stokes objected especially to Leadbeater's tendency to treat HPB as a sort of John the Baptist to his own Jesus Christ, and criticised Annie severely for supporting him. The two of them, according to Stokes, were hijacking Theosophy for their own ends, Annie pushing her social agenda, Leadbeater his own occult ambitions. They had even suggested that new members should read books by themselves (in fact, their complete works) before they touched a word of Blavatsky, and they had the cheek to 'edit' *The Secret Doctrine* by making thousands of amendments to the third edition. The three great objectives of the Society had now been replaced, Stokes suggested, by three more:

> First. – To form a nucleus for talking about the Universal Brotherhood of humanity, and to leave it to others to practise it. Second. – To encourage the study of the writings of Annie Besant and Charles W Leadbeater, and to discourage comparing them with other religious,

philosophical or scientific writers, including the Founders
of the Society. Third. – To accept without investigation the
unproved assertions of clairvoyants about the unexplained
laws of nature, and the powers which they claim for
themselves.[18]

Stokes was not the only critic. Bhagavan Das, formerly the
Secretary of the Indian Section and a close colleague of Annie's, was
increasingly alarmed by her political ambitions, Leadbeater's pretensions and Krishnamurti's deification. Attempting to reason with
Mrs Besant, he found her obdurate and concluded that her natural
altruism had given way to egotism since she became President.[19]
Alice Cleather conducted a vigorous campaign against Besant and
Leadbeater. Cleather pointed out that although Annie had recanted
her notorious views on birth control when she joined the Society,
she had effectively espoused them again in order to defend Leadbeater's teaching on masturbation. Leadbeater himself she dismissed as a 'sex pervert and pseudo-occultist'.[20] She also mocked
Annie's need for a male intermediary with the Masters and
suggested that Leadbeater and his patron were no better than
vampires, crazed with power and feeding on the worship of devotees
as Dracula feeds on the blood of his victims.

No hostages were taken in the theosophical battle. Katherine
Tingley herself continued her missionary campaign against Adyar
in general and Leadbeaterism in particular, by discrediting several
representatives of the Indian Society previously associated with
Leadbeater, including Alex Fullerton, who was convicted of homosexual assault and then committed to a lunatic asylum at her
instigation. Now Tingley's chief pamphleteer, Joseph Fussell,
waged war against the Bishop with bitter hatred.

The battle was intensified by desertions from the Purple Mother's
own army to rival theosophical factions, most of them sickened by
the endless feuding with Adyar. In 1904 she had lost (or ejected,
according to which account you believe) Robert Crosbie, an early
Judgeite and formerly one of her strongest supporters, who formed
his own United Lodge of Theosophists in 1909. This organisation
pointedly discouraged personality cults – even its official history was

published anonymously – and it had no constitution or hierarchy. It soon attracted disgruntled Tingleyites and Adyar refugees and continues to function. Crosbie was followed by others.

But Tingley had far less to lose than Besant in the way of members and reputation, and it was against Besant that the fiercest attacks continued, covering everything from her policies to her clothes. T. M. Nair's *The Evolution of Mrs Besant* and F. T. Brooks's *Neotheosophy* were only the fiercest of many pamphlets attacking Annie personally. The criticisms were always the same: on the one hand the President involved Theosophy in ridiculous occult claims, self-aggrandising rituals and even immorality, while on the other she used the Society's name for her own political and social causes, which, however worthy they might be, had nothing to do with Theosophy or with HPB's legacy, which she had so impertinently appropriated to herself. Several critics quoted as self-evidently ludicrous Leadbeater's assertion that 'I have stood beside your President in the presence of the Supreme Director of Evolution on this globe . . . the plans she is carrying our are [His] plans for the welfare of the world . . .'[21]

The criticism and the defections made no difference to Annie. She shrugged off the attacks and continued her political and social work in India, where in November 1913 she had encountered the Master Rishi Agastya, the member of the Great White Brotherhood responsible for India. He arranged for her to have an interview at Shamballa with the Lord of the World. The Lord had asked Mrs Besant to work for Indian self-government and she had agreed to do so. News of this meeting only increased the unhappiness of Theosophists dissatisfied with Annie's leadership. Angrily pointing out that HPB had repeatedly excluded politics from the Society's work, Stokes, Das and Cleather thought their President should pay a little more attention to their spiritual welfare and a little less to her grandiose political schemes. They were also aware of unpleasant rumours coming out of Australia, where Leadbeater was once again under investigation for immorality – this time by the police.

EIGHT

Ahriman and Lucifer

There is a theosophical myth concerning the beings known as Lords of the Dark Face, evil angels whose cosmic role is to lead humanity astray. Vaguely adumbrated by early Theosophists as the 'Dark Forces' who fight an unyielding war with the Great White Brotherhood of Masters, these Lords were given positive identities by a second-generation member of the Society, the Austrian philosopher Rudolf Steiner (1861–1925). Steiner named the main enemies of mankind as Lucifer and Ahriman, personifications of the spirit of pride and the spirit of materialism.[1] Ahriman tempts human beings to reject the spiritual by inducing them to trust only in the realm of the mind and the senses, thereby involving them in his own contradiction as a spirit-denying spirit. He is the presiding deity of modern science and technology, and of all those who would describe Man as no more or less than animal. Lucifer the light-bearer more subtly seduces mankind to overestimate their spiritual powers by persuading them they can transcend human limitations by their own efforts. He dominates modern literature, philosophy and art.

It was easy for Theosophists to conclude that anyone who disagreed with them, however well intentioned, was working in the service of the Dark Forces. The charge was eventually to be levelled against Steiner himself, when he rejected Theosophy in favour of his own new society. He was an unlikely rebel: a small, quiet, earnest, visionary ascetic, an obsessively hard-working scholar trained in the German idealist tradition. But though he briefly headed the German Section and would certainly have become a dominant Theosophist had he stayed there, Steiner left the Society

when he found it cramping his own grand vision. For Steiner was
not only a spiritual teacher, but also an artist, architect, political
theorist and intellectual polymath who dreamt of building a new
world order on the basis of his communications from the spirit
world.

If this description suggests a dreamer out of touch with reality,
the impression is unfair. Although Steiner was a romantic who
relieved his otherwise drab appearance with a flowing artist's tie, he
was also a realist who created an empire which has since outstripped
Theosophy in power and popularity. His reaction against Theosophy pinpointed everything wrong with the Society. And although
he produced a body of occult literature whose fantastic claims rival
or even exceed Leadbeater's, there could be no greater contrast to
the *fin-de-siècle* frivolity and decadence of the Leadbeater-
Wedgwood circle than Steiner's high-minded, plain-living hetero-
sexuality, his lofty philosophy and dedication to work.

Perhaps the only thing Steiner and Leadbeater had in common
apart from membership of the Society was a father who worked on
the railways.[2] The eldest child of a village station master, Steiner
was born in the remote mountains of Styria and brought up on the
Austro-Hungarian border, in isolated villages where strangers were
disliked. His parents were peasants from the estate of Horn, north
of Vienna, whence they had fled when their feudal master Count
von Hoyos Sprinzenburg forbade them to marry. Their life was
hard. There was little money and young Rudolf had to walk several
miles to school and back, often through deep snow.

A solitary, serious, reflective child, Steiner was a visionary from
his earliest youth, communing with spirits in the hills surrounding
his home. Later, he became the adult Wordsworth had dreamt of
being: one who never lost the sense that there is beyond – and yet
somehow immanent in – the visible world a celestial realm accessible to the spiritual eye. This eye usually closes in maturity,
remaining open only for the few. When Steiner realised that he was
one of the privileged minority, he decided to devote his life to
teaching others how to cultivate the faculty of spiritual sight – which
makes it all the more surprising that he became not a Words-

worthian poet but a Kantian philosopher who cultivated rationality, detachment and objectivity.

Steiner was a slow, careful and pedantic thinker, whose natural qualities were intensified by training in the German academic tradition. He adored his father, who was anxious that Rudolf should get on: equating advancement with railway technology, he insisted that his son should study sciences at university. This the boy did, but the battle to make him an engineer had been lost years earlier when he discovered the great classics of German literature and philosophy in the library of the local doctor, an eccentric figure who diagnosed patients from a moving train as it passed the station platforms on which they were standing.

Goethe, Schiller and Lessing – the staple authors of the German literary tradition – all fed Steiner's visionary experience with their lofty moral idealism and their sense of a transcendent inner world. But the first decisive moment in his spiritual development came at the age of fifteen as he pondered the discovery that, for most people, this 'inner world' does not seem to have any real existence, except as a fantastic or imaginary realm. This discovery led him to question the relationship between the commonplace world others saw and his own visionary experience, which he perceived as having equal or even greater reality than the everyday world. Was he merely imagining his visions, he wondered, or did they possess the reality he ascribed to them? And if they did, what conclusions were to be drawn from that fact?

By asking such questions, Steiner was instinctively drawn into an ancient philosophical and religious controversy concerning the relationship of appearance and reality, and he found his puzzles formulated as philosophical problems in the work of Kant. Attempting to refute Hume's sceptical claim that the human mind can possess no certain knowledge of the world, Kant had asserted that it can; but in so doing he was forced to postulate a theory of two worlds: the phenomenal and the noumenal. The phenomenal world is the world of appearances which the organs of perception, regulated by the understanding, present to the mind as reality. But behind this world there is a realm of ultimate realities or noumena –

sometimes called 'things-in-themselves' – which the mind can never know.

This formula suggested to Steiner the possibility of a solution to his problem. Kant had been right, he argued, to postulate the existence of noumena, but wrong to argue that they can never be known. For Steiner was convinced that his spiritual visions *were* the perception of ultimate reality, and he rejected Kant's belief that we cannot experience things-in-themselves. Others might have been content to leave it at that, but the intellectual Steiner – who inherited the passionate Kantian belief in the importance of knowledge and enquiry – wanted an explanation of *how* such visions could be perceived, if not through the ordinary organs of perception. And he wanted a philosophical theory that would provide a comprehensive account of the relationship between phenomena and noumena.

By the time he reached university he had discovered some preliminary but, as it seemed to him, inescapable answers to these questions. He concluded, first, that the spirit world is real, not illusory; second, that the only way to understand and learn from it is to observe it closely as a scientist would observe the material world; third, that the only limits on such observation are the limits of our perceptive organs; and fourth, that there must therefore exist special organs of spiritual perception which are simply atrophied in most individuals. These organs Steiner imagined to be mental equivalents of the appendix. The logical conclusion was that the prevailing orthodoxy of materialism, which explained all knowledge as the product of physical perceptive organs, must be wrong.

These views were severely tested by his scientific studies at the Technical University of Vienna, where materialism was the fashion and the dominant influence was the Australian Darwinian, Ernst Haeckel.[3] Steiner could not accept materialist theories of evolution. More unusually, he rejected mechanical theories of heat and light in physics for the same reason: that none of these theories took into account spiritual realities. This was an extreme position, since even the most committed of Christians was normally relaxed about mechanical explanations of such phenomena on the grounds that God could be said to have created the mechanisms. But the acceptance of a distinction between spirit and matter entailed all sorts of other philosophical problems, which Steiner solved by concluding that because everything was created from spirit and spirit had priority, therefore spirit was present in everything. For the same reason he rejected current epistemological theories: in the spiritual realm, knowledge and experience were one.

He was able to combat the challenge of materialism by invoking the other formative influence on his intellectual and spiritual life: Goethe – not as poet and dramatist, but as scientist and philosopher. His encounter with Goethe solved the problems posed by Darwin and Haeckel. Goethe's anti-Newtonian (and generally discredited) optics proposed a theory of light as the medium between the sensible and the supersensible, while his notion of plant metamorphoses envisaged lower forms evolving into higher forms through the workings of some spiritual or supersensible force. Above all, Goethe's passion was for wholeness and unity. He wanted to find an account that would unite the separate phenomenal and noumenal worlds of Kantian philosophy, and this he found in the idea of spiritual metamorphosis, a notion with affinities to Lamarck's theory of evolution, which holds that there is a creative purpose in the universe and that distinct species are an illusion produced out of the ever-changing flux by the shortness of human life.[4]

For Steiner as for Shaw, metamorphosis was the acceptable face of evolution, and it led him to conclude (in a lecture of 1905) that he quarrelled not with neo-Darwinism but only with its materialistic explanations. What Haeckel and his colleagues failed to take into account, according to Steiner, was the miracle of Christ.[5] Originally endowed with clairvoyance, the human race had eventually lost this power, becoming as time went on ever more involuted, i.e. bound up in their material bodies, until Christ's direct intervention in human affairs from the spiritual world set them once more on the upward path of evolution. For evolution, in Steiner's understanding of the term, must entail increased understanding and spiritual insight. There is no such thing as purely material evolution: the very fact that something evolves implies (indeed, is proof of) the presence of spirit, purpose and at least nascent consciousness.

Part of Goethe's appeal to Steiner was his rejection of cloudy mysticism and subjectivity in favour of clear thinking and the objective study of supersensible phenomena. Here again Steiner invoked the idea of science. His encounters with spirits, he believed, were given to him as knowledge through organs of spiritual perception as valid as any other organs. He accordingly rejected spiritualism as arbitrary and irrational. The meditation he practised to develop his own encounters with the spirit world increased the effectiveness of psychic organs just as use increased the efficiency of material organs. Thus Goethe made it possible for Steiner to see science not as a bar to spiritual development but as a contribution towards it.

Steiner believed that Goethe had been deeply influenced by the Rosicrucian and other esoteric traditions, hidden since the Renaissance. This belief eventually convinced him that the right way forward for Europeans was not the eastern path of Theosophy but the route of what he called western esotericism – a formula very similar to Anna Kingsford's. Such esotericism has been the dominant philosophy in three periods: in the days of Pythagoras and Plato, in the Renaissance, and in our own time, beginning in the later nineteenth century. Otherwise it had gone underground. Theosophy was merely the sign of its re-emergence.

After leaving university in 1884, Steiner became tutor to the four sons of Pauline and Ladislas Specht in Vienna. One of the boys was a backward ten-year-old with water on the brain. Steiner lived in close intimacy with the family for six years and the experience of teaching this boy helped him devise the theory of curative education which became the foundation of his schools and the basis of his spiritual pedagogy. Steiner found that the child's powers of concentration and absorption were severely limited, and that before he could learn anything he had to be prepared to receive it. This preparation took more time than the learning process itself. Their relationship makes an interesting contrast with Leadbeater's tuition of Krishnamurti – another child thought by many people, including himself, to be comparably disadvantaged. Unfortunately Steiner is maddeningly unspecific about his methods, though they appear to have consisted largely of gaining the boy's confidence and establish-

1. Madame Blavatsky

2. Maloney and Jack, the chums

3. *and* 4. Masters Koot Hoomi and Morya

5. A caricature of Charles Darwin as an ape

6. Annie Besant, Colonel Olcott and William Quan Judge

7. Krishna, Nitya and Leadbeater at Adyar, 1910

8. Sir Edwin and Lady Emily Lutyens (*centre*)

9. Croquet at Wimbledon, 1911:
Nitya (*left*), George Arundale, Krishna, Mrs Besant (*centre*)

10. Rudolf Steiner

11. The first Goetheanum

12. The new Goetheanum

13. Annie Besant, *c.* 1868

14. Katherine Tingley, *c.* 1897

15. Leadbeater and students on a picnic

ing the closest personal rapport with him. The crucial lessons for Steiner himself were, first, that the teacher must understand the relationship between body, mind and soul; and, second, that each child is different. These are perhaps lessons which every great educator learns anew, though they had special value in an age of rote learning, when the old humanist pedagogy had faded without being replaced by an equally coherent and comprehensive educational theory.

Throughout his six years with the Spechts, Steiner worked closely with Pauline, whose influence was crucial to her child's progress and to Steiner's own. Throughout his life he was involved with a series of strong supportive women, beginning with the wife of his professor in Vienna, and although he liked to insist on the absolute distinction between his own development and the spiritual revelation vouchsafed to him, it is clear that there were connections. Each stage of his career is associated with a new woman.

In 1890 he was ready to move on from Vienna and migrated to Weimar to work in the Goethe archive at the invitation of the Grand Duke of Saxony. The Saxon government was in the process of issuing a complete edition of Goethe's works and appointed Steiner to edit the scientific writings. In Weimar he encountered not only a rich cultural and social circle but also the third woman in his life, Anna Eunicke. In 1897 he followed Frau Eunicke, by this time a widow, to Berlin, where he became her lodger and lived by journalism and lecturing.

They married in 1899. She was a simple, motherly woman, who took the greatest care of Steiner and was forever producing cakes and pastries to tempt the ascetic scholar. Steiner himself remained throughout life a courteous, reserved and outwardly conventional figure, his eccentricities extending to little more than his flowing cravats and the occasional simplicity of manners revealing proletarian origins.[6] Though he later had a number of aristocratic patrons and followers, he was not at home in the drawing-room. Even those who found him sympathetic and charismatic noted that he remained curiously unworldly even after forty years in good society. Steiner was a peasant, and from this he drew much of his strength. Spending his early maturity among the intelligentsia of Vienna,

Weimar and Berlin, where he frequented salons and cafés for a while, he nevertheless cultivated his distance from them, remaining completely his own man and making no concessions. The sense of his own apartness and uniqueness can make him look either self-important or dedicated, according to point of view.

At about the time he married Frau Eunicke, Steiner began to teach in the Berlin Working Men's College established by Marx's former colleague Wilhelm Liebknecht, a founder of the German Social Democratic Party. The purpose of the college was to bring higher education to the proletariat, and Steiner lectured in philosophy and literature. Frau Eunicke took a full part in this work, attending some of his talks and dispensing hospitality to the students, but she was unhappy about his increasing interest in Theosophy, as were the Marxist-inclined governors of the college.

Steiner had encountered Theosophy in the 1880s through the writings of Sinnett and Blavatsky, most of which he later rejected – with the exception of *The Secret Doctrine*, which he regarded as the most remarkable esoteric text (apart from his own) published in modern times. These books provided him with at least a partial contemporary explanation of the psychic phenomena he had been experiencing since childhood. More particularly, they strengthened his own belief in the possibility of a rapprochement between science and religion through the cultivation of a new kind of knowledge. In 1898, after going through a mental and spiritual crisis, he began to turn away from cultural education towards his spiritual vocation. This process reached a climax in July 1902 when, after attending a Theosophical congress in London where he met Annie Besant, Steiner took over leadership of the Theosophical Society in Germany, Switzerland and the Austro-Hungarian Empire.

The jump from tacit socialism to explicit Theosophy was not easy to explain. Like Annie Besant before him, Steiner had to endure contempt and ridicule from his former socialist associates. He announced his change of direction in a lecture to his former students, during which he praised Madame Blavatsky, dissociated himself from spiritualism and referred to the German philosopher I. H. Fichte, who had proclaimed that the task of German scholars was to refine their philosophy into a new theosophy (Fichte actually uses this word). But Steiner hardly needed to proclaim the change. His old students noticed that he had returned from London without his moustache but with a bowler hat, as if to signal his shift of interest from the world below to the world above. Nor could he look them in the eye, they thought. Instead he stared straight out into the hall during the lecture. It was not long before he gave up lecturing to the Working Men.

Steiner was accompanied to the 1902 congress by Marie von Sievers, a Baltic aristocrat and drama student who had been working with him since 1900. In 1903 he moved out of Anna Eunicke's house and into the Berlin Theosophical headquarters, where Fraulein von Sievers also lived.[7] From then on she became his inseparable companion, organising his life and listening to his lectures. The audiences for these were at first very small. Happily, Steiner showed no concern, claiming that the audience was swelled by invisible spiritual beings and the dead, eager for the occult knowledge they could not, apparently, acquire in the Other World.

Over the next ten years Steiner had a difficult relationship with Mrs Besant. Though they recognised their doctrinal differences, the two were at first on friendly terms. Annie visited Berlin in 1904 and Steiner translated her talks into German. Meanwhile, Olcott continued to reiterate the Society's policy of tolerance for all opinions. But Steiner was outraged by the Leadbeater scandal of 1906 and disliked Annie's orientalising tendencies, while she mistrusted his ambitions within the Society. There was also conflict between Steiner and many of his own German lodges, which resented the reduction of their independence under his rule and had no interest in his esoteric brand of Christian mysticism. While Olcott lived, there was peace between them, but at the Theosophical Congress of May 1907, held three months after the colonel's death while Annie was standing for election as his successor, it became clear that a breach was unavoidable.

The congress was staged in Munich by Steiner himself, and the occasion made his attitude to Theosophy plain. He dressed the conference hall with the seals described by St John in the Apocalypse and with busts of his own heroes, the German idealist philosophers Hegel, Fichte and Schelling. There was no sign of the Masters or any of the Hindu deities Annie cultivated. On the contrary: the central feature of the congress was a performance of Edmond Schuré's *Sacred Drama of Eleusis*, translated by Marie von Sievers and revised by Steiner.[8] The message was quite clear: Steiner had decided to swing the Theosophical focus westwards.

Schuré had attempted to recreate the Greek Mysteries. Steiner's revision of the text infuses it with his own Rosicrucian symbolism, and the play caused uproar. Steiner was accused of attempting to hijack the Society in favour of his own neo-Christian beliefs. He meanwhile became increasingly alarmed at what he saw as the personality cult of the new President. Annie was diplomatically silent in public, but she made her views known in private. For the time being they agreed to go their own ways, but by 1910 the split was open.

The break was hastened by the lawsuit brought against Besant by Krishnamurti's father. Steiner and his friends shared Narianiah's view of Krishnamurti's relationship with Leadbeater – that it brought the boy, his family and the Society into disrepute. But to Steiner the real offence was Leadbeater's claim that the Lord Maitreya supposedly reincarnating in Krishnamurti was identical with Jesus Christ. Steiner's cosmology was christological: he regarded Christ neither as a rather special human being (the tendency of humanist theology), nor as merely another avatar of the world spirit, but as a unique figure in the spiritual history of the universe. He also distinguished between the human body of Jesus and the spirit of Christ which had entered into that body for the last three years of Jesus's life. He was therefore quite unable to accept the idea that Krishnamurti was the latest – and in that sense the best – reappearance of the Christ Spirit in the world, or that this spirit was subordinate to the Lord of the World who resided at Shamballa.

The Order of the Star in the East had been formed to promote these ideas, and the crisis came when Steiner flatly refused to allow the order to operate in Germany, requiring any German members who were already members of the OSE to withdraw from it. At the same time he sent a telegram to Annie Besant in Adyar, requesting her resignation from the presidency of the Society. She responded by cancelling the German Section's charter and expelling Steiner from the parent society. He then severed his links with Theosophy, and in February 1913 founded the Anthroposophical Society. Many German Theosophists followed Steiner, leaving the rest in the care of HPB's old friend Dr Huebbe Schleiden, a Munich factory owner.

But if Krishnamurti was the immediate occasion of Steiner's break with Theosophy, there were deeper causes. Steiner had long believed that the Society had two vital weaknesses, which he unsuccessfully tried to remedy. First there was the need for a sound conceptual scheme integrating theosophical doctrine with valuable elements from the European philosophical tradition. The mixture of eastern terminology and personal inspiration which characterised most early theosophical writing had served its purpose in awakening Westerners to the vast gaps in their understanding produced by the decline of religion and the rise of materialism, but it was not enough in itself. A truly ecumenical doctrine must start from what people knew already. European formulations of spiritual truths could not simply be brushed away. The task was to sort the wheat from the chaff, and that required scholarship.

The second problem was a matter of spiritual pedagogy. As we have seen, Blavatsky and Leadbeater between them went some way to providing this, but their methods were vague and rested almost entirely on personal authority. There were no established teaching methods, no clearly visible pedagogic traditions: just Leadbeater's secretive initiations, which were anyway largely ceremonial and bestowed for reasons apparent only to the bestower. To be fair to Leadbeater, this is typical of esoteric traditions which, by def- inition, transmit intangible wisdom rather than methodical know- ledge and do so in secret, the results known only to teacher and pupil. Nevertheless, it was clear to Steiner that, if Theosophy were to be more than a collection of confusingly stated doctrines plus a whimsically directed journey along the uncertain path to Master- ship (anyway a dubious honour), something more than this or that gifted individual teacher was needed. That 'something' was a teaching method: a body of cognitive techniques that could be

recognisably transmitted. He therefore looked for a spiritual practice that would combine coherent doctrines accessible to western
disciples with a method of learning from those doctrines.

Anthroposophy was intended to provide such a practice and it
signalled its difference from Theosophy in its very name. Crucially,
it took from Theosophy the notion of spiritual science. Steiner
understands the word 'science' in both common senses: as a body of
knowledge and as a methodology. Indeed, this was one of the ways
in which he distinguished eastern occultism from western esotericism – the first seeking to transcend the material world in a purely
spiritual realm, the second accepting that human life is in part a
material life and must be worked out in material terms. Man is
precisely the being in whom the sensible and supersensible worlds
are united: that is what distinguishes him from animals and from
angels. The supersensible realm has objective reality but so does the
phenomenal world. Anthroposophy is the study of man's place in
the relationship between them. This is not the wisdom of the gods,
which by definition we can never have, but the humbler wisdom of
man – or rather, wisdom *about* man.

If the new society differed from the old in vital respects, it was at
first very similar in style. Steiner's entourage had the usual
constituents familiar from Theosophy: bossy matrons, artistic
maiden ladies, wealthy idealists, and faddists of every variety; but
the tone of his enterprise was altogether higher than anything to be
found in Theosophy, and from the start Steiner was surrounded by
an atmosphere compounded of reverence, earnestness and optimism. The slightly raffish, metropolitan atmosphere of Theosophy
gave way in Anthroposophy to nature-worship and the simple life.
Many Theosophists were vegetarians, dress reformers or anti-
vivisectionists, but in what amounted to a parody of German
thoroughness, Steinerism provided a complete way of life which
included all these things in a coherent pattern. The polymath found
himself giving guidance on every aspect of life, from the colour of
auras to the colour of kitchen cupboards, as he extended his
influence from the spiritual lives of his followers to the food on their
tables.

*

Rudolf Steiner was that unusual thing among alternative spiritual teachers: a rigorous and highly trained western intellectual. The other would-be savant in this period who tried to build a new religious synthesis on theosophical foundations was Peter Damien Ouspensky.[9] As Steiner himself admitted, his own education made him especially susceptible to Ahrimanic spirits who tried hard to persuade him to accept positivist science. The self-taught Ouspensky was tempted more by Luciferean visions of self-transcendence, dreaming of a humanity remade in the image of gods by its own strenuous efforts. The two men were complementary types, contrasted in their characters, differing widely in their means, but united by their objectives. In the end, both rebelled against Theosophy – Steiner from within, Ouspensky from without – and their efforts to open new routes to esoteric wisdom have proved profoundly influential ever since.

Even so, Ouspensky's name is not well known outside esoteric circles today. He left no schools or hospitals bearing his name. He was not a bohemian aristocrat or an exotic spirit medium but an earnest metropolitan bourgeois who founded no society of his own and died a self-proclaimed failure. Yet his books still sell over forty thousand copies each year in English alone, and there is every indication that sales are on the increase. Never officially a member of the Theosophical Society (which was banned in Russia until 1908), he was nevertheless deeply read in Theosophy and absorbed its doctrine into his own odd synthesis of Kantian idealism, four-dimensional mathematics, Sufism and Buddhism. Yet he eventually reacted against the institution on exactly the same grounds as Steiner, finding the doctrine inconsistent and the pedagogy inadequate. His solutions to these problems, however, were radically different to Steiner's.

Ouspensky was born into a cultured upper-middle-class Moscow family in 1878. His parents, a land surveyor and a painter, died during his childhood and he was brought up by his grandmother. He was a lazy, dreamy child who could only work at what he fancied. His formal education ended when he was expelled from school in his mid-teens and continued after that as a private adventure, especially in philosophy, physics and mathematics, the only subjects that interested him. His lack of schooling may have influenced his own insistence in later life on the need to know exactly the rules that govern human existence.

The portrait of his own childhood in Ouspensky's novel *The Strange Life of Ivan Osokin* and his account of early manhood in another book, *In Search of the Miraculous*, suggest a character riven by contradictions. Ouspensky was both lazy and restless, sceptical yet credulous, intellectually vigorous yet eager for reassurance, wilful yet submissive, a logical thinker and a dreamer, gregarious and solitary, autocratic and remote yet craving cheer and good company: an intellectual *flâneur*, a domineering slave and an ascetic sybarite. In appearance he was a small, powerfully built man, with a massive head, bull-neck, thin lips and penetrating eyes. He loved cats and wine, dressed fastidiously and cultivated the manners of a professor by day and a bohemian by night. He was obsessed with the experience of déjà vu, and his two intellectual interests were mathematics and mysticism. Both seemed to offer the possibility of providing keys to a complete understanding of things, one through numbers and the other through visions. Both had the appeal of relative secrecy, being couched in languages closed to all but the few.

Ouspensky studied the fourth dimension in the hope of explaining the origin of the feeling that we have 'been here before'. He was well-read in the fanciful literature of the subject popular at the time, including E. A. Abbott's novel *Flatland* (1884) and the popular scientific works of C. W. Hinton.[10] Flatland is a place inhabited by two-dimensional beings who would regard any incursion from the world of three dimensions as miraculous. By extension, it can be conjectured that three-dimensional beings – such as humans – would regard a creature from the fourth dimension in the same way. Ouspensky developed the idea in his first precocious publication, *The Fourth Dimension*, postulating from three dimensions the existence of a fourth, a fifth, and perhaps any number more.

The fourth dimension itself he posits as time, of which we occasionally become aware in moments of heightened consciousness. But like so many of his contemporaries – Proust, Bergson, Freud, Einstein, Wells, Joyce and Eliot (on the last of whom he later had some influence) – Ouspensky was fascinated less by time itself than by notions of the extra- or super-temporal which define it.[11] He explored these in practice through the analysis of dreams and the use of consciousness-altering drugs, concluding from his researches that dreams continue in daytime. According to Ouspensky we are usually 'asleep', even when we think ourselves awake: what we take for consciousness is itself a sort of dream. The glimpses of déjà vu, the momentary visions which come to us in sleep, dreams and hallucinations: these are signs of the reality to which we could gain access were we truly awake. How then can we rouse ourselves from waking dreams? What would real consciousness be like? And what would it be consciousness *of*?

Mathematics provided no answers to such questions, and Ouspensky looked for help in the then fashionable theories of Nietzsche concerning eternal recurrence and soul-making. Nietzsche argues that to have even the semblance of freedom we must live our lives in a spirit of joyful acceptance, as though we were ready to repeat even the most painful moments again and again. Only then, when we have conquered ourselves and achieved willing acceptance of necessity, can we become real individuals.[12]

For Nietzsche, the notion of eternal recurrence is a necessary metaphor. Ouspensky took the idea literally and turned it on its head. Invoking eastern notions of reincarnation, karma and the wheel of existence, Ouspensky argued that we really have lived our lives before, and will live them again, endlessly, unless we can find a way out of the circle. To do this we must somehow learn to raise the level of our consciousness so that we become permanently aware of what is happening to us – at which point we will encounter ultimate reality (a notion Nietzsche would have found absurd and self-contradictory).

But once again, the problem for Ouspensky was how to proceed. Nietzscheanism provided no more help with spiritual and psychological technology than mathematics did. At this point he discovered Theosophy. In 1907, while working as a journalist on a Moscow daily, *The Morning*, his desk drawer gradually filled with theosophical publications. These included books by Sinnett (*The Occult World*) and Steiner (*Atlantis and Lemuria*). Deputed to write articles on the current European political situation, he found himself constantly drawn back to his secret reading on the occult.

Theosophy's millennial and occult tendencies sat well with the atmosphere of frenzied eschatological doom pervading Russia in the first decades of this century, and many intellectuals and writers were attracted to it, including Blok, Pasternak, Berdyaev, Soloviev, Rozanov, Florensky, Merezhkovsky and, most famously, Bely and Skriabin.[13] Ouspensky belongs to the generation – born between 1870 and 1900 – moulded and often destroyed by the Revolution, whose advent almost everyone expected for half a century before 1917. Indeed, it was Ouspensky's contemporaries who made the Revolution, which broke out when he was thirty-nine. Those who survived it for the most part went into exile or perished in Stalin's purges.

Those men did not necessarily expect revolution to take political form. The inheritance of Gogol and Dostoievsky was still strong: both had envisaged the apocalyptic transformation of the country into a vast religious community through the renewal of Russian Orthodoxy. Like Ouspensky, Andrey Bely (1880–1934) was fascinated by the relationship between science and mysticism, but saw the barbarian horde as a more likely outcome of contemporary events than progressive revolution – and said as much in his novel *Petersburg*, written at this time. The composer Alexander Skriabin (1872–1915) was closer to the Gogol/Dostoievsky tradition. An ardent if ignorant Theosophist, he put his faith into his music and looked forward to the imminent end of the world, perhaps because he expected to accompany and perhaps even precipitate this event with a performance of his own masterpiece, a theatrical 'Mystery' which fortunately remained unfinished.

Ouspensky took a more measured view. For him, Theosophy's charm was a systematic cosmology which enabled him to mould fragments of fourth-dimension mathematics, Nietzschean theories of recurrence and self-making, symbolism, psychology and personal experience into an apparently coherent whole embracing every level of existence. For a man armed with fragments of knowledge and obsessed with system, method and coherence, here at last was a philosophy that held things together. There really was a secret wisdom tradition, and Theosophy was the way to gain access to it.

Yet even this was not enough. For despite its promise, Theosophy remained obstinately abstract and even the intellectual Ouspensky was hungry for the certainty which comes from direct experience. In 1908 this hunger drove him eastwards, armed with a roving journalistic commission to write about his travels. His quest was rewarded with little more than a moment on a boat in the Sea of Marmora, when he had a mystical experience of unity with the elements. The moment was fleeting, as were the intimations of wisdom he felt on the occult tourist route while visiting the Sphinx, the Taj Mahal and an emerald-eyed Buddha in Ceylon. Yet at least these experiences convinced him that he was right to believe in the existence of the esoteric wisdom crudely sketched by Theosophy. But if there really were a secret wisdom, where was its source, and how could one contact that source?

Ouspensky was already convinced that esoteric truth could not be acquired by individuals on their own. It was necessary to attach oneself to a 'school' such as the Brotherhood of Masters. Though he believed that there might be many such schools, the problem was to find a genuine one. This was not only a matter of sorting out the real from the fraudulent: it also involved distinguishing genuine but non-esoteric schools from those with a direct line to the source of cosmic wisdom.

In India he visited the disciples of Ramakrishna and other yogis, but concluded that meditation and devotion were not the route to illumination. Occult wisdom, he believed, lay in activity not contemplation. The dervishes of Constantinople and Scutari seemed to take him nearer to this route, and what Steiner found in the renewal of esoteric Christianity Ouspensky searched for in the mystical sects of Islam. He was especially impressed by dervish dancing, which united mathematics and movement in an ineffable experience of Being which might also be a symbolic language – if only one could translate it. Furthermore, the cryptic sayings and arduous discipleship of the dervish orders looked suspiciously like evidence of the school he was searching for. There were, however, many rival dervish orders. Even assuming each had partial access to the source, they could not themselves *be* the source. Which raised another problem – for how, anyway, would you recognise the source or the school when you found it?

In 1913 he set out again on his eastern travels, this time visiting Adyar, where he was privileged to stay on the top floor of HPB's old house with members of the Esoteric School. Like everything else in the Society, the building was arranged hierarchically: the leaders lived above the shop, their close assistants dwelt in the wings, and menials were scattered through the grounds in cottages, some of them little more than hovels. By 1913 Adyar had become a prototype of the prosperous contemporary commune: a mixture of ashram and holiday inn where suitable visitors passing through Madras were allowed to stay. Ouspensky recognised in what he heard of the Theosophical Esoteric School a pale reflection of what he was looking for.

At Adyar he met the German mystical philosopher Count Herman Keyserling, who was on a similar quest.[14] The visit was decisive for both. While they recognised Theosophy's pioneering value as the movement which opened up eastern religion to the West, Keyserling and Ouspensky concluded that the object of their quest was not to be found in the Society. They were united in the opinion that the only alternative was to continue the search elsewhere. But their unity on this and other matters was soon to be shattered, for while they were working out their spiritual destinies in the East, political events were moving rapidly at home. Within a few months of their first meeting, the two men found themselves on opposite sides in the greatest war in history.

NINE

War Games

The 1914 war turned out to be a considerable embarrassment to Theosophy. While political fraternity and religious universalism remained official policy, chauvinism flourished within the Society and Theosophists were just as likely as anyone else to assume that God was on their side.

Some went still further, turning the catastrophe to their own advantage. In tough social Darwinist fashion, the fanatically imperialistic Leadbeater not only identified the Germans with the Dark Forces, but announced that the conflict was part of the evolutionary process, a kind of dialectic from which a higher human synthesis would emerge.[1] He even took a leaf out the Muslim book, asserting that to kill German soldiers was to do them a favour by hastening their occult advancement, whereas being a live Hun did you no good at all. British victory thus coincided neatly with the divine plan.

On the other side of the North Sea, Rudolf Steiner, who agreed with Leadbeater about the role of the Dark Forces in bringing about the war despite the best efforts of helpless statesmen,[2] nevertheless proclaimed the superiority of Teutonic culture and the spiritual world-mission of the German people;[3] and although he was careful not to exalt militarism and nationalism, others sharing his views were ready to lay responsibility for the carnage firmly at Britain's door. It was well known in anthroposophical circles that Edward VII's frivolity and decadent francophilia were at the root of the European problem – a confusing variation on the view long popular among the German intelligentsia that the British were a nation of pleasure-loving grocers, quite below the moral and spiritual level of their Saxon cousins (and also in comic contrast to the British view of Edward as an honorary German).

Whatever his subsequent apologists may say, Steiner's extensive writings on European politics before the war gave tacit approval to milder versions of such crazy ideas. His mystical view of national destinies as part of a cosmic scheme makes it impossible to distinguish his fervour for Teutonic culture from cruder forms of patriotism. He endorsed, for example, the view expounded by Hegel and Fichte that the Germans are innately more philosophical than other European peoples. This claim is based on the assumption that philosophy is the highest human activity; which makes the Germans the greatest European nation.

Steiner also followed his philosophical masters in distinguishing national historical 'tasks', adding the piquant theory that each nation is guided from above by an archangel who is somehow also the folk-spirit of that nation. Prince Max of Baden, the last Chancellor of the German Empire, particularly asked for a copy of his lectures on this topic.[4] Other European nations, according to this argument, have been appointed to develop certain 'aspects' of humanity as their contribution to world evolution – an interesting idea which is let down by the banality of Steiner's conclusion that the Italians were given feeling, the French thought, the English consciousness, and so on. Of course, only the Germans combine all these aspects at the highest level.

When war broke out, Steiner based himself in Switzerland, where he married Marie von Sievers in December 1914.[5] During the war he maintained a degree of neutrality by using his lectures to set the conflict in a world-historical and cosmic perspective and by praying for combatants on all sides; though he travelled and lectured frequently in Germany and Austria, where public neutrality was of course out of the question. He was also a family friend and adviser to the Chief of the German General Staff, Helmut von Moltke, hardly an acquaintance that suggests detachment. Whether Steiner liked it or not, Anthroposophy was identified with German war aims, just as Theosophy was with the Allied cause. Though there were a few English members of the Anthroposophical Society in wartime Britain, they kept very quiet about it.

At first Steiner shared a common view that something pure and noble might arise out of the conflict between nations; but as the apparently unstoppable carnage became ever more horrifying he modified his instinctive nationalism in favour of a broader perspective. After the war he was ready to support the League of Nations, and in his later writings he takes more care to distinguish the political from the spiritual. From 1919 on, we hear less about the spiritual mission of the German people and more about the idea that German political power must be sustained in order to balance America and Britain in the West against Russia in the East.[6] This idea – hardly original – emerged from Steiner's increasing interest in social and political organisation. His thinking is based on the traditional comparison between the political system and the human body, which is said to need all its major elements in equilibrium for good health.

Arguments about national character were part of a larger, older and darker controversy about the Aryans, and they underline the racist side of occultism. Nineteenth-century research into the origins of European peoples and their languages had suggested that both derived from a single pure source – the Sanskrit-speaking Aryans – whose purity had gradually been diluted (and, as some thought, polluted) by miscegenation as they swept westwards through Europe. Since theorists from Rousseau to Gobineau were agreed that racial purity equalled strength and vigour, nations vied in their claims to ethnic purity and Aryan origin.

The competition produced some bizarre assertions. In the later nineteenth century, the Germans – torn between priding themselves on Teutonic exclusiveness and envying the prosperity and political stability of their less immaculate English cousins whose bloodlines were polluted with Celtic and Roman strains – worked hard to prove that the greatest Englishmen, such as Shakespeare, were really Germans. The French, patronised by Saxons on either side, responded by insisting that their Frankish and Gallic ancestors were really Germans too. And everyone could unite in despising inferior races such as Slavs and Jews.

This contempt, which was soon to have such horrific consequences in Hitler's Germany and Stalin's Russia, was reflected in the absurdities of occult controversy. Trying to preserve Jesus from his apparently undeniable Jewish origins, for example, Steiner and the racial theorist Houston Stewart Chamberlain agreed that he had both Semitic *and* Aryan features, and was therefore as good as an honorary German.[8] The next stage was to deny that Jesus was a Jew at all, and there were plenty of people ready to take that step. Even the Himalayan Masters of Theosophy combined their handsome Indian looks with suspiciously pale skin and European features.

In short, the war was about more than imperial or economic rivalries. It was a Darwinian struggle for racial, moral and spiritual supremacy. Such ideas may not have interested the men in the trenches, but they sustained many of the politicians who sent them there, and the jingoistic public who supported the politicians, exacerbating the bitterness of the struggle.

Despite his preoccupation with the Liberal Catholic Church from 1915 onwards, Leadbeater was eager to be involved in the war effort. One way was by pulling strings with the powerful. Rudolf Steiner had access to General von Moltke and Prince Max of Baden; Annie Besant and Emily Lutyens had British friends in high places. But as usual Leadbeater, who never did things by halves and hated to be outdone, played the occult ace of trumps, announcing that *he* had been in communion not only with the influential living but also with the mighty dead, talking on the astral plane with Otto von Bismarck, who had discussed the struggle with him at length.

It turned out that Germany's former ruler, once identified by HPB herself as a distinguished occultist, was one of the Lords of the Dark Face, the agents of evil who were battling against mankind in twentieth-century Europe as they had done in Atlantis thirteen thousand years before. Their battle was not merely a spiritual one: according to Leadbeater, Bismarck had planted magnetic talismans at the four corners of Germany to prevent resistance to the Fatherland's armies – to no avail, as it happened. But Leadbeater was anxious that no trick, of this world or the next, should give victory to the Huns (though, since he also argued that their machinations were anyway only part of the Divine Plan for a Second Coming, it is hard to see what he was worried about). Why the Lords of the Dark Face should have revealed their stratagems so willingly to an enemy, we are not told.

As to practical help, there could be no question of Leadbeater taking part in the battle, of course, but there was something useful he *might* do. From his fastness in Australia, the Bishop nobly agreed to patrol the Front in his astral body in order to guide the souls of the dead on their way into the afterlife, as a sort of Stygian major-domo. Although it became timely in 1914, this was already a recognised theosophical activity, and there was yet another organisation within the Society specifically devoted to it: the Invisible Helpers.[9] Emily Lutyens was an enthusiastic Helper, though her pacifism and her refusal to hate the enemy put her in a quandary when war broke out, because Leadbeater took the view that the Helpers should assist Allied spirits first. The Bishop hated pacifists and eventually forced Emily Lutyens out of the editorship of the *Herald of the Star* on the grounds that she was too sympathetic to Germans. That journal, said his spokesman Jinarajadasa, should declare 'uncompromisingly on the side of the Brotherhood', i.e. the Allies.[10]

Krishnamurti, who was to go public as an unrepentant and absolute pacifist during World War Two, found himself in a difficult position in 1914. He was ready to fight, and old enough to do so, but Annie refused to allow him to enlist in any capacity, not because he might have to kill but because living off army rations meant eating meat, and his vocation (not to mention his brahminism) required him to be strictly vegetarian. This did not prevent his dashing brother Nitya serving briefly as a cycle rider for the Red Cross Unit in Flanders, but Annie eventually put a stop to that too, and the brothers spent most of the war studying for their examinations or idling in London and the country.

Annie was not the only obstacle in the way of their efforts to help. Although he joined in scrubbing out the Endsleigh Palace Hotel when it was turned over to medical use for the duration, Krishna was not permitted to work in the hospital set up there, because of his colour. It was thought that the patients would object to being nursed by an Indian, especially one who claimed to be the Messiah. What made him exotic and alluring to spiritually inclined aristocrats was apparently unacceptable to the wounded lower middle classes. Krishna and Nitya were well-used to ridicule and to racial discrimination. Though it upset them, they treated unpleasant incidents with impressive diplomacy. Lady Emily, who shared Queen Victoria's passion for all things Indian, found her feelings harder to control.

The upshot of Annie's interference, combined with the strangeness of his surroundings, the eccentric behaviour of his English guardians and the strain of living up to his high destiny, left Krishnamurti confused and depressed. While the fighting went on and he fretted unhappily on the sidelines, ordinary life – in so far as he had one – was impossible. Like other civilians, he was deeply affected by the hostilities, though not directly involved in them. As Proust wrote at the time, people lived in the war as mystics used to speak of living in God. It consumed all their attention, leaving them no energy for anything else.[11]

Ironically, the end of the conflict made things even worse, when economic and political chaos was accompanied by an enormous emotional vacuum. The energies of individuals and whole societies, so completely engaged in the life-or-death struggle, now had nowhere to go. There was the necessity of reconstruction – social and political, physical and financial, human and personal – but the real question in everyone's mind was: How much do we *want* to reconstruct a system which has recently involved us in such catastrophe? Was it not better to build a new world? And if so, how was this to be done? A new world was, by definition, unknown. There was no pattern to build it from. Everyone was working in the dark.

Theosophy and Anthroposophy were both to profit from the spiritual hunger aroused by the end of the war, and from the vague feeling that the old religious and political institutions had been finally discredited. Both societies expanded rapidly through the 1920s, developing popular youth movements in the process. But the same appetite also produced another wave of alternative spiritual teachers who, though owing more to Theosophy than they liked to admit, threatened to replace its bland generalities with something altogether more vigorous. This new wave came once again from a vaguely defined 'East', but preferred the energy of militant mystical Islam to the kindly synthesis of Hinduism and Buddhism dreamt up by Madame Blavatsky.

These new teachers touched a raw nerve in western Europe. It was as though the violence of war, now calmed on the battlefields, was erupting instead into private life. Freud had already begun to chart the psychic route of such violence, and of its repression.[12] The war, he believed, was the result of no military accident or political miscalculation, but a mass slaughter unconsciously willed by whole nations, unable to cope with the demands of their own moral and social codes. Now the religious implications of their unconscious wishes were to be made clear. The era of gentle Jesus was drawing to a close.

No nation was more horribly involved in the brutality of the war than Russia, where the revolution it helped to precipitate was followed by a long and bitter battle in which White and Red Armies struggled for supremacy. Yet ironically, the western tendency to identify Russia in this period with all things barbaric had less to do with soldiers than with dancers. For the most exciting cultural event in pre-war Europe had been the appearance of the Russian Ballet, which dominated the artistic scene and led the avant-garde from its first appearance in Paris in 1906 to the death of its founder-director, Sergei Diaghilev, in Venice in 1929.[13]

Diaghilev was the ultimate impresario. Nothing like the Russian Ballet had been seen since the French opera-ballets written to glorify Louis XIV. In the works he commissioned for his company, Diaghilev achieved the synthesis of all the arts that Wagner had only dreamt of, while at the same time transcending the earnest realism of late-nineteenth-century Wagnerism in a dazzling new blend of fantasy, comedy, fairy tale, barbaric splendour and spectacle. Central to this miracle was the dance, an art hitherto usually relegated to the cultural margins of operatic interludes and variety turns. Tchaikovsky had already explored the ballet's theatrical possibilities, but it was left to Diaghilev and his troupe to transform dance into a revolutionary new art.

Diaghilev himself was a volcanic character, a charming, sinister, flamboyant homosexual dilettante who thrived on tantrums and scandal; effortlessly dominating both his artists and the rich patrons who paid for them, while at the same time flouting all the usual rules of moral and social conduct as of right. Observing his relationship with his lover and principal dancer, the wretched Nijinsky, some people compared him to Svengali, others to Rasputin.

But Diaghilev was not the only impresario and man of power to emerge from Russia in this period. Though known now as a spiritual teacher, George Ivanovitch Gurdjieff liked to refer to himself as a dancing master, and dance is indeed central to his teaching. Even as Diaghilev was sweeping triumphantly through western Europe, Gurdjieff was trying unsuccessfully to stage his own ballet, *The Struggle of the Magicians*, in Moscow and St Petersburg.

Nothing could be further from the good works and brotherly love of Theosophy than the teaching of Gurdjieff. However bitter their factional antagonisms, the various theosophical and anthroposophical groups still preached the gospel of peace and fraternity; and however chauvinistic the two sides became during the war, this was their official line again in 1919. Gurdjieff would have none of it. If Theosophy represents the idealistic tendencies in early-twentieth-century Europe – the currents of feeling which gave birth to the League of Nations, social democracy and youth movements – Gurdjieff is part of the complementary fascination with barbarism and primitivism which colours the politics of Fascism and works of art from Lawrence's novels to Stravinsky's early ballets. Gurdjieff's doctrine was war and his method of teaching was to stir up productive strife with all the means at his disposal.

Yet though he avowedly rejected Theosophy, Gurdjieff turned a similar ideology – including a universal doctrine, a detailed cosmology and (crucially) a Brotherhood of Masters – to good account. How far he took this ideology from HPB it is impossible to say. Theosophy was flourishing in Russia in the first two decades of this century when Gurdjieff formulated his teaching, but the notion of a

Hidden Brotherhood, located by Blavatsky in Egypt and the Himalayas, is also to be found among the mystics of Central Asia where Gurdjieff was born – a fact which perhaps reinforces the theosophical claim that there is in all world religions a common doctrine. And given the proliferation of occult societies and secret fraternities in the late nineteenth century, it would be unwise to derive Gurdjieff's teaching too closely from Blavatsky's, especially as his teaching methods developed in a very different way.[14]

What cannot be denied is the very striking similarity between their characters and the patterns of their lives. Equally arresting are the parallels between HPB's fanciful if amateurish creation of her own mythology and Gurdjieff's masterly staging of his career. That Gurdjieff was well-acquainted with HPB's writings and reputation is clear from scattered remarks to pupils. On occasions he even jokingly claimed to have had an affair with the Old Lady. At many points it is as though he had modelled himself on her, but in each case he improved on his model. If Blavatsky had travelled in Central Asia, Gurdjieff came from the region; if Blavatsky set up a mere society to study phenomena, Gurdjieff established a true esoteric school to practise them; if she was in contact with the Masters, he claimed to be one. Without insisting on a lineage, one can therefore legitimately claim an inheritance – or, perhaps more subtly, what the philosopher Ludwig Wittgenstein would have called a family resemblance: a set of correspondences which suggest a kinship they do not necessarily prove.

The first forty or so years of his life are shrouded in a mystery he was happy to compound.[15] Like Blavatsky and Leadbeater, he was a fertile story-teller, and nothing gave him more scope for invention than the public blanks of his own history. Even the date of his birth is uncertain. One recent authority suggests 1873, another prefers 1877, and a third 1866; while a fourth plumps for 1874, with the proviso that any year between 1870 and 1886 would be a plausible guess. This uncertainty, which Gurdjieff did nothing to dispel, contributed to his aura of mystery. Passing through US Customs on one occasion, it was discovered that Gurdjieff's passport assigned his birth to a date in the distant future. 'No mistake,' said the delighted time-traveller to the customs official, 'you go arrange.'[16]

For the other facts of his life between birth and the first meeting with Ouspensky, shortly before the Revolution, we have only his own testimony, much of it wrapped in fantastic stories lifted from Central Asian folklore and the *Arabian Nights*. However, it seems likely that he really was the child of a Greek father and an Armenian mother, born at Alexandropol (now in the republic of Armenia) and brought up in the 'remote and very boring town' of Kars near the Russian–Turkish border.

Though the town itself may have been dull, the region is complex and dangerous. Fought over for centuries by Russians and Turks, crossed by nomads and disturbed by ethnic movements caused by wars, trade and natural disasters, this region was a racial, religious and linguistic hotchpotch, a crossroads for the merchants and travellers of Central Asia – which possibly helps to explain Gurdjieff's later linguistic skill, his talent for self-preservation and his cosmopolitanism. Greeks, Armenians, Turks, Russians, Kurds, Tartars and Georgians mingled in small towns set in a vast tract of plain, bog and mountain; the passing tribesmen were fantastically diverse; and the indigenous religions encompassed everything from Nestorian Christianity to Sufism, from Buddhism to Shamanism and Devil worship.

Gurdjieff described his father as the descendant of a fabulously rich and ancient family, who inherited great flocks which were then decimated by pestilence, ruining their owner in the process. After that, he took to a number of other trades, including carpentry; but all his business ventures failed, largely because Gurdjieff *père* was too honourable a man to profit from the gullibility of others, according to his son – though why success in business should necessarily involve deception Gurdjieff *fils* does not say, which is perhaps not surprising in view of his own experience.

More to the point, his father was also said to be an *ashokh*, or poet and story-teller, with a vast stock of verses committed to memory, including the ancient epic of Gilgamesh. This provided his son with a palpable link to the remote past which no amount of lost and fabled wealth could offer. It also suggested to him, he says, the continuity of cultural tradition which he interpreted in religious terms as the preservation of ancient wisdom in contemporary formulas and rituals whose meaning has been forgotten. Whether his recitations really included the story of Gilgamesh, as Gurdjieff later asserted, we cannot know. This may be one of the points at which fantasy takes over from fact. As with Blavatsky, it hardly matters. What does matter is the part Gurdjieff wanted his father to play in Gurdjieffian mythology: the Rousseauian noble savage in touch with the deepest springs of life.

This role also explains the father's greatest gift to his son, according to its recipient: a harsh domestic regime which taught the boy how to take care of himself in a hostile adult world. Cold baths and early rising were the order of the day, supported by severe punishments for non-compliance. Old Mr Gurdjieff's idea of a character-building joke seems to have been the schoolboy standby of a toad in the bed, or a venomous snake to hold while Dad finished his lunch – severities for which the boy was later touchingly grateful. These rough methods he was later to reproduce with his own followers.

The young Gurdjieff, then, was essentially a tough, worldly-wise street urchin who excelled at looking after himself. Like all towns in the region, Kars and Alexandropol were divided according to differences of class, custom and worship, and the boy was sensitive to such differences, as well he might be. For despite the boasts of a distinguished lineage, he grew up in poverty and soon learnt to turn his hand to whatever came along, from cobbling to hypnosis, acquiring in the process manual skills which made a profound impression on the middle-class intellectuals who later gathered round him.

His education was picked up largely on the wing, though he claims to have spent some time in the choir school at Kars, until the dean of the cathedral there advised his father to take the boy away from the school and educate him at home, on the grounds that the teaching was not up to standard for such a bright pupil. The dean then became his unofficial tutor, instilling in him ten principles (the exactness of the number is very typical of Gurdjieff): an unremarkable list of scriptural injunctions to obey parents and work hard, leavened only by a sixth commandment which enjoins *Fearlessness towards devils, snakes and mice.*

His formal education soon concluded, Gurdjieff set out on his travels. As with Blavatsky, these may or may not have taken him to Tibet. The idea that he visited the country is based on claims that he worked there under an alias, either as a Tibetan lama involved in political intrigue or as the Tsarist secret agent Ovshe Narzounoff. At least one recent writer accepts that Gurdjieff and Narzounoff were the same man. His best and most recent biographer is more circumspect, though he concedes the probability that Gurdjieff worked as a Tsarist agent under one name or another.[17]

Gurdjieff himself let the matter go by default, claiming only to have been wounded in Tibet in 1902 while on a mission there to study occult lore. But meeting Achmed Abdullah, a flamboyant member of the Younghusband expedition, in New York many years later, Gurdjieff gave him to understand that he had indeed been an agent (though Abdullah's testimony is at least as suspect as Gurdjieff's own).[18] All we know for certain is that Gurdjieff had to live off something, that he was often involved in shady business dealings, that he may have been mixed up in political intrigues, and that he had an almost magical ability to survive without obvious means of support. He also knew how to strengthen his own allure by deepening the mysteries and scandals attached to his name.

Gurdjieff's own account of his early life pictures it as a quest for Hidden Masters of Wisdom. Keeping a straight face, he describes in *Meetings With Remarkable Men* his early ambition to discover the purpose and meaning of life by travelling (inevitably) in Egypt with a mysterious map discovered in an out-of-the-way village. The book details a number of more or less incredible adventures in which even the author's Kurdish sheepdog figures as an amazing phenomenon. But Professor Skridlov the archaeologist and Prince Lubovedsky the spiritual pilgrim, Ekim Bey, Bogga Eddin, Bogacheksky and all the other so-called Seekers for Truth he encountered on the way are important now only in so far as they embody facets of an archetypal life-journey. Disguised by pseudonyms, it can never be known whether they really existed.

The focus of attention in the book eventually turns from Egypt to Central Asia and northern India, when Gurdjieff meets a certain Father Giovanni, formerly a Christian priest but now settled in an

Islamic monastic order in Kafiristan, one of four such orders scattered along the Pamir and Himalayan mountains. But Father Giovanni refers to the rites and doctrines of a 'World Brotherhood', leaving it unclear whether or not its members – of whom he is one – are identical with the Masters of Wisdom.

The account of Gurdjieff's years in the wilderness echoes Blavatsky's tall tales of her own early life. The only difference is that whereas the aristocratic HPB at least had to make an effort to disappear from public view and hardly bothered to keep her narrative credible, Gurdjieff's humbler origins and remote birthplace simply kept him out of sight until he forced his way to public attention with stories well-anchored to circumstantial detail of manners and places. That said, it is obviously all too easy to dress up a vacant period in one's life as a mystical retreat or an occult apprenticeship when there is no one to gainsay the fact; and even if there is, it can always be claimed that witnesses do not see what is 'really' happening in such cases, given that the occult is by definition hidden from public view. This is a favourite tack. What matters, we are told, is not appearance but reality, not phenomena but interpretation, not history but meaning. There is no way of refuting such claims, though the lengths to which people will go to sustain them give pause for thought.

Gurdjieff's pupils, later trying to account for their difficulties with his teaching, were variously inclined to describe the map and the search as realities, as parables or as metaphors for the spiritual quest. He himself remained teasingly ambiguous on the subject, and followers have suggested that this ambiguity is itself a sort of test to distinguish the wise from the foolish by means of their skill in interpretation. Those who can discern the truth in the Master's fantastic tales are those who thereby prove they have the right to it. Hardly surprising, perhaps, that Gurdjieff was apt to refer to his pupils as sheep fit for shearing.

Early in 1912 Gurdjieff reached Moscow, where he set himself up as a dealer in carpets and Central Asian artefacts. He first enters history in the autobiography of the Englishman Paul Dukes,[19] and in an anonymous essay called 'Glimpses of Truth'.[20] Dukes, a music student at the Moscow Conservatoire who subsequently became a British secret agent, had read *The Secret Doctrine* and experimented with spiritualism. His piano teacher introduced him to Theosophy and, after dabbling in various esoteric sects, he encountered Gurdjieff and became his first foreign pupil. Dukes and the author of 'Glimpses of Truth' describe similar encounters with the Master, one in a country house outside Moscow, the other in a drab street near the city's Nikolaevski Station, whither they were taken under conditions of secrecy.

Arriving at their rendezvous, they were led through dark passages into dimly lit rooms richly adorned with carpets and shawls, the ceilings draped like tents in the eastern fashion, orientalia scattered round the walls. The anonymous writer describes one of the lamps, which had a glass shade in the form of a lotus flower, and there was a cabinet with icons and ivory statues of Moses, Mahomet, Buddha and Christ: the pantheon of Hidden Masters. Opposite the final door, staring straight at the visitor with penetrating but not unfriendly eyes, a silent middle-aged man sat cross-legged on an ottoman smoking a water pipe. Dukes found the Master playing chess opposite a mysterious bearded guest with high cheekbones and slanting eyes. Gurdjieff then demonstrated a breathing and singing exercise, intoning the Lord's Prayer in a way that induced in Dukes a sort of mild electric current.

The episode suggests parallels with Thomas Lake Harris which were to become marked in later years as Gurdjieff's ascendancy over his pupils became absolute, but much in these scenes comes straight out of Bulwer Lytton via Blavatsky, and they show clearly that at this stage Gurdjieff was cultivating the image of an indiscriminately mysterious 'oriental', in the manner of the fictional Fu Manchu and the real HPB. He later jettisoned his stage props and learnt to make an effect by sheer force of personality, though he retained a weakness for carpets. Theatre was central to Gurdjieff's life in more ways than one. He was always performing. If this provoked doubts in those who met him, it was also the source of their fascination. And despite the dilettantism of his setting, Gurdjieff's teaching already had a serious side. He taught breathing and chanting exercises to Dukes, who continued to take lessons from him for several years.

Ouspensky's first encounter with Gurdjieff was less promising. Returning to Moscow from his travels in late 1914, shortly after the outbreak of war, Ouspensky went back to work in journalism. Noticing the announcement of *The Struggle of the Magicians*, he included it as an item in his own paper, but it was not until the following spring that the two men were introduced through a mutual friend, the sculptor Mercourov (who may also have been Gurdjieff's cousin).[21]

They met in the spring of 1915 in a cheap Moscow café, where Ouspensky found

> a man of an oriental type, no longer young, with a black mustache and piercing eyes, who astonished me because he seemed to be completely disguised . . . with the face of an Indian raja or an Arab sheik . . .[22]

Gurdjieff, who immediately impressed Ouspensky as a man who 'knew everything and could do everything',[23] spoke carefully, precisely and with authority. Not only did he seem to be omniscient: more to the point, he knew what was important and what was not. When Gurdjieff spoke, things also seemed to be *connected*; he communicated a sense of the wholeness of creation; each remark implied a vast, unified and coherent system of thought, which corresponded in turn to the very nature of reality. He was ready to discuss the deepest topics with his new acquaintance without further ado, and they immediately got on to Ouspensky's obsession with the search for an esoteric school. Gurdjieff made it clear that Ouspensky had at last come to the right man: he, Gurdjieff, was in direct touch with the true esoteric tradition.

But though Ouspensky was impressed by Gurdjieff's personal authority, a persistent hint of fraudulence repelled him. This was to be a common response in the years ahead. Searching for an explanation of this contradiction – and sensing that his new friend was an actor who never showed his true self – Ouspensky was perplexed. Role-playing normally produced a sense of falsity: in

Gurdjieff it suggested authenticity. The man had an aura of innate power and dignity which overcame the fastidious Ouspensky's distaste for what could otherwise only be called charlatanry: the stagily mysterious manner, the hints of occult powers, the boasting. Yet it seemed to be impossible to distinguish the strengths from the weaknesses, and Ouspensky wondered whether the very theatricality of the man wasn't some sort of testimony to his genuineness, on the grounds that no half-way competent confidence trickster would sink to such nonsense. Later, he concluded that ordinary standards could not be applied to Gurdjieff; that the tricks were part of a deliberate and complex stratagem to test others; and that the source of Gurdjieff's power lay ultimately in his naturalness and simplicity.

Yet, when they left the café to meet Gurdjieff's small band of followers in a dingy flat above a municipal school, Ouspensky was struck by the absurd disparity between the teacher's grandiose description of his important pupils and the dismal band of no-hopers gathered there. And when Ouspensky asked these people what their master taught them, they talked vaguely about a system of ideas, about group work and 'work on oneself', but appeared unable to say more. Gurdjieff also made it clear that he expected his disciples to pay well for his services (without specifying what these services were), on the grounds that people do not value what they have not paid for.

This depressing scene increased Ouspensky's doubts. He was well aware that Gurdjieff was out to impress him: as a successful journalist, a well-known lecturer on the esoteric and a member of the St Petersburg intelligentsia, he would be a good catch for the unknown Gurdjieff. It was also quite clear that the existing pupils lacked the money Gurdjieff was looking for. Ouspensky wondered whether he was being used by a mountebank. Yet despite his misgivings – could this seedy, flashy figure who stooped to tricks out of cheap fiction really have the occult credentials he claimed? – he accepted Gurdjieff as his master. For Ouspensky's rational reservations were swept away by an extraordinary sensation: Gurdjieff's presence made this normally staid intellectual want to laugh, shout and sing 'as though I had escaped from school or from some strange detention'.[24] He was soon meeting Gurdjieff for instruction every day.

At these meetings it became clear that 'work on oneself' involved a good deal more than learning Gurdjieff's 'system' – which was anyway almost impossible for Ouspensky to grasp: every time he thought he had mastered some of it, there was more. Gurdjieff himself insisted that this was deliberate: it would be a mistake to diminish the value of understanding by making it too easy. He also demanded and exacted submission from his pupils, and the more abjectly they obeyed, the more aggressive and capricious he became. Ouspensky discovered what this meant when he went to St Petersburg in the winter of 1915 to form a group for the purpose of putting Gurdjieffian principles into practice. His teacher visited the city from Moscow to give talks every fortnight, leaving Ouspensky to organise attendance and venue, often at the last minute, while he drank in the café or organised the sale of carpets. Sometimes he left his wretched lieutenant in suspense about whether or not there would be a talk until the last minute. For the disciplined Ouspensky this must have been torment. Nevertheless, he gradually built up through his contacts a group of between thirty and forty pupils. Some quickly became devoted to Gurdjieff, others were birds of passage.

But what did these pupils do? For much of the time they listened to Gurdjieff talking, expounding the cosmology and psychology described by Ouspensky in his book about these years, *In Search of the Miraculous*. Gurdjieff's system impressed his new pupil with exactly the qualities he had been looking for: detail, extent, connectedness and comprehensiveness. It seemed that Gurdjieff quite literally had an explanation of everything and could always show how one thing related to another. But even more important was the practical training he offered. Explaining why Ouspensky had so far failed to find such an education elsewhere, Gurdjieff told him that from ancient times the Indians had had a monopoly of spiritual philosophy, the Egyptians of spiritual theory and the Persians and Mesapotamians of spiritual practice. The region of 'Turkestan' from which Gurdjieff hailed was therefore the home of spiritual practice, and Gurdjieff himself the inheritor of the tradition.[25]

To prove the point he began assigning tasks to the pupils. These tasks – which comprised the 'work on oneself' of which they had spoken to Ouspensky – included the chanting and breathing exercises described by Dukes, and a range of movements designed to co-ordinate mental, spiritual and physical aptitudes. The exercises were to be vital to Gurdjieff's teaching, and they mark the distinctive break with Theosophy. The core of Gurdjieff's doctrine concerns the integration of all the vital forces in order to bring them into harmony with one another and with the cosmic order, so that each individual can learn to Be. This idea had a powerful appeal to the intellectual Ouspensky, who had so far pursued the Theosophical ideal of esoteric knowledge as a route to spiritual enlightenment. But real knowledge, according to Gurdjieff, is a function of being. What a man knows relates directly to what he is. Distinguishing between essential being and superficial identity or personality, Gurdjieff therefore designed his exercises to weaken the imprisoning power of acquired characteristics, thus restoring the fundamental sense of being which those characteristics usually block or obscure.

The exercises were made no easier by growing civil unrest in Russia. Hardship at home, the manifest incompetence of the civil and military authorities and the hideous carnage of the war provoked riots in Moscow. Confidence in the government, already weak, collapsed. Indeed, it seems extraordinary that anyone could take an interest in esoteric activity at such a time, when just staying alive and securing one's future became daily more perilous. Yet it was precisely this peril that focused interest in Gurdjieff's teaching. For here was someone who could explain the terrifying chaos into which life was rapidly sliding and – perhaps even more to the point – who could also rise above it.

Gurdjieff, like Steiner, attributed the war to occult powers – more specifically to hostile planetary influence[26] – but he also argued that, because of these occult forces, there was nothing individuals could do about the situation directly, be they peasants or cabinet ministers. Things happen.[27] For the most part, men behave like machines or sleep-walkers, blindly running into disaster. Under the circumstances, the only logical course of action was to ignore the chaos without while trying to preserve oneself so as to establish order within. It was only by freeing oneself from the arbitrary course of events that one had any hope either of developing spiritually through the experience of being, or of affecting those events. He supported this consoling if fatalistic doctrine by inviting his pupils to put their absolute confidence in him. His behaviour might at times appear arbitrary, but only because the logic of it was hidden from their eyes. Given the complete absence of any other dependable support to lean on, there was no reason why they should not trust Gurdjieff.

Although deeply involved, Ouspensky was still sceptical. As the months went by, his teacher's methods did not seem to be producing results. These methods were also bizarre in the extreme. As the group grew in numbers during 1916, Gurdjieff supplemented his occasional talks with intensive group therapy. Pupils who came to him for esoteric instruction were told that all their ideas about occultism and mysticism were nonsense, that their professional and personal talents were trash, and that the only way forward was to strip away everything familiar in the hope of discovering their essential selves. This was not to be done by study or meditation but by living and working together in a group, performing menial tasks assigned by their teacher. They were also instructed in the movements Gurdjieff claimed to have learnt in remote monasteries during his travels in Central Asia, and drilled in ever more gruelling mental and physical exercises. As the political situation worsened, Gurdjieff's regime became tougher. In addition, he constantly took pupils to task for their failings, sometimes in private but more often in front of their fellows, requiring the public confession of faults and insulting with particular vigour those who tried hardest to please. He even encouraged their squabbles, as a way of breaking up the normal behaviour which forms part of the individual's imprisoning personality.

The purpose of these methods was to promote self-observation and 'self-remembering' so that pupils could begin to wake up from their deep slumber and become conscious of their true selves. Only then would they cease to be human machines. Gurdjieff's distinction between being – or essence – and superficial personality acquired from heredity and environment depends on the fact that most of us most of the time identify with our surface life, which is entirely subject to external influences. Before we can develop spiritually we must find our true self. This can never be a comfortable or pleasant process. Stress, pain, tension and conflict are all needed to promote it. Gurdjieff's regime was therefore quite literally a course of shock therapy.

His pupils were perplexed. This was a long way from the excitement of the occult or the consolations of Theosophy with which most were familiar, and many soon abandoned their new teacher. Others accepted Gurdjieff's view that disciples must unquestioningly obey the Master, however unreasonable he may seem, if real spiritual progress is to be made. Such trust, he claimed, was in itself both an essential hurdle to be surmounted and a sign of the acolyte's suitability for the work. Ouspensky was among those who accepted this claim, though he could not quite rid himself of the intellectual's residual doubts about submitting to authority without question.

In the summer of 1916 the core members of the group retreated to a Finnish country house belonging to one of their members for a period of intensive study. By this time Gurdjieff's main pupils included the mathematician A. A. Zaharoff; Dr Stjoernval, a specialist in mental disorders who had become (according to his own wife) the new teacher's devoted slave; one of Stjoernval's patients; Ouspensky's friend Sophia Grigorievna; and a Polish prostitute, Madame Ostrowska, who had become Gurdjieff's mistress.

The atmosphere in Finland was tense. Gurdjieff's little party was subject to the gossip, hysteria and claustrophobia that commonly afflicts such groups even in ordinary times, especially under the leadership of an inscrutable charismatic figure who may or may not know what he is doing. The war, which was going badly for Russia, could only make things worse. There were food shortages and travel was becoming increasingly difficult. Yet it was precisely these conditions that concentrated the minds of Gurdjieff's pupils – especially as several, including Ouspensky, were already fasting and practising the consciousness-heightening exercises prescribed by their master. The result was that they all became highly suggestible, and Ouspensky found himself in direct mental contact with his teacher, hearing Gurdjieff's voice within his own body, and answering out loud questions that the other pupils had not heard Gurdjieff ask.

According to Ouspensky himself, Gurdjieff made it clear in this way that his best pupil must now either give way or get out. He could no longer stand slightly outside the work. Challenging and even dismissing pupils were to become familiar Gurdjieffian ploys in an often repeated sequence which is one of the more sinister aspects of his approach. Followers were first seduced by the Master, then subordinated, and finally thrown out, often for no apparent reason. Many, unable to do without Gurdjieff's support, begged to return, and some were allowed to do so for a while, but in the end Gurdjieff himself sent away all his major pupils or provoked them into leaving by making their situation intolerable. On this occasion Ouspensky left Finland and returned to St Petersburg, where he continued to communicate telepathically with Gurdjieff for several weeks – or so he thought. Whatever its nature and however it came about, the episode signalled Ouspensky's complete submission to his teacher.

The beginning of Ouspensky's real esoteric education coincided with the end of his old life in Russia. In October 1916 he was briefly called up for military service in the Sappers. At about the same time he began to share his apartment with Sophia Grigorievna and her daughter, though they never married. Pupils continued to join the group, but conditions in the Russian capital were becoming impossible. Within six months of the Finnish trip the whole country began to collapse as the political crisis deepened. In February Gurdjieff left for Moscow. A week later the Tsar abdicated, giving way to a provisional government. On 16 April that other man of power, Lenin, arrived at the capital's Finland Station and the Revolution proper had begun.

TEN

Travels

Gurdjieff was a man who thrived on adversity, and the Revolution brought out the best in him. Leaving Moscow in the spring of 1917 to join his family in Alexandropol, he eventually summoned his pupils to follow him south.[1] Many of them did so. Ouspensky arrived in June 1917, shaken by the summary executions he witnessed in the railway station at Tbilisi. By July, however, the two men had decided to return to St Petersburg but Gurdjieff changed his mind at the last minute and remained in Essentuki, a town on the railway line to the Black Sea, sending Ouspensky on alone to the capital, where he was to gather the other pupils for the journey south.

Ouspensky soon returned and others followed, including Zaharoff, and Thomas and Olga de Hartmann, who had joined the group not long before. The Hartmanns, who came from the same aristocratic Russo-German background as Madame Blavatsky, were Gurdjieff's most distinguished catches to date. Olga had trained as an opera singer and her husband was a successful composer whose ballet, *The Pink Flower*, had been performed at the Imperial Opera with Nijinsky and Karsavina in the cast. Rich, charming and independent, with no idea of what to expect, they arrived in the Crimea accompanied by a chambermaid and two carriages full of luggage. The social status of Gurdjieff's pupils was beginning to rise.

The group settled first in Essentuki, where their leader took a villa and established the pattern of life he was to follow for the next decade. As chaos closed in on the outside world during the summer of 1917, Gurdjieff set up an autocratic commune in which members combined household chores with exercises, discussions and dances, all under the Master's close supervision. In their country excursions from St Petersburg, household tasks had been a kind of game for the middle-class pupils in an age when all but the poorest employed servants. Chopping wood, cooking, gardening and cleaning were familiar to them only from the Tolstoyan cult of voluntary manual work as a route to moral improvement. Now their labours were in deadly earnest. Spiritual growth and self-preservation had become identical.

Gurdjieff required little sleep himself and his pupils got no more: five hours a night if they were lucky. When not working in the vegetable gardens or bargaining for scarce food in the markets they went for brisk walks, returning home to practise movements and breathing exercises. The austerity was punctuated – and accentuated – by occasional bouts of indulgence, when the Master rewarded his devotees with treats: a rest from their labours or a delicious dinner, something increasingly rare among the privations of a country descending into anarchy. In better times, the dinners were to become a focal point of Gurdjieffian life. The Master would preside over a table groaning with exotic food and huge quantities of brandy, like a combination of tribal chief and Victorian family autocrat, alternately teasing, bullying and ignoring his dependents. Lengthy ritual feasts, interspersed with elaborate toasts, reinforced the sense among his pupils that their teacher was a godlike figure, dispensing wisdom, wit and justice, preserving them from evil and conjuring bounty out of thin air.

In August 1917 Gurdjieff and most of his followers left Essentuki for Tuapse, a resort on the Black Sea coast. Ouspensky returned to the capital to see what he could salvage of property and other pupils. The political and military situation was changing all the time and Gurdjieff presumably moved to the coast to avoid being trapped inland. But once arrived in Tuapse he told the Hartmanns that he intended to *walk* from there to the safety of Persia – which meant a long and dangerous journey through the war zone. He also said that he would break stones on the road to earn a living. Who would come with him? Zaharoff and the Hartmanns, now mesmerised by

Gurdjieff and quite unable to fend for themselves, agreed to go. The others stayed behind.

Guided by Gurdjieff, the party walked inland for days, lacerating their feet and ruining their clothes on the mountain paths, only to find themselves in another village by the Black Sea not far from Tuapse: they had travelled in a virtual circle. As soon as they reached the coast Thomas de Hartmann went down with typhoid and Gurdjieff summoned Ouspensky and the Stjoernvals to join his party. Hartmann recovered, but the Civil War had begun to rage through the Caucasus; in order to escape it Gurdjieff kept his party on the move for the following months, once Hartmann could travel, until they ended up once more in Essentuki, exhausted by their trip and pauperised by the Bolshevik government which had in the mean time confiscated all private property.

In February 1918 Gurdjieff sent out a circular inviting all his pupils to join him in Essentuki, where his family were already gathering from Alexandropol. The commune re-formed and the old regime began again: dances, movements, hard labour and periods of enforced silence, this time supplemented with folk music from Turkestan and the conjuror's repertoire of fancy tricks their teacher had picked up on his travels. The band of followers now numbered over a hundred and their mixture of classes and characters produced Chekovian absurdity, as fine ladies worried about their few remaining jewels or dresses while Armenian peasants chattered in corners about eggs and flour, intellectuals struggled with spiritual exercises, and everyone earnestly discussed the meaning of life. Gurdjieff himself gave spiritual instruction and chewed sunflower seeds while he thought up schemes to support his growing entourage.

The numbers in the group were not constant. As more pupils and relations arrived in Essentuki, others left. In July 1918 Gurdjieff's sister and her husband reached the nearby town of Mineralni Vodni with their six children, reduced to living skeletons by the journey from Alexandropol – a distance of less than four hundred miles as the crow flies, but beset by every kind of peril, from regular soldiers to bandits. They also brought with them the news that the Turkish Army had slaughtered the male population of Alexandropol, including Gurdjieff's father, who had declined to leave his house. Everyone else had fled.

The party was then depleted by Ouspensky's defection: when Gurdjieff left Essentuki to return yet again to the Black Sea, in August 1918, his pupil remained behind. It is not easy to say why Ouspensky was convinced that the time had come for him to break with the Master, and why at that moment. Ouspensky himself says quite simply that he no longer trusted Gurdjieff – though his own evidence suggests that he never had. They had been living and working together in close proximity for just over a year; but while Ouspensky believed more fervently than ever in what he called the System, he had begun to fear its transmitter. Certainly the two men were incompatible characters, and the very traits that had once attracted Ouspensky to Gurdjieff in spite of himself had now begun to grate intolerably. Besides, both were autocrats, and neither could tolerate being directed by others. Though emotionally vulnerable, Ouspensky had the intellectual arrogance of a successful autodidact. He also found Gurdjieff's massive inconsistencies hard to take. Eventually he concluded that the only solution to his problem was to divide the man from the teaching, a move justified on the grounds that everything of value in the teaching belonged not to the teacher himself but to the traditions of the ancient school in which he had been trained. In future, therefore, Ouspensky would promote and develop Gurdjieff's System, free from Gurdjieff's own overwhelming and often sinister influence – or so he would claim.

As the Civil War came closer, Gurdjieff made plans to leave the area altogether with a small group of pupils. His family and the rest of the party stayed behind. The extreme difficulty and danger of travelling through the war zone made a good reason for travel necessary, and Gurdjieff managed to convince the Bolshevik authorities that, in the middle of a civil war, he was about to lead an archaeological expedition. He also hinted that he proposed to prospect for gold by the way. It is a testimony to his powers of persuasion (or bribery: we shall never know) that they believed him. Not only was he given the necessary permission: the authorities also supplied camping and digging equipment including tents, spades and twenty-one hatchets. At Ouspensky's suggestion Gurdjieff cheekily asked for alcohol to wash the gold. This, too, they provided in large quantities, despite the imminent famine. On Tuesday 6 August 1918, an expedition consisting of a donkey and fifteen people, including the Hartmanns and the Stjoernvals, left Tuapse by railway goods-wagon, travelling inland at four miles an hour.

Eventually they reached Maikop, a hundred miles north-east of the coast, where it turned out that anarchists had blown up the railway line and White and Red guards were fighting over the town. The engine driver wisely abandoning the train, they were left to fend for themselves. Finding an abandoned farmhouse, they fell into their accustomed routine. The donkey grazed, the pupils worked, and in the distance the noise of gunfire signified that the war was continuing. Yet even in their solitude they were not alone. The area was swarming with refugees of every kind, all trying to judge which way to jump as the local towns changed hands with successive changes of government. Hartmann met a fellow Guards officer turned tramp, while Dr Stjoernval came across a Finn become Buddhist monk, *en route* to India in monkish robes.

After three weeks in the farmhouse it became clear that they would have to move on. Having taken Maikop, the White Army was hanging all suspected Bolsheviks and it would only be a matter of time before the Reds retook the town and started shooting all Tsarist traitors. Whichever side one chose, there was mortal danger. Though Gurdjieff typically succeeded in coaxing travelling passes out of both parties written on two sides of the same piece of paper, gambling on which side to show each time they were stopped on the road, even his ingenuity could not sustain the juggling act for ever. The only thing for it was somehow to escape from Russia altogether. This meant crossing the hills to the Black Sea yet again; now the railway was out of action, the only way to do *that* was to pack their carts and walk.

The journey involved crossing military lines several times, carrying their own luggage, negotiating steep hills and thick woods, eating wild mushrooms and berries by day and camping by night in the tents supplied by the Bolshevik authorities in Essentuki. On the way they 'discovered' a series of dolmens – it is not clear whether

Gurdjieff already knew of their existence – justifying their original description as an archaeological expedition, should anyone enquire.

At last, in October 1918, they reached Sochi on the Black Sea, sliding down the steep hills outside the town 'on their arses' at Gurdjieff's suggestion. Once more they had travelled in a circle. They took rooms in the best hotel and that same evening after dinner Gurdjieff asked Olga de Hartmann to sing the Bell Song from *Lakme*, as though everything were quite normal. It was a minor task after what he had recently required of her.

Within days the group began to disperse – whether on their own account or at Gurdjieff's request is not clear. Gurdjieff was left with only Julia Ostrowska, the Stjoernvals and the Hartmanns. But Sochi was no safer than anywhere else. Though the Bolsheviks were not threatening the town, the newly independent Georgians and the White Guards were. In January 1919 the diminished group set off on their travels once more, this time taking a boat to Poti and then making their way to Tbilisi, the capital of Georgia, where (according to his account in *Meetings With Remarkable Men*) Gurdjieff had worked on the railways thirty years before. In Tbilisi he found refuge with cousins and was soon in business again as a carpet dealer, on capital advanced by his brother's father-in-law, who happened to be the local archbishop. Dr Stjoernval set up in medical practice and the Hartmanns found musical work, Thomas in the conservatoire and Olga at the opera, where she was immediately cast as Micaela in *Carmen*. She took on the role despite signs of incipient TB, and was soon cured under Gurdjieff's direction by eating bacon and sleeping on the cold verandah.

Her irrepressible leader at once began negotiations with the Georgian government for the establishment of the first of his 'institutes' which were to be such a feature of the following decade. The days of *ad hoc* groups were over: Gurdjieff now wanted a proper school and official recognition. Having spent his life fixing and dealing, he took to the negotiations with great gusto, and his experience with the shaky Georgian administration was to come in useful when he embarked on grander overtures to the French, German, British and American governments at various times during the 1920s. Eventually the Georgians, apparently flattered by Gurdjieff's suggestion that he could help to make their capital a centre of world culture, gave him a building in Tbilisi where he set up the grandly named Institute for the Harmonious Development of Man. The institute promptly folded for lack of public interest, despite an outrageously optimistic – not to say dishonest – prospectus which announced that it was already operating in the world's major cities including Bombay, Cabul, Alexandria, New York, Chicago, Moscow, Christiania, Stockholm – and Essentuki.[2]

Behind the fraudulence of the prospectus there was a real educational programme of sorts, based on Gurdjieff's theory of personality, according to which man has three centres: physical, emotional and intellectual. The purpose of his exercises – and at this time he was more therapist than occult teacher – is to bring these centres into balance through movement and self-understanding.

According to Gurdjieff, who was fond of threes, there are three traditional ways to awaken the human machine from its sleep and promote the growth of consciousness: the way of the fakir, which concentrates on the physical centre; the way of the monk, which concentrates on the emotional centre; and the way of the yogi, which concentrates on the intellectual centre. But all these ways produce one-sided development. In his Central Asian *Wanderjahre* Gurdjieff claimed to have studied a Fourth Way by means of which the three centres could be harmoniously developed.[3] If harmony seems an unlikely objective for one who was always at the storm's centre and never hesitated to provoke conflict, Gurdjieff would argue that what normally looks like harmony is in fact sleep; and that real harmony is not the absence of discord but the concordance of dynamic forces.

But although Gurdjieff was not able to establish his institute successfully, he did continue to develop his role as a dancing master. The sets and lighting for Olga de Hartmann's *Carmen* had been designed by Alexandre Salzmann, whose wife, Jeanne, rapidly became one of Gurdjieff's most enthusiastic pupils. Born in 1874, Salzmann was something of a wild card, a wanderer who combined his artistic talents with an interest in ju-jitsu, healing and occultism. A friend of Kandinsky's, he had been at various times forest ranger, inventor and Benedictine monk. His much younger wife (born in

1889) was a dancer who had studied with Emile Jaques-Dalcroze at the School of Eurythmics in Hellerau near Dresden.[4] When Gurdjieff arrived in Tbilisi she was rehearsing her students for a performance of Dalcrozian dances. Deeply impressed by her husband's new friend, she turned over her class to his direction for a performance of the Sacred Dances, so long practised but never seen. The performance took place in Tbilisi Opera House on 22 June 1919.

Meanwhile Olga de Hartmann had been dispatched on a journey. That spring Gurdjieff's brother Dmitri reached Tbilisi from Essentuki where his mother and sister had just about survived the purges, plagues and famines. Most of their belongings had been sold or plundered, but a few of Gurdjieff's carpets and Olga's miniatures survived, and Olga, now one of the Master's most trusted lieutenants, was sent through the war zone to fetch them. She later saw the journey, like all the challenges Gurdjieff produced for her, as a test – the view of their adventures in the Caucasus taken retrospectively by all the pupils who remained loyal.

The less credulous Ouspensky was also demonstrating his powers of survival in Essentuki. Within a few days of Gurdjieff's departure the Civil War had engulfed the town, and conditions rapidly deteriorated as the Red and White Armies fought over the territory and random Cossack raids terrorised the population. Responding to desperate circumstances with Gurdjieffian panache, Ouspensky commandeered a room in the local school, where he arranged all the books he could find in what he called the official library of the Essentuki Soviet, announcing the fact on a banner over the door. This gave him an official role which may have saved what life was left in his starving body, though books were of little use when it came to providing food and clothing. In one of the articles he contributed to an English journal describing conditions in Russia at the time, Ouspensky wrote that 'I personally am still alive only because my boots and my trousers and other articles of clothing – all "old campaigners" – are still holding together. When they end their existence I shall evidently end mine.'[5] His friend Zaharoff was not so lucky, dying of smallpox in Novorossiysk in November 1919.

In June of that year, after nearly ten months of suffering and many rival claims of victory, Essentuki had been briefly 'liberated' by Denikin, the general in command of the White Russian armies, and Ouspensky was able to make his escape as adviser to Major Pinder, head of the British Economic Mission to Denikin's army. Pinder had been alerted to Ouspensky's condition and whereabouts by a fellow-Englishman, A. R. Orage, who had published Ouspensky's six 'Letters From Russia' in his magazine the *New Age* between September and December 1919. So fluid was the military situation in the Caucasus that Pinder himself was soon afterwards captured by Red troops, imprisoned and very nearly executed; but both men eventually extricated themselves from the war and retreated westwards across the Black Sea.

By March 1920 Ouspensky had reached the safety of Constantinople. Gurdjieff meanwhile had formally disbanded the Institute for the Harmonious Development of Man in Tbilisi, abandoning yet another attempt to stage his ballet. There was no time left for dancing and he was now seriously considering his flight from Georgia, where conditions were rapidly deteriorating. Pinder, appointed British Cultural Attaché to the short-lived Georgian government, passed briefly through Tbilisi, where he shared a bottle of Johnny Walker whisky with the Master,[6] but it was not long before both men had to leave the capital in a hurry. Gurdjieff's companions sold their property, converting the proceeds into rare carpets; Hartmann gave a farewell piano recital; and they set out again for the Black Sea and the port of Batum. Here they had a narrow escape. The boats leaving with refugees were packed, places almost impossible to come by. While they negotiated for berths, soldiers stole most of their valuables. Despite this they still had enough to pay for tickets, and on 7 June 1920 Pinder and Gurdjieff, with about thirty of Gurdjieff's followers, many of them acquired in Tbilisi itself, managed to reach the comparative safety of Constantinople. Ouspensky and his feared master were together once more. They were never to enter Russia again.

The Turkish capital was swarming with refugees and official representatives of the great western powers awaiting the final collapse of the Ottoman Empire. Turkey had sided with Germany in the war, making it legitimate prey for the victorious Allies, and France and Britain both had military missions in Constantinople to look after their interests. Nominally these missions were intended to promote stability in a highly volatile region. In fact, they were engaged in intelligence work and political agitation on their own account. Southern Russia, Turkey and the Balkans were all in chaos following the war, and it looked as though the whole of Central Asia would soon be dismembered by mandating powers, imperial colonists or the subtler manipulators of 'spheres of influence'. Besides the Russian Civil War, which stretched across the Crimea and Caucasus and down into Asia, there were ethnic squabbles throughout the disintegrating empire. In Turkey itself, though the last Sultan was still on his throne, it would not be long before a republic was declared.

Gurdjieff, who claimed to have visited Constantinople in his youth to investigate the dervishes as part of his quest for truth,[7] settled in Pera, a section of the city where he found a community of impoverished White Russians gathered in the cafés, Ouspensky among them. His former pupil lived in lodgings on Prinkipo Island, supporting himself and Madame Ouspensky's family by giving lessons in English and mathematics. The city was swarming with Tsarist exiles. In the autumn of 1920 the defeated White Army retreated to the Bosporus and over a hundred thousand people were added to the exodus from Russia into Turkey, forming a city within a city.

Whatever the tragic consequences for others, this was good news for Gurdjieff. Earning his living as a healer and dealer, he again went to work to establish an institute, entering as usual into complicated negotiations for premises. These he found in the autumn of 1920, giving lectures and organising rehearsals of the sacred dances in another room near by. Pupils were less difficult to come by than rooms. The ground in Constantinople had been prepared for him by Ouspensky, whose escape from Gurdjieff was not to be the simple matter he had planned. Ouspensky was already at work on the System, with more than twenty pupils who met in the White Russian Club. Whatever his misgivings, he obediently handed this group over to the Master, falling back for a while into his old role of touting for Gurdjieff's pupils.

The two men also worked together on the everlasting *Struggle of the Magicians*, writing verses for the scenario and devising songs influenced by the music of the *tekkes* (the dervish monasteries, of which there were over 250 in Constantinople alone). Thomas de Hartmann was also at work on *The Struggle*, filling out the musical sketches supplied by Gurdjieff. Exposed by the Master to Armenian and Georgian folk music during his months in Tbilisi, he now absorbed dervish influences. But Ouspensky's alliance with Gurdjieff was not to last long. Gradually withdrawing from his teacher, he left the city for London in the summer of 1921, twelve months after Gurdjieff's arrival.

It hardly mattered. By this time Gurdjieff was discovering new friends and pupils, and not only among the White Russian community. Many people found him intriguing, not to say sinister, and even in a city full of exotics he stood out. One of his long-standing contacts in the city was the Sultan's nephew, Prince Mehmet Sabeheddin.[8] Sabeheddin later told a mutual friend that he had known Gurdjieff since 1908, which is possible, given the reported involvement of both men in shady dealings of every kind. They may even have met through the Dashnakzutiun, the fierce Armenian secret society which fought against Turkish rule. Though a member of the ruling family, Sabeheddin was a political intriguer, involved with the Young Turk opposition to the sultanate and implicated in plots against the regime. For his involvement in one of these plots he had been tried and sentenced to death *in absentia* in 1913. Living mainly in Europe during the war years, he was restored to favour in 1918 by the accession of his uncle, Mehmet VI. Returning to Constantinople, he lived at Kuru Chesme, an imperial villa overlooking the Bosporus.

It was here that Gurdjieff dined with him in January 1921. A small, fine-boned, melancholy man in a fez and a frock-coat, Sabeheddin was then in his mid-forties. His interests were divided between Eastern religion and Western politics. Dabbling in Theosophy and Anthroposophy, he had met and corresponded with

Rudolf Steiner and Edmond Schuré, besides making a study of Islamic mysticism, Buddhism and Christianity. But it seems likely that such interests, however sincere, were desultory: everything about the unfortunate Sabeheddin suggests dilettantism. He made a cult of Jesus and the Virgin Mary, but his passion for the English was almost as strong.

England figured largely on the guest list that evening. Captain J. G. Bennett was a regular guest at Kuru Chesme.[9] Bennett had arrived in Constantinople in February 1919, aged twenty-three, on secondment to the British Army of Occupation as one of the few officers with knowledge of Turkish. He was a talented and charming man with impressive mathematical and linguistic skills, who had served with distinction in the war before being invalided out with injuries that produced a curious mystical by-product: the temporary sense of being removed from his own body and observing it from above. This experience, recurring throughout his life, prompted Bennett to wonder whether there was something more to human existence than everyday experience. While convalescing in Cambridge, his work on five-dimensional mathematics also suggested a realm beyond normal notions of time and space.

When the Allies began to squabble over their spoils in Asia Minor, Bennett's linguistic expertise made him an obvious candidate for service overseas, and despite his recent marriage he took the opportunity. His easy mastery of Turkish secured him rapid promotion and he was soon effective head of British Military Intelligence in Constantinople – a posting which eventually brought a remit over the whole sphere of Turkish influence. His activities in Constantinople included spying, surveillance and making contacts with all political groups, and Bennett was able to develop a natural taste for mystery and intrigue. In the course of his work he also investigated the various dervish orders Ouspensky had visited a decade earlier.

These orders were reputed to conceal political secret societies, but there was more than intelligence-gathering to Bennett's interest. The notion of a spiritual quest which already figured largely in his life was fed by his research into Sufism. Like other people in this book, Bennett lived much of his life in a twilight zone where intelligence work blended into vague belief in hidden brotherhoods and occult societies. And, as any comparison of his autobiography with Foreign Office records will show, he was no better than Blavatsky, Leadbeater or Gurdjieff at distinguishing public reality from personal fantasy.

Bennett's researches into the Mevlevi Order were encouraged by Sabeheddin, who introduced him to occult texts, including Schuré's neo-theosophical *Les Grands Initiés*, which expounds the theory that all religions are basically the same and that there is a line of great initiates through whom the wisdom of the ages is transmitted. These theories chimed in with Bennett's own instincts, setting him off on a lifelong search for the initiates who held the secret of existence in their hands.

There was also an English woman at Prince Sabeheddin's that evening: a white-haired and distinguished matron in her forties. Educated in India, where her father had been tutor to the Maharaja of Baroda, Winifred Elliott had trained as a painter at the Slade School of Fine Art and married in England. After an adventurous career, including marriage to a Mr Beaumont, she had come to Turkey as companion to Sabeheddin's emancipated daughter, Princess Fethiye. Mrs Beaumont shared Sabeheddin's interest in social reform, spiritual enlightenment and radical politics. She may also have been his mistress. Twenty-four years older than Bennett, she was a committed and experienced socialist and a friend of European socialist leaders, including Arthur Henderson and Philip Snowdon (later Foreign Secretary and Chancellor of the Exchequer in Ramsay MacDonald's Labour cabinet). Despite the age difference, the susceptible Bennett found Mrs Beaumont's low voice, her intelligent talk – and her fine complexion – most attractive.

It was a curious party: the tiny Sabeheddin, the refined Mrs Beaumont, the cocky young captain and the overwhelming Gurdjieff, who talked at length about hypnotism and higher states of consciousness. By now the Master had taken on his distinctive appearance and manner – a cross between guru and carpet dealer. Strongly built and swarthy, with curled black moustaches, a domed, shaven head and piercing eyes, he always made an immediate impression, whether for good or ill. Both Bennett and Mrs

Beaumont were especially struck by his gaze, quite different to anything they had ever seen. Ouspensky had described him as having the face of an Indian raja or an Arab sheikh – perhaps a fanciful way of saying that Gurdjieff radiated power, assurance and authority. Yet Ouspensky had also noted the disturbing sense of a veiled or hidden power, something at once esoteric and exotic.

Gurdjieff's reputation had gone before him. Intelligence reports from the imperial government in India alerted the British authorities in Constantinople that a notorious Russian agent was on his way there, though the charges against him were vague. These reports were almost certainly in Bennett's office even as he dined with the prince, though he claims in his autobiography not to have been aware of this until afterwards – a claim that does not sit well with boasts about his influence on and knowledge of the Turkish *demi-monde*.

By chance, and unknown to Gurdjieff, Bennett had already come across Ouspensky. Among the lodgers who passed through Mrs Beaumont's flat was the silent and withdrawn Mikhail Alexandrovitch Lvow. Lvow was poorer than most of the émigrés, though better equipped to cope with his poverty, having years before the Revolution abandoned both his fortune and his post as Colonel of the Imperial Horse Guards to follow Tolstoy. Now about fifty and ekeing out his living as a cobbler, he lived in a cupboard under the staircase at the Russian Club, the Russky Mayak, until Mrs Beaumont gave him a tiny room in her apartment. It was through Lvow that Bennett met Ouspensky, when Lvow asked if his friend could use Mrs Beaumont's drawing-room for group meetings – though Lvow stipulated that the other occupants of the flat must not eavesdrop on these meetings, which were 'private'. Mrs Beaumont agreed, Ouspensky and his group moved in, and the talks began.

Captain Bennett and Mrs Beaumont had already been holding informal meetings of their own in the apartment to investigate hypnotism, and, despite or because of the stipulation that he should not listen to Lvow's friend, Bennett was soon involved with the group – perhaps impressed by Ouspensky's claim that their purpose was no less than the Transformation of Man. Bennett had also met the Hartmanns because of his involvement in organising concerts, and they talked to him about Skriabin, whom they had known, and Skriabin's theosophical ideas. Curiously, neither Ouspensky nor the Hartmanns mentioned Gurdjieff to Bennett. It seemed they had all learnt the better part of valour. Yet, on Bennett's own account, though he spent far less time with Gurdjieff than with Ouspensky during the next twenty-five years, it was Gurdjieff who was to shape Bennett's life.

This time their paths crossed only briefly. By August 1921 Ouspensky and Gurdjieff had both left Turkey by different routes for the same destination: western Europe. In the spring of that year a translation of Ouspensky's *Tertium Organum* published in America by Claude Bragdon, a future Gurdjieff pupil, had enjoyed a *succès d'estime* and – more to the point – made some royalties, which reached the author in Constantinople. Bragdon and Ouspensky corresponded, and when Lady Rothermere, wife of the newspaper proprietor, read the book and became a fan, Bragdon told her about Ouspensky's desire to leave Turkey, which she was happy to finance.[10] A classic if well-meaning enthusiast for short-lived good causes, estrangement from her husband and the loss of two sons in the war had sharpened Lady Rothermere's spiritual appetite, and she was constantly looking for means to assuage it. Bennett wangled a visa and Ouspensky left for London, establishing himself, again courtesy of Lady Rothermere, in a dreary West Kensington flat. 'Madame Ouspensky' remained in Constantinople with Gurdjieff.

Meanwhile Bennett himself had taken leave to visit England, prior to retiring from Military Intelligence altogether. While there he saw his six-month-old daughter and estranged wife, only to conclude that there was no hope of rapprochement between them: the encounter made him decide to return to Constantinople. Though technically not on duty, he also attended the London Conference for the Pacification of the Near East, where he advised the Prime Minister, Lloyd George, on how to handle the Turkish delegation; and later met Ramsay MacDonald (through Philip Snowdon), who suggested he stand for Parliament as a Labour candidate. Though tempted by the prospect, Bennett found life in Turkey more exciting for the present. The pleasures of being an MP could hardly compare, he thought, with his prestige in Constantinople, where he was popularly supposed to be the personal envoy of George V, and courted accordingly with comic and magnificent consequences. The ex-Khedive of Egypt, for example, had begged him to accept a thousand gold sovereigns in a suitcase in return for exerting his general influence on the Khedive's behalf; while the Albanians, always at a loss for suitable candidates, had offered him their throne. He wisely refused the crown but kept the money, using it to import figs from Asia to London, then investing the profits in a coal mine which he later sold for a good sum. It was just as well that the business came his way: having left the Army, he was now in need of employment.

Gurdjieff too was at a loose end, and had decided to settle in Germany. With no Lady Rothermere in sight to pay his bills, he once again sold up and took the train westward, leaving Constantinople on 13 August 1921 and arriving in Berlin on the 22nd. There were good reasons to choose Germany. The total collapse of the old order after the defeat of World War One had given rise to a frantic period of experiment and freedom in every form, tolerated (when not actively encouraged) by the Weimar government. Religion was no exception, and spiritual communities, schools and communes were springing up all over Germany, many of them drawing like Anthroposophy on the nation's rich philosophical tradition.

The immediate spur to Gurdjieff's choice of destination was an invitation from Emile Jaques-Dalcroze, arranged through the Salzmanns, to work in his premises at Hellerau. The Swiss musician and dance teacher Jaques-Dalcroze (1865–1950) had studied composition with Bruckner and Fauré, and taught harmony in the conservatoire at Geneva, where he devised his system of rhythmical movements christened Eurythmics in the decades before the war. In 1911 he set up his institute in a sort of mock Greek temple at Hellerau, financed by two Polish brothers, Harald and Wolff Dorn. Bernard Shaw, Stanislavsky and the American novelist Upton Sinclair visited the institute and were favourably impressed by Dalcroze's work, which explored the spiritual, therapeutic and symbolic properties of dance in an attempt to synchronise human movement with natural rhythms.[11]

Dance was very much to the taste of the time, perhaps because it combined exercise, ritual and craft in ways that simultaneously met the old hunger for sacramentalism and high art and the new fashions for health and hygiene. Dance was also an integral part of the avant-garde movement which dwelt on the ideals of freedom, expressiveness and integration with nature. Though the Russian Ballet dominated the theatre from 1910 to 1930, other dances, companies, teachers and theorists abounded. Ballet was only one of the forms dance took. The improvisations of Isadora Duncan, Josephine Baker and Louie Fuller were celebrated by poets and painters from Degas to Yeats as embodiments of sensuous liberation and instinctive being, while theorists such as Jaques-Dalcroze and Rudolph Laban attempted to devise systems of movement that incorporated freedom and complexity.

Dalcroze had moved his institute to Geneva during the war and decided to stay there in 1919. His former quarters at Hellerau were tenanted by a number of other 'progressive' movements, including independent Dalcrozians and a school under the directorship of A. S. Neill.[12] One of the disquieting farces so common in Gurdjieff's life now ensued, when he persuaded the Dorns to revoke the existing leases and assign them to him. Neill and his colleagues threatened legal action; the owners changed their minds, alleging that Gurdjieff had hypnotised them; and there was a lawsuit, which Gurdjieff lost. The charge of hypnotism was a common one, suggesting that he had unusual persuasive powers, whatever their nature – a point possibly substantiated by the fact that some of the Dalcrozians at Hellerau were so impressed by Gurdjieff they abandoned Dalcroze to follow him, becoming lifelong pupils.

Quite why Gurdjieff did not persist in Germany after the failure of his attempts to set up shop at Dresden is not clear. The country's radical instability may have played a part – though Gurdjieff was no stranger to such instability: as we have seen, he even relished it. In February 1922 he crossed the Channel to inspect London, where Ouspensky was already ensconced – no doubt congratulating himself on the distance he had put between himself and his worrying teacher. But the English did not suit the Master – which was just as well, because, despite Lady Rothermere's best efforts and support from several substantial citizens, the Home Secretary refused to allow Gurdjieff's party to settle in London, though he eventually indicated that Gurdjieff himself could stay if he wished. The intelligence reports which passed through Bennett's office in Constantinople had percolated back to London, and even Bennett's own efforts – he had returned from Turkey in June – were no help.

This must have been a relief to Ouspensky, who contemplated moving to America if Gurdjieff settled in Britain. For though Ouspensky fell into his usual subordinate role, arranging meetings for Gurdjieff at the Theosophical Hall in Warwick Gardens and filling them with his own pupils while Olga de Hartmann or Pinder translated and took notes, Gurdjieff did not hesitate to attack him. Ouspensky, he insisted at a public meeting, had misappropriated and misinterpreted Gurdjieff's ideas. He had no business setting himself up as a teacher of anything but his own theories and he would do better to submit once more to the Master. As for the audience, they must choose between the false prophet and the real one.

The staging of this confrontation was a classic Gurdjieffian occasion – so much so that some of those present later wondered whether Ouspensky and his master were in collusion; but it seems unlikely that Gurdjieff ever colluded with anyone. The combination of bullying threats with persuasive eloquence and personal magnetism was to become familiar to all his pupils in the years ahead and it is hardly surprising – apart from the personal humiliation involved – that Ouspensky mistrusted it. But, as so often before, Gurdjieff carried the day by sheer strength of character and the audience gave way.

Apart from Lady Rothermere, one or two minor aristocrats and a northern millionaire, Ralph Philipson, the gathering consisted mainly of journalists, psychiatrists and doctors, and their wives and husbands. The majority either sided with Gurdjieff in this quarrel of his making, or at least sympathised with him. At one stroke Gurdjieff had acquired many of his most zealous pupils. From Gurdjieff's point of view, however, though he didn't yet know it, the most important member of the audience was A. R. Orage, who later said that 'After Gurdjieff's first visit to Ouspensky's group, I *knew* that Gurdjieff was the teacher.'[13] Such was the strength of the impression he made.

Orage was an archetypal convert. Born in 1873, he grew up in a village near Cambridge. The family were badly off and the talented boy was educated at the local squire's expense. Orage had expectations of this childless man's further generosity, but when the squire married late and sired a child his protégé had to give up hopes of university in favour of training college, becoming a teacher in Leeds in 1893. The disappointment coloured his outlook, encouraging a native melancholia. Orage's moods in later life were marked by the alternation of euphoric confidence and gloomy self-doubt. He became a romantic who, as he said, wanted 'to live in a world of miracles and to be a miracle himself'.[14]

In Leeds Orage worked for the Independent Labour Party, gave lectures on Nietzsche and Plato, joined the Society for Psychical Research and the Fabians, and in 1901 founded the Leeds Art Club with his friend Holbrook Jackson (1874–1948), the literary historian and critic.[15] He also became an ardent Theosophist. At the same time, he began evolving his own philosophy. As Jackson remarked, Orage wanted 'a Nietzsche circle in which Plato and Blavatsky, Fabianism and Hinduism, Shaw and Wells and Edward Carpenter should be blended, with Nietzsche as the catalytic'.[16] Though the names in the synthesis changed, his ambition remained constant over the years, and Orage gradually developed a somewhat Shavian theory of creative evolution, in which Man appears as simply the highest mundane vehicle through which cosmic consciousness can develop. When the Superman emerges – as he will – this creature will not be another Napoleon or Bismarck, but a creature with all its mental faculties intensified to an unimaginably high level.[17]

In 1905 Orage left Leeds and his wife for London, with nothing but a three-volume translation of Nietzsche for luggage. For a decade from the mid-1890s, he had been a pillar of Theosophy in England, though a scourge of Besantian and Leadbeaterian excesses, which he criticised vigorously in print; and in London he became a member of the Section Committee, though increasingly disillusioned with the leadership. Soon afterwards he came under the influence of Beatrice Hastings, whom he encountered at a theosophical meeting in 1906.[18] A wild South African briefly married to a boxer, Beatrice suffered from delusions of literary grandeur which were strong enough to dominate Orage and the *New Age*, the influential magazine he founded with Holbrook Jackson in 1907, partly on money borrowed from George Bernard Shaw.

Over the next decade literary journalism displaced spiritual questions in the lives of Orage and Hastings. The *New Age* became the most prestigious literary magazine of its time and Orage was the centre of a circle which included T. S. Eliot and Ezra Pound. He only resumed his interest in the esoteric when his relationship with Beatrice began to crumble at the beginning of the war, which she spent in Paris while he remained in London. But by that time his ardour for Theosophy had cooled. Always intellectually restless and ambitious, he was looking for a metaphysical solution to life's problems: a grand synthesis that would go beyond Theosophy – but to what?

First he took up Dmitri Mitrinovic, a swarthy Serbian mystic with piercing eyes and a domed, shaven head in the Gurdjieff manner.[19] During the war Mitrinovic contributed a series of articles on the spiritual aspect of European politics to the *New Age*, but most readers, including the Editor, found them incomprehensible. Orage also hoped for great things from one of the magazine's backers, Lewis Wallace, who had written articles on what he called Psycho Egyptology and a massive book about *Cosmic Anatomy*, but Wallace satisfied him no better than Mitrinovic. Then he turned to a variant of psychoanalysis devised by some Jungian friends who later became followers of Gurdjieff. Whereas Freudian practice was devoted to analysing the psyche in quasi-medical terms, the more optimistic purpose of psychosynthesis, as the Jungians christened their new method, was to reconstitute the patient spiritually. Though more promising than the work of Mitrinovic and Wallace, this, too, failed to interest Orage for long. But each failure sharpened his spiritual hunger. By the early 1920s he was a soul frantically in search of salvation, and Gurdjieff – who had, as it were, shadowed all Orage's earlier attempts to find a solution – arrived in London at just the right moment to save him.

Orage was not Gurdjieff's only English convert, but he was the crucial one. Where he led, other intellectuals followed. There were many in need of help. The war had left a spiritual desert in its wake, peopled by lost souls looking for leadership. Millions were soon to turn to Fascism and Communism as a direct result. The more fastidious looked to different solutions. Many were frustrated Theosophists weary of the endless rows within the Society, which had been in semi-permanent upheaval throughout the previous decade. And though Theosophy continued to attract young people in large numbers, many older members were disillusioned with it. Steiner's seriousness had attracted some of them into Anthroposophy; now Ouspensky and Gurdjieff were also in a position to capitalise on theosophical disaffection.

One momentous consequence of their growing influence was a major shift in emphasis among subsequent western gurus. Theosophy had been dominated by Hinduism and Buddhism, partly because of Blavatsky's original emphasis, partly because of Besant's later political interests and Olcott's work in Ceylon and Japan. Despite the huge Muslim population of the subcontinent and the Middle and Near East, and the efforts of isolated individuals such as Laurence Oliphant, Islam had so far been largely excluded from the alternative synthesis, perhaps because this monotheistic faith looked too close to Christianity and Judaism to be sufficiently exotic. But from now on the mystical forms of Islam found in Sufism and the active and contemplative practices of dervish communities were to play an increasingly important role in shaping the traditions of western guruism. The geographical centre of gravity had shifted once more. Just as Blavatsky moved it eastwards from Egypt to the Himalayas, now it had relocated westwards from the Far East to the Middle East and Central Asia.

Gurdjieff, now that he had thrown down the gauntlet to Ouspensky and his pupils, retreated to the Continent. Having decided that if Britain and Germany would not receive him he would try France, he arrived in Paris on 14 July 1922. Three months later a celebrated experiment in living had begun.

ELEVEN

Affairs

Krishnamurti spent the war years in the English Home Counties, safe, sound, bored and profoundly unhappy. As an Indian in Europe, a black man among whites, a Theosophist among Christians, a colonial among the ruling classes, a poor boy among the rich, he was inevitably an outsider and therefore lonely. But his worst problem was coming to terms with his role in a culture profoundly hostile to the idea of holiness. Accepted in India, holy men outside the Church were seen as aberrations in England, to put it mildly. And while there were some Englishmen who took this distinguished, exquisitely dressed young man for a visiting maharaja, many more pointed out the 'chocolate-coloured Jesus', often with ribald comments. There was no getting away from it: Krishna was a freak.

Inevitably the pressure sometimes made him self-pitying, egotistical and humourless. Even in childhood he had taken his role seriously, and he could be priggish and self-important when surrounded by adults who constantly reminded him of his great destiny. Lady Emily's daughter Elisabeth, who rebelled against the stifling worship of the boy-god, reproached him for the way he presumed to lecture others about their duty. She preferred Nitya, whom she found 'aloof and terribly fastidious'.[1] The younger Lutyens children saw a different side of Krishnamurti, who had not lost the taste for silly jokes. While Elisabeth stood somewhat apart, Mary loved her new friends. Coming home from school each afternoon, she would hope to find on the hall table their fine grey Homburgs and gold-headed canes: signs that they were visiting the house. Later she cherished a stronger passion for Nitya, whom she found less good-looking than his brother but even more charming.[2]

In Lady Emily's exotic black-walled drawing-room with its painted floor designed by Sir Edwin, the brothers could relax. Though inclined to be sentimental and intense, Emily gave the young men the warmth she felt she had unwittingly denied her own children. When Sir Edwin was about, the atmosphere was livelier. Though he respected his wife's belief, he had no time for the 'Sunday feeling' she cultivated.[3] But despite his distaste for Theosophy, he was always kind to the young Indians. Sir Edwin loved company, filling the house with friends whenever he could. A man of strong tastes with a passion for jokes, his pet hates included long-stemmed glasses, fish-knives, cut flowers, silk lampshades, pile carpets, the seaside, statistics, painted nails, the diagonal placing of furniture – and, of course, religious enthusiasm.[4]

Edwin's irreverent attitude was reflected in the nursery, where the children would invariably greet Krishnamurti's arrival by singing:

> Cowardy, cowardy custard,
> Your face is the colour of mustard;
> Your hair is black and greasy too;
> Cowardy, cowardy custard.[5]

Krishna took the song in good part. The Lutyenses were his surrogate family and he was close at different times to Barbara, Robert and Mary, though in the end it was only with his brother that he could really relax completely. Nitya was his one link with the past and with the dead mother he called for in moments of sickness and stress.

The company of the Lutyens family was all the more important because, with Leadbeater in Australia and Annie in India, Krishna no longer had their support to lean on. In one respect this was a good thing. He had never liked the old man and was gradually drawing away from him. Though in public he still accepted Leadbeater's judgement in all things theosophical, in private he chafed against his

old teacher's autocratic ways. Nor was Annie always a good
influence, partly because she herself was so easily influenced by
others – especially by Leadbeater – and ready to try out their
prescriptions on Krishna; and partly because she was too deeply
involved in her pet causes to spare much time for individual
problems. To the end of her life Krishna called Annie 'Amma' –
Mother – and he remained personally devoted to her, but they were
already drifting apart doctrinally.

But the main difficulty concerned his relations with others,
especially with girls of his own age. Though it was taken for granted
that Krishnamurti would remain celibate, there were usually several
girls competing for his favour, and he was quite ready to respond.
These girls were known to the more ironic of the theosophical
faithful as *gopis*, after the milkmaids who traditionally serve Sri
Krishna in Hindu mythology, and at least one of them was briefly
claimed to be the reincarnation of HPB, which presumably made
her flirtation acceptable.

His frustrations, doubts and sufferings were not eased by Leadbeater's tendency to promote the claims of new protégés. The main
contender for his favour was Desikacharya Rajagopalacharya.[6]
Raja, as he understandably preferred to be called, was the son of a
distinguished high-caste Hindu Theosophist. An intelligent,
exceptionally handsome boy born in 1900, he belonged to the
Society's élite, attending the theosophical school in Benares with
Yagna Shastri, whose sister Rukmini later married George Arundale. Though Leadbeater left for Australia soon after discovering
Raja in 1913, he kept up his interest in the boy, who seemed to be an
altogether more tractable candidate for messiahship than Krishna.
In 1920 Raja moved to London, where he stayed with Miss Dodge,
whose protégé he also became. She financed his years at Cambridge
and later made a financial settlement in his favour.[7]

Inevitably there was trouble. Raja's academic success underlined
the failures of Krishnamurti, who now had to share the limelight
with his rival. Even worse, he found himself in the painful position
of an heir apparent threatened with supersession. In the face of this
threat, Krishna and Nitya (who had to accept the newcomer as a
flatmate) reverted to their assumed roles as English public school-

boys, making fun of Raja's name and calling him a 'blinker'.*
Perhaps they were now able to understand how the dispossessed
Hubert van Hook had felt when he was forbidden by Leadbeater to
touch any of Krishna's belongings so as not to taint them with bad
vibrations.

The brothers were not the only ones to be put out by Raja's
appearance. Almost as soon as he discovered the boy, Leadbeater
decided that not only had Raja been St Bernard of Clairvaux in a
previous incarnation, but that he was to follow Krishna as the
incarnation of Buddha on the planet Mercury in a future existence –
an announcement which greatly upset George Arundale, who had
already been promised the same job. Arundale's distress – he was a
tough, virile young man, who became an army officer during the
war – is typical of the hysterical atmosphere the unpredictable
Leadbeater maintained among his flock, with the positive encouragement of petty rivalries, blatant favouritism, and an honours
system which kept everyone on their toes wondering who was next
for advancement on the Path or demotion from a plum cosmic job.

This whimsical bullying extended to the very highest reaches of
the Society, and neither Annie nor Krishna was exempt. On one
absurd occasion in 1914 when the Theosophical circus had moved to
Taormina for a spiritual holiday – a sort of luxury version of
Gurdjieff's Essentuki with tennis and charades taking the place of
housework and spiritual exercises – the party consisted of Krishna,
Nitya, George Arundale and his aunt Francesca, Dr Mary Rocke
and Lady Emily. As so often, they were all in a state of mild
communal hysteria, hoping for great developments on 11 January,
the anniversary of Krishna's first initiation.

On the evening of the 10th Krishna announced that he expected
something to happen that night. Retiring to bed in the belief that
they were to visit the Masters and take several steps along the Path,
they could none of them say the next morning whether anything had
actually happened, so they wired to Bishop Leadbeater for clari-
fication. Krishna, however, had recently written to his teacher
hinting that he wanted more independence and Leadbeater was still

* 'Blinking' being a polite substitute for 'bloody'.

in a sulk about it.[8] This may explain why his cross reply to the wire said that nothing had happened to anyone in Taormina, though various Indian pupils of his own had received promotion that night. The party lapsed from euphoria into depression.

This atmosphere was maintained to a greater or lesser degree throughout the war, as Krishna moved round England in a bizarre combination of praetorian guard, permanent house party and travelling circus. The circle of friends, mentors, admirers and hangers-on who made up this fluctuating ménage included the Taormina party plus Lady Emily's children, Muriel De La Warr, Miss Dodge and a changing ensemble of bit-players. Miss Dodge usually remained in Wimbledon because of her crippling arthritis, and Krishna and his brother often stayed with her there, under the stern eye of Lady De La Warr. By the end of the war, the dominant figures in this circle were George Arundale and Emily Lutyens, and a struggle for ascendancy developed between them, complicated by Arundale's unsuccessful wooing of Emily's daughter Barbara. The struggle reached a climax in 1915 when Arundale forbade Emily to visit Krishna, who was staying at Bude in Cornwall, swotting for yet another attempt at matriculation, because of the distress it allegedly caused the boy. Deploring Emily's sentimentalism, Arundale wrote to his rival that 'you have used Krishna more for your own convenience and satisfaction than for any other purpose . . . you have hindered the Master's work by emphasizing Krishna's lower nature . . .' and he rebuked the self-centred way in which she caused such 'whirlpools' of emotion, interfering with the boy's occult progress.[9]

Shattered by these accusations, Emily Lutyens nevertheless recognised the truth in them, however exaggerated, and withdrew somewhat from her beloved boy, but in fact she had won the battle with Arundale; depressed by Barbara's rejection, angry at his demotion from Mercury and preoccupied with his new job as General Secretary of the British Section, Arundale began to lose interest in Krishnamurti. Soon he was beginning to wonder whether the new Messiah's whole heart was really in the job. After all, Arundale had his own great role to play in the glorious future of the cosmos, a role which required neither meddling middle-aged women nor naïve messiahs. But in the long term Emily found that she, too, had lost Krishna; and as the years passed it became clear that no one would possess this aloof, mysterious stranger. Many people were to think of him as a close friend, only to discover that things were not quite what they seemed.

Fortunately Lady Emily was distracted for the time being by her interest in Indian Home Rule, which she took up in the footsteps of her heroine Annie Besant. Annie's chance entrapment in India when war broke out had turned out well. Always unable to resist the lure of public life, she was becoming ever more involved in Indian nationalist politics. As usual, she was able to claim that her political activities were a response to divine guidance. While in the midst of her lawsuit with Narianiah in 1913, the Lord of the World asked her to work for Indian self-government. This she enthusiastically agreed to do. The timing was excellent. She had won her final appeal to the Privy Council in the lawsuit with Narianiah and could turn her full attention to other things. Her new mission was clear, and it occupied much of her attention for the next decade.

Enthusiastically supporting her chief, Lady Emily held tactless Home Rule League parties in her London house while Sir Edwin was in Delhi designing the new imperial capital. Once again she was to be rebuffed. Encouraged by an angry *Times* leader which denounced her parties, she was crestfallen when Mrs Besant, annoyed by the hostile publicity and the prospect of a rival, told her to keep her nose out of politics – not for Annie's sake, of course, but in order to avoid embarrassing Sir Edwin.

Krishnamurti was also having to come to terms with Mrs Besant. For all the love and admiration she inspired, Annie's need to have her own way made her a figure of fear even to her closest associates. While she genuinely continued to revere Krishna as a divinity and bowed to his spiritual authority, in all practical matters she was not above bullying him for his own good. The combination of coercion and indulgence was echoed in different forms by the other powerful figures in his life – Leadbeater, Arundale, Lady De La Warr – many of them further confused by the need to look up to a boy they regarded instinctively as their social and racial inferior. The inevitable result was a painful sense of unreality which only intensified Krishnamurti's resentful sense that he wanted a life of his own.

The situation was not helped by Annie's post-war tendency to treat the now adult Krishna as a god at one moment and as her own adjutant at the next. This process began in earnest on her return to Europe from India in June 1919, when she began a long and strenuous series of the meetings she so much relished. She dragged the World Teacher in her wake, forcing him to address public meetings and encouraging him to learn French so that he could address the crowds in Paris. These meetings were agony for the shy boy, but they inaugurated a pattern of incessant talk and travel which would occupy the rest of his life. There were compensations. Many of the speaking-tours took in extended Swiss and Italian holidays in the company of Nitya and assorted Theosophists. But even the holidays could become vexatious. They usually took the form of reading and meditation parties, during which Krishna held intense discussions with his fellow-holiday-makers with intervals of tennis or golf. His companions badgered him with endless requests for group talks and private consultations about their spiritual condition, and the time seemed to pass in a state of febrile spiritual excitement.

This excitement was induced partly by the simple fact of Krishna's proximity and partly because all concerned, including Krishnamurti himself, were on a rapidly accelerating train to spiritual bliss. In the early days of Theosophy HPB had stressed that apprenticeship was long and hard – though she usually made exceptions for her favourites. Probation – the first stage of initiation – took seven years, and subsequent stages depended on spiritual progress. Leadbeater had speeded things up considerably, especially since Krishnamurti's arrival. By the 1920s the Theosophical movement was in a permanent state of millenarian enthusiasm, with its leaders looking for new spiritual honours and adventures at every turn. The spiritual fever was also shared by millions grieving for sons, husbands and brothers and hoping to find evidence of their survival in some other form. Spiritualism became popular again and that helped the Theosophical Society to expand. It seemed that HPB's grand ambitions really were about to be realised.

Theosophy was not unique. The years between the wars saw a huge increase in evangelising mass movements throughout the western hemisphere, as charismatic leaders from Hitler and Mussolini to Frank Buchman and Amy Semple MacPherson drummed up support for their different roads to salvation.[10] The decade was also an age of youth movements, as the nineteenth-century discovery of 'the child' was followed by the twentieth century's discovery of the adolescent. Religious and political leaders began to see the importance of influencing the young, all the more so because the emerging generation had been decimated in the war. Youth culture therefore represented both a symbolic new beginning and a practical reality. Associations of every kind sprang up, while those already in existence flourished. Some, such as the Scouts and Guides, the Boys' Brigade and the YMCA, were devoted to exercise and character-building. They emphasised group loyalty, sexual purity and practical skills, but they also promoted national solidarity and social reform. Though many of the children involved were middle-class, many more were from deprived urban backgrounds. The new associations held weekly meetings and summer camps, providing millions of slum children with their first taste of fresh air. Other movements, including the Hitler Youth, the Young Communists and various League of Nations societies, used the same methods to inculcate political lessons. For a brief period the Theosophical Society appeared to be in the vanguard of such movements, but this turned out to be an illusion. Though the youth membership increased hugely after the war, this was in response to Krishnamurti's personal appeal and to a general enthusiasm for humanitarian movements. But Theosophy's leaders were increasingly out of touch with their own members. They were also getting on in years. By the end of the war Annie Besant was seventy-two and Leadbeater sixty-five. They had been in effective control of the Society for almost twenty years.

There were those who said Annie was losing her grip, as her old weakness for fancy uniforms and occult ceremonies increased. Yet for all her crankiness she still had the populist touch, understanding instinctively that Krishna was her greatest new asset. He was not in these years an effective speaker, but his very diffidence, combined with youth, courtesy and dark good looks, had a powerful effect. Here was no demagogue, no ranting missionary, but a spiritual figure who quietly spoke a truth that came from within. Into the bargain, he looked and behaved like that new phenomenon, a film star, but without a film star's vulgarity.

In 1921 Krishnamurti was offered a magnificent opportunity to show off his talents to a world audience when Baron Philip van Pallandt, a Dutch aristocrat, offered the Society his property at Ommen in the Netherlands. Holland was becoming an important theosophical centre and Castle Eerde, an exquisite moated seventeenth-century house with an estate of five thousand acres, made an excellent HQ for the Society's élite, while the grounds could be used for mass meetings of the Order of the Star in the East. Throughout the 1920s the Society held yearly international gatherings at Ommen – known as the Star camps – often attended by thousands of people, most of them young and sleeping under canvas, while the ruling elders slept comfortably in the tapestry-hung chambers of the castle or in specially constructed huts in the grounds.

The camps combined religious uplift, political idealism and youthful high spirits with the post-war craze for self-improvement and plain living, and the atmosphere was often electric. There were lectures and discussions and other theosophical activities, but the highlights of each camp were the starlit talks Krishna himself would give by the camp fire. These talks were the effective beginning of his own career as a public teacher, and they taught him how to manipulate a crowd. While the campers sat round him in a ring, he would wait in silence, often for several minutes, until the inspiration came and the audience were ready: then he began to speak. His near-contemporary Hitler used precisely the same technique to rather different effect in his Nuremberg Rally speeches, silently waiting while the tension rose.

Unlike Hitler, Krishnamurti never raised his voice, and the effect of his words was not to work the crowd into a frenzy but to lift them to a state of individual exaltation. The beginning of the talk was often hesitant, the speaker warming to his theme as he proceeded. He did not rehearse or use notes, though he would sometimes elaborate a topic announced in advance, constantly returning to the same themes: compassion for all living things, sincerity, honest self-knowledge and the need for each individual to find his or her own way to enlightenment. What he had to say affected his audiences all the more powerfully because he seemed to embody his own ideals so well. In stark contrast to the theatrical Besant and Leadbeater, the slight, unassuming, modestly dressed and quietly spoken young man struck no poses but spoke from the heart.

There was some understandable murmuring among Theosophical grandees about the content of the talks, which clearly went against the Society's insistence on a hierarchical path with a period of probation, stages of initiation, and so on; but most of the audience hung on every word. Curiously, no two of them could afterwards agree what Krishnamurti had said; and when transcripts were produced, what had seemed supremely lucid and inspiring in delivery often struck readers as confusing and flat. Some people concluded that the magic was all in the moment, others that it lay in Krishnamurti's personality; while a minority believed him to be possessed by the divine spirit when he spoke.

Whatever the explanation, it was clear that, without specifically addressing individuals, he persuaded each listener that the talk was especially relevant to him or her. As a result, many of Krishna's most enthusiastic followers *thought* they heard him say exactly the opposite of what he had said. Perhaps this is the definition of charisma: that each person can so easily invest its object with his own dreams. For, in a curious way, the beautiful young man who insisted so fervently on the necessity of sincerity, transparency and honesty was just as much a creature of theatrical illusion as Annie Besant herself. Though his acting was involuntary where hers was calculated, this made it all the more potent. The crowd elicited from both something not otherwise on view, even to themselves – a point vividly illustrated by the occasions when the otherwise demure Krishnamurti preceded his talk by lighting the evening camp fire at Ommen in a flamboyant gesture of spiritual authority quite alien to his everyday manner.

As with great actors, the phenomenon had something to do with Krishnamurti's own emotional and psychological constitution. His constant injunction to others to empty themselves of all prejudices and illusions was in part prompted by the Hindu doctrines he imbibed in youth, but in part by his own natural inclination and by the curious vacancy so many noticed when he was a child. Years later, one associate was to observe that the World Teacher, who had long since abandoned theosophical play-acting, reacted to other individuals like a mirror, reflecting their own psychic states back to them,[11] but the solitary figure who spoke to the crowds at Ommen was already in a sense the creation of an audience in permanent attendance on him since Leadbeater's discovery by the River Adyar in 1909.

While the approval of the crowd can be exhilarating, its demands are often painful, depressing and exhausting, as any actor or teacher will testify, and Krishnamurti was soon beginning to show signs of near-collapse. This was hardly surprising, given the combined pressure of his public appearance with two other debilitating constraints. First, there was his increasing remoteness from his own childhood and everything associated with it. Unlike Gurdjieff, a stronger character who carried his family with him, and Steiner, who never strayed far from a supportive woman and the German-speaking culture in which he grew up, Krishnamurti was isolated from his origins, and this isolation turned him increasingly in on himself. Only his brother Nitya stood between him and complete exile from the world in which he grew up.

In addition, he was barred from the usual means of compensating for such exile by marriage. Flirtation was one thing, but a sexual partner was out of the question for the World Teacher. Theosophical leaders eventually countenanced Arundale's union with an Indian girl and Raja's romance with an American; but it was decreed that Krishnamurti had to be above all worldly concerns. Krishna himself fully supported this view in theory, though that didn't prevent him from falling in love with a series of attractive theosophical offspring.[12] But the nearest any of them came to consummating their passion was lying chastely in bed beside its object.

Frustration pays a high price, and Krishnamurti's emotional situation reached crisis point in 1922, when he and Nitya visited America on their way back to Europe from Australia following a Theosophical congress. Krishna was under even more strain than usual because of his brother's deteriorating health. The lively and energetic Nitya had long suffered from TB. Hitherto kept under control, the disease was now worsening and it had become imperative that he return to Switzerland for treatment. It was thought that travelling via India would be too hot and exhausting for him. The brothers therefore took the Pacific route from Australia to Europe, breaking their journey on the west coast of America, where they could rest and be sure of a welcome.

California was already home to several rebel brands of Theosophy, founded after Judge's decision to break away from Adyar. At Point Loma Katherine Tingley was still struggling with an ever-deepening financial crisis. There was also a cultural and missionary centre established by the Adyar Society at Krotona: it had been a source of satisfaction for Annie Besant to plant her orthodox flag in enemy territory. But rivalry with Point Loma and native competitiveness were not the only reasons for her zeal. Though Leadbeater preferred to live in Australia, California was still important in theosophical mythology as the home of the future southern Pacific root race which was to replace the currently dominant European/Aryan root race. There were enough members of the parent society in California to carry on the good work of preparing the way for this new race, including the local Secretary George Warrington, who arranged for the brothers to stay in the healthy climate of the Ojai valley in the hills beyond Los Angeles.

After the usual unpleasantness aboard ship, where white travellers were inclined to object to sharing an ocean liner with coons, darkies and niggers who weren't safely stowed in the stoke-hole, the openness of California made an overwhelming impression on Krishnamurti. By no means free from racial prejudice, Los Angeles nevertheless breathed a freer air than Australia and Europe.

Ojai, then largely deserted, is about eighty miles from the coast, a paradise of hills and orange groves with brisk mountain air and a dry summer climate. The brothers settled there in a cottage belonging to Mary Gray, a local landowner. Unable to do anything for themselves, they were looked after by Mr Warrington's daughter, but Nitya's health began to decline further as the TB advanced into his lungs and extra help was needed. This was provided by Rosalind Williams, whose family were staying in another of Mrs Gray's cottages at Montecito. Though Rosalind was not a Theosophist, her sister Erma was. Erma, who introduced Rosalind to Nitya and Krishna, claimed that the family's connection with Theosophy dated back to its earliest days. Their grandfather Carl Waldo, an aristocratic German exile who settled in Buffalo and made money out of cabs, had attended the New York funeral that Olcott organised for his fellow-countryman Baron de Palm in 1876. Waldo was not converted to Theosophy on that occasion, but the personal link with Blavatsky appealed to at least one of his descendants and Erma joined the Society.

Fair, blue-eyed and just nineteen, Erma's sister Rosalind was an attractive, energetic girl with a passion for sport, a liking for animals, and no particular inclination to the spiritual life, which must have been rather a relief for the two brothers, hot from the absurdities of Leadbeater's regime in Australia. Rosalind's vitality and naturalness appealed to them both and they were soon in competition for her attention. She spent her days at the cottage, sleeping in Mrs Gray's house near by. While Krishna meditated and Nitya recuperated she cleaned and cooked for them. For relaxation, the three read poetry together and took leisurely walks through the valley.

So strong was their affinity with Rosalind that both the brothers wrote to Leadbeater asking if she might be their reincarnated mother. The Bishop doubted this, because that lady had died two years *after* Rosalind's birth. Perhaps this was just as well, because spiritual maternity might have excluded warmer passions, and there seemed to be a special attraction between Nitya and their new friend. Whether it was this attraction (as her daughter believes), or whether (as seems more likely) it was a combination of all the frustrating factors that made his life increasingly oppressive suddenly brought into unbearable focus by the simultaneous proximity of everything unattainable Rosalind represented, and the fear that he might lose his brother (whether to her or to death), Krishna soon developed an illness of his own which kept him in retreat at Ojai for almost a year.

This illness appears to have been wholly psychosomatic in origin but its recurrent symptoms, known in his circle as the Process, were to play a major role in his life from then on. As described in memoranda written by both the brothers and sent to Annie Besant, Leadbeater, Miss Dodge and Lady Emily, these symptoms combined excruciating physical pain with mystical experience.[13] Lasting for several days in the first instance, they continued intermittently for months, recurring throughout Krishnamurti's life whenever he was under stress.

The trouble usually began with a sensation of weakness and pain in the neck, which gradually spread down the spine. As the pain worsened, Krishna periodically lost consciousness. When awake he alternately experienced a mystical sense of leaving his body and union with all creation, and violent physical disgust with the filthiness of his surroundings. He also developed a fear of sunlight and a feeling of suffocating heat, cowering in dark corners and refusing to leave the cottage. His only relief from the symptoms came when Rosalind cradled his head in her lap.

After several days, during which the tension in the small cottage had risen to unbearable levels, the Process culminated in a moment of Forsterian muddle. Mr Warrington, Nitya and Rosalind were sitting on the verandah in the cool of the evening. Krishna, who had been complaining of the filth in the cottage all day, was eventually prevailed upon to join them and sat chanting mantrams near by but apart. As he chanted, Nitya, who claimed that he had sensed a great and growing power in the house, gradually became ever more vividly aware of a specific presence and of Rosalind saying repeatedly, 'Do you see him?' When Krishna got up and came towards them, according to Nitya she fainted, and he assumed that she had been overwhelmed by the manifestation of a divine figure: of Krishna transformed into a divine figure.

Much later, Rosalind denied that most of what Nitya supposedly saw and heard had ever happened. There had been no figure. Far from fainting, she said, she had been asleep the whole time and only heard about the advancing divinity when woken by Nitya. And if she had spoken, she insisted that it must have been in her sleep. At the time, however, she seems to have accepted Nitya's account of events, as did his brother. Evidently she kept her counsel then or changed her mind later. Whatever the truth of the matter, it seems unlikely that any one of the three deliberately deceived the others, and despite this farcical misunderstanding the episode took on major significance for all three of them, reinforcing Nitya's sense of Krishna's divinity and encouraging Rosalind's feeling for Nitya. Only Krishna was left out of this bonding – and he was the most deeply affected of the three. Accepting his brother's interpretation of events, he was confirmed in a belief in his own extraordinary spiritual status – a belief which lasted throughout his life. Though the Process continued during the following months only in physical form, without accompanying visions, he interpreted it, with support from Annie, as a sign of his occult progress along the Path.

There was some justification for this interpretation. Yogic philosophy locates the vital powers of life – called *kundalini* – at the base of the spine. Personifying kundalini as a coiled snake, yoga seeks to awaken this power as a route to spiritual enlightenment. The Process could therefore be interpreted as the awakening of *kundalini* and the beginning of true enlightenment. Leadbeater, however, was dubious. Though he believed that progress on the Path was slow and difficult, it was not meant to involve physical pain, and neither he nor Annie had experienced any such difficulties – so why should anyone else? While accepting its importance, Leadbeater therefore warned against investing the Process with too much importance. Perhaps he sensed that it signalled not so much progress on the Path as its imminent abandonment – for there were already hints of Krishnamurti's gradual discovery of his own apartness from Theosophy as he withdrew into mystical experience. Seen from this viewpoint, pain signified the agony of separation, not growth. Leadbeater was presumably also aware that *kundalini* includes sexual powers, though he could not have known that the pains of the Process were to affect Krishnamurti only in the company of women.

Not realising their implications, Annie was at first impressed by signs of what she took to be a new maturity and insight on her protégé's part. She was also enchanted by Ojai when she visited Krishna there. Determined to acquire the site of such profound spiritual experience, she soon raised the money to buy several acres in the valley. Perhaps she was reminded of those idyllic mountain fastnesses where the Masters dwell when she set up a trust fund called the Brothers Association, punning on relationships human and divine. The land included the cottage where the Process began, and this they repaired and called Arya Vihara – the House of the Aryan. Theosophists never did things by halves, and gradually an estate was acquired at Ojai (largely with help from Miss Dodge) which was to become a spiritual centre to rival and even surpass Adyar. It was not Annie's fault that Theosophy was not to be its objective.

Perhaps Mrs Besant needed a distraction from her other troubles as much as Krishnamurti did. The Theosophical Congress of 1922 had been particularly exhausting, as a new row about Leadbeater, brewing for almost five years, finally came to a head. Her colleague had been under attack by the Point Loma Theosophists almost continuously since 1906. Katherine Tingley had encouraged one of her lieutenants, Joseph Fussell, to write two scandalous pamphlets about him in 1913 and 1914, in which eight serious charges against Leadbeater and Besant were listed. The exotic charge-sheet included claims of near-divinity and impossible occult powers, the abandonment of 'Mosaic prohibitions' against murder and adultery in favour of pseudo-Buddhism, endangering the innocence of youth, promoting such untheosophical activities as buggery, and generally associating the Society with perverts and madmen. Fussell was especially shocked by the *Lives of Alcyone*, in which the characters seemed to change identity, sex and relationship with an ease suggesting loose thinking if not loose living.

In 1917 Fussell had sent his pamphlets to the Attorney General of New South Wales, who ordered an investigation into Leadbeater's activities. The police were not able to interview Bishop Leadbeater, whose health fluctuated on demand, but they did speak to a Mr and Mrs T. H. Martyn, rich Sydney Theosophists with whom the Bishop had been staying until forced to move out by an outbreak of scarlet fever. Mrs Martyn said that she had disliked the Bishop from the start, which is not surprising, given his insistence that she and her husband sleep in separate rooms while he stayed with them, in order not to pollute Leadbeater's purity. The instruction was all the more offensive because, having heard of his reputation, she swore that she had seen him take naked boys into his bed while under her roof.

Martyn, who effectively bank-rolled the Sydney Lodge, was more reluctant to believe rumours that threatened to blow apart the Society in Australia, though one boy described his own experiences with Leadbeater. But even Martyn had to accept the truth when he went to America in 1919. There he met Hubert van Hook, now a young man. Embittered by his shabby treatment at Leadbeater's hands, Hubert bluntly accused the Bishop of fraud and pederasty. Arriving in London that autumn, Martyn heard worse things about Leadbeater's friend Wedgwood – rumours which Annie confirmed. Following recent sex scandals involving four Liberal Catholic priests, Wedgwood had escaped to Holland to avoid arrest in Britain. Wedgwood could not possibly be an Initiate, said Annie, and must be expelled from the Society. She deputed Martyn to tell Jinarajadasa, Deputy Head of the Esoteric Section in Australia, to cast him out.

Jinarajadasa had naturally consulted his old teacher about the matter, and Leadbeater came to Wedgwood's aid. In December 1919 the bemused Jinarajadasa had cabled Annie: 'Martyn reports you said W not initiate. Leadbeater asserts you were present at initiation.'[14] It was the old conundrum: if Annie proceeded against Wedgwood she would be denying the truth of her own occult experience. As she depended on Leadbeater to tell her what that experience was, there was only one way out. Within the week she had replied to Jinarajadasa: 'Brother's statement enough accept fact. Cancel message sent.'[15]

It is difficult to assess Annie's state of mind at this time. Though vigorous and in full possession of her faculties, she was now an old woman of seventy-four approaching the last stage in a full and often exhausting life. Surely she was tired of these endless squalid dramas involving her friend, which were in such embarrassing contrast to the Initiate's need for purity? Even if she didn't believe them, she must have wondered at Leadbeater's phenomenal indiscretion. Not only did he associate with Wedgwood; he was still surrounded by boys and handsome young men – although, as Nitya ironically wrote to his Italian friend Ruspoli, 'he goes out of his way now to talk to all the ugly old women'.[16] That was all Leadbeater did. He still refused to shake hands with a woman, or stay in a room alone with one (except Annie) on the grounds they might pollute him. Yet oddly enough, the Bishop was genuinely devoted to Emily's daughter Barbara Lutyens (to her father's dismay); and although he disliked women as such, he was always prepared to make exceptions. But the row rumbled on through 1920, and in May 1921, convinced that Leadbeater was as guilty as Wedgwood, Martyn wrote to Annie formally stating his suspicions and marshalling the evidence.[17]

His letter is a devastating document which articulates what many people must have been thinking. Wedgwood is accused of flagrant sodomy, Leadbeater of protecting him and practising his own vices into the bargain. Martyn then widens his charges to accuse Leadbeater of fraud in his alleged transmissions of messages from the Masters, personal disloyalty to Annie and general dishonesty. He also tells Annie that she is too credulous where the Bishop is concerned and questions the validity of their occult relationship.

A few months later the letter leaked out, published by the Editor of the *OE Library Critic* together with other attacks on Leadbeater and Wedgwood. There was also stern criticism of Annie. Then, less than two months before the 1922 Australian Convention was due to open, Reginald Farrer, a Liberal Catholic priest and friend of Wedgwood and Leadbeater who had briefly tutored Krishna, wrote to Annie, with copies of his letter to all concerned, resigning as the English head of the Co-Masons, confessing to sodomy and accusing Wedgwood of the same crime.

Four months after this bombshell, Annie received yet another letter from a Liberal Catholic bishop, Rupert Gauntlett, reiterating the charges against Wedgwood. This was followed by a public circular from the President of the Nottingham Theosophical Lodge demanding the investigation of rampant homosexuality in the Society. By then the Australian convention had taken place. Summoned by Leadbeater to support him, Annie, Krishna, Nitya and their party arrived in Sydney, where the police were investigating charges of immorality against Wedgwood and Leadbeater, though the Bishop was as usual too ill to see them.

The only first-hand evidence against Leadbeater was offered by the Martyns, who reported seeing him in bed with Oscar Kollerström, the son of a Liberal Catholic priest, but even this evidence was inconclusive and no charges were brought. Sharing a bed was not held to be a crime in itself. Wedgwood, on the other hand, trailed by the Society's own private detective, had been seen to visit no less than eighteen public lavatories in two hours. When questioned, he told police that he was searching for a friend he had known in a previous life. This friend had 'gone wrong' and it was Wedgwood's mission to rescue him.

At the convention Leadbeater was accused of everything from ventriloquism to pederasty, which he allegedly used less for pleasure than for building up reserves of astral power. As usual he denied the charges, but feelings were running high. When Leadbeater, supported by Annie, refused to step down, the inevitable result was the splitting of the Australian Lodge and many resignations from the Society world-wide. In retaliation against the rebels for flouting her authority, Annie cancelled the Sydney Lodge's diploma and most of the members responded by leaving with Martyn to form an independent society. Given the size of Martyn's financial contribution, this was a serious blow to the parent society. The remnants joined Mrs Besant's newly formed Blavatsky Lodge.

Loftily ignoring all these difficulties, Leadbeater turned his attention instead to building a giant Greek amphitheatre near Sydney harbour, complete with arena, library and tea-room. The complex was opened at a ceremony in which the Bishop played a starring role, inaugurating the new building with the words

> In the Name of all the Buddhas, past and future, in the
> Name of the Great Master of the Wisdom, and in the
> Name of the Father, and of the Son, and of the Holy
> Ghost, I turn this sod.[18]

Most of Leadbeater's time was spent at his hideous but imposing Sydney house, The Manor, where a theosophical commune had been established. Despite scandals, the commune continued to flourish. In 1925 Emily Lutyens took several of her children – including Mary and Betty – to stay there for that year's Theosophical convention, held once again in Sydney. They travelled from Europe with Rosalind Williams, Krishna and Nitya, who was secluded from the other passengers because of his recurrent illness. After the convention Emily and her children stayed on at the Manor for the sake of their occult advancement. It couldn't have been for the sake of anything else. Betty Lutyens, who disliked the Bishop, revolted against his dreary regime, which included compulsory attendance at St Alban's Liberal Catholic Cathedral, Masonic meetings and silent vegetarian dinners in a copper-lined dining-room where Leadbeater glared at anyone who made the slightest noise. Mary Lutyens was more impressed by the old man, who exactly resembled her childhood image of God, despite his booming voice and vile temper; but even she found the place intolerably boring.

Her stay at The Manor wasn't made any easier by the arrival of Rosalind Williams. Shortly after he had arrived in Sydney, Nitya's doctors had dispatched him to the hills in Rosalind's care. Even on board the boat out, Mary had hardly seen her beloved. Now he remained in the hills while his guardian came to the Manor. Frustrated by her separation from him, the adoring Mary felt bitterly jealous of Rosalind, yet she could not help admiring her rival. Still a plain schoolgirl, Mary was unable to compete with the older woman in looks or charm. With blue eyes like a Siamese cat, pink cheeks and fair wavy hair, Rosalind conformed to an image of northern beauty which exactly complemented the dark looks of the Indian brothers.[19] But she skilfully dispelled Mary's envy by taking the young girl into her confidence and talking to her about Nitya. Soon Mary was in love with Rosalind too.

However dull, a house filled with young people encouraged romantic dreams. Despite their seriousness, Mary noticed that most of the younger pupils were very good-looking, though she wondered why so many Theosophists cultivated the centre parting. When Leadbeater met Lady Emily and her children on their arrival, he came to the harbour wearing his purple robes and amethyst ring, 'prancing like a great lion'[20] and leaning on the shoulder of an exceptionally handsome fifteen-year-old boy, Theodore St John. At The Manor the young people spent their time hanging around waiting for interviews with Leadbeater or for 'another message to come through on the astral ticker-tape'.[21] These messages, later described by Betty as 'banal bromides', were then typed out by a favoured girl. Typing was the only skill most of them learnt during their stay.

Occasionally Leadbeater would emerge from his room and invite someone to accompany him on a walk. There was competition for this honour – partly because (as even Betty admitted) Leadbeater told marvellous stories, which were the only thing to break the atmosphere of monotony and jealousy at the Manor; partly because to be chosen as the Bishop's companion was a sign of honour; and partly because there was nothing else to do. His imagination was certainly as fanciful as ever. One day, according to Mary Lutyens, he pointed out a large rock in the park which had fallen in love with one of the Manor boys who sat on it.[22]

Edwin Lutyens thought the dreariness of the Bishop's regime very bad for his daughters, describing it as 'no fun at all allowed – a sort of Church-all-day feeling and solemnity of a royal code',[23] but perhaps it was just as well that Lady Emily was with Leadbeater in Australia, given the exploits in Europe of her former colleague Wedgwood. Now disowned by the Society and on the run from the police because of criminal charges including drug abuse and buggery, Wedgwood had left England at very short notice, briefly taking refuge with Gurdjieff at Fontainebleau before setting up with his minions in Paris, where he indulged in a riot of promiscuity and drugs. When money ran low he turned to the long-suffering Annie

Besant for help and she put him in touch with Dutch Theosophists. But it was not long before their patience or their funds ran out, and Bishop Wedgwood was reduced to paying bills by smuggling cocaine in the head of his episcopal crozier.

TWELVE

Life Classes

One consequence of the post-war enthusiasm for youth noted in the last chapter was a general interest in educational reform, based on the belief that shaping the minds of young people might be the best way to prevent another war. Experimental pedagogy was therefore high on the popular agenda, as theorists and teachers debated how to produce that ancient desideratum: the community of complete human beings, the world of rounded individuals whose creativity, openness of mind and spiritual evolution would defeat the selfishness that had undoubtedly promoted the last war.

As theories multiplied, western gurus found themselves well placed to contribute to the debate. Theosophy and Anthroposophy had always emphasised the ideal of the balanced person, whose physical and mental capacities are not developed at the expense of his spiritual welfare. They had also devised organisations to embody their ideals. These ranged from voluntary lodge meetings, summer schools and conferences to the kindergartens and primary schools opened by Besant, Tingley and Steiner, and included elaborate universities complete with their own research departments. The two societies now argued that the best way forward was a pedagogy that blended modern teaching methods with ancient spiritual truths.

Not everyone shared in the general optimism. Gurdjieff regarded high-minded talk about world peace and the Brotherhood of Man as so much hot air. He also shared Freud's pessimistic view that the cult of such notions had actually played a significant role in precipitating the war. Widening the gap between ideals and actual behaviour had imposed an intolerable strain on individuals and whole societies, producing the characteristic hypocrisy of late-nineteenth-century society and intensifying hidden conflicts. But even Gurdjieff subscribed to the fashionable interest in educational reform, albeit in his own idiosyncratic way.

Establishing your school was not necessarily a matter of bricks and mortar, though many spiritual academies found new uses for old country houses and required appropriately substantial funding; they still do. Krishnamurti taught at times in the open air, his schools doubling as summer camps; Annie Besant and Anna Kingsford lectured in drawing-rooms; and Steiner even set his followers to construct their own building.

What mattered most, though, was not the place but the style of teaching. Ouspensky articulated this preoccupation in his theory of 'school', which held that it was impossible to acquire true esoteric knowledge without access to a legitimate pedagogic tradition.[1] The core of spiritual education was not to be found in dogma but in the transmission of living ancient wisdom, which was unlikely to be in purely verbal form – hence the interest in movements and exercises. The difficulty was that such wisdom could not be acquired by the individual on his own, either by study or by introspection: you could not sum up universal truth in a set of phrases to be learnt by heart. Everyone needed a teacher who had himself been taught. The teacher was therefore vital, as was his place in the apostolic succession.

But where do you find such a teacher? How do you go about your quest? And – most puzzling of all – how do you know when and whether you have been successful? For what, after all, can count for 'success' in such a venture? The esoteric knowledge you seek is, by definition, hidden – so much so that you may not recognise what you are looking for even when you find it. This involves, at the very least, trusting your soul to an unproven authority, as Ouspensky had done – unproven because, however successful he or she might appear to have been with other pupils, there was no way of knowing: the fugitive nature of spiritual growth means that all its appearances are deceptive.

Furthermore, in the western liberal traditions which formed all the teachers in this book to a greater or lesser degree, each individual is held to be unique. This means that even if X is genuinely in touch with the esoteric tradition and demonstrably the right teacher for Y, there is no certainty he will be the teacher for Z. Last, there is the formidable problem of what constitutes 'wisdom' in the spiritual sphere. A piano teacher's skill might be measured by the prowess of his pupils, a doctor's by the health of his patients. But how do you measure the success of a spiritual school – assuming that the very notion of 'success' in such a context isn't anyway a gross vulgarism at odds with the nature of the enterprise to which it refers?

Blavatsky and Leadbeater had relied on claims to direct inter-course with the Masters and their own powers of persuasion to support their authority. Gurdjieff took much the same line. The more scrupulous Ouspensky and Steiner, sensitive to claims of charlatanry, struggled to establish an authentic esoteric lineage and pedagogic tradition.

Krishnamurti came to exactly the opposite conclusion. Instead of looking for an esoteric tradition, he believed it was up to individuals to find their own way forward. Indeed, tradition and doctrine might be positive barriers to personal progress, for each person could only find their own path and no one else's. It was precisely Theosophy's downfall that each day in the Society brought a new article of faith for its members to swallow. But the passion with which he expounded this idea put Krishnamurti himself in an awkward dilemma, for though he increasingly disclaimed personal dominion he was well aware that his followers regarded him as their master. And if he were not a master, why did he go on teaching?

He sometimes tried to resolve this paradox by withdrawing from his public mission as a teacher, or by insisting that he wanted no disciples and that his purpose was not to impart a specific doctrine but to invite those who might chance to hear him speak to reflect on their own situation and then find their own way. On these occasions he presented himself not as a teacher but as an example. For most of his audiences the distinction was unconvincing. The very passion with which he spoke, reproaching his hearers with their failings, was enough to suggest moral and spiritual command; and his implicit rejection of positive doctrine was in itself a constructive teaching.

There were also cynics who hinted that he was hardly likely to abandon such a profitable career. For Krishna was now becoming big business. Throughout the 1920s, especially after he began to travel through America, where religious revivalism is usually the order of the day, he gradually became a kind of star, combining the appeal of good looks, exotic origins and religious charisma. Skilfully organised by Raja, who metamorphosed during the decade from Krishna's rival to his friend and business manager, his appearances drew ever larger crowds. His fame brought substantial financial rewards but made it even more difficult to convince audiences that he had no positive doctrines.

The problem of teaching pupils without simply moulding them in the teacher's own image was an abiding preoccupation for anyone who saw spiritual evolution and not personal aggrandisement as their objective. Western culture's emphasis on the primacy of selves made this inevitable, providing another source of paradoxes for those who cultivated eastern religious doctrines which dwelt on the necessity of ridding oneself of personality as a first step to enlightenment. Indeed, this was ironically one of the earliest stages on the Theosophical Path, though Krishnamurti was the only major Theosophist who made any attempt to realise it.

Count Herman Keyserling tried to resolve these paradoxes by presenting his work not as instruction but as dialogue, and himself as a master of ceremonies not a pedagogue.[2] The function of his School of Wisdom in the small central German town of Darmstadt was to promote understanding and enlightenment through discussion. Born in 1880, Keyserling was an intellectual Baltic nobleman who travelled extensively in the East, and lived mainly on his remote Estonian estates until driven out by a revolution which impelled him to Berlin in 1918. There in the following year he married Bismarck's granddaughter.

A student at the Universities of Dorpat and Heidelberg, Keyser-

ling had been trained as a Kantian Idealist. Like Steiner, he drew
heavily on Goethe for his philosophical and spiritual nourishment.
He was also deeply influenced by Houston Stewart Chamberlain's
Foundations of the Nineteenth Century, and by the Austrian philosopher and mystic Rudolph Kassner.[3]

What little of his fame survives derives from the Philosophy of
Significance, the dismally unpromising Germanic name for a mode
of thought which its inventor was never able to define satisfactorily
in all his enormously prolific writings, though it seems to come very
close to the basis of Theosophy – the sense that there is a
recognisable and eternal value or meaning underlying all phenomena, which can be intuited though never fully articulated. This
value or meaning is the fundamental reality common to all cultures.

Keyserling took a close interest in the Society, especially after his
visit to Adyar in 1913. He was strongly attracted by oriental
philosophy, especially Buddhism, which he contrasted favourably
with the materialist philosophies of the West. At the same time, like
Steiner, he warned against trying to adopt eastern ways and insisted
that we must find a way forward through our own spiritual and
philosophical traditions. Nevertheless, he believed that Orientals
can teach us two vital truths – truths which look surprisingly like the
doctrines of the German Idealist philosophy Keyserling imbibed in
his university days.

First, there is the fact that understanding – the perception of
significance – exists beyond words: like our response to music, it
cannot usually be expressed in language. The highest poetry
conveys a sense of it – though, precisely for that reason, such poetry
is untranslatable. Westerners, who set more store by expression
than understanding, deny this: they think that what cannot be
articulated in words has not been – and perhaps cannot be –
understood. Second, there is the doctrine that truth as wisdom is
subjective. But Westerners see truth as objective fact, and they want
to express it in the form of knowledge. The ultimate forms of
western knowledge are science and technology, and the more these
forms of knowledge dominate western thinking, the more they
marginalise other notions of what truth might be.

According to Keyserling, these two ideas – that understanding exists beyond words, and that truth is subjective – can be found together in Indian philosophies, in the notion that thought is not merely a means of articulating reality; it *is* reality. For Westerners thought is a means to an end – mastery of the material world – which distracts them from understanding the spiritual world or even noticing its existence.

Keyserling agreed with Yeats that Theosophy's error was to attempt a rapprochement between religion and western science, between the truth of subjective wisdom and the truth of objective fact. This attempt inevitably entailed trying to reach inner reality from outside, the spiritual through the material. It aims at knowledge, not at being. Here Keyserling comes near to his contemporary, the philosopher Martin Heidegger, who approached these questions through the route of academic philosophy. Both take the view that science can only produce knowledge, not understanding or wisdom.

According to Keyserling, two classes of men know this and approach adequate articulation of significance by different routes. These classes consist of artists, and what Plato called philosopher kings: those whose wisdom gives them the right to govern others. Artists are the discoverers or even the creators of meaning (Keyserling blurs the distinction), and art embodies eternal 'significance', always instinctively recognisable for what it is. But higher than artists are philosopher kings, who bestow meaning on a whole way of life. Plato and Buddha are two such – and no doubt Keyserling had a sneaking suspicion that he was another.

In the ferment of new ideas which swept Germany after the war Keyserling became fashionable. Like Steiner, he succeeded in grafting popular interest in all things oriental on to the native cultural tradition. In 1919 he was invited to settle in Darmstadt by the Grand Duke of Hesse, who took a serious interest in spiritual matters (as his descendants still do). The grand duke lent Keyserling a villa, where the philosopher established what he called his Free School of Philosophy – free in the sense that all topics were open to discussion and there was no fixed syllabus. By 1920 this had evolved into the School of Wisdom, though after a brief life as a sort of college at Darmstadt, the school became a yearly colloquium convened in locations throughout Europe – meeting one year on the beach at Formentor.

The most interesting feature of this school, which never quite threw off its drawing-room origins, was its founder's determination to let every voice be heard. Keyserling wanted to avoid imposing his own views. Instead he introduced the notion of creative polyphony which the school would harmonise in its colloquia. The objective was not to produce philosophers – thinkers with rounded coherent systems – but philosophical men: individuals capable of formulating questions and looking at problems from many angles. This, in Keyserling's view, was the only sound basis of spiritual and social progress. The discussions were published in the magazine *Leuchter*, and the same approach is reflected in Keyserling's own later writings, which value the fragment over the treatise, the aphorism over the paragraph. Despite his admiration for Goethe, Keyserling's literary ideal, like Heidegger's, was the gnomic Hölderlin. Completeness can only be achieved in death. Indeed, completeness *is* death. Life is inevitably partial, subjective, fragmentary.

Nothing could be more different from Steiner's attempt to establish his own school of wisdom not far away from Darmstadt, at Dornach near Basle in Switzerland. Steiner had already founded an anthroposophical group associated with his theosophical work, and in 1911, some time before leaving the Society, he dedicated a building for it in Stuttgart, where he had a strong personal following. Soon after cutting his links with Theosophy he began to raise funds for an HQ in Switzerland. The foundation stone of the new building was laid at an afternoon ceremony in September 1913 amid a howling gale and premature darkness, but these omens were disregarded and Steiner completed models for the main structure by the end of that year. Work soon began, and the buildings, intended to incarnate Goethean artistic and spiritual ideals, were named the Goetheanum.[4]

Calling on a wide range of talents from wood-carving to glass-staining, the actual process of construction was visible evidence of Anthroposophy's practical and communitarian ideals in action: artists and intellectuals, artisans and amateurs, lay members and leaders, all working together to produce a wooden palace over sixty-five thousand cubic metres in size, erected on stone foundations and roofed with Norwegian slate. Steiner not only designed the building: he directed every aspect of the work, including the intricate decoration. He also laboured on the building himself in the intervals from touring Germany and Central Europe to preach his doctrine. Nothing like it had ever been seen before, and in its brief life – it was burnt to the ground in December 1922 and immediately replaced with a concrete successor – it became a place of both spiritual and aesthetic pilgrimage, a visible expression of the Steinerian world view.

Following Goethe, who derives the idea from cabbalistic notions of creation as God's inhalation and exhalation, Steiner envisages the earth as an organism which breathes in and out with the seasons.[5] In summer the earth exhales, in winter she inhales. Human life is incorporated into this process of respiration, developing according to cycles which are seasonal, historical, global and cosmic. Man changes psychically and spiritually at the equinoxes. Humanity is therefore part of an evolving macrocosmic spiritual/physical organism which it recapitulates microcosmically. The spiritual history of mankind is part of this process. Steiner believed that in the modern era mankind had lost the spiritual, aesthetic and cognitive unity for which it now pined. All artefacts – from spoons to buildings – should in his view contribute to the restoration of that unity by every available means.

The design of the Goetheanum was meant to express Man's organic involvement in nature and the building's own role as a focus of spiritual energy. Every aspect of the building therefore had to be both functional and expressive. Despite extravagant claims for the uniqueness of Steiner's vision, there were strong hints of art nouveau in both the decoration and the incidental structural features, such as columns and window-frames, each of which was distinguished from the others by detail. But underpinning these decorative features is Steiner's conviction that artistic forms must flow from inner spiritual necessity if they are to be great and significant, in the way the best German art always must be. Everything about the building was therefore meant to flow, embodying Goethe's theory of metamorphosis, according to which all organic things are endlessly changing and evolving, and Steiner's own perception of the auras or lines of force which, he believed, surround living creatures. The basic design feature was consequently the absence of straight lines where these could be avoided. Everything was decorated. Even the glass in the windows, the walls and the ceilings were coloured according to Steiner's Goethean theory of colour, different shades indicating different soul-states and producing different psychological and spiritual effects. The building materials, including glass, were specially made, and the dyes were produced only from plants.

The demand for curves caused considerable engineering problems, not least when it came to mounting the two intersecting wooden domes of different sizes which crown the main building (one of them larger than the dome of St Peter's). Because the domes cut into one another, they could not be strengthened by the usual hidden support of tension rings, and a new method had to be found so that they supported one another. But these engineering problems were subordinate to the larger consideration of the building's multiple purposes. The space under the domes, which seated over a thousand people, was both lecture hall and meeting-place for anthroposophical congresses on the theosophical model. There were also living quarters and extensive studios and workshops, and like the site at Point Loma the Goetheanum soon became not just a temple but a social, artistic and educational centre, as the activities involved in constructing it were continued for other purposes once the buildings were complete. For Steiner, like Gurdjieff, was both therapist and mage. His objective was the integration of all aspects of life into a unity. By this means, the spiritual evolution of the individual could contribute to the evolution of the community. The Goetheanum was therefore envisaged quite literally as a cosmic project.

This *folie de grandeur* certainly owed something to Wagner. When deciding to settle in Switzerland after the authorities in Munich refused him a building permit, Steiner had spoken to the donors of the land at Dornach about establishing a new Bayreuth there, and soon afterwards he attended a performance of *Parsifal* in Wagner's own theatre. *Parsifal* is the opera in which the composer's theory of the *Gesamtkunstwerk*, or total art work, in which all the arts unite to produce a sacramental drama, is applied to the Grail myth. It made a profound impact on Steiner, who was already interested in the notion of drama as a route to religious understanding and a sacramental celebration of that understanding. He had found something of the sort in Edmond Schuré's attempt to re-create the Orphic rituals on the contemporary stage. Combining ideas from Wagner and Schuré with his own doctrine, he produced the Mystery Plays, which were to become the focal point of activity at Dornach and have remained in the anthroposophical repertoire to this day.

These plays, which trace the spiritual evolution of the same characters through four stages (a fifth was never written), combine the arts of speech, movement, colour and design in a Wagnerian synthesis which is given a new twist by Eurythmy.[6] Steinerian Eurythmy (as distinct from Dalcrozian Eurythmics) is defined as visible speech and song; it is based on the idea that we are affected not only by the sense of words but also by their sound. This sound is produced as invisible waves disturbing the air, and the waves can be translated into visible shapes, resembling the natural lines of force embodied in Steinerian painting and sculpture. But words also signify something, and the shapes can therefore be used simultaneously to articulate meaning.

Like Gurdjieff, Steiner believed that dance rhythms were involved in – and therefore disclose – the origins of the cosmos; and that ancient temple dances now lost or degenerated beyond recognition expressed both this, and man's relationship to that cosmos. Everything in creation is rhythmically inflected: the calamity of modern life is that we have lost our sense of natural rhythms, both in the world and in our own bodies. Recovering them in dance – an art in which all human faculties are involved – would teach us something about both cosmology and cosmogony. And because it is also the art which sharpens our sense of space and time (and the relationship between them), dance is potentially the medium in which meaning, history and expressiveness are all most potently combined in the movement of the human body – a way, perhaps, of recovering that ancient mathematical formula which had stirred Mr

Felt and his friends to establish the Theosophical Society forty years earlier. It is therefore the essential medium for Anthroposophy: the means by which the discursive science of spirit can be translated into the immediate apprehension of Being.

An enhanced sense of *Being* – as opposed to mere existence – was also the objective of the epoch's most notorious school, based at the Château du Prieuré des Basses-Loges. Here Gurdjieff established the new version of his Institute for the Harmonious Development of Man in October 1922, beginning (as he said himself) 'one of the maddest periods of my life' – and, he might have added, of anyone else's.

In sharp contrast to Steiner's mobile art-nouveau vortex of force-lines, the château is a severe but elegant mansion whose balanced windows and elaborate decoration express the hierarchical, worldly ambience of seventeenth-century France. Yet Gurdjieff was to turn it into his own version of the Goetheanum. About forty miles from Paris and set in a large park at Avon near Fontainebleau, the building is surrounded by a high stone wall and approached through gates opening on to a courtyard with a fountain. Taking it first on a lease, Gurdjieff eventually bought the place for seven hundred thousand francs from the widow of Maître Labori, the lawyer who had represented Dreyfus.

The surrounding estate extended to about 250 acres, but although the house was structurally sound and luxuriously appointed, with fine formal salons and an orangery, it had not been lived in since 1914 and the rooms were dirty, the gardens almost derelict. Gurdjieff therefore took a house in Auteuil and began work at once, setting some pupils to clean the château while others worked on the sacred dances, using the Dalcroze Institute in Paris for their rehearsals. Eventually these were transferred to a disused aircraft hangar, dismantled and re-erected in the grounds of the château and equipped with stoves, a fountain, coloured-glass windows and a dais covered with fine carpets which ran right round the room. The floor of this building – known as the Study House – was made by flattening and drying the earth on which the structure stood, and the walls were decorated with designs and improving texts, rather like an enormous exotic sampler. It held three hundred people.

The usual lying and skulduggery also started straight away, a new prospectus for the institute claiming a world-wide membership of five thousand, a resident staff of experts on every conceivable subject, and a dazzling medical department in which patients could undergo psychotherapy, hydrotherapy, magnetotherapy, electrotherapy, dietotherapy and duliotherapy.[8] In fact, the staff consisted of Gurdjieff and his older pupils: Stjoernval, the Hartmanns and the Salzmanns; the institute's syllabus looks like an exotic rehash of theosophical doctrine and Sufi exercises; and the total membership probably amounted to little more than 150. But since the divergence between appearance and reality was one of the Master's most serious themes, perhaps these discrepancies were in order.

Of 150 or so pupils, about forty eventually became residents at the Prieuré (though the number fluctuated considerably), and a bizarre mixture they made, about half of them hailing from Russia and eastern Europe and the other half from the English upper middle classes. The eastern Europeans were mainly Slavs and Armenians, most of whom spoke neither French nor English. In 1923 they were joined by the surviving members of Gurdjieff's family, who made the trip from Georgia. If nothing else, the eastern contingent added the required exotic colour to the institute. Keeping to themselves, few of them learnt French, and when the Master periodically threw them out they were very much at a loose end. In the mean time they staged his sacred dances and lived off his bounty.

Thirty years earlier most of the English contingent would have taken to Theosophy. Many were indeed dissatisfied members of the Society in search of a more rigorous doctrine and a more stringent personal discipline. They had come to the right place. For Gurdjieff offered precisely what Theosophy now lacked: hardship, difficulty, excitement, novelty – and the distinctive blend of supportive control and exhilarating freedom which results from abandoning one's comfortable life and submitting to another's will.

Above all, he provided just what many Theosophists, disciplined or otherwise, had always fruitlessly craved: contact with a real

Master of Wisdom; a being who, if not quite one of the Immortal Brotherhood himself, appeared to be in direct communion with them, or with whatever Ouspensky meant when he referred to the Source. But it was only in part that Gurdjieff drew his authority from this communion. What really counted was his own personality: the power that persuaded even many of his enemies that he was a force to be reckoned with. Nothing less than absolute submission to that was demanded.

Life in the Prieuré followed the patterns established at Brocton and Essentuki, and the residents lived as though under permanent siege, which in a sense they were. The enemy was Gurdjieff himself. He imposed his usual intermittently benevolent despotism, now also insisting that the inmates observe not only his arbitrary will but a whole series of prison-regulations administered by subordinates. These regulations prevented pupils from being in certain places at certain times or from leaving the premises without permission. They also extended to daily life within the house and gardens. Many of the rooms were luxuriously furnished, Gurdjieff having acquired some contents with the house, but these were reserved for rich visitors, new arrivals, occasional favoured pupils, and Gurdjieff himself. They were christened 'the Ritz' by the other inhabitants, themselves relegated to attics on what was appropriately known as the Monk's Corridor, where they were segregated according to sex and slept in monastic austerity. Children lived apart from their parents in a small house in the park, and were cared for by adults on a rota basis.

Though the routine at the Prieuré was occasionally varied by the Master's whim, its basic pattern was predictable and spartan.[9] Work began after a breakfast of coffee and dry toast between six and seven. It continued until lunch at twelve. This usually consisted of bread and soup. There was more work after lunch, and pupils then had some free time before dinner in the evening at seven. Dinner was followed by gymnastic exercises, dances, talks and discussions from about nine, often lasting until far into the night. Sometimes it was three or four in the morning before they got to bed. This regime operated on weekdays. On Saturdays it was varied with communal Russian baths and a feast with dances, when Sparta gave way to

Central Asia. The visits of distinguished strangers were often marked by banquets. On the other hand, Gurdjieff imposed a severe fast for Lent: an enema followed by several days on only oranges or sour milk, several days more on nothing at all, one day on bouillon and one day on beef steak. Sunday was always a day of rest.

The meals were cooked and the rooms cleaned by the pupils, who worked hard. To prepare breakfast, the cook had to rise by four-thirty to stoke the ovens, fill the coal scuttles and make the coffee and toast. Immediately after breakfast, twenty-five-litre tureens of soup were set to simmer, and the kitchens cleaned. While some pupils were cooking, others were growing vegetables, tending and killing chickens for the pot, chopping wood, polishing furniture and floors and repairing the large house.

In sharp contrast to the spiritualising, disembodying tendencies of Theosophy, which disdains human existence as an unfortunate necessity in the scheme of things, the Work,[10] as it came to be known, emphasises physical labour and communal projects. While Keyserling's followers indulged in aristocratic dialogue and Steiner's found God through art and good works, Gurdjieff's pupils lived in a bracing frenzy of hard labour, group meetings and psychological exercises designed to waken the soul from its slumber. It was this – rather than his elaborate doctrines – that gripped the members of the English contingent, inured as most of them were to the buttoned-up life of the British upper middle classes. These men and women came from the comfortable world then being satirised in the novels of Aldous Huxley, D. H. Lawrence and E. M. Forster: a world where menials did everything for their employers short of performing their bodily functions, and the employers in consequence experienced a spiritual death.

A. R. Orage was among the earliest pupils at the Prieuré. He saw his adventure in a heroic light, telling his devoted secretary at the *Little Review* as he left England for the Prieuré that he was 'going to find God'.[11] Having arrived at the château equipped with little more than this desire in his heart and a wonderfully appropriate copy of *Alice in Wonderland* in his pocket, he was surprised to discover that the search for God involved him in nothing more than heavy digging all day and every day in a completely pointless hole.

When Orage complained to the Master about the depression and fatigue induced by weeks of this futile exercise, Gurdjieff told him to stop moaning, put his back into the work and dig harder. Near to collapse and rebellion, Orage obeyed, and just when it seemed he could continue no longer, the pain barrier was passed and he began to discover deep satisfaction in a labour which was no longer exhausting, a job well done and obedience to his master's will.[12]

Imposing impossible tasks was only one of the ways in which Gurdjieff continued to create friction. He delighted in insisting on an uncongenial regime, humiliating his pupils in public and even encouraging quarrels between them. These were supposedly all part of a therapeutic grand strategy of shock treatment which took the official form of mental, emotional and spiritual exercises.

The exercises, which took up a good part of the day for those who were not doing housework or gardening, ranged from simple ordeals, like Orage's digging, to confusing multiple tasks. Society ladies who had never done a day's work would be set to peel potatoes or weed a flower border with teaspoons while learning a few Tibetan words or memorising Morse code. Others were given complicated exercises in mental arithmetic while performing certain move-ments. A Harley Street doctor was deputed to light the boiler, writers cooked and chopped, and eminent psychiatrists shovelled manure or scrubbed the kitchen floor. The place had the atmo-sphere of a savage boarding-school run by a demented if genial headmaster, and most of the pupils loved it – for a while.

Personalities were taken into account when assigning trials, and Gurdjieff ignored the usual distinctions between important and trivial, serious and humorous. Individuals assigned to certain jobs were told to do them in half the usual time, and then in a quarter. Others were put to work in groups with colleagues they detested. Intellectuals were forbidden to read, while sensitive souls mucked out byres and slaughtered animals. The basic pedagogical principle was contradiction: do what you hate, whatever seems hostile. Do the impossible; then do more of it; or work at two impossible tasks together.

The exercises were based on two principles. First, there was the need for voluntary conscious suffering, which Gurdjieff says we must undergo if we are to wake up to reality and stay awake. But few individuals can achieve this on their own. So the second principle follows: that suffering must be induced in them by a teacher to whom they give absolute obedience. Hence the necessity for 'school'. Without faith in the teacher, Gurdjieff argued, there is no evidence of a real will to suffer. As we have seen, Ouspensky had already rebelled against this prescription several times. Others were perplexed when Gurdjieff mischievously pointed out that the tendency of his pupils to obey him, however capricious his commands, showed that they needed and deserved their suffering. Revolt was sometimes greeted with banishment, sometimes with the announcement that *at long last* the rebel had made some progress, had learnt to stand on his own two feet.

The effects of this teaching were variable. Delighted society ladies often found that they were indeed more self-aware for a day or two, but the effect wore off as soon as they returned to Paris or London and turned to the next fad, which usually happened when the Master insulted them, as he invariably did. For Gurdjieff believed not only in making life difficult for his pupils but also in making himself difficult. He had no time, he said, for triflers, though he took their money all the same: 'shearing his sheep', as he called it.

Serious students found themselves apparently making spiritual progress under this torture, but that was only the beginning. Gurdjieff always found new afflictions for them, driving everyone under him to the limit and beyond. There could be no question of relaxation. Constant vigilance was the watchword, constant striving, constant strife. The journalist Carl Bechofer Roberts, a colleague of Orage's who had met Ouspensky and Gurdjieff while reporting the Russian Civil War, describes the Master constantly urging his English pupils on at their tasks with the injunction to 'Skorry' and to go 'Queeker.'[13] If this was the strategy of the Fourth Way it was also spiritual Darwinism gone mad.

In its extreme form Gurdjieff's teaching could undoubtedly have serious consequences for those who were neither able to cope with it nor to escape from the Master, and there were to be breakdowns and even suspected suicides among his pupils.[14] Yet these consequences are the measure of his power. It can, of course, be argued that the breakdowns and suicides would have occurred anyway, that in such cases it is precisely the neurotic and the vulnerable who are attracted to such a man. Once under his spell, many of the weaker and more credulous pupils regarded him as possessing godlike powers. They explained everything that happened in terms of his will. When, for example, he released them from a painful task imposed by himself, it was as though a benevolent deity had intervened in their lives. Some even greeted the mending of an erratic car engine as evidence of his wizardry.

The mixture of seriousness and outrageous frivolity is Gurdjieff's puzzling hallmark, and it made superb copy. Journalists loved the Prieuré and it featured extensively in the popular papers between 1922 and 1925. Both the *Daily Mirror* and the *Daily News* ran articles on Gurdjieff, discovering everything from Satanism to nudity at the Prieuré. There was a more dignified though no less inaccurate piece in the *New Statesman*, which made the inmates of the Prieuré famous as the 'Forest Philosophers'.[15] But however much the press misrepresented his activities, Gurdjieff played up to the notoriety. Like HPB he also enjoyed confusing the issue with outrageous stories of his own. Much of the news value was self-generating, and had more to do with the interest in Gurdjieff's rich and titled sponsors than with the Work itself. When Lady Rother-mere came to inspect her investment during January and February 1923, that was definitely news.

The appearance of Gertrude Stein and Upton Sinclair at the Prieuré also attracted press attention, as did a flying visit from Diaghilev, who considered staging the sacred dances. The majority of the visitors were less celebrated. J. G. Bennett turned up for a five-week stay in the summer of 1923, and later the same year Gurdjieff briefly took in Bishop Wedgwood of the Liberal Catholic Church, keeping a low profile after the latest scandal. Many people came from Paris for the day or the evening in expensive cars to observe the exercises and dances, and Gurdjieff and the Prieuré were definitely in fashion – very much part of the Parisian circus.

The visitors were sumptuously fed and wined, and when they stayed the night it was of course in the Ritz. But the food and flattery Gurdjieff handed out didn't please everyone, and many wondered whether their host's elaborate politeness and tall stories were not ways of making fun of them. Some visitors were frankly hostile. Curious about the new guru and earth-father so many of his friends were talking about, and egged on by Mabel Dodge Luhan – who made the mistake of assuming that their common abrasiveness would produce affinity – D. H. Lawrence and his wife Frieda visited the château in January 1925.[16] They hated every minute of it. Lawrence called the Prieuré a 'rotten, false, self-conscious place' filled with people 'playing a sickly stunt'.[17] The only oddity about this reaction is that anyone should ever have expected Lawrence and Gurdjieff to get on in the first place: they were rivals, not soulmates. Others shared Lawrence's scepticism, though few expressed it in the violent language of Wyndham Lewis, who called the Prieuré's proprietor a 'Levantine psychic shark'. Bechofer Roberts more temperately and amusingly described the English at the Prieuré as 'mystical Micawbers [waiting] patiently for something super-conscious to turn up'.[18]

One who waited in the almost certain knowledge that this 'something' would be death was the establishment's most famous resident, Katherine Mansfield, who died there. Mansfield went to Fontainebleau because of Orage, who had published her first stories in the *New Age*. By the time she arrived she was dying with TB and she knew it. Throughout the previous year she had been looking for a miracle, as she wrote to Dorothy Brett, in the form of a doctor who could cure her. At the same time, she suspected that it was more than her body which needed curing, and there was a sense in which, at the very end of her life, she was beginning to identify her own 'cure' with the world's. At the very least she wanted a doctor she could believe in, who would be sympathetic and understanding, not merely a clinical physician – a man of power, rather than a man of skill.

Her first candidate was the Russian Dr Manoukhin, who treated his patients with X-rays directed at the spleen. Manoukhin was recommended by her friend Serge Koteliansky; and Mansfield, who had a weakness for Russians, envisaged him as a sort of Chekhov: tender, wise and powerful. She travelled to Paris in January 1922 to see him, and he promised he could cure her. Reporting the good news back to Middleton Murry, her husband, Mansfield nevertheless confided to her diary that her feelings about the doctor were divided. Half of her saw him as a good man, half as an unscrupulous impostor. Even so, she began a course of treatment, while taking the precaution of consulting a doctor in England.

She was also taking other measures. Just as she began her consultations with Dr Manoukhin, Orage sent her an anonymously published book about the psychic control of physical ailments. *Cosmic Anatomy, or the Structure of the Ego* by Lewis Wallace, one of the *New Age*'s backers, made a profound impression on Mansfield, who included quotations from it in her scrapbook. But Wallace was soon to be superseded by Gurdjieff.

Mansfield arrived in Paris at the beginning of October just as Gurdjieff was establishing himself at the château. Orage reached the city on the 14th, *en route* for the Prieuré, and other Gurdjieff pupils visited Mansfield at her hotel. She moved into the château on 17 October, where they installed her in the Ritz, and she was immediately drawn to Gurdjieff, though she described him when they first met as looking 'exactly like a desert chief'.[19] The house itself was cold – there was already ice on the fountains – and she treasured the warm clothes her friend Ida Baker sent from Paris; but she was comfortable and apparently happy, though her letters reveal a certain understandable irritability. For by this time Mansfield had only a few weeks to live.

Perhaps her condition is best described as febrile. She wrote to Ida Baker several times in a Gurdjieffian spirit, reproaching her for being self-indulgently gloomy:

> Why are you so tragic? It does not help. It only hinders
> you. If you suffer, learn to understand your suffering but
> don't give way to it. The part of you that lived through me
> has to die – then *you* will be born. Get the dying over![20]

Mansfield herself had entered into life at the Prieuré as well as she could, despite being moved from the Ritz after her short stay there to a small bedroom on the general corridor on the top floor, with bare boards and a scrubbed table. (She was moved back to the Ritz when her condition perceptibly worsened in December.) To add to her difficulties Gurdjieff then changed the routine of the inmates, announcing that in future the work involved in the daily running of the house would be done at night. Mansfield found herself scrubbing carrots in cold water at midnight, and sharing her rough food with the other pupils – a considerable change from the invalid fare of the last few months: 'You eat what you get and that is the end of it.'[21]

Everyone took part in the housework and cooking on a basis of turn and turn-about. The castle was run like a true commune, and futile tasks – such as Orage's digging – were, she thought, the exception. There were vegetables to be grown, logs to be chopped for fuel, repairs to be carried out and a large garden and park to be maintained. Gurdjieff even kept livestock, including cows, which figured in Mansfield's life when the Master ordered her to spend part of her days on a specially constructed platform over the cowbyres where she could inhale the odours: a traditional peasant remedy in eastern Europe according to one of her biographers, who observes that Mansfield has little to say about the effect of the remedy in her letters and diaries. The little balcony was gilded and painted with birds and insects and supplied with rugs and mattresses; and two of the female pupils, Adèle Kafian and Olga Ivanovna Hinzenburg (who later married Frank Lloyd Wright), were instructed to look after her there.

Mansfield was certainly changing in the last weeks of her life. She saw Orage almost every day, and referred in their conversations to her old self as dead: 'the late lamented Katherine Mansfield'.[22] She regretted the partiality and malice of her earlier stories and wanted to become a new sort of writer who showed characters struggling with Gurdjieffian notions of consciousness and self-remembering in stories she could 'show to God'.[23] It was not to be.

Gurdjieff had a passion for banquets and festivals of every kind, but he made a special feature of Christmas, with elaborate decorations, meals and ceremonies. Mansfield joined in the celebrations, looking forward also to the Russian New Year on 13 January, when the little Prieuré theatre was to be opened. She invited her husband for the occasion, and he arrived on the 9th, finding her 'a being transfigured by love'.[24] While Mansfield had been living at the Prieuré, Murry had been following his own search for God, in a cottage at Ditchling in Surrey with a sort of English provincial Gurdjieff, Miller Dunning, who practised yoga and had just published his mystical tract *The Earth Spirit* (1920). Dunning told a friend that Ouspensky's teaching was evil. Favourably affected by Gurdjieff at the time of Mansfield's death, Murry himself was later to dismiss the Work as 'spiritual quackery'.

That evening there was dancing. Walking up to her room afterwards with Murry, Mansfield was seized by a spasm of coughing on the stairs. By the time they reached her room, blood was welling out of her mouth, and within a few minutes she was dead, aged just thirty-five. They buried her three days later, on 12 January 1923, in the Protestant cemetery near by, in the presence of her husband, her sisters and a few of her friends from the château, including Gurdjieff, who might have taken her short life as an omen for the Prieuré.

THIRTEEN

Calamities

If the 1920s were years of hope and excitement, they were also a time of violent débâcles. The Wall Street Crash was symbolic of a general tendency to abrupt swings of mood which affected everything from finance to religion. After the brief post-war boom and the political optimism aroused by the founding of the League of Nations, the late '20s saw a swing towards rampant inflation, agricultural depression, industrial slump, mass unemployment and political upheaval. Spiritual teachers were affected, as religion gave way to politics in popular interest. By 1933, when Hitler came to power and the developed world was rapidly polarising into three camps – liberal democracies, Fascist and Communist dictatorships – the Theosophical Society was in decline, the Work over, the Darmstadt School of Wisdom closed, Anthroposophy heavily repressed, and many of the leading figures in this book dead, mad, silent or in exile.

Violence first struck Anthroposophy in the form of a fire which burnt most of the first Goetheanum to the ground on New Year's Eve 1922. The unfinished wooden building was extremely vulnerable to sparks from workmen's tools or the heating system, but arson was suspected and with some reason. A virulent pamphlet campaign against Steiner was under way in Germany, where he was threatened with retribution for crimes which ranged from being a Jew, a traitor, a black magician, a Carbonarist, a Communist and a Fabian to staging financial frauds and – best of all – supporting the IRA.[1]

Most Anthroposophists attributed the disaster to sabotage, and some suggested that there was more to the fire than mere human agency. They put the blame on Ahriman, Lord of the Dark Face. According to Steiner, Ahriman had been making trouble in the world since 1879 when the Archangel Michael took over the divine guidance of mankind and began a cosmic process of enlightenment.[2] He was fiercely resisted (in incidents such as this one) by the powers of evil. The physical destruction of the Goetheanum was thus accounted for in terms of a *meta*physical war – an explanation which did not prevent the Anthroposophical Society from collecting the heavy insurance due on the building.

The sedateness of Steiner's life, which consisted almost entirely of lecturing on esoteric subjects and building the Goetheanum, makes a grotesque contrast with the hysteria generated by the charges and counter-charges that flew about his head. Anthroposophists replied to their critics in equally vigorous terms, accusing them of spiritual and physical sabotage and assassination attempts on their leader. It seems that some of the charges were justified. Political murder was common in Germany, where defeat, rampant inflation and political chaos were prompting all sides to look for someone to blame for failure in the war. In September 1921 Hitler had become Chairman of the Nazi Party on a programme of anti-Communism, anti-Semitism and national regeneration. By November 1923 he was one of the leaders of a right-wing uprising against the government, for which he was gaoled the following year. It is a vivid illustration of the electric atmosphere in Germany during the '20s that even Steiner's staid meetings, like Communist and Nazi Party rallies, now had to be patrolled by discreet bands of burly young men, ready to fall on any troublemakers.

On the other hand, it was this very agitation that stimulated interest in Steiner's work in German-speaking countries just after the war; especially in his native Austria, where the whole political structure had collapsed. Though defeated and riven by political conflict, Germany remained unified; despite the loss of territory, it was essentially the country it had been before 1914. The Austro-Hungarian Empire was completely destroyed, Vienna reduced at a stroke from the imperial capital of central and eastern Europe to the status of a remote provincial city in a minor country vulnerable to more or less permanent regional upheavals.

Steiner turned his mind increasingly to social and political affairs, exercised by the urgency of establishing a stable world order in central Europe if another round of wars and revolutions were to be avoided. His interest in these matters was sharpened by Lenin's success in Russia and by the spread of atheism through Europe that was expected to follow the Russian Revolution. Already in 1917 and 1918 he had discussed his plans with high-ranking politicians in Munich and Berlin, including the then Chancellor of the German Empire, Prince Max of Baden, and there is some evidence that his papers on the topic eventually reached the last Austrian Emperor, Charles VI, who is unlikely to have read what was anyway too late and too fantastic to save his dynasty.

The basis of Steiner's thinking was the Threefold Social Order or Commonwealth, about which he published a book in 1919.[3] This founded political and social organisation on the tripartite division of the human organism into thinking, feeling and willing faculties which correspond to the cultural, political and economic spheres. Just as thinking, willing and feeling are inescapably connected in the human being, so the cultural, political and economic are connected in the state.

This is a familiar idea and the Threefold Commonwealth is, of course, a variant on the oldest way of thinking about the state in terms of the human body. But whereas ancient theorists tend to equate the ruler with the head and the other classes with bodily parts and organs, Steiner suggests that in the modern age of what he calls the consciousness soul a less hierarchical analogy is required. The terms for this analogy were, he thinks, established during the French Revolution, whose makers nevertheless misunderstood them. 'Liberty, Equality, Fraternity' is indeed the right slogan for the modern age, but only if we realise that each belongs to a different sphere of existence.

Steiner's ideal state involves spiritual and cultural liberty, political equality and economic fraternity, i.e. co-operation. Communities that attach the wrong value to the wrong sphere (such as the English with their passion for political liberty, or Communists who work for economic equality) are bound to miss the spiritual path, which can only appear when all three spheres are in the right relationship. Broadly speaking, Steiner's scheme reduces the role of the state to the enforcement of political rights, sharply increasing the importance of individual effort and voluntary associations, making it look curiously like later twentieth-century Conservatism.

This tripartite structure, which was also to provide the basis for Steiner's system of 'curative' medicine, was much elaborated by its originator and his followers, but its significance in the present context is that it exists at all. Far from turning his back on society by retreating to an Ojai or a Prieuré, Steiner ambitiously proposed his scheme as a way of redeeming the world from chaos. At the same time he accepted that it could not be imposed – that, on the contrary, to inaugurate by force the huge changes necessary in social organisation would be to vitiate the whole raison d'être of freedom on which it was based. In keeping with anthroposophical principles, the Threefold Order could only be of value were it to emerge organically from communal need. But this was not to be. The doctrinal subtleties of the Commonwealth were easily eclipsed by the harsher doctrines of Communism and National Socialism.

Steiner's own days were also numbered. Though he threw himself into raising money to rebuild the Goetheanum almost at once, he was shattered by the fire and may well already have contracted the mysterious illness which was soon to kill him. Nevertheless, on New Year's Day 1923, the lecture and play scheduled to celebrate the solstice were performed, more or less in the smouldering ruins, and business thereafter went on as usual. Steiner also took the opportunity of the fire to reform the Anthroposophical Society, which had so far been an extremely loose organisation of which he himself, rather bizarrely, was not technically even a member. The anomaly arose because Steiner distinguished between the Anthroposophical *Movement*, which he saw as a legacy to mankind, and the Anthroposophical *Society*, which was merely its local vehicle. Steiner led the Movement while claiming to be detached from the organisation of the Society. The new Goetheanum was to bring the two together, becoming not only the spiritual focus of Anthroposophy but the society's administrative and financial centre. At the same time, the School of Spiritual Science was to be firmly established. The school corresponds to the Theosophical Society's Esoteric Section and is restricted to privileged members who are sworn to secrecy about its teaching.

Steiner also attended to the establishment of more children's schools.[4] These were devoted to putting into practice the principles he had developed while working as a private tutor, and they emphasised the cultural and spiritual development of the child. Visiting England for this purpose with Marie von Sievers in August 1923, he stayed first in the Yorkshire town of Ilkley and then at Penmaenmawr on the Welsh coast, where it rained. He and Marie enthused over the Druid circles in the mountains overlooking the town. Struggling up the hill with his successor-to-be, the worthy Gunter Wachsmuth, Steiner even relived Druid ceremonies by means of clairvoyance, effortlessly incorporating them thereafter into his esoteric synthesis. Inevitably, he had a similar experience at Tintagel in the following year, when he visited the West Country from Torquay and found the sodden air filled with spiritual beings who gave a glitter to the raindrops. The astral light showed him where the castle had stood and even provided him with a vision of Merlin and the Knights sitting at their Round Table, each with an appropriate sign of the zodiac over his head. He later compared the Arthurian court with the Knights of the Grail, hinting that the Anthroposophical Society was following in their footsteps.

The new Goetheanum was inaugurated on Christmas Day 1923, less than two months after Hitler's first bid for power in the Munich *putsch* of 8 November. It was completed five years after Steiner's death and stands to this day as Anthroposophy's centre. The original wooden structure had given way to concrete, but in certain respects this was an improvement, for concrete is a more congenial medium than wood for the flowing lines of Steinerian art. But Steiner was now sixty-three and so ill that he could not digest his food and took hardly any nourishment. He spent most of the last months in his room writing an autobiography and dictating letters and lectures to Wachsmuth. He refused orthodox medical treatment.

A pioneer of holistic therapy, he devised his own pharmacopoeia.[5] He also established a school of anthroposophical medicine. One of its first students was Ita Wegman, the woman who came closest to him in the last months of his life. Like Mesmer and Baker Eddy, Steiner insisted that the root of serious illness is not organic but spiritual. It has two main causes. The first is bad karma. Having rejected Leadbeater's *Lives of Alcyone* fifteen years earlier, to the extent of making it one reason for his departure from Theosophy, Steiner nevertheless gave his own lectures on *Karmic Relationships* in which he traces the line of civilisations through which different spirits reincarnate, refraining however from Leadbeaterian snobbery and favouritism. He also emphasises the role of Christ the Healer in modifying the chain of incarnations.[6] Though the doctrine of karma – responsibility for past misdeeds – seems to conflict with the belief that Christ died once and for all to redeem our sins, Steiner explains that the contradiction is only apparent: we do indeed pay for the past but Christ intervenes to prevent our evil deeds building up into a sort of credit account for Ahriman, who would otherwise overwhelm the world with the tide of negative etheric energy arising from past iniquities. Our 'payment' can take the form of mental and/or physical illness.

But the second possible cause of serious illness is the onset of a new stage in spiritual evolution, which can produce symptoms such as the 'Process' Krishnamurti took to be a sign of his progress along the Path. That is how Steiner saw his own illness: death was simply a matter of taking the next step and Crossing the Threshold, as Anthroposophists call it. This he did on 30 March 1925, just fourteen weeks after Hitler's release from gaol.

Though the Prieuré was never physically threatened, its problems were just as acute. After a brilliant beginning, the community there was soon in deep financial trouble. Gurdjieff's activities were always very expensive, and the running-costs of an establishment which often numbered upwards of forty permanent residents and a shifting population of a hundred students must have been high, even though the inmates did all the menial work themselves and attempted to grow some of the food. According to reports in the press, there were fixed charges for staying at the institute – a minimum of £17. 10s. per month for regular pupils, and a great deal more for occasional guests in the Ritz – and the proprietor charged large fees for the occasional cures he was asked to perform on alcoholics and drug addicts. Rich supporters also continued to help out now and then, and some of those who intended to settle at the Prieuré on a long-term basis seem to have invested their own capital.

The real problem, however, was Gurdjieff himself. The regular running-costs of the château were trivial beside its proprietor's vast and uncontrolled occasional expenditure. Like Blavatsky, Gurdjieff lived for the moment – and each moment involved luxurious personal tastes and big ideas. He drank vast quantities of brandy, travelled a good deal and staged innumerable banquets. He also indulged his pupils. When loose cash was available, instead of paying bills he was inclined to blow it – on a huge collection of bicycles, for example, a group holiday for selected inmates or a general hand-out.[7] Returning from one trip, he summoned the residents to a meeting and asked for a report on each from the deputy left in charge, who recorded their crimes in a small black book. He then gave each of them a sum of 'pocket money' in inverse proportion to their alleged good behaviour and left them to puzzle over his action. Though Gurdjieff had a sharp commercial nose and a genius for raising money, funds were therefore always in short supply. Many members of the community – including the Master's own family and his poverty-stricken Russian followers – were in no position to contribute anything but labour and their empty bellies, and the Prieuré's (and his own) constant need for more funds increasingly diverted Gurdjieff's energies from his teaching.

It is at this point that the puzzling relationship between Gurdjieff's pedagogy, his erratic behaviour and his financial juggling becomes impenetrable. From 1917 to 1922 it had been possible to argue that the difficulties his pupils encountered were all part of a great scheme designed to wake them from their slumbers: Gurdjieff turned the dangers of the time to their advantage. But it is also true that he had a positive relish for living from hand to mouth which continued even when existence was less hectic. Improvisation and the unexpected may have been vital to his method; they also happened to suit his way of life. Ouspensky had understood this from the beginning: it prompted him to distinguish the man from the method. Once Gurdjieff was settled in France – and, indeed, for the rest of his life – he continued from choice to live at a prodigal rate.

It can be argued that such recklessness eventually destroyed all his grand projects, such as the Prieuré. Prodigal with money; capriciously rude to potential backers; shocking, disgusting and rude; and subject to violent swings of mood and interest, Gurdjieff's own character was the source of all his troubles. Yet it was also clear to his admirers that this dangerous, headlong progress through life was the source of his electrifying effect on them. What Gurdjieff produced in others was vitality, excitement, an enhanced sense of being. The distribution of bicycles was not important in itself: the constant expectation of the unexpected was.

The only way to pay for this flamboyance was to mine American gold. In December 1923 a reconnoitring party was sent to prepare the way, consisting of his old friend Stjoernval and his new John the Baptist, A. R. Orage. Orage, who announced in America that 'At least one of Jesus's preaching trips was financed by rich women',[8] was clearly well suited to his new task and he at once began attracting interest through his old intellectual and journalistic network. But the blatantly publicity-seeking nature of the trip contrasts strangely with the secretive nature of earlier (and later) Gurdjieffian practice, with its emphasis on the difficulty, serious-ness and exclusiveness of the Work. The American trips of the later 1920s were determined attempts to popularise Gurdjieff's doctrine. As such, they failed.

In the spring of 1924, the Master took between thirty and forty of his pupils to America to give public demonstrations of the sacred dances. Despite advance publicity, free tickets, a receptive audience and the newsworthy presence of a policeman, sent by the authorities to ensure that no erotic displays took place on stage, the visit was not a popular success. The press amused themselves with fantastic accounts of the Prieuré but the general public took little notice.

It was a different story with the intelligentsia.[9] Credit for this must go to Orage, who introduced Gurdjieff to a wide range of literary contacts, many of whom showed an interest. In November 1924 Orage followed up his teacher's visit and returned to America to set up a network of Gurdjieffian groups. In December of that year he published an article about 'Religion in America' in the *New Republic*, the first of many which underlined – sometimes tacitly, sometimes explicitly – the need for a man like Gurdjieff. He also acquired a new companion, Jessie Dwight. Orage had met Jessie in the Sunwise Turn Bookshop, where he held court in New York during his 1923 visit. She was a partner in the shop, where one of the temporary employees, C. S. Nott, also became a devoted follower of Gurdjieff. It was not long before Orage, with Nott's support, acquired a band of distinguished pupils and interested observers.

The novelist and critic Waldo Frank came to Gurdjieff through reading Ouspensky's *Tertium Organum*. Frank was married to Margaret Naumberg, founder of a New York school that based its pedagogy on psychoanalysis and the educational theories of Steiner and the American philosopher John Dewey. He was a visionary who studied mysticism and oriental religions; he and his friend Gorham Munson were introduced to Ouspensky's work by the poet Hart Crane, a brief visitor to the Work. Frank, Munson and Crane were all preoccupied with a mystical interpretation of American history in which America appears as a visionary place where the spiritual regeneration impossible in the old world is a real possibility, and they wondered whether Gurdjieff might not be the agent of this spiritual renewal. Other writers, including Zona Gale, Kenneth Burke, Schuyler Jackson, Carl Zigrosser and Muriel Draper (in whose studio many meetings were held), stood more aloof, though their work shows signs of Gurdjieff's influence. Herbert Croly, Editor of the *New Republic*, also followed the Work for a while, but he was still in quest of the old grail of union between science and religion, and Gurdjieff's example offered him little.

Croly was a conservative: a public figure concerned with social renewal. At the other end of the cultural and political spectrum stood Jane Heap and her companion Margaret Anderson. Heap and Anderson were the Editors of the influential *Little Review*. This radical journal, founded by Anderson in 1914 – the golden age of literary magazines – at first dabbled in both politics and literature with a strong leftward slant. But after Anderson met Heap in 1916, they focused more on moral and religious matters. Under Gurd- jieff's influence, public affairs gave way entirely to private develop- ment. Heap was the stronger character, supporting Anderson through a breakdown and more or less taking over the magazine after World War One. Their links with the Prieuré were streng- thened when Anderson's nephews, Tom and Fritz Peters, were boarded out there after the divorce of their parents. Heap's interest in the Work was further stimulated by friendship with Maeter- linck's former mistress Georgette Leblanc, who became a devoted follower of Gurdjieff, and the three were leaders of a lesbian Work group operating mainly in Paris during the 1930s and '40s.[10]

Perhaps the most interesting member of this (very loosely constituted) circle of American writers and intellectuals was Jean Toomer, a mixed-race misfit whose one published novel, *Cane* (1923), caused something of a stir. For several years Toomer was Gurdjieff's most devoted follower, exerting himself to find money and members for the Work. Mabel Luhan was one source of funds. She took an interest in every new development, talking vivaciously while her current Indian husband, Tony, sat silently by. Although her efforts to persuade D. H. Lawrence to take an interest in Gurdjieff had been unsuccessful, this didn't dampen her own enthusiasm, partly because she was besotted by Toomer.

Through Toomer's agency, the ever-generous Mabel even offered her famous ranch at Taos as the site for a Gurdjieffian institute, plus $15,000 to set up a foundation. Gurdjieff characteristically turned down the ranch and took the money, to finance publication of his proposed literary works. Some time later he decided to accept the ranch, but it was no longer on offer. Though one of Ouspensky's dottier later followers was to set up an institute in Mexico, it is hard to imagine Gurdjieff among the cactuses.

Most of these contacts came through Orage, who set up in America as a teacher in his own right after Gurdjieff returned to Paris. Though he taught Gurdjieff's ideas, he taught them in his own way. In character Orage was closer to Ouspensky than to Gurdjieff – an autodidactic intellectual with a passion for order and coherence. Just as Ouspensky had arranged Gurdjieff's ideas into a System within which there were logical relationships and a hierarchy of concepts, so Orage turned his teacher's work into a clearly defined scheme which he expounded to his group.[11] On the other hand, Orage resembled Gurdjieff in the hypnotic power of his personality and his drive to dominate others, either by charm or will, though he lacked entirely Gurdjieff's earthiness. It was Orage and Ouspensky between them who interpreted Gurdjieff to the wider world in the 1920s.

Orage's role was to prove crucial when the brief glory days of the Prieuré ground to a halt in a typically violent way. In July 1924, shortly after his return from America, Gurdjieff was involved in a bizarre accident on the Paris–Fontainebleau road. Gurdjieff's driving was like his life.[12] Whenever he decided on an excursion, companions would be chosen, the car piled high with luggage and exotic picnics, and they would set off for Vichy or Nice or the mountains at breakneck speed with Gurdjieff at the wheel. He refused to slow down at signposts or to take any notice of the petrol gauge. When the car ran out of fuel, as it always did, one of the party had to walk to a garage and fetch a mechanic, because the driver insisted there must be a mechanical failure. If a tyre punctured it was changed, but the punctured tyre was not replaced. When both the spares were damaged, subsequent punctures had to be repaired *en route*. Each missed road, each breakdown, necessitated a stop, while the passengers dismounted to argue about a course of action and Gurdjieff directed operations or sat quietly by, watching the discussion. Arriving at their destination, invariably after all the hotels had closed, some would be ordered to knock up the manager of the best hotel, whom Gurdjieff would then charm into providing an enormous and elaborate meal, proposing endless toasts and tipping the waiters lavishly at every opportunity. After a few days, the party would pack the car and repeat the whole process on the journey back to Fontainebleau.

On this occasion Gurdjieff was driving alone. The facts of the incident have never been clearly established and never will be, but its very obscurity plays an important part in Gurdjieff mythology. It was the Master's practice during the middle of the week to visit

Paris, where he kept a flat, leaving the running of the Prieuré in the hands of his devoted follower Miss Ethel Merston, an English-woman of Portuguese and German-Jewish origins who later became a pupil of Sri Ramana Maharshi.[13] Gurdjieff often took Olga de Hartmann with him on these journeys as secretary/companion, but on 5 July 1924 he travelled back from Paris to the Prieuré alone, arranging for Madame de Hartmann to return on the train in the stifling summer heat. No explanation was given for this, but Gurdjieff's followers were accustomed to respect his every whim without explanation, which is what she did. Nor did he explain why he had asked the Prieuré mechanic to check the car with particular care before leaving, or why he had taken the curious step of giving Olga power of attorney over his affairs that very day.[14]

That night, he was found lying under a blanket on the side of the road near his crashed car, with his head on a pillow and what seemed to be serious injuries, including acute concussion. How he came to be there and not in the ruins of his car, or simply flung to one side, was never accounted for. Some people assumed that a sympathetic passer-by had arranged the cushion and blanket while going for help. Others said that a guilty motorist had made Gurdjieff comfortable before fleeing from the consequences of the crash. Yet others – including the incredulous gendarme who found him – credited the Master with the superhuman power to crawl from the car and dispose himself under the blanket with a last titanic effort before collapsing. Gurdjieff himself simply commented later that 'this battered physical body of mine crashed with an automobile going at a speed of ninety kilometres an hour with a very thick tree'.[15]

The Master was brought home, apparently close to death. Without their teacher's will to guide them, many of the Prieuré residents fell into despair and apathy. Others continued with their work, in the spirit of Fritz Peters, who had taken to heart Gurdjieff's injunction to stick at his labour whatever befell. At eleven Fritz was a difficult and lonely child who had warmed to the owner of the Prieuré in their brief acquaintance, taking everything he said with the utmost seriousness. His assigned task was to mow the huge lawns of the château in as short a time as possible. When

Gurdjieff was brought home from his accident, Fritz went on cutting the grass with renewed intensity. Gurdjieff had been ordered to rest in complete quiet and Madame de Hartmann asked the boy to stop his noisy mowing. He refused: his orders were to cut the grass, and that he would do, come what may. Madame de Hartmann warned him of possible consequences to the patient, whose life was said to be in the balance, if the noise continued; but Fritz was not compelled to stop. By now he was mastering the task: soon he would be able to cut all the grass in three days, as Gurdjieff had originally ordered. So it was another setback when the gradually recovering Gurdjieff told him that he must now reduce the mowing-time from three days to one. Nevertheless, he achieved this goal. Such was Gurdjieff's influence on those who loved him.[16]

There were those, however, who wondered whether the accident had not been an elaborate ruse.[17] They suspected that Gurdjieff had set up the crash and exaggerated his injuries for his own reasons. But if so, what was his purpose? The answer may lie in subsequent events. The normally bustling Prieuré was hushed and numbed as the pupils wondered what would happen to them if the Master died. In fact he recovered with surprising speed – a minor miracle that he attributed equally to his strong constitution and his spiritual powers.

But no sooner had he recovered than the pupils, still shocked by the apparent vulnerability of their hitherto impregnable teacher, found their fears for the future confirmed in an unexpected way. In September 1924 Gurdjieff announced the 'liquidation' of the institute and set about banishing most of its members, including the Russians. Broadly speaking, those who could afford to support themselves and contribute to the general upkeep – which increasingly meant Americans, dollar-rich in inflationary Europe – were retained, the others dismissed. This was not Gurdjieff's first clean-out of personnel: many had left when funds ran low in the previous year. It was not to be the last.

Though the Prieuré remained in operation for several more years, its great days were already over. Symptomatically it vanished from the front pages of the popular press as abruptly as it had appeared there. Eventually the principle of communality was restored, as disciples began to trickle back after the mass expulsions of 1924. But whatever it meant to the pupils, the institute had become a secondary interest for Gurdjieff: a place where pupils hung around on sufferance in the hope of crumbs from the esoteric table. His own attention had turned from teaching to writing.

The financial crisis of the mid-'20s played its part in this change. So, perhaps, did the death of Gurdjieff's mother at the Prieuré in 1925, and the illness and death of his companion Madame Ostrowska, in 1926. Both may have encouraged him to turn away from his public mission to a sort of private life. Everyone at the Prieuré observed that their teacher was subdued by his losses, though Madame Ostrowska's long and painful death from cancer did not prevent him siring a child by another woman in the mean time.

America also affected him. Writing and America were inextricably linked in Gurdjieff's career during the second half of the '20s. It was American writers who espoused his ideas and financed his writing, and many of them visited the Prieuré. Associating so much with writers, it was inevitable that Gurdjieff, always one to learn from his experiences, should turn to writing himself. The move from teaching to writing – or rather, from teaching in person to teaching by writing – was a major shift of emphasis, given his earlier habit of suiting teaching to individuals, for writing could only be concerned with general doctrine, not with particular cases. It also sat uneasily with his injunctions to Ouspensky and others not to falsify his message by putting it into print. Presumably he hoped for higher things from his own work.

Circulating in manuscript, his writings provided the material for Orage's American classes, at which sections would be read aloud and commented on by Orage, who expounded them in the light of his version of Gurdjieff's System. Between 1924 and 1931 Gurdjieff and Orage spent increasing amounts of time in America or with their attention directed there. Their American followers returned the compliment by crossing the Atlantic to seek out the Master in Paris. The Prieuré gradually revived, but it was now less of a dynamic spiritual powerhouse and more like a refuge for the remaining members of Gurdjieff's entourage and an expensive religious rest-home for rich, confused Americans who paid $100 per week to stay there.[18] The regime of working and feasting, bathing and talking, continued in a gentler form while the Master, more and more preoccupied with writing and financial troubles, spent his days in the Café de la Paix or its Fontainebleau equivalent, drinking coffee and armagnac, filling notebooks and dictating to a changing procession of amanuenses.

By 1929 Gurdjieff was again desperately short of money and general interest in his Work was waning, though there were still enthusiastic individual followers. During the second half of the decade, Orage and Toomer between them had raised over $20,000 and others made contributions according to their means, but it still wasn't enough. Between January and April 1929, the year of the Wall Street Crash and the Great Depression, Gurdjieff again visited America to raise funds.

He returned several times for the same purpose over the next few years, but his task was increasingly difficult. For one thing, even the American middle classes were feeling the financial pinch. For another, by the mid-'30s Gurdjieff had alienated almost all of his major pupils and old followers, except for Madame de Salzmann. Toomer was disillusioned, Ouspensky exiled, Frank had given up Gurdjieff years before, shaking his fist and telling his erstwhile teacher to go back to hell where he belonged.[19] Even the Hartmanns had been expelled from their paradise – for 'impertinence', according to the mischievous Gurdjieff.[20] Thomas de Hartmann remained unswervingly loyal to his master from a distance, spending the rest of his life in a touching attempt to explain the break with Gurdjieff without in any way criticising the cause of their grief. His wife even continued to visit her teacher at the Prieuré regularly, despite the fact that he shouted at her every time they met. The final break came when she refused to leave her seriously ill husband to perform some minor task at Gurdjieff's insistence.[21]

At last the faithful Orage, too, was dismissed from service. Orage's loyalty had been tested to the limit by Gurdjieff's endless peremptory demands for money, his deliberate rudeness to the sensitive American pupils so carefully cultivated by his disciple, and his habit of humiliating Orage in private and in public. Fritz Peters records an occasion at the Prieuré when he answered a summons to Gurdjieff's room, only to find the Master like a man possessed, screaming furiously at a pale and trembling Orage.[22] Pausing only momentarily to thank Fritz with a charming smile for the coffee he had brought, Gurdjieff resumed his screaming. The episode made the boy speculate about Gurdjieff's powers as an actor, just as Ouspensky had done a decade earlier. No doubt Orage took the lesson on board. Despite his weariness he regularly sent Gurdjieff dollar cheques, but by 1929 he was not sure he could tolerate the constant badgering any longer.

Jessie Dwight, by now his wife, was certain he could not. Jessie, who disliked Gurdjieff, had a mind of her own, and this hastened the break. Demanding submission, Gurdjieff could not abide rivals for his pupils' attention. Furthermore, he never allowed his lieutenants to leave of their own volition, preferring to precipitate the break as a sign of his own authority. Returning to America in the winter of 1930, he suddenly demanded that Orage's pupils sign a paper repudiating their teacher and his teaching. Orage, it was said, had fallen into Ouspensky's error: his System had nothing to do with Gurdjieff. It was too complicated, too intellectual, too clever. Yet even this dramatic move did not force the break. The mixed reactions of the pupils were superbly put in the shade when Orage, returning hastily to New York from a holiday in England, rose to the occasion and willingly signed the paper – thus repudiating himself.[23]

Magnificent and absurd as a gesture, it was little more than that, and it signalled the end of their relationship, which came on 13 March 1931, when Orage and his teacher met for the last time. Orage returned to Theosophy and journalism, but though he founded yet another literary magazine, the *New English Weekly*; took up the economic theory of Social Credit[24] which also obsessed Ezra Pound; and contributed to occult journals, the fire had gone out of him. He died in 1934. Yet even then his family could not quite escape the Master's long arm. When Jessie Dwight visited Gurdjieff in Paris after the Second World War, perhaps hoping for an explanation of his behaviour to her husband, he told her the tragic story of a brilliant man who was just too clever to grasp simple truths, and made her cry.[25]

FOURTEEN

The End of the Path

Nineteen thirty-one was also a turning-point for Krishnamurti. It marked a decisive break between the past and the future, signalled by the discovery that he could no longer remember most of his childhood and youth – and, in particular, his initiation into the Theosophical Society. His close friends, to whom he confided the discovery, found the oblivion to be selective and sometimes caught him out referring to people and events from the years he claimed to have forgotten. But whether the black-out was feigned or genuine, there could be no doubt about what it meant: Krishnamurti was turning from irritable tolerance of Theosophy to outright rejection. This was a painful process, and not only for his old friends. Krishna's role and character since the age of fourteen had been shaped by the Society and its rulers. As a result, his sense of identity was inextricably bound up with his attitude to Theosophy: a crisis in one inevitably meant a crisis in the other.

Forgetting the past was one way of coping with Krishnamurti's problems. Moving away from them was another. Since his first visit to California in 1923, he had come more and more to regard Ojai as his home, in so far as anywhere could be so regarded by a man constantly on the move and spending long periods in Europe and India. In 1931 Ojai became his permanent base and so it remained for nearly thirty years. From now on, the Atlantic and the Pacific were to separate him from his old patrons. With Leadbeater in Australia and Annie Besant increasingly frail at Adyar or in London, the World Teacher found himself making his own new life in America.

He could not have found a better place for his purpose. The climate was kind to Nitya's TB and the landscape reminded them of India. The cultural vacancy of California also gave Krishnamurti complete freedom to develop in any direction, or in no direction at all: his mind could become as empty as the desert. And the solitude of the mountains provided a welcome escape from the increasingly bizarre antics of European Theosophy.

Trouble between Krishna and his patrons had been brewing for some time. His disenchantment set in after the First World War with the embarrassing Leadbeater scandals and the absurdities of the Liberal Catholic Church, but though these offended his puritanism they were peripheral to the real problem. What concerned him more immediately was his own situation. For although Krishnamurti was increasingly inclined to dismiss theosophical practices and to question theosophical doctrine, he still tacitly accepted the idea of his vocation as *a* world teacher, if not perhaps *the* World Teacher. This vocation, however, had been defined by Besant and Leadbeater in specifically theosophical terms: the World Teacher's role, in their view, was simply to spread knowledge of Theosophy throughout the cosmos. Having rejected such a role, Krishnamurti had to find another, distancing himself from Theosophy without destroying his own credentials.

The first stage of this process was his rebellion against the Society's accelerating ceremonialism and triumphalism. Throughout the early 1920s he showed his distaste for the rituals of the Liberal Catholic Church, the Co-Masons and Theosophy's other proliferating sister-organisations, but matters only began to come to a head in 1925, after an absurd dispute with George Arundale. A strong and ambitious character who was eventually to become President of the Society, Arundale was already well-advanced in its hierarchy, despite breaching the tacit rule which said that Theosophy's leading figures should remain celibate.[1] He had done so in especially dramatic fashion by marrying an Indian girl, Rukmini Shastri, simultaneously violating Hindu caste, Theosophical convention and English racial prejudice. Nevertheless, Arundale was now a bishop in the LCC and permanently based at Adyar. As a means of consolidating his authority he had learnt to cultivate his psychic powers and 'brought through' messages from the Brother-hood of Masters at every opportunity.

During a visit to Huizen in July 1925 Arundale brought through fraternal directives thick and fast, ranging from the announcement of twelve Theosophical Apostles whom the Lord had chosen to work with him, to the order that Liberal Catholic priests must wear silk underwear for psychic reasons. (The underwear plan fell through when Miss Dodge finally baulked and refused to foot the bill for clerical vests and drawers.) He also entered into detailed communication with Master the Count in Hungary, discovering from this source that his new ally Wedgwood – and not Jinarajadasa, as announced by Leadbeater – was to be the next Mahachohan or Lord of the Five Rays. It was on this occasion that Krishna and others were confirmed in their fourth initiation and said to be *en route* for the final lap to complete divinity, while Annie, Wedgwood and the Arundales were forbidden to eat eggs.[2]

At seventy-eight the ever-suggestible Annie Besant was now firmly under Arundale's influence, and when the Ommen camp opened in August 1925 she proclaimed at his suggestion not only the names of seven new apostles – chosen, of course, from among the theosophical élite – but also the founding of a World Religion with New Mysteries (unspecified) and a World University, described by Arundale as a reincarnation of the University of Alexandria.[3] Nothing was said about the location, funding, teaching staff or accreditation of the university. No doubt the Masters would see to all practical details and there was plenty of blue ribbon left for the degree diplomas. However, the President did refer mysteriously to the Lords of the Dark Face, who were up to their old tricks and apparently wanted to interfere with these glorious new projects and even with the coming of the World Teacher.

Mrs Besant then left for Hungary to visit the castle of Master the Count, again at Arundale's behest, accompanied by a party including George and Rukmini, Wedgwood and Wedgwood's Polish boyfriend. Arundale had been instructed by Master the Count himself to ascertain the location of this castle by opening the continental railway timetable and choosing a destination at random. The destination was accordingly settled and the party set off. Lady

Emily Lutyens and Annie's old friend Miss Bright were told to await instructions to join them, and for the next few days the two women hardly slept a wink for excitement. A week later the travellers returned, having got no further than Innsbruck. Annie told Lady Emily, who had never seen her friend so agitated, that the Dark Forces had defeated them,[4] but she also said to another friend who had declined to go on the trip that he was the only sensible person among them.

Leadbeater was naturally displeased by these turbulent priests and their doings, most of which he had explicitly forbidden in a string of angry telegrams from Australia, but Wedgwood and Arundale were now beyond his control. He was not the only one to be annoyed. By the time the Apostles and his own fourth initiation were announced, Krishnamurti was ready to rebel against what he regarded as cynical, self-interested lies. Asked to confirm the Huizen initiations from Ojai where he was then staying, he refused point blank. With Nitya's deteriorating health on his mind, he had no more time for niceties.[5]

The difficulty was how and what to tell Annie, whom he still dearly loved. He shrank from upsetting her. Perhaps he also realised what pressure the old woman was under from her new advisers. Eager for power, Arundale had told her that it was the Master's wish that she resign the presidency of the Society in his favour; while Wedgwood, aware of Krishna's opposition to his schemes, whispered to Annie that not even the World Teacher was immune to the evil influences of the Dark Forces.

Krishna was unmoved by this campaign against him, though he found Lady Emily distressed by it when he arrived in England with Raja and Rosalind Williams in October 1925. But Lady Emily was also upset by his rejection of the Apostles and promotions, in which she fervently believed; and she doubted the wisdom of confronting Mrs Besant with the unwelcome news. Despite his anger, even Krishnamurti dreaded telling Annie about his views face to face. According to one report, he persuaded an official from the new World University to break the news, while he waited in a car outside Mrs Besant's house – a method bitterly pilloried by later critics, who used it to present Krishnamurti as dishonest, weak and evasive.

Hearing that Krishna could not accept either the so-called Apostles or the initiations, it is probable that Annie drew the logical conclusion: that her protégé also rejected the whole panoply of the Brothers, their psychic message and therefore the theosophical hierarchy itself – the whole structure of beliefs on which she had built her life. It was too much to take in, and Lady Emily later reported to Krishna tht she did not think Mrs Besant had really understood the bad news.[6] But others noted that Annie became physically ill after the visit and went into a rapid and perceptible decline from that moment.

Krishna was less reluctant to speak his mind to Wedgwood and Arundale, and they hinted in return that he was spoiling his own chances in the Society – an appeal to self-interest which outraged him further and confirmed his doubts. With Annie he continued to be more circumspect, suggesting to her when they met that Arundale was well-meaning but mistaken. When she persisted in referring to the Apostles at public meetings he finally decided that he must tackle her about the matter directly, but she seemed confused and unable to take in what he was saying. Emily Lutyens wondered whether she had been hypnotised by Arundale.

It was the sort of conclusion Theosophists were inclined to reach in the fervid atmosphere of the times, but it seemed to those about her that Annie was, more mundanely, in the grip of old age. Though she continued to travel and to address public meetings, nothing was quite the same. Even her power to hold things together within the Society began to flag. At the end of 1925 the whole Czech Section seceded in disgust at the squabbling among its leaders, the absurdities of the LCC and the reported immorality of notorious Theosophists, just as the Germans had twelve years before. With the Australians split, the Americans alienated and the whole Society in permanent uproar over the behaviour of Wedgwood, Arundale and Leadbeater, the task of running it became more and more difficult and Annie no longer had the energy to conciliate the conflicts or to conceal them.

Yet, strangely enough, the total membership continued to increase. Ironically, this owed something to the publicity which resulted from unsavoury scandals, but more to the popularity of its youth movement, to the OSE (whose members were not necessarily Theosophists) and to the growing personal prestige of Krishnamurti himself. In its early days (as now) the Society was very much the preserve of the elderly. For a brief, glorious decade from 1919 to 1928 it flourished among the world's youth as a sort of junior League of Nations. For what appealed to young people was not Theosophy's ceremonial and the psychic mumbo-jumbo but its humanitarian, pacifist and internationalist ideals, embodied in the summer camps and in the fetching person of Krishnamurti himself. His quiet, improvised talks about the need for peace and the conquest of egotism and desire contrasted sharply with the noisy formal rhetoric of conventional political and religious leaders. Krishnamurti stood, apparently, for freedom, happiness, mutual tolerance and self-fulfilment.

It is thus even more ironic that precisely this decade was the most difficult in his own life. No year was worse than 1925, when, as he wrestled with his distress and disillusion, surrounded by the very people who had brought them about, a bitter blow struck him. On 8 November 1925 he left Europe by steamer for Adyar with the usual entourage: Annie, Emily Lutyens, the Arundales, Wedgwood and the Rajagopals. Only Nitya was not with them as usual. He was thought to be too frail to leave Ojai. Worries about his brother's condition were hardly dispelled by Arundale, who brought through a cynical message saying that if Krishna confirmed the Huizen promotions his brother's life would be spared. Despite a wire from Ojai saying that Nitya had the flu and asking his friends to pray for him, and the ominous portent of a violent thunderstorm as they entered the Suez Canal, the party were optimistic, but on 14 November, shortly after George had communicated the Master's promise to Krishna, the news of Nitya's death reached the ship.

Krishnamurti was shattered. Not only was Nitya his one link with childhood: he was also the only person the World Teacher could trust to speak frankly and in confidence about the extraordinary life they were now living together. Constantly surrounded by admirers, and especially by adoring women, Krishna was nevertheless a lonely figure. Nitya's death made his solitude complete. Though he was to have other close advisers, and though he was soon to claim that Nitya himself, together with the whole of their past, had become a hazy memory, he was never again to be fully intimate with anyone.

Yet despite the initial shock, his friends noticed that he took the blow calmly. And in the long term the disaster did not annul Krishna's sense of his own great destiny. The fact that the Brotherhood of Masters had not protected Nitya as promised confirmed his mistrust of Arundale and his suspicion that the Masters were not what they were said to be by Theosophy; but it did not weaken his belief in the reality of spiritual powers and their inclination to single him out. On the contrary, Nitya's death seems to have strengthened his trust in his own destiny by cutting the final close link with his pre-Theosophical days, which in turn helped him to cast off Theosophy itself. Within weeks of his brother's funeral he had an inkling of what this destiny might be, when he spoke at the Adyar convention on 28 December. Referring to the Lord Maitreya, he suddenly slipped from the third person to the first, referring to 'I' and not 'he'. Everyone present instinctively recognised that something momentous had happened – that this was not Krishna himself speaking but the Lord Maitreya in him.[7]

Or almost everyone. Wedgwood and Arundale affected to notice nothing but an attractive young Indian speaking in his usual halting manner. They were very much in the minority. Even Leadbeater, who had arrived from Sydney in episcopal grandeur with a party of seventy, pointedly ignored Wedgwood and Arundale at the convention, saying to Krishna, 'At least you are an Arhat.'[8] He had every reason to be furious with his former friends, who had not only made themselves officially divine with five spurious initiations, but grossly flouted his occult authority. This didn't prevent him from accelerating his own stream of promotions and initiations, and the two parties openly accused one another of co-operating with the Dark Forces. In the past Annie had patched up quarrels in her flock, but this time rivalry had gone too far, the peacemaker was too weak, and the convention broke up in January without reconciliation.

Krishnamurti himself was confused about what had happened, but his confusion masked a crucial change of stance, a change he did not understand until it was complete. Something other than 'Krishna' had spoken through him at Adyar, that he was sure of: something which continued to speak throughout his life. He must therefore be a vehicle of some sort. But he was not *the* Vehicle of Leadbeater's expectations: therefore he was a teacher not by virtue of his role in the Theosophical Society but in his own right. By means of this shift of emphasis he abandoned his theosophical luggage while holding on to his spiritual status and remaining above the factional disputes within the Society.

The conflict continued to worsen in the following year, when the first of several annual meetings was held in Castle Eerde for a party of thirty-five invited members of the Society, followed by the usual summer camp at Ommen. Krishna also spoke each morning in the castle to a small group selected from the thirty-five. Annie was not asked to these meetings – for fear, he said, of upsetting her; for Krishna no longer talked of her favourite themes, the Path and Discipleship, and barely mentioned the Masters, urging each individual to find his or her own way without recourse to higher authority. This was to be the core of his teaching for the rest of a long life. But Annie inevitably felt hurt and excluded, and her advisers equally inevitably pointed to Krishna's behaviour as evidence of his pretensions, his betrayal of the Society's ideals and his personal disloyalty.

On 27 July 1926 the Lord Maitreya once again spoke through Krishnamurti as he addressed the crowd by the Ommen camp fire. This time Wedgwood took a stand and told Annie privately that the agency speaking through Krishnamurti was not the Lord Maitreya at all but a Black Magician. When Annie in turn confided this to Krishna he was horrified and told her that if she believed it he would never speak in public again. Once more the poor woman was trapped between opposing parties, but though her loyalty to Krishnamurti wavered this time, she nevertheless supported him. There was no question of giving up his teaching now that his incarnation as the World Teacher was at hand.

In the end Annie always put her trust in her boy – and for that one must admire her. Nevertheless, weary of the conflicts within the Society and doubtful of her own role now Krishna was ready to take up his mission – as she thought – she again considered resigning the presidency. Leadbeater advised her against this move. He was ready neither to give full power to the World Teacher nor to contemplate the possibility of Arundale's election as President. It was not the Master's will, he told her, that she should give up her burden yet, and to that authority she bowed.[9]

Krishnamurti, too, claimed to be weary of the strife and talked to Lady Emily about becoming a sannyasi, a wandering holy man who renounces the world to meditate on spiritual matters.[10] The idea of giving up everything was becoming increasingly attractive to the fraught young man, in proportion as Arundale and Wedgwood and their followers indulged their worldly passions. He spent his time at Ojai, especially in the winter, writing poetry and contemplating. Not that his contemplation had any content. His mind was instead a vacancy, an empty space in which the universal powers could work their will.[11] Krishnamurti thought of himself more and more, he said, not as a self but as a vessel, one whose task in the world was not to teach but to be a means for others, a mirror they might look into to find their own truth. This was a further move away from the Society: if they had made him what he was, then he would become nothing. From Theosophical Vehicle to universal vessel was but a short step.

The succeeding years of suffering and isolation, and the institutional shambles of the Theosophical Society, were to confirm Krishnamurti in his new role. Supported by a few close associates, he was to emerge by the early 1930s, like a brilliant butterfly from the crumbling chrysalis of Theosophy, with a public career which quite eclipsed even Blavatsky and Besant. There were to be those who saw this emergence as a portent and a pattern for his later relationships, which he was alleged to abandon as soon as they ceased to serve his purpose and his own greater glory.[12] Many in the years to come, including some of those closest to him, were to end by agreeing with Arundale and Wedgwood, in spirit if not in language, that Krishnamurti was a fake, though the bitterest accusations were published only after his death.

To Annie's considerable distress, Krishna's estrangement from Theosophy became overt at the 1927 Ommen camp. Though she had always prophesied accurately that the World Teacher's message might be unwelcome when it came, she no longer had quite the strength to face this fact herself. There were almost three thousand people present at the camp, including the British Labour Party leader George Lansbury, when Krishnamurti explained his situation in dramatic language. On 12 July he proclaimed that 'I am the Teacher. I have entered into the flame – I am the flame, I have united the source and the goal.'[13] A few days later he explained what these gnomic phrases meant in words that some found even more gnomic. In childhood, under his mother's influence, he had had a vision of Sri Krishna. Later, guided by Leadbeater, he saw the Master Koot Hoomi. Then, in maturity, the Lord Maitreya and the Buddha appeared to him. These persons, he had discovered, are all one and the same and he was now in union with them and with 'the Beloved', which is itself a mystic sense of union with reality. Krishna continued to use the image of the flame to express his condition, repeating at the same camp two years later that 'I am that full flame which is the glory of life . . .', a phrase which is intended to signify exactly the opposite of the egotism it seems to convey. The emphasis here is not on the 'I' but on the flame. The individual known as 'Krishnamurti' has vanished.

Though there was enthusiasm, even delirious excitement, at the camp, as usual not everyone was pleased. Some saw his words as a ludicrous arrogation of personal authority. Others were distressed by the implication that the ladder of Theosophy could be kicked away now it had served the purpose of producing Krishnamurti. The comforting doctrine of the Masters and Theosophy in general had become irrelevant because, as Annie herself had proclaimed in America only a few months earlier: 'The World Teacher is here.'[14] Unfortunately, his arrival had not taken the form she hoped. Wedgwood and Arundale naturally resisted the threat to the very organisation and doctrine that made them what they were, but Annie's distress went far deeper. It was not Krishnamurti's new-found authority she feared – far from it – but his insistence that the Masters and the Path were things of the past.

Leadbeater took a much subtler view, despite Jinarajadasa's angry complaints about Krishna's ungrateful behaviour.[15] Leadbeater not only accepted Krishna's words as proof that he really was the World Teacher, but treated him with a new reverence. He preferred to explain his differences with Krishnamurti by minimising the importance of the Teacher and by making a distinction between the mystic path, which Krishna followed, and the occult path open to Initiates.

Perhaps such casuistry was too much for Annie Besant, who had always been stronger on rhetoric than on logic. Unable to make subtle distinctions, she simply continued to love Krishna as an individual in private and to revere him as a great spiritual teacher in public. Acknowledging Krishna's defection and accepting that each individual must follow his own path, she proceeded to invent yet more new orders and organisations. Thus in the very same year that she closed the Esoteric Section throughout the world on the grounds that there was no further need for it now the World Teacher was here to fulfil his mission, the woman who had once sternly rejected sacerdotalism reformed the Order of the Star to accommodate the World Teacher's new needs, and announced the foundation of World Mother Day and the World Mother organisation and journal in a sermon given in the Liberal Catholic church at Adyar.

The World Mother was the high point of theosophical absurdity. Recognising this, newspapers predicted the imminent birth of a World Father, a World Infant and a World Great Aunt. The role of World Mother was meant by Annie and George as a job for Rukmini Arundale, who was said to be the Mother's representative on earth, presumably because, despite her initiations and honours, she hadn't yet got a suitably important post in the Society. Aware of the ridicule she was attracting, Rukmini soon quietly abandoned the enterprise and later explained to one of Annie Besant's biographers that the whole thing had been a misunderstanding.[16] Lady Emily continued to take it seriously, which is curious in view of her later admission that she had neglected her own six children, but perhaps the anomaly is a measure of just how completely Theosophy had taken over her life. This was the Temple of the Rosy Cross all over again, but better: being a mother herself, she could take a full part.

She wrote a book entitled *The Call of the Mother*, and wanted to launch a league of motherhood. She imagined herself as a maternal abbess at the head of a sacred order – with the additional advantage of 'wearing some kind of becoming nun's habit so that I would never have to worry about my clothes again'.[17] It was not to be. After one issue of the *World Mother* journal and a few articles by Annie and Leadbeater, the whole matter was quietly forgotten.

Amidst her confusion Annie still had a good grip on business. She arranged speaking-tours in America for Krishnamurti and herself with fees of up to $1,000 per lecture. She also delighted in touring Europe in a small aeroplane, giving talks at each stop.[18] Despite internal upheavals money was pouring in to the Society, through donations, legacies, subscriptions, the sale of publications and shrewd investments. Both Annie and Krishna attracted rich admirers with plenty of loose cash, who were ready to use it either for their daily expenses or for ambitious projects such as schools. By 1927 the Society owned five hundred acres at Ojai; houses in Wimbledon; schools, colleges and other real estate in England, America and India, besides the growing property at Adyar. Krishnamurti himself was becoming big business. Though he claimed to have turned down an offer of $5,000 a week to play Buddha in a silent film (an offer which led him to brag in later life that he could have been a film star), his writings were beginning to earn big money – so big that it was decided proper financial arrangements must be made to deal with the flow of cash. There was also the question of Krishnamurti's own future. Though he had £500 p.a. from Miss Dodge, which would meet his personal expenses, it would not begin to cover the cost of his world-wide travels, or the outlay entailed in publishing his speeches and poems.

The problem was solved by Rajagopal, who had been turned from Krishnamurti's rival to his closest friend, adviser and business manager after Nitya's death. A talented man who had taken a good degree at Cambridge, he gradually took over the OSE and the various business and publishing enterprises that arose from the talks given by the World Teacher. He also organised Krishna's personal itinerary: planning his trips, booking tickets and hotels, arranging talks and paying bills.

A trust was set up under the name of Krishnamurti Writings Incorporated, or KWINC for short, with Raja and Krishna on the board, plus three other trustees appointed by them. KWINC was a registered charity and took up increasing amounts of Rajagopal's time over succeeding years, as the relatively modest enterprise became a multi-million-dollar concern.[19] Eventually he became President of the Board of Trustees and Krishnamurti resigned his trusteeship to concentrate on teaching – moves that were to have serious consequences for both many years later. Krishnamurti's financial arrangements were complicated and variable, but basically he possessed, as he liked to claim, almost nothing of his own but a Pathek Philippe watch presented by an admirer. Needless to say, everything was paid for either by the trust or by generous sponsors, many of whom continued to provide extensive hospitality throughout the world for the rest of his life. Krishnamurti never went short of anything he wanted, from hotel rooms to luxury motor cars.

The emotional arrangements surrounding Krishnamurti were equally complicated. To some extent, Raja took the place of his dead brother – and not only with Krishna. Rosalind Williams, like Mary Lutyens, had been in love with Nitya. After his death she came closer to Rajagopal. Within two years, Raja, Rosalind and Krishna were sharing their lives at Ojai. With the support of Annie Besant, Rosalind and Raja were married in London in 1927. Their daughter Radha was born in 1930. Krishna lived with the three of them *en famille* at Arya Vihara, the tumbledown cottage with its six surrounding acres that Mrs Besant had bought at Ojai in 1923. Here Krishna acted as a second father to Radha during Raja's frequent absences on business – to such an extent that she assumed everyone must have a second father at home such as Krinsh, as she called him.

Throughout the 1930s and '40s Krishnamurti was to find with the Rajagopals the pleasures of domestic life and close friendship with contemporaries previously denied him. Life at Ojai revolved around the farm and garden. Raja lived in Hollywood during the week, managing the various businesses connected with the Krishnamurti Foundation, while Krishna himself looked after the menagerie of animals which gradually accumulated, or played with Radha. The luxurious holidays of the past were now replaced by a more spartan though still idyllic regime.

But Krishnamurti was also able to continue his work at Ojai. The valley's isolation promoted meditation and writing, while its comparative proximity to Los Angeles allowed for some social life. It was also the ideal place to hold summer camps on the Ommen model. The small tract of land bought by Annie Besant had been gradually extended until the Society owned a medium-sized estate in the valley, and the Order of the Star held its first annual meeting there in 1928. The Ojai camps were opened to the public in 1930. Their importance increased in 1931, when Castle van Eerde was handed back to Baron van Pallandt, who had married and produced an heir. Although camps continued at Ommen until 1939, Ojai was now the focus of Krishnamurti's attention.

It was just as well that proper financial arrangements had been made when they were, for the split between Krishnamurti and the Theosophical Society was imminent. In 1928 there was a bad-tempered gathering at Ommen in which Krishna threatened to disband the OSE if its officials continued to insist on their monopoly of the truth. Despite that and the increasing uproar within the Society, Annie accepted in public Krishna's doctrine of the variousness of truth – though ironically the text from the *Bhagavadgita* she chose to make her case ('Mankind comes to me along many roads') hints at precisely the theosophical metaphor of the Path which Krishna was to deny in the following year.

The final parting of the ways came on 2 August 1929. At the Ommen camp that year, in front of three thousand people in a talk which was also broadcast, Krishnamurti announced his belief that 'truth is a pathless land' and rejected study of the occult, acceptance of authority and religious ceremonial as ways to spiritual growth.[20] Acknowledging that many of his followers would be upset, he urged them to confront the absolute necessity of freedom. In future, he said, he would accept no pupils or followers, and he urged them to join no sect or church. Belief must be an individual matter: organisations cripple it. All he wished to do was to set himself and others free from bondage, whether mental or emotional, political or religious. He then formally dissolved the Order of the Star in the East. This was quite literally the end of the Path.

It was not a spontaneous move – the administrative changes it required were already in train, though Krishna was careful in his farewell speech to disclaim any financial motives for his change of heart – but it came as a shock to an audience composed largely of Theosophists, even though they had been listening to Krishna's message for some years. Theosophists were ill-equipped to cope with freedom. They had joined the Society to seek guidance from the Masters and from their appointed representative on earth, Krishnamurti. When he now told them that the Masters had no real existence, they felt betrayed and abandoned. Even those like Lady Emily and Mrs Besant who respected Krishna's decision to leave Theosophy found it difficult to understand the manner of his going, and the general feeling was summed up in Leadbeater's terse pronouncement that 'The Coming has gone wrong.'[21]

The inevitable bitterness spilt over into rows about money. Krishna's lofty claim that he owned nothing was now turned against him by George Arundale, who pointed out that most of the assets on which Krishnamurti depended were legally the property of the Society. Raja responded by citing the power of trustees to decide who should be the beneficiary of their funds. By the time the OSE was dissolved he had already ensured the transference of its assets to the Star Publishing Trust, controlled by himself.

The severing of Krishnamurti's links with the Theosophical Society was formalised in 1930 when he resigned from all its organisations. By 1931 the World Teacher was dead and buried and Krishnamurti was ready to begin his new life as an independent guru. Rather curiously, Raja remained a member of the Society and continued to cultivate good relations with Adyar, but Krishnamurti's spectacular defection sent the membership figures plummeting. Old members left in disgust or bewilderment and few new ones came forward.

Poor Annie, now almost completely senile, continued to endorse Krishna's words and actions without understanding them. This was just as well: what she did understand she disliked. They continued to see one another occasionally. When he visited his Amma for the last time, early in 1933, she hardly knew who he was. Mrs Besant died on 20 September 1933. Leadbeater, too, was ailing, and followed her on 1 March 1934. Krishnamurti attended the Bishop's funeral in Sydney but refused to enter the Liberal Catholic chapel where the service was conducted, standing outside instead. Other old-timers were also falling by the way. Lady De La Warr died in December 1930, Miss Dodge in 1935. Katherine Tingley had been killed in a car crash that same year and without her Point Loma rapidly began to crumble.

For some the end was also a beginning. Hubert van Hook threw off the theosophical yoke and made a new start, as a successful lawyer. George Arundale achieved his ambition and succeeded Annie as President of the Society. Although he entered on to a sadly depleted inheritance, at least he had the satisfaction of banning Krishnamurti from Adyar. But many of those who survived the débâcle lived on in limbo. The best time of Emily Lutyens's life was over and she knew it. Although she continued to love Krishna-murti, she never again understood him or his teachings and never found a substitute for the Society. Theosophy had brought her hope and happiness, the sense that there is a purpose in things and that she was serving that purpose. But though she could not follow Krishna, she found it impossible to remain a Theosophist. Still valuing theosophical ideals, she found them intolerably com-promised by the Society itself. As if awakening from a dream, she slowly saw all Theosophy's absurdities for what they were, and her misery was compounded by the knowledge that she had shamefully neglected her husband and children to follow an illusion.[22]

There must have been many like Lady Emily, cast adrift in a hostile universe. Perhaps their condition was best symbolised by Wedgwood. Finally driven into madness by the strains and excesses of his life, he lingered until 1951 at Tekels Park, the genteel theosophical estate near Camberley, where he wandered in a twilight world haunted by ghosts of the past and the shades of spectral Masters.

FIFTEEN

Private Lives

If youth was the keynote of the 1920s, and modernity the rage, in politics the fashion was for internationalist, socialist and pacifist movements. Communism had conquered in Russia. Democracy flourished in America, given a new lease of life by President Wilson's intervention in the war. Liberalism was triumphant in the nations of Europe. Even China and Japan were taking steps towards political reform. The League of Nations was set up to patrol the world in the cause of justice everywhere. There might even be hope of liberal treatment for the colonial empires. In the early '20s it seemed that perhaps the age of political enlightenment fore-shadowed by eighteenth-century philosophers had arrived at last.

Towards the end of the decade however, the political atmosphere darkened once more. Stalin tightened his grip on Russia, China lapsed into chaos, the military took over in Japan, America retreated into isolation, and the central European nations created by the Versailles Peace Treaty of 1919 revealed their weakness. The whole edifice of international relations was shaken to the founda-tions by the Wall Street Crash of 1929 and the slump which followed. Unemployment soared throughout the world; and in Germany, already plagued by the struggle between Left and Right, financial chaos and hyper-inflation, slump created the conditions for Hitler's rise to power. While Germany and Russia were undermined by civil war, America remained indifferent and Japan was preoccu-pied with the conquest of China, an uneasy peace prevailed in Europe in the early '30s. But as soon as Hitler and Stalin felt strong enough to threaten their neighbours, they revealed the vulnerability of liberal empires in Britain and France.

In such circumstances, spiritual teachers were faced by a dilemma. Their work with individuals and small groups was overshadowed by the huge political problems of the time – yet it was precisely these problems to which answers were most urgently required. The trouble was that most people tended to identify the spiritual with the private, assuming that it had little bearing on the public domain of politics. This was a tendency encouraged by Ouspensky, Gurdjieff and Krishnamurti, who all made a point in their work of addressing the individual – of claiming, indeed, that it was only through individuals that any real change could take place in the world, and that it was worse than useless to address problems at the political level. Caught between the necessity of responding to political challenges and the impossibility of doing so, most western gurus retreated into private life during the '30s, that characteristically political decade.

The darkening of the world scene between the mid-'20s and mid-'30s cast an especially ironic shadow over Annie Besant's decline and death. Despite the quietist tendencies of most Theosophical Society members, she had pursued a vigorous policy of social and political engagement during the twenty-seven years of her presidency. In the early twentieth century, Theosophy had been a major political force in the British Empire, with powerful friends in the Indian Home Rule movement, six MPs at Westminster and a future leader of the Labour Party (George Lansbury) to represent it, not to speak of influential supporters in the professions and high society. Yet, at the very time when the taking of sides had become essential if the liberal reforms and freedom of conscience espoused by the Society were to be preserved, Annie was deserted by Krishnamurti, who *taught* the doctrine of non-involvement, and succeeded by Arundale, who effectively *practised* it. As a result, the Society's mass support collapsed. Deprived of its romantic Indian figurehead and its social mission, the Society lost its raisons d'être. From then on, Theosophy was to be just another cranky religious group among many, with a loyal following in India and Ceylon and rapidly declining membership in the West.

If the Society was now finished as a major social and political force in Britain, its influence on spiritual trends was also in decline. Christian evangelism was reviving, in the shape of Moral Rearmament, the Oxford Group and their Catholic equivalents,[1] while youthful idealism went into the Communist Party and the Peace Pledge Union[2] – or into their right-wing counterpart, Sir Oswald Mosley's Union of Fascists. This pattern was repeated throughout Europe. In France opinion was polarising between socialism and the Catholic Right, while in Germany Hitler moved against all organisations showing the slightest sign of resistance to his regime, including Theosophy and Anthroposophy, which shared the fate of the Christian resistance. Churches of the Steinerite Christian Community were early victims, not least because Hitler detested pacifists. After the Anschluss and the annexations of Poland and Czechoslovakia, Waldorf schools were closed throughout the Reich and its dependencies. Even Keyserling was persecuted by the state. The Nazi Party was too confident of its own ability to embody the German Mission to need help or competition from elsewhere.[3]

For Gurdjieff, the early 1930s were a very low point indeed. It was as though his life reflected in its own curve the turn from glitz to gloom. He had quarrelled with most of his major pupils and rich backers, he was perpetually short of money, he was no longer a seven-day wonder in the press, and such reputation as he had was blackening rapidly. Disgruntled former followers had sinister tales to tell about the Master's bullying ways and his undue influence. Persistent rumours circulated about suicides and illegitimate children. Some said he was mad, others that he was bad, and all agreed that he was dangerous to know. The voices raised in his favour were muted or unheard or just out of fashion. Ouspensky claimed that Gurdjieff had gone mad, and English Ouspenskyites thought of this as a charitable explanation.[4]

In 1933 even the Prieuré was lost, when the Fontainebleau coal merchant forced its sale to retrieve a few hundred francs.[5] The triviality of the debt and the disproportion of its consequences are typical of a man who delighted in absurdity and extremes. No doubt

Gurdjieff could have found a way to pay the bill, or to charm the creditor as he had charmed so many others, but the truth was that he didn't care any more. The Prieuré experiment had lasted ten years – longer than any other stage of his career – and it had come to the end of its natural life. If allowing his coal merchant to force the issue over a trifle was a characteristic victory of impulse over policy, it also gave Gurdjieff an opportunity to present the event as another triumphant leap into the unknown. By letting the château go in this apparently humiliating way he demonstrated his ability to put chance adversity and submission to material circumstances to good spiritual use – just as he taught others to do.

More mundanely, he was almost certainly bored and tired. His remaining pupils observed that he was out of shape physically and emotionally: fat, ageing, bored, apathetic and often irritable. Age was one problem, money another, but the main enemy was almost certainly tedium. Gurdjieff needed his pupils as much as they needed him: to combat the ordinariness of life. But now, even staging the unexpected had become repetitious.

Yet the old fire was still there. An American woman unknown to the Master felt that even his gaze from an adjacent restaurant table stirred her 'sexual centre' more than she had ever known – an incident that especially gratified his taste for offending American prudery.[6] On another occasion, a party of rich and respectable New Yorkers dining with Gurdjieff were shocked by a recital of his most obscene stories, liberally decorated with four-letter words. Nevertheless, they gradually succumbed to his power of suggestion and threw themselves into an orgy under Gurdjieff's direction – until violently and humiliatingly interrupted by his harangue on the slavery of all Americans to the sex instinct.[7]

The orgy episode was characteristic of Gurdjieff's sadistic urges to keep his own pupils in constant uproar and to *épater les bourgeois* in general. Travelling on a night train from New York to Chicago with his erstwhile pupil Fritz Peters in the mid-'30s, he made the young man's life a misery, first demanding that Peters delay the train while Gurdjieff said his goodbyes to the usual crowd of well-wishers, then waking up everybody already asleep on the train with his noisy progress from one end to the other in search of his cabin.

After reaching his berth, the Master proceeded to talk, smoke, drink and eat smelly cheeses for much of the night, making so much disturbance that the porter and the conductor finally threatened to eject him at the next stop. At last coaxed into bed, he summoned the porter on several pretexts throughout the night, repeating the performance next morning in the breakfast car, where he demanded unobtainable food, calling for the steward and complaining at the top of his voice when his wants could not be supplied. Throughout the sixteen hours of the trip Peters could only seethe with his own anger while he registered the fury of the other passengers and vowed never to see his teacher again.[8]

Gurdjieff spent most of his time between 1933 and 1935 in the United States, trying unsuccessfully to restore his fortunes. Despite alienating loyal supporters such as Orage, Toomer and the hero-worshipping Peters, he was well placed to do so. There were still Work groups in the major cities – the loyal remains of Orage's missionary trips – and they met regularly to read and discuss pirated manuscript extracts from the Master's writings. But these meetings were, for the most part, dour occasions, devoted to mutual criticism and the discussion of sexual problems. As one former pupil who occasionally joined the New York and Chicago groups observed, they seemed to have lost their founder's dynamic spirit and turned their gatherings into dreary group-therapy sessions.[9]

Nevertheless, Gurdjieff still had influential connections in America, and he might well have settled there. One of his most devoted students was Olga Ivanovna Hinzenburg, who had joined the Master in Tbilisi in 1919. By way of Constantinople and the Prieuré, 'Olgivanna' had now completed the long journey from her aristocratic Montenegrin origins to Wisconsin in the American Midwest, where she held court with her new husband, the sagacious architect Frank Lloyd Wright.

In the early '30s Wright was keen to establish a progressive school of architecture at Taliesin, his estate on the Wisconsin river. Olgivanna was equally determined that any new school should be run on Gurdjieffian lines. Wright agreed, and the result was a community which cultivated the ideals of the Prieuré, though organised and financed on more practical lines. At Taliesin the study of architecture became a way of life: the relationship between space, line and material was seen to be a spiritual product and a function of the architect's organic sensibility.

Though never in any sense a pupil of Gurdjieff's – he was himself too powerful a character for that – Wright admired him as a fellow-guru and fell under his influence, describing him (after his death) as 'the greatest man in the world'[10] – a judgement fulsomely supported in his wife's memoir of Katherine Mansfield. The two men crossed the Atlantic to visit one another. During the Second World War, Taliesin became a refuge for the Hartmanns, Notts and other Work exiles, but it is impossible to imagine Gurdjieff settling there. Apart from the fact that this child of the Central Asian wilderness had become invincibly metropolitan, there was the presence of Wright himself to contend with. Two such egotistical *monstres sacrés* could never have lived in harmony, however strong their mutual respect.

Even if Gurdjieff had wanted to take up the offer, his visits to the United States were brought to a dramatic temporary halt by a series of scandals involving female 'patients'. Working once again as a healer in order to supplement his income, he treated a supposedly alcoholic woman in her fifties who had been forbidden to drink by her doctor. Contradicting the treatment, Gurdjieff recommended a moderate daily dose of spirits, on the grounds that the woman was not an addict but genuinely needed alcohol to sustain her chemical balance; he instructed her to follow his prescription in secret. This she did, seeming to improve, until a friend told her doctor about the alternative treatment. He persuaded her that Gurdjieff was a quack and took her back off alcohol. She died shortly afterwards – though no one could say for certain why.

A second patient fortunately survived his treatment, though she blamed Gurdjieff for getting her into trouble with the doctors; but a third was not so lucky and committed suicide. It may well be that Gurdjieff gave his patients sound advice, but he was unwise to put them in conflict with their doctors. His sensational reputation laid him open to charges of causing her death and the authorities took these charges seriously. He was briefly imprisoned on Ellis Island as an undesirable alien and then left the country. He was not to return to the United States until after the war.[11]

Shut out of America, he briefly explored the possibility of returning to the USSR. While the Soviet authorities indicated that this might be possible, they made it clear that if he came back he must renounce his teaching and accept state direction – probably a euphemism for Siberian exile or even liquidation. It is easy to imagine Gurdjieff relishing such dangers, but presumably even he realised that the odds were stacked impossibly against him. Instead of accepting what later camp prisoners were to call Stalin's hospitality, he returned to the dull safety of a Paris flat.

American trips and Russian dreams apart, Paris was still the centre of Gurdjieff's activities, and he drew a small band of Americans there like a magnet. He lived in a tiny flat in the rue Labie, spending much of the day in favourite cafés. 1933 was the year of his first publication: an embarrassingly awful pamphlet called *Herald of Coming Good*, which was indeed the herald of several major books. He worked on them in his 'office' at the Café de la Paix, where he watched the world from a banquette, drinking huge amounts of coffee and armagnac and tipping the waiters in a parody of Proustian lavishness with piles of bonbons and candied fruits (a lifelong habit). Sometimes he would receive pupils in the café. Abandoning the old pattern of large gatherings and complex gymnastic exercises, he confined himself to teaching individuals and small groups, in particular a French following directed by his most loyal lieutenant, Jeanne de Salzmann, and a small but influential band of foreigners led by Jane Heap. Lacking the glamour of the Prieuré, this period of intimate teaching was perhaps his most valuable achievement.

Jeanne Matignon de Salzmann was established at Sèvres with a new band of pupils in a mini-version of the Prieuré. These pupils she put at his disposal, just as Ouspensky and Orage had done before her. Gurdjieff's relationship with Madame de Salzmann strengthened further after her husband's death, despite an unpleasant but obscure episode in which Gurdjieff brutally rejected his old comrade, refusing to visit him in his final illness. There is a curious parallel here to the history of his relationship with Madame Ouspensky, which improved dramatically after the breach with her husband. Though the causes of the quarrel with Salzmann are unknown, it was so virulent that in his fantastic book *Beelzebub's Tales* Gurdjieff describes a lethal gas which pervades the universe as *salzmanino*.[12]

Yet it was Alexandre Salzmann who had finally broken down the barriers between Gurdjieff and the French by introducing him in the early 1930s to René Daumal. During his short life, Daumal himself became one of the Master's most enthusiastic followers, but the meeting was to have more than personal significance. Until the late 1930s, almost all Gurdjieff's pupils had been American and British. In the following years and especially after his death, he was to become the jealously guarded property of the Parisian intellectuals who had hitherto despised him.

Born in 1908, Daumal made a poor living by translation. In 1928, together with friends, including the novelist Roger Vailland,[13] he founded the literary review *Le Grand Jeu*, devoted to the loftiest Mallarméan ideal of poetry as a quest for the Absolute. The founders of the new review announced their belief in miracles and issued a quasi-existential manifesto which insisted that everything must be placed in question at every moment: when it came to the Absolute, after all, there could by definition be no half-measures. Daumal found his new teacher's rigour especially sympathetic. His unfinished novel *Mount Analogue* recalls the Master's own *Meetings With Remarkable Men*. The novel – if it can be called such – is about a band of explorers searching for a mountain from whose summit the universe looks quite different. Climbing to the top demands almost superhuman effort: the reward is an otherwise unimaginable new perspective. Daumal's work thus synthesises Central Asian occultism with the sublime vapourings of French symbolism. This is Parnassianism on the grand scale.

Salzmann and Daumal led two interlocking French groups. An expatriate American contingent was directed by Jane Heap and Margaret Anderson, now members of a lesbian circle which included the writers Djuna Barnes and Janet Flanner,[14] and Georgette Leblanc, a pre-Raphaelite figure who moved with equal ease in esoteric and *demi-mondaine* worlds. Gurdjieff's influence over these women puts an interesting gloss on claims that his power consisted largely of sexual magnetism. Whatever affected them, it was certainly not virile charm in the usual sense of that term.

The American novelist Kathryn Hulme joined the Heap-Anderson group in 1933.[15] Hulme had encountered Gurdjieff some years earlier while travelling in France as companion to a rich milliner. Acquaintance with Barnes and Flanner resulted in a meeting with Jane Heap, now spending much of her time in Paris, and Heap in turn led Kathryn and her friend 'Wendy' to Gurdjieff. Hulme later wrote a detailed account of this circle and their work with Gurdjieff. Heap was a passionate devotee who inspired them all; and although he disliked male homosexuality – not on grounds of bourgeois morality, of course, but because it violates the laws of cosmic harmony, in which normal sexual polarity plays an important part – Gurdjieff seems to have kept his opinions about lesbians to himself.

To begin with, he subjected his new pupils to a softening-up process, alternately charming and spurning them. Before selling the Prieuré, for example, he drove there at high speed, with Hulme following in her own car. She marvelled at the power of the Master's eyes, the persuasiveness of his talk and the recklessness of his driving. Yet despite this intimate occasion, Gurdjieff usually kept Hulme at a distance, and at first she was too shy to ask him to accept her as a pupil. On at least one occasion he treated the whole group to a dinner of crayfish and armagnac, complete with ritual toasts to the different orders of idiots that had been a feature of Prieuré feasts. This menu became a standard feature of Hulme's years with the Master. At other times he ignored his new admirers, establishing himself in a corner of the Café de la Paix to write while they watched from a distance, not daring to approach.

At first Hulme met Gurdjieff only as a friend of Jane Heap's. Late in 1935 Heap left Paris to live in London, bidding Katherine Hulme goodbye at the railway station with the portentous words: 'We in this method are like Lucifer, cast out from the mechanical heaven in which we live.'[16] It was then that Hulme plucked up the courage to approach Gurdjieff, asking to be accepted as a pupil. The Master agreed and Hulme formed a small Work group that included an Englishwoman, Miss Gordon, a former *habituée* of the Prieuré. They called themselves The Rope, because they were roped together on a dangerous inner journey up the Daumalian mountain. Their instruction took place in the Café de la Paix, in Gurdjieff's tiny rue Labie flat where he prepared elaborate meals, or anywhere they happened to be. The meals were consumed in silence, punctuated by Gurdjieff's toasts and *obiter dicta*. It sometimes seemed to Hulme that these sayings were commonplace, if not downright banal. On reflection, she always discovered their profundity, and she was outraged when Rom Landau's book *God Is My Adventure* presented her teacher as a latter-day Rasputin.

In fact, by Margaret Anderson's account, the foundations of Gurdjieff's theology differed little from Blavatsky's. In *The Unknowable Gurdjieff* Anderson writes of his hermetic 'science' – sometimes she calls it 'super-science' – which 'belongs to the knowledge of antiquity'.[17] She quotes Eliphas Lévi to the effect that there is 'a formidable secret . . . a science and a force . . . one sole, universal and imperishable doctrine', and she reports Gurdjieff himself as declaring that 'All the great general religions . . . are all based on the same truths.' Where her teacher differed from others, she thought, was in the matter of his genuine connection with a remote occult tradition – with the Brothers of Wisdom who had once populated the Sarmoung Monastery described in *Meetings With Remarkable Men*. The 'evidence' for this claim was based on nothing more than the powerful effect Gurdjieff produced on Anderson, filling the otherwise burning emptiness of her life with an untranslatable sense of meaning and significance. There was, she thought, something in the way he played melancholy oriental tunes on his hand accordion after dinner that transcended all the intellectual discourse in the world.

Gurdjieff flirted ruthlessly with the group, individually and together, giving them animal nicknames: one became Canary, another Sardine and Hulme was called Crocodile. The nicknames were symbolic of characters and character defects. Each woman was subjected to a public analysis of these defects and a withering critique of her weaknesses. As usual, spiritual instruction merged seamlessly with the teacher's own current preoccupations, and his new pupils were soon immersed in the details of his daily life. Sometimes Gurdjieff taught the doctrines of intentional suffering, self-observation and the laws of three and seven by direct exposition; and sometimes by involving his pupils in the purchase of his new motor car.

But what impressed them most was neither the doctrine nor his exotic manners but Gurdjieff's psychological acuity and his insistence that they should act without reflection. He gave them his usual message: they must learn to Know less and Be more. Hulme thought it extraordinary how he seemed to see into their deepest natures, to know them better than they knew themselves, to understand what their problems were and what must be done about them. But given the neurotic introspection of most of these pupils – several had undergone severe breakdowns in the previous decade – the injunction against reflection was just as sensible and effective as it had been with the febrile Russian intelligentsia of twenty years earlier.

By the spring of 1936 their meetings were taking place almost every day, usually in the rue Labie flat.[18] Though other pupils appeared there, Hulme's milliner friend Wendy, who joined in on her trips to Paris, wondered why there were so few. Her queries were given added point by the presence of a box on the kitchen table into which everyone put what they could afford. Though the usual shady business deals appear to have been going on in the background – by their nature they were never recorded and Gurdjieff kept no accounts – the days of Lady Rothermere were long since gone, and the Master was everlastingly strapped for cash. That summer he abruptly dismissed his pupils for three months, on condition they return in the autumn. How he lived in their absence one can only conjecture. The women were miserable. Visiting America, Kathryn and Wendy couldn't wait to return to their teacher, as he no doubt anticipated. Having been conditioned to Gurdjieff's ways by a subtle mixture of cosseting, bullying, flirting and sheer charisma – spoiling with one hand and scolding with the other, as Hulme put it – they were alienated from their old lives and addicted to the new one.

The high point of each year was Christmas, which Gurdjieff celebrated with every ceremony. For the 1936 festival, he summoned The Rope and his other pupils to pack forty boxes in the tiny sitting-room at rue Labie. These boxes, containing bonbons, banknotes and other small gifts, were presents for his family and pupils, and for the poor émigrés to whom he acted as a father figure. By the time the packing ceremony was completed in a flurry of activity by Gurdjieff himself there were more than forty people crammed into the flat and everyone joined in a rich and ceremonial meal, after which their host entertained them on his accordion. The boxes were presented in another elaborate ceremony, and the proceedings took up much of the night. They were briefly interrupted when Gurdjieff's niece supplemented the long series of customary toasts by proposing Gurdjieff's own health, and her uncle rounded furiously on the girl for presuming. When the grand guests had gone, according to the maid, Mr Gurdjieff's poor dependants would arrive for their share of his generosity. Such incidents were the small change of Gurdjieffian occasions.

Christmas in the rue Labie sums up the sense of life Gurdjieff induced in his pupils at its best: intimate, elaborate, mysterious, generous, dangerous and magical. It also underlines the complex dilemma which confronted his pupils, as Katherine Hulme noted from her own experience. On the one hand the Master exerted such a strong pull over those around him, and created such a complete universe for them to live in, that for his devotees to be apart from him was to be miserable. He made the rest of the world – other people, the past, everyday life – seem positively unreal, while his own presence was imbued with the visionary intensity of the truly authentic. At the same time, it was Hulme's life with Gurdjieff that often felt 'unreal' in another sense: because it was so remote from that other world to which they both knew she would eventually return.

The upshot was that Gurdjieff – whether deliberately or not – made his pupils dependent by weaving them into his life, and then despised their dependence while demanding their absolute loyalty. He was thus both the liberating teacher and the possessive father, the creating god and the destroying devil. This could create unbearable conflicts within pupils: under their pressure all but the hardiest tended to fall away, especially after separation from what Hulme calls Gurdjieff's magnetic field. When they did so, the consequences could be brutal. Wendy left the Work after a serious illness in America, leaving Kathryn Hulme to return alone to Paris in 1938, and her teacher responded by blotting out the memory of his erstwhile admirer. After discussing the matter with Hulme once, the Master simply said, 'And about her, now we do not speak.'[9] Though briefly troubled by divided loyalties and by Gurdjieff's cruelty, Hulme did not hesitate to prefer her teacher to her old friend. When she left Paris in 1939 and found herself separated from the Master by war and the Atlantic, she felt as though she had been cast out of paradise.

SIXTEEN

Sinners

The person about whom Gurdjieff most conspicuously 'did not speak' in these years was, of course, Ouspensky. He too was excluded from bliss, a permanent exile from the happiness he had glimpsed in 1915.[1] In other respects, the outcast prospered between the wars as his English following grew, yet his gloom deepened by the year. Groups were started, country houses found, lectures given, but it was all just more of the same. That was the trouble with formulating a system: what could you do but repeat it? And though his life was now comfortable and even luxurious, it lacked the one essential element that Gurdjieff provided: danger.

Ouspensky also disliked the English. Indeed, they embodied his problem. Though he relished the ease and regularity of middle-class English life after his troubles in Russia and Turkey, he also found the sheer comfort and lack of intellectual curiosity oppressive. In one of his books Ouspensky remarks that the significance of life is in the quest for meaning, not in meaning itself. For him the quest was over. He responded to failure by gratefully accepting English indifference and relieved the monotony of life by taking to the bottle.

He was not helped by his wife. Although she had left Gurdjieff to join Ouspensky in England in 1929, by the mid-1930s they were once more living independent lives and Madame Ouspensky was blossoming into a teacher in her own right. She was far closer in character to Gurdjieff than her husband, as many pupils noticed: a strong woman with a generous spirit and a peremptory manner. In the autumn of 1935 Sophia Grigorievna had moved out of London to a country house at Lyne Place, Virginia Water, which became a sort of weekend Prieuré where the residents were joined on Saturdays by scores of pupils from London, who worked in the house and garden under the direction of a chatelaine whose fierce tongue was feared and obeyed.

To begin with, Ouspensky himself preferred to remain in town, though he eventually took to the life of a country gentleman, Virginia Water not then being the suburb it has become. By 1939 over a hundred people were meeting at Lyne at the weekends for lectures and questions.[2] Ouspensky was at last able to indulge his passion for animals, especially horses and cats. But despite Madame Ouspensky's bracing regime he slid ever deeper into depression. Boredom was certainly one cause, drink another; but, as subsequent events were to show, these were only symptoms of the disease. The real problem was a growing sense of bafflement and failure, which could only be exacerbated by his wife's calm certainty.

For Ouspensky had always oscillated between a passionate desire to believe in Gurdjieff's teaching and an ineradicable scepticism about it. His uncertainty had been concealed by his cool public manner. Now his doubts began to spread. He wondered whether the System itself, so long his bedrock, was not as dubious as its transmitter. He did not at first make these doubts public, but they cast a shadow over his later life, a shadow deepened by his wife. After the many years he had spent simultaneously revering and resenting Gurdjieff, he now found himself in a similar situation *vis-à-vis* Madame Ouspensky, hardly a cosy companion for his old age. He spent much of the time in his sitting-room, alone or with pupils, who sat in respectful silence while their teacher consumed incredible amounts of white wine and vodka and reminisced about the past or delivered withering critiques of their failings.

Ouspensky's relationship with his pupils ironically recapitulates his own conflicts with Gurdjieff, illustrating the problems of spiritual pedagogy. How far must the teacher instruct students and how far put them in situations from which they can learn – assuming they have the capacity to do so? To what extent should the pupils follow or even imitate the master and to what extent do they reward his teaching by showing their independence? How do they recognise what it is they are learning? These questions remind us that there is another sense to the word 'privacy' than mere disengagement from public life. Esoteric or occult wisdom is by definition secret, hidden, apart. As Blavatsky had found, its transmission – which must be intelligible to the acolyte yet concealed from the vulgar gaze – is therefore fraught with difficulties.

Perhaps the most intractable of these difficulties results from the attempt to turn occult teaching into a public mission, an attempt likely to be beset by misunderstanding and charges of fraud. No one struggled more seriously – or more comically – with this problem than Captain J. G. Bennett, formerly of the British Secret Service, and now somewhat incongruously combining the roles of spiritual teacher and mining engineer. Bennett's life embodies Gurdjieff's principle that the truly spiritual man does not withdraw from the fray into contemplation but finds opportunities for self-observation and intentional suffering in every circumstance that comes to hand. Yet though Bennett led what might be called a public life in two respects, becoming a prominent figure in both business and alternative religion; and though he was charming, urbane and gregarious in manner, to himself he remained essentially a private, even tortured figure, for whom the twin paths of his life embodied the painful dilemma of one perpetually compelled to choose.

After leaving government service, Bennett spent the early 1920s pressing the vast property claims of the deposed Osmanli royal family, including the late Sultan's eight widows, whose estates, confiscated by the new Turkish republican government, covered large areas of the Mediterranean coast.[3] Much of this coast was now controlled or influenced by the British. As a former representative of the British government, with inside knowledge of the post-war Middle East, where business was dominated by baksheesh and politics by secret agents, Bennett was well placed for the work. He was persuaded to take it on by the imperial family's dentist, a passionate royalist who kept him in the operating chair for almost two hours one afternoon in 1921 on the pretext of treating an abscess, while persuading his patient to help the Sultan's huge family of deposed and mostly corrupt royal princes regain their property.

As a partner in this enterprise – which if successful promised to make them a vast fortune – Bennett took on the financier and businessman John De Kay, a friend of Mrs Beaumont and Prince Sabeheddin. The idea was that Bennett would manage the political negotiations while De Kay looked after the financial dealings. Given Bennett's political experience and his partner's vaunted business expertise, the partnership looked promising. There were, however, flies in the ointment.

Born in North Dakota in 1872, De Kay was a complex character: a passionate socialist, a visionary and a crook, always full of great schemes and always overstepping the thin lines between business, politics and crime. According to his own account he had made his fortune in newspapers, beginning aged twelve as a paper-boy, progressing to journalism at nineteen and achieving the ownership of three provincial newspapers by the age of twenty-two. After using his newspapers to support the unsuccessful presidential campaign of William Jennings Bryan,[4] he sold up and moved on to Mexico, where he enlisted the support of the ruling dictator, Porfirio Díaz, to set up in the meat-packing business. This did well until De Kay backed the wrong side in the civil war which erupted in Mexico when Díaz retired, forcing him to move on to Europe, where he became an arms dealer and traded in Mexican government bonds to finance his deals.

By the way he wrote a play for Sarah Bernhardt, had the obligatory affair with her, and tried to acquire the Château de Coucy, in the Marne valley north of Paris, claiming descent from its medieval builders, the Sieurs de Coucy. He also entered into a liaison with Bennett's future wife, Winifred Beaumont, whom he took back to Mexico. A charming, eloquent and theatrical man, he was fond of dressing in what Bennett calls Midwestern costume, with a Stetson and a six-shooter, which he took with him into banks and boardrooms when raising money.

The war caught De Kay and Mrs Beaumont behind German lines in France, and the fighting made such an impact on them that De Kay decided to forswear arms-dealing and became a pacifist. This was not enough to assuage Mrs Beaumont's dismay when she discovered that De Kay already had two children by a mutual friend. In 1919 she left him to join Prince Sabeheddin in Switzerland, moving from there to Constantinople. By the time she introduced him to Bennett, De Kay was living in Berlin.

It is clear that De Kay expected his relationship with Bennett and the Turkish imperial house to help him with other business schemes that were in difficulties. The two men got on all the better because they had been in the same line of business: De Kay is described in World War One intelligence files as 'chief of the sabotage and murder section of the German Secret Service'[5] – a point omitted from Bennett's account of these years. And although Bennett mentions that De Kay was imprisoned in London at the end of the war on charges of trading in false Mexican bonds, he tactfully – and incorrectly – presents the charges as unjustified. In fact, almost everything De Kay told Bennett about himself is either untrue or distorted. This time he got away with it because of flaws in the extradition treaties between London, Washington and Mexico City. He was not always to be so lucky.

De Kay immediately set up a company to press the Osmanlis' claim. Abdul Hamid Estates Incorporated, registered in Delaware, was capitalised at the value of the confiscated estates, estimated by De Kay to be in the region of $150,000,000. Quite naturally, the new Turkish government was bitterly opposed to their claims, but the two men knew how to use their good connections and believed they had a reasonable chance of retrieving at least some of the property, which meant, in relative terms, an enormous amount.

The affair dragged on through 1922, 1923 and 1924 with no tangible result. In the summer of 1923, hoping to further his case, Bennett attended the Lausanne Conference at which the Allies negotiated a new peace treaty with Turkey. He whiled away the long hours between meetings by taking dancing lessons from a Russian lady, in the company of a Japanese baron and the Turkish Chief Rabbi. But though he learnt to dance, nothing came of the conference for his clients. Nevertheless, Bennett remained confident. He knew how protracted such negotiations always were in the best of circumstances, and nowhere more so than in the former

Ottoman Empire, where nothing was straightforward, everyone wanted their cut and every palm required greasing. Even under the puritanical new regime, what Westerners regarded as corruption was still rife.

What Bennett didn't know – or claims he didn't know – was that his own partner was under investigation once more by the American federal authorities, for issuing fraudulent Mexican bonds and other fiscal offences. The crash came in 1924 with the election of a British Labour government, which should have proved propitious. Both De Kay and Bennett knew leading members of the Cabinet – Bennett had canvassed for Ramsay MacDonald – and De Kay expected his newly powerful friends to help with the claims of Abdul Hamid Estates Inc. to the Middle Eastern territories – formerly part of the Turkish Empire – which the British now controlled. De Kay also hoped to make whatever influential friends he could for other more pressing reasons. But it was too late. The combination of fraud and socialism did not endear him to the conservative American administration. Once in Britain, he was arrested and imprisoned at the request of the US authorities, who then extradited him to the States for trial. Though eventually acquitted for lack of evidence, De Kay spent many months in prison and his partner never saw him again. The princes' claim was stalled until Bennett could find new backers to form another company.

This was only the beginning of his troubles. Bennett was now very short of money – even shorter than he would have been had he never met De Kay, who was inclined to make extravagant promises of financial support and then renege on them. Pursuing the claims of the Turkish heirs in Greece (where he married Mrs Beamont in April 1925), and assured by his associates there that they would get quick recognition of the princes' claims by promising to the government to develop tracts of the land they claimed, Bennett involved himself with Nico Nicolopoulos, who had formerly worked for him and for Compton Mackenzie in the British Secret Service. A handsome fellow given to lying, bravado and acts of real courage, Nicolopoulos offered to help by gathering together the widely dispersed title deeds to the land, much of it owned in small plots by many different proprietors.

Nicolopoulos was not over-scrupulous about his methods, and the inevitable followed. In March 1928 Bennett was arrested and imprisoned on charges of forging title deeds. He only managed to escape from the fetid cell where he was locked in with murderers and prostitutes by taking iodine to feign appendicitis (though Bennett claims he had to take it twice because the prison doctor wouldn't take any notice the first time). Nicolopoulos, who had also been arrested, died in prison, helped on no doubt by his treatment there. Bennett was eventually brought to trial, and though acquitted for lack of evidence the delays put an end to his work for Abdul Hamid Estates Inc.

However, this absurd episode was also the beginning of Bennett's long career in mining. During the trial he had been visited by a certain Dmitri Diamandopoulos, an engineer who explained to him that he, Bennett, was the victim of a political plot. Diamandopoulos, who had been impressed by Bennett's demeanour in court, owned a brown-coal mine in the hills a hundred miles west of Salonika, but couldn't find the capital to develop it. He offered Bennett a half-share in the mine in return for help financing the extraction of the coal. Bennett agreed. Once out of prison he returned to England and formed a partnership with James Douglas Henry, a mining engineer. They decided to turn the coal into charcoal for domestic use in Greece and formed a company for that purpose.

At first the company prospered. Bennett found a profitable method of making brown coal into charcoal, and even managed to interest the Greek Prime Minister Venizelos, who visited the firm's British works in Birmingham. But in 1931 Venizelos fell from power and an anti-British government took power in Greece, raising the taxes on coal and lignite. Coincidentally the manager of the Bennett mine was arrested for financial irregularities, and that was the end of the Grecian Mining Co. Ltd.

In 1932, on the strength of his Greek experiences, Bennett took a job as engineer-estimator with H. Tollemache, specialists in powdered coal, and began research into the possible uses of coal-dust. It was the first step in a twenty-year involvement with the British coal industry in public and private capacities, which included serving on government committees and heading research laboratories. Two years later, in 1934, he became Director of the Coalburning Appliance Makers Association, which he helped to found, and started the British Coal Utilization Research Association (BCURA) with the help of Lord Rutherford, who was then Chairman of the British government's Scientific Advisory Council. BCURA looked into ways of making coal-burning more efficient while exploring other possible uses for the fuel.

All this time, from 1921 onwards, Bennett was also pursuing his spiritual investigations. Shortly before setting to work on the Osmanli claims he had experienced a moment of mystical illumination in a cemetery overlooking the Bosporus while recovering from foot-and-mouth disease caught by eating Bulgarian cheese. A disembodied voice – the first of many – told him that he had seven years to prepare for the commencement of his spiritual life, when he was to embark on a great task whose meaning would only be revealed to him at the age of sixty.

He rehearsed for his great task by spending several weeks at the newly opened Prieuré in 1923, where Gurdjieff told him – as usual – that he had too much Knowledge and too little Being, and Bennett suffered from a recurrence of the dysentery he had contracted in Asia Minor. Nevertheless, he joined in all the hard work, meditated and – not surprisingly – had out-of-body experiences. When Mrs Beaumont arrived to join him she was horrified at Bennett's condition. Taking against Gurdjieff, she decided that he was either a very good man or a very bad man. And though Ouspensky later told her that Gurdjieff was a good man, he added that Bennett was not yet ready for that master's teaching. Mrs Beaumont was also disgusted by the squalid conditions at the Prieuré, where flies were swarming in the kitchens and the doctor treating Bennett had dirty hands. Having draped the kitchen in fly-papers, she nevertheless decided that stronger measures were needed and took her friend to Paris to recuperate.

Abandoning Gurdjieff, Bennett began to attend Ouspensky's meetings in London. It was not long before Ouspensky decided that his pupils must choose between him and Gurdjieff, telling them in 1924 that, though Gurdjieff was an extraordinary man with great possibilities, these possibilities could be developed for good or ill. It seemed that Ouspensky had changed his mind since speaking to Mrs Beaumont a few months earlier, for now he told his students that the two sides in Gurdjieff – the good and the bad – were at war, and the battle could go either way. While it raged, they should stay away from him.

Choosing to follow this advice, Bennett became a leading member of Ouspensky's London group throughout the 1920s. In West Kensington he struggled with objective consciousness, self-remembering and work on himself, and dreamt of setting up his own institute to research the fifth dimension. As we have seen, institutitis was a catching disease. Under Bennett's influence even De Kay talked of establishing a school called Intellectus et Labor to promote the ideals of the Second Socialist International (and, presumably, the German Secret Service). The polymathic Bennett, who never did things by halves, also studied Sanskrit and took lessons in Pali, the language of Buddhist scriptures, from the wife of a distinguished Oriental scholar, a Mrs Rhys Davies, who believed herself to be the reincarnation of a Buddhist nun.

Business impinged on his spiritual life when he discovered on his return to London from Greece, after his 1929 trial, that Ouspensky had severed relations between them. The cause was a telegram Ouspensky sent Bennett while he was awaiting trial, reading 'Sympathy to Bennett under 96 laws', a reference to Gurdjieff's theory of the planetary limitations under which men live. Finding this sinister message when they searched Bennett's flat – and no doubt aware of his work in intelligence – the Greek police had turned it over to the British Embassy, together with other papers. As a result Ouspensky was summoned to the Foreign Office in London and interviewed about his possible sympathies with British socialists and Russian Bolsheviks, considered by many in the Foreign Office to be more or less identical. Rattled and furious, he immediately excommunicated the absent Bennett – not for the last time.

Despite constant rebuffs from Ouspensky and from Sophia Grigorievna, who drew attention to what she called his 'mechanicalness', his lack of spirituality, his obtuseness and his general inadequacy, Bennett persevered in his spiritual quest. But, battered by this application of the Gurdjieffian critical method, he decided to form a group of his own. Its first members were a man his wife had met on the train and a woman she once sat next to on a number 16 bus: appropriate beginnings in a way, given the role rapid travel (from place to place, idea to idea, faith to faith) was to play in Bennett's life. Later the group became a family affair, when Mrs Bennett's sister joined, bringing two friends with her, thereby increasing the total membership to seven.

Bennett sent regular reports of his meetings to Ouspensky, who usually ignored them. When he did finally acknowledge these communications, Ouspensky's response was to follow Gurdjieff's example and absorb Bennett and his best pupils into his own group. After that Bennett rapidly became one of Ouspensky's chief lieutenants, finding pupils, arranging meetings and drinking with his chief into the small hours. On one occasion they finished five bottles of claret, which may have had something to do with the out-of-body sensations Bennett experienced that night.

When Madame Ouspensky moved to Lyne in 1935, Bennett began to work with her there at weekends, drifting more and more under her influence in the late '30s. His wife, however, was made unwelcome in the house for three years for unstated reasons. Like Gurdjieff, the Ouspenskys often insisted on parting spouses or stirring up trouble between them. But Bennett, who believed in the value of unquestioning obedience to a spiritual teacher, accepted the situation, though it meant spending apart the only part of the week when he and his wife might have been together. Eager not to stand in the way of his spiritual development, Winifred Bennett offered to leave her husband.

She was finally welcomed into the house at Lyne in 1937 only after trying to kill herself. In the three-day coma which followed her attempted suicide Winifred went to heaven and stood in the presence of Jesus, until Bennett selfishly called her back. After this episode Ouspensky welcomed her at Lyne, where she spent her time making quilted curtains and telling the master about her jaunt to heaven, which made him cry with frustration because he longed to visit the celestial regions himself and knew he never would.

By this time Bennett himself had also drifted away from Ouspensky and into the orbit of Sophia Grigorievna. Nevertheless, Ouspensky's treatment of Winifred impressed him with his former teacher's sensitivity, compared with his own obtuseness, which he put down to the urgency and coarseness of physical desires, revealing themselves in psychic impurity. He had gradually become convinced that there was a relationship between mystical experience and the 'sex function' – though what the relationship was he could not say. According to Mrs Bennett part of the problem was her husband's 'negative attitude towards sex',[6] which prevented him from understanding women – and, presumably, the profounder forms of mystical experience. To judge from the stories one hears about Bennett, she might well say that: in his case a negative attitude seems to have meant an all too positive appetite.

Sex was also causing problems in the orange groves of Ojai. Raja's work for KWINC kept him in Hollywood for most of the week, in an office next to the house he had bought for his mother- and sister-in-law. Though she visited Hollywood, Rosalind lived mainly at Ojai, where she shared Arya Vihara with Krishna and Radha. Raja joined them at weekends, but even then he and his wife lived very much apart. Raja liked to get up very late and work into the night; sometimes he ate alone. Krishna and Rosalind, on the other hand, rose at dawn and lived in one another's pockets, holding aloof both from the local citrus farmers and from the Theosophical enclave with which they shared the valley. In consequence, Krishna, Rosalind and Radha become a tightly knit emotional unit over whom the shade of Nitya constantly hovered. At the child's birth Krishna had wondered whether she was the reincarnation of his brother. Now he transferred to Rosalind and her daughter all the affection once bestowed on Nitya, just as Rosalind had transferred her love from Nitya to Raja. It was at Ojai, according to Radha, that Krishna and her mother became lovers in 1932, the year after her own birth.

This claim cannot be confirmed or denied until the relevant papers become available – and perhaps not even then. On the other hand, it would explain a good deal about his life that is otherwise difficult to understand. Having parted from Annie, Krishna was also drifting away from his other surrogate mother, Lady Emily.

Rosalind had taken a maternal role towards Krishna ever since the beginning of the Process and, according to Radha, he had often shared Rosalind's bed – chastely – when unwell, like a sick child going to its mother. Now a mother herself, with an absent husband and a child Krishna treated as his own, she was – or so the story goes – ready to become Krishna's mistress. They had been cast as possible lovers in the early days of their friendship by a press ever watchful for the sensational news of a black messiah with a 'blonde bombshell': now the tide of circumstances bore them on. If there was an affair it was easily kept secret in the small and very private community at Ojai, though some of Krishna's old friends and Rosalind's family had their suspicions. But Krishna had always required the intimate friendship and support of women, and it seemed to most observers even in their inner circle that this was simply a peculiarly close version of his relationships with Annie, Emily and others.

If Krishna and Rosalind *were* having an affair, they and Raja sustained a delicate situation for thirty years. It is however hard to see how the three of them reconciled that situation with Krishna's public mission. Though Krishnamurti was no longer a Theosophist, there was a tacit assumption that he would never marry – far less engage in adultery – remaining celibate in order to fulfil his spiritual destiny. This is certainly what his followers continued to believe. Raja's daughter exonerates her parents from any responsibility for what amounts to deliberate deception. She had no doubt that Krishna was to blame; and though she pays tribute to the loving care he took of her in childhood, she paints the picture of a monster of dishonesty and selfishness, who bent others ruthlessly to his will and told any lie to save his own reputation.

These failings affected everything in his life, from the trivial to the serious. When Krishna failed to carry out engagements Raja had organised for him, for example, Raja had to take the blame. One might put such behaviour down to self-absorption or naïvety – but what are we to make of the claim that, when Rosalind conceived

Krishna's children, he not only made it clear she must get rid of them, but left her to arrange the abortions on her own? Radha also convicts Krishna of gross disloyalty to Annie Besant, to Leadbeater and to the Theosophical Society, contrasting this betrayal with her father's continuing reverence for the roguish old Bishop and his good relations with Adyar. In her book, Krishnamurti is a mystical Harold Skimpole, posing as a childlike saint to outsiders while Raja and Rosalind suffer from his vanity, his fantasy and his pathological lying, because of their unstinting loyalty to the man who betrayed them both.

This account is hard to take, if only for the reason that the Rajagopals can scarcely be excused for condoning the situation as their daughter describes it for almost thirty years, unless they were venal, idle, stupid or quite unbelievably naïve – and they were clearly none of these. They also had plenty of chances to escape. Financially, they were independent, with incomes settled on them both by the prodigal Miss Dodge and later inheritances from elsewhere. Both worked successfully outside the Society, and after Krishna's break with Theosophy Raja was invited back to take a leading role (which he refused). Neither was extravagant, and though Radha makes a good deal of how plain life was at Ojai – long hours on the farm, simple food and home-made clothes – she seems unaware that the endless procession of houses and holidays enjoyed by her parents – not to speak of the subventions from followers and friends which she herself describes – would strike anyone else as good fortune.

Besides, Radha herself claims that Krishna proposed marriage to Rosalind in 1933, but that Raja refused to take the idea seriously. She also says that Raja frequently offered to leave but was dissuaded from doing so by Krishnamurti – because, she thinks, her father was convinced that it was his fate and duty to stay. But if *that* were the case, we must wonder why Raja was not able to submit himself entirely to his fate to the end? One can only conclude from the evidence that, though he may not have been happy with the situation, he was content for it to continue.

This is confirmed by the fact that, though they drifted apart from one another, Raja still clung to his relationship with Krishna in the mid-1970s, by which time they were enmeshed in complicated litigation over Raja's administration of the various Krishnamurti trusts. Raja's possessiveness suggests that the triangle was not simply one in which Krishna – however badly he may have behaved when judged by standards he set himself – betrayed his friend and abused his mistress, practising a hypocritical fraud on the rest of the world into the bargain. The dynamics of their relationship were subtler than that: there were complex mutual needs between the three of them which reached back into the past. There is also the probability that, once they had settled into a rhythm of life, all three found it difficult and inconvenient to break the pattern, until Krishna began to move away from his friends.

But that moment was far in the future. For the time being, all three led full and interesting lives, following their own interests. Lady Emily, indeed, wondered whether Krishna realised just how much his life looked to outsiders like one long holiday, as the intervals between public appearances became longer and more luxurious. Despite the complications of their private affairs and Krishna's long retreats at Ojai, the three also cultivated an elaborate social life, coming into contact with a wide range of people on the west coast.

In summer the Ojai family often stayed at Peter Pan Lodge, Carmel, where they met among others the writers Robinson Jeffers, Rom Landau and Lincoln Steffens. They also made friends in Hollywood, especially among the émigré community, whose numbers were increased by Nazi persecution and the threat of war in Europe. Many of the émigrés worked in the cinema: the novelists Christopher Isherwood and Aldous Huxley and the film star Luise Rainer were all close friends. Others, such as the philosopher Bertrand Russell and the Thomas Manns, were passing acquaintances. Krishnamurti was also befriended by natives and adopted natives such as Anita Loos and Greta Garbo, and his friendships extended as far as New Mexico, whence Frieda Lawrence wrote to compare him with her husband.[7]

Most of the people he met instinctively deferred to Krishnamurti's reputation as a spiritual teacher. It was easy for him to feel at ease with the famous, having long experienced the pains and pleasures of celebrity himself. He knew what it was to be a freak and the west coast was willy-nilly a world of freaks. Gradually, the talks, writings and public appearances turned his early notoriety into stardom. By 1939 he had reached the curious condition of being famous because he was a star and a star because he was famous. But the price of stardom is a painful and damaging dislocation between the individual's self-consciousness and the way others see him – between the public persona and the private life. As the years passed, the gap between the image of Krishnamurti's saintliness and the reality of his sin, however interpreted, was to grow ever larger.

SEVENTEEN

Gurus in the War

The outbreak of war in 1939 put the political choices of the previous decade in stark form. This was to be no 'civilised' war of armies in the field, but Hitler's *Blitzkrieg*: a life-and-death struggle between whole nations during which millions of civilians were casually swept away. Yet even now the wily Gurdjieff managed to stay out of the battle, just as he had always done, though living under the very nose of the enemy. Refusing offers of American refuge, he spent the war years keeping his head down in occupied Paris. It remains a mystery why he was not interned as an alien or arrested as a black marketeer, especially given the Nazi distaste for Slavs and Asians. He also acquired a suspiciously well-stocked larder. When the war ended there were rumours about collaboration with the occupying authorities. Briefly arrested on suspicion of currency offences after the Liberation, when large amounts of dollars were found concealed in his apartment, he was released without charge the next day – an outcome which could point either to his innocence or to police complicity.

Throughout the war Gurdjieff continued to teach, receiving at his flat those pupils who remained in occupied Paris. Others were less fortunate. Georgette Leblanc died of cancer in 1941. René Daumal, on the run from the Gestapo because of his marriage to a Jewish girl, succumbed to TB in 1944 at the age of thirty-six, his Gurdjieffian novel *Mount Analogue* still unfinished. Perhaps the failure of Daumal's literary ambitions was of no importance: visiting another dying pupil, the young novelist Luc Dietrich, the Master produced two oranges and told him that 'All your life has been a preparation for this moment.'[1]

More obviously men of principle than Gurdjieff, Ouspensky and Krishnamurti agreed that what mattered about the war was not the glamourised battle between good and evil but the fact that it was a horrifying distraction from issues of real importance. All the parties involved were 'wrong'. The allied empires – British, French and American – might be taking the better part in the struggle, relatively speaking, but why had it come about in the first place? Hitler was only the spark igniting a tinder-box created and maintained by others. If Fascism and Communism were undoubtedly forms of thuggery, what was liberal democracy but the deluded pursuit of freedom and materialism, fatally lacking in any sense of cosmic purpose?[2]

Besides, mass conflicts were spiritually meaningless, signifying little more than the migration of swallows or the wars of cats and mice. The only thing that mattered in life was the cultivation of individual enlightenment, whether by means of Ouspenskian self-observation or through Krishnamurti's method of 'choiceless awareness'.[3] The two approaches can seem very similar: both entail minute, objective and undeviating scrutiny of mental life and both can trace their descent from ancient spiritual practices. But there the resemblance ends. While Ouspensky's teaching is positively and brutally strenuous – 'negative emotions' are fiercely discouraged[4] – Krishnamurti follows Wordsworth's injunction to cultivate a wise passiveness. In wartime this doctrine led him naturally to pacifism.

Gurdjieff and Ouspensky were neither combatants nor pacifists. They simply continued to insist that men could do nothing about the situation, but only (perhaps) about themselves. Here, too, there was a link with Krishnamurti's seemingly very different doctrine. As Ouspensky's disciple Kenneth Walker put it, in several books published during the war, world reform could only be achieved by reforming human consciousness: the internal changes must come first.

Krishnamurti, on the other hand, was a committed pacifist in the Indian tradition of *satyagrahi*. This was an important matter now

16. G. I. Gurdjieff

17. P. D. Ouspensky

18. *and* 19. Olga and Thomas de Hartmann

20. J. G. Bennett (*second from right*), 1919

21. A. R. Orage

22. Jane Heap

23. Viscountess Rothermere

24. Katherine Mansfield

25. A symposium at Point Loma

26. Bishops Wedgwood and Arundale of the
Liberal Catholic Church (*left and centre*)

27. Aldous Huxley

28. Christopher Isherwood (*left*) and W. H. Auden

29. Raja, Radha and Krishna in Los Angeles, 1932

30. Jeanne de Salzmann

31. Gurdjieff on a journey

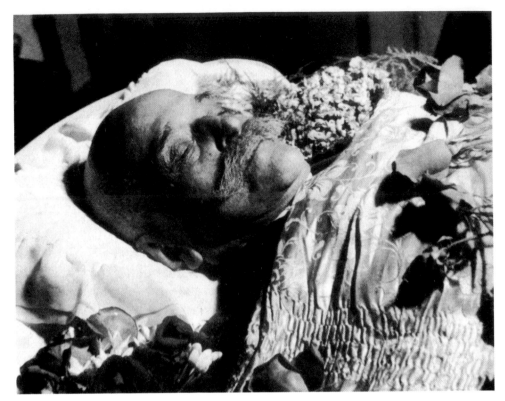

32. Gurdjieff in his coffin

33. Krishnamurti, 1986

that he was an established and respected figure. For, whatever the secret peccadilloes of his private life, by the mid-'30s he was increasingly perceived by the public as a latter-day saint (it was this perception, indeed, that was to so enrage the Rajagopals). Even Ouspensky, who was much impressed by the younger man, formed this view at their one meeting. Thus Krishnamurti had succeeded in throwing off his theosophical inheritance, emerging as a major spiritual teacher in his own right. His declared pacifism was therefore a matter of public interest.

Conscientious objection was an honourable if unpopular choice. Combatants could respect sincere pacifism even after war broke out. What they could not respect – or condone – was a refusal to take sides morally. Krishnamurti could find no difference in practice between British imperialism and German.[5] Having experienced the crudest forms of racialism and class distinction at close quarters among the British, he believed that what the Nazis did was only the brutal manifestation of what other Europeans felt in their hearts.

While he still had European supporters, old friends now committed to the struggle concluded that his American exile – not to speak of his pampered, protected life in country houses and grand hotels, watched over by a praetorian guard of rich women – had shielded him from the uniquely horrible wickedness of Nazism: he ought to be able to see that for once this really was a war between good and evil, however compromised and relative the 'good' might be.

Emily Lutyens took this view.[6] She found it hard to understand Krishnamurti's wider philosophical point: that there is in the end no difference between good and evil, all worldly experience being a form of illusion or *maya*. Less tolerant observers – especially those who railed against Auden, Isherwood and the British expatriates who spent the war in America – went further still, suggesting that pacifism, like emigration, was simply an easy way out of a hard choice. Others saw in the absurdity of refusing to distinguish between Fascists and decent people the inevitable result of dabbling in occult nonsense. Yet ironically, Krishnamurti was to find a timely apologist for both the theory and the practice of his pacifism on his California doorstep, in the most brilliant and celebrated European sceptic of his day.

His new ally was Aldous Huxley, whom he met in the winter of 1937/8.[7] Immensely tall, with a beautiful blind face and a fluting voice in which he was given to describing almost everything as 'Extraordinary!', Huxley had arrived in America at the age of forty-three with a glittering reputation. Immensely talented himself, he came from the huge and privileged clan of Darwins, Huxleys, Stracheys, Stephens, Arnolds, Wedgwoods and Sidgwicks who had dominated Victorian Britain's intellectual life and still exerted enormous influence over it. The scientist T. H. Huxley, the novelist Mrs Humphry Ward, the poet Matthew Arnold and his father Thomas, Headmaster of Rugby, were all Aldous's close relations.[8] The biologist Julian Huxley was his brother, many of the Blooms-berries his distant cousins, and even Darwin himself a connection.

In some ways Aldous was the most remarkable member of the clan. Despite a troubled childhood, which included the early death of his mother, the suicide of an adored elder brother and virtual blindness as the result of an untreated eye infection, he took first-class honours at Oxford, having studied mostly by Braille; and after a brief career as a schoolmaster established himself in the years following the First World War as the coming novelist with *Crome Yellow* (1921), *Antic Hay* (1923) and *Those Barren Leaves* (1925).

For many readers these early stories, like the contemporary novels of Scott Fitzgerald, epitomise the tone of the 1920s: brilliant, bitter and zany. Characters are suspended in what the title of his first book aptly calls *Limbo* (1920), and that is where Huxley remained himself in his twenties and early thirties. Indeed, the sound of clever men chattering in a void is an effect which pursues one through almost all his work, often to wearisome effect. But like his near-contemporary Evelyn Waugh – though by a very different route – Huxley gradually moved from near-nihilism to a form of religious conversion.

With such an intellectual pedigree, his quest for faith was inevitably conducted in terms of late-Victorian debates about the relationship between religion and science. Huxley was too sophist-icated to accept either the unqualified belief in scientific progress which sustained some of his contemporaries or the religious beliefs which consoled others. Temperament, understanding and family background all inclined him to rational pessimism. It was, after all, Aldous's grandfather T. H. Huxley who had coined the word 'agnostic' in the 1890s to describe the problems of religion that could not be solved but would not go away.[9]

Somewhat uneasily, the young Aldous Huxley accepted that Christianity might provide a usable moral code, always providing it was stripped of its metaphysical mumbo-jumbo, though he pointed out that Buddhism or even Theosophy might be a better help in this respect. As early as 1917, writing to his father from Eton College, where he was teaching, he described a conversation about Theosophy with some of the boys, including the fearsome Muriel De La Warr's son, a passionate socialist (and later a Labour minister) who had recently succeeded to his father's title:

> I have long discussions with De La Warr and other boys on the subject of Theosophy, which appears to have excited a number of the more serious minded and thoughtful of the boys. One has to go to work with care: it is no good being too violent. I point out Mrs Besant's errors in science and history, which thickly encrust her books, and try to wean them from the merely superstitious side of it. Except for the bunkum about astral bodies, spiritual hierarchies, reincarnations and so forth, theosophy seems to be a good enough religion – its main principles being that all religions contain some truth and that we ought to be tolerant, which is the sort of thing to be encouraged in an Anglican stronghold like this. A little judicious theosophy seems on the whole an excellent thing.[10]

Huxley was especially impressed by the principled pacifism of many TS members. Born in 1894, he belonged to the generation of young men decimated by the carnage of World War One, which so deeply scarred all who survived it, even those excluded from military service like Huxley himself. What increasingly exercised him after the war was the possibility of doing something practical about the spread of militarism, which could only contribute to another and possibly even bloodier conflict. This was more than a matter of preaching pacifism. War, Huxley perceived, was not some unfortunate accident that occasionally took place, killing unfortunate bystanders. Nor was it forced on unwilling nations, as many people thought, by wicked statesmen or profiteering businessmen (though these had a good deal to answer for). On the contrary: war sprang from the hearts of ordinary people and was regarded by them as an integral, inevitable and even desirable feature of human existence. Of course people *rationally* wanted peace – but they also, somewhere deep inside them, *irrationally* wanted war. Given the power of the irrational over the rational, as recently demonstrated by Freud, it was likely that the urge to self-destruction (which is what the taste for war amounts to) would triumph unless someone did something positive to change attitudes.[11]

The immediate aim for anti-war campaigners, in Huxley's opinion, was to create a climate of feeling in which the desire for peace could become a positive political reality which outweighed the fatalistic drive towards war. With this aim in mind, he joined the Peace Pledge Union, an organisation founded in 1935 by the Reverend Dick Shepherd, Dean of Canterbury.[12] An outspoken maverick who refused to toe the Anglican line despite his high preferment, Shepherd was Britain's most popular and respected churchman between the wars. When he died prematurely in 1937 the streets of London were lined with mourners and a large cortège followed the coffin.

In 1934, worried about the international situation, Shepherd had written to the press, asking how many people would be prepared to take the following pledge:

> We renounce war, and never again, directly or indirectly,
> will we support or sanction another.

Over a hundred thousand letters came pouring in and Shepherd arranged meetings in the Albert Hall to inaugurate the new movement. Its supporters included Siegfried Sassoon, Eric Gill, Vera Brittain, John Middleton Murry and George Lansbury.

Huxley appeared on the platform at one of these meetings, and soon became the union's leading propagandist. *Ends and Means*, his collection of essays about the application of pacifist principles to every aspect of life, has been called the organisation's bible. Huxley also began to give talks on 'The Case for Constructive Peace', as he called a later pamphlet. Arguing against Hobbes and the continental dictators that war is *not* the law of nature, he pointed out that it is a purely man-made thing, and those who make it may refrain from doing so – if they wish. The problem is that many do not so wish. How are they to be persuaded otherwise?

In the long term, what Huxley calls preventive pacifism will only be achieved when individuals and governments understand that peace is ultimately in their own best interests. It is hard to see this happening. Good intentions and even strong arguments, however popular, are virtually powerless against the entrenched economic and political interests driving the world to war. If lasting peace is to be established and sustained it requires a complete overhaul of all the old arrangements, especially the national relationships established by the Treaty of Versailles negotiated at the end of the last war, supposedly to maintain the peace in Europe but in fact to take revenge on the Germans.

In the short term, there are practical courses of action open to peace-loving states. Huxley and his friend Gerald Heard had discovered, for example, that Nazi armament engineers were desperate for nickel, of which they possessed only small supplies. The vital stocks were in Canada. Why could not the British government simply corner the market in nickel and stymie the German war effort? Through family connections Heard and Huxley managed to convey the plan to Chamberlain, but the Prime Minister replied in one word that their proposals were 'Impractical.'[13]

As the likelihood of another European conflict increased with every day that passed, Huxley hoped in vain for a generous gesture from one of the major states to galvanise public opinion, but his private thoughts turned from prevention to the predicament of pacifists when war broke out. Two things were becoming clear to him. First, that it was no use telling governments to behave peacefully when the individuals who supported them had murder in their hearts. Men who hated their wives or their employers could hardly be expected to will real peace, whatever they might say in public. Personal reform from within was therefore vital, and this must be continued even – and especially – in the midst of the coming conflict.

Second, he realised that the agnostic humanism of his youth no longer provided an adequate philosophy to support his beliefs. Whatever Kantian philosophers may say, he concluded, morality cannot be divorced entirely from metaphysics. This conclusion is reflected in Huxley's early novels, when the cynical heroes and heroines try to live by bread alone and find themselves unable to do so. Formulating the grounds of his pacifism had led Huxley to the conclusion that we must recognise the reality of the spiritual domain, however we explain or describe it, for only at the spiritual level can men be united. Whether as metaphysical fact or psychological conviction, the idea of God is essential. But God, whatever His nature, is not to be discovered in the heavens or the churches. He is present in the deepest depths of the self.

Huxley had been working towards this view for some time. *Those Barren Leaves* concludes with Calamy's discovery that the spiritual life is the only solution to the worldly problems that have plagued the other characters in the body of the book. The questions posed by this conclusion are: how to live such a life when there is no god, and what does religion mean in such a context? There are strong echoes of Theosophy. When Calamy's former fellow-guests at the *castello* visit him in his hillside retirement he lectures them, as Huxley's positive characters are apt to do, on the similarities between the essential elements of all the great religions. Jesus, Buddha and Lao Tzu agree in every important respect. The novel ends with a symbol of hope, and there is no sign of the expected irony.[14]

In the years between publication of *Those Barren Leaves* and the outbreak of war in 1939, Huxley's novels and essays returned obsessively to the exploration of ultimate truth within the self. In *Do What You Will* (1930) he writes of 'the truth – the inward truth, I mean, since that is the only truth we can know'.[15] People have for too long sought salvation in churches, books, friends, science, art and politics; but only within ourselves are we likely to find any illumination – and that will be fleeting at best. For the rest of his life his work was shaped by the ironic tension between the aspirations of human knowledge – at its most triumphal in western science and technology – and the finally unknowable depths of the self.

Huxley thus encountered Krishnamurti at the moment when their philosophies were converging. The ex-Theosophist and the former sceptic both now believed that the only route to peace and spiritual truth was subjective. Institutions were, at best, miserable necessities which could achieve nothing by themselves. Knowledge was a means too often mistaken for an end in itself, especially in the form of science.

The two were alike in other ways. Almost exact contemporaries, they were shy, retiring men who had both led sheltered and privileged yet painful lives, losing their mothers in early childhood. Both had been forced into public roles that went against their natures. And although Krishnamurti had successfully resisted the intensive education system of which Huxley was such a triumphant product, both belonged to the Victorian liberal intelligentsia from which Huxley was descended by blood and Krishnamurti by affinity.

Their relationship was facilitated by the close friendship which developed between Rosalind Rajagopal and Huxley's saintly Belgian wife Maria. The house at Ojai became a second home to the itinerant Huxleys, and parts of several books by Aldous, including *After Many a Summer*, in which one of the characters is based on Rosalind and another (partly) on Ouspensky, were bashed out on an old typewriter as he sat on the lawn outside Arya Vihara.[16]

The two couples were part of a close-knit social circle in California during the war years. Bertrand Russell (another PPU supporter), Christopher Isherwood and his boyfriends, the Brechts, the Thomas Manns, the Stravinskys, the Charles Chaplins, Anita Loos, Iris Tree and Greta Garbo all belonged more or less to this circle, whose centres were Huxley and Krishnamurti – a fine irony given the detachment practised by both men. There was a round of social events, including communal holidays, lunches and dinners, plays and concerts, and picnics in the hills and deserts round Los Angeles. Though Krishnamurti was theoretically in retreat for much of the time, he enjoyed social life. He also liked to be up and doing. When not working in the garden at Ojai – incorporated into the citrus farm in wartime to increase food production – he looked after young Radha and her menagerie of animals.

The Huxleys had moved to America from the south of France in 1937, settling in California with their fellow-emigrant Gerald Heard. Huxley and Heard were both brilliant, talkative, witty and endlessly learned, their incisiveness a world away from the absurdities of Leadbeaterian cosmology and the simple faith which motivated many Theosophists. Yet they had followed a very familiar track among twentieth-century intellectuals and writers, a track which leads from scepticism and agnosticism through and beyond intellectual questioning to the rediscovery of religion in a form which is ironically close to the theosophical ideal of a synthetic wisdom religion, combining the common doctrines and best aspects of all faiths. This journey found literary expression in Huxley's anthology of mystical writings, *The Perennial Philosophy*, published in 1946. Expounding the theory that knowledge is a function of being and that the cultivation of being is essentially a religious activity, *The Perennial Philosophy*'s introduction includes paragraphs that might be lifted from the works of Blavatsky or Besant.

In later life Huxley came round to the view that the mystical and magical aspects of religious experience are not only real but vital. Nevertheless, he complained to the psychic investigator J. B. Rhine, in whose work he took a keen interest, about the pathetic susceptibility of much of the human race to the 'Baconian-pyramidological-cryptographic-spiritualist-theosophical syndrome'.[17] To this susceptibility he saw no limit.

Gerald Heard was more tolerant of such absurdities: indeed, tolerance was in general something he made a point of.[18] Though he shared a house with his friend Christopher Wood, the two men lived very different lives. Wood was a hedonistic homosexual, Heard an ascetic celibate: the saint who needed his sinner, as Isherwood later saw it. But Heard's saintliness – like Huxley's – extended to more than chastity. In Europe the two men had been liberal agnostics – sharp, witty sceptics, with an endless fund of weary tolerance for the equally endless foolishness of a world they contemplated and analysed with such fascination. Both were polymaths, always stocked with scientific facts, social and economic statistics, obscure anecdotes and an extraordinary range of knowledge in all the arts and sciences, and both had concluded that human life was a foolish post-Nietzschean charade in which rational men must just do their best to improve things, while understanding all the while that this best was likely to be frustrated by human folly. They were also intellectual magpies, ready to snap up whatever took their fancy into a vast, idiosyncratic learning.

Olympian in their knowledge, culture and sensibility, they rose above circumstances with perhaps just a little too much wry indulgence. But in the absurd, sensuous air of California, which tempts so many to abandon the life of the mind in favour of the body, gratified or mortified, they found themselves confronted with another kind of reality altogether. In the vacancy of the desert they encountered the reality of God. This was not an experience conducive to informed detachment, and each man devoted the rest of his life to understanding the encounter.

Born in 1889, Heard was five years older than Huxley, but it was not only his seniority in years which gave him such influence over his more famous and successful friend. An opinionated, learned, histrionic Irishman, everyone agreed that Heard had an extraordinary air of authority. Like his friend Wystan Auden, he produced *dicta* on almost any subject, and even such a man as Huxley acknowledged his superiority. Though always polite and considerate, he liked to sway others to his views – and Heard had views on everything.

Once he became interested in God, his moral authority acquired an added spiritual dimension; symbolised, as Isherwood noted, by the Christ-like beard he grew in America, which seemed to point his face to the heavens above. America and religion worked other changes in Heard, a fastidious but theatrical man who dressed formally in London but took to shabby denim on the west coast. His new life soon transformed his appearance from metropolitan intellectual to man of God. He followed an appropriately ascetic regime, eating, drinking and sleeping little and meditating three times a day for two-hour stretches. If there was play-acting in all this, it was a necessary preliminary to the real thing. By behaving like a saint Heard might hope to become one.

*

Though Huxley and Heard were immediately impressed by Krishnamurti, they were already followers of another, more orthodox Indian guru, Swami Prabhavananda, head of the Ramakrishna Order in Los Angeles.[19] Hindu missions had been established in America at the end of the nineteenth century by Ramakrishna's disciples, who settled mainly on the west coast. Ministering at first to migrant Indian workers, they began to make native converts. Prabhavananda, a pupil of Brahmanandra, who was in turn a disciple of Ramakrishna himself, was Huxley's near-contemporary. Born in Bengal in 1893, he had been sent to America thirty years later to lead one of the missions founded by Vivekananda – another Ramakrishna disciple – on his second visit to the States in 1899. Shortly after this visit, one of Vivekananda's converts, the widowed Mrs Carrie Mead Wyckhoff, gave her house in Hollywood to the Swami, and here, at 1946 Ivar Avenue on the hills overlooking Hollywood Boulevard, the Los Angeles Vedanta Center was established. In 1938 a temple with onion domes was built in the garden and Mrs Wyckhoff still lived in the community as a nun under the name of Sister Lalita.[20]

Prabhavananda taught his pupils the doctrines of Vedanta. Drawn from the sacred texts of the Vedas, India's ancient scriptures, which are the foundation of Hindu religion and philosophy, Vedanta – which means literally 'the end of the Vedas' – signifies both the sum and the crown of human knowledge. The aim of Vedanta is *moksa*, or liberation from suffering. It teaches that the *atman* (essential self) and the Absolute are one; that true reality is accessible only to intuition (and not to logical thought); and that appearances are illusory. The tasks of an enlightened individual are to discriminate between the eternal and the temporal, to renounce non-spiritual desires, to cultivate self-control and to strive after *moksa*.

Converts were comparatively few at first. The residents in the new centre pooled their resources and lived very simply. Most Californians simply assumed that the Swami was another Hollywood character, and when the telephone rang at the centre it was often someone requesting a horoscope or a demonstration of the

Indian rope trick. Gradually the community became known and people took it more seriously. There were applications to join – some applicants wanting to become full-blown monks or nuns living at Ivar Avenue, others visiting the temple for devotions and spiritual advice. The community never numbered more than twenty, but the Swami's influence began to spread, especially among European émigrés. Most of those who contacted him, like Heard and Huxley, were interested though not committed. But his most celebrated convert was a real catch, another English émigré introduced to Vedanta by Heard.

As he was later to admit, Christopher Isherwood was at this time a sort of spiritual tourist, much as he and his friends had been political tourists in the early 1930s, dallying with all the radical ideologies on offer but never settling down with one for long. He had emigrated to America just before the war. Arriving in New York with Auden in January 1939, he found himself for once at a loose end while his friend prospered. This was an unusual experience for the handsome, charming novelist, who was used to success and having his own way; but while Auden flourished in the free air of America, released for good from the family ties (real and imagined) which had oppressed him at home, Isherwood seems to have found that his background had sustained him more than he suspected. It was one thing to be an *enfant terrible* among a familiar and indulgent audience; quite another to be an unknown quantity in a hostile city.

Auden – hugely prolific and a natural solitary – thrived on hard work and his new-found social success. Isherwood, by contrast, was unable to write. Instead he turned to sex, alternating bouts of promiscuity with the attempt to find a long-lasting relationship. It was militant homosexuality that eventually brought him to the doctrinaire pacifism of Heard and Huxley. But whereas their crusade for peace was a matter of intellectual principle, carefully thought through, Isherwood's was typically the product of strong personal feeling. It was possible that his former lover Heinz would be conscripted into the German Army. How could Isherwood fight in a war that might involve him in shooting at the boy and his old friends? The odds against this happening point to the irrational streak in Isherwood's approach to the question. They also suggest his ability to find good personal reasons for justifying his attachment to unpopular causes.

But irrational pacifism led Isherwood rationally to religion when he found that, like Huxley, he needed a surer foundation for his beliefs, and (unlike Huxley) deliverance from his rackety life. Detesting most forms of Christianity – not least for their association with the life he had abandoned in England – he was drawn to Hinduism by what seemed to be the combination of moral freedom, doctrinal subtlety and sheer exoticism. Once again the overwhelming reasons were personal: enticed by the idea of Vedanta, he was soon enchanted by Prabhavananda's personal charm.

Typically, neither Huxley nor Heard was in any way committed to the Swami, and by 1941 Heard had dissociated himself from the centre on the grounds that the Swami wasn't austere enough to lead a truly religious life. This charge understandably made the Swami extremely angry. He replied to Heard (in print) that 'A man of true renunciation concerns himself neither with poverty nor riches,'[21] implying (with considerable justice) that his former follower was a little too demonstratively ascetic. Isherwood agreed, though he puts it another way. Heard, he thought, was a life-hater who recoiled from the good-natured bustle of the daily round at the Vedanta Center, where a seemingly endless series of rites and devotions involved the female followers in preparing meals and offerings, the males in practising pointless ceremonies. Isherwood liked precisely this aspect of life in the community. Even when he tired of what he described to Maria Huxley as the 'endless yacking about God'[22] indulged in by his intellectual friends, Christopher could revel in the cosy muddle of Ivar Avenue.

While Heard enjoyed the drama of a definite break with the Swami, Huxley drifted away from Vedanta gradually, having taken from it what he wanted: a method of meditation, and support for his existing religious views. But it was while his older friends were moving away from Hinduism that Isherwood was reaching the moment of his closest commitment to it. He took a while to come round to the idea of being involved at all. For one thing, his whole past life seemed to be against it. For another, his sexual habits and his work in the film studios seemed to be at odds with it.

First he tried working in a Quaker community, but found this uncomfortable. He couldn't help sensing among these saintly people their unspoken disapproval of his way of life – as well he might: before joining them he had been sharing a flat with Denny Fouts, a high-class male tart. Yet even that period in his life was not without its religious commitment. In the spring of 1941 Isherwood and Denny decided to put into practice Heard's receipt for 'intentional living', meditating for long periods each day, and keeping to a strict regime involving complete abstinence from sex and alcohol. Not surprisingly, the experiment was a failure. For the next few years Isherwood alternated between periods of complete celibacy (he once managed six months) and riotous promiscuity.

Meanwhile Heard was trying to persuade Isherwood – and even Denny – to join his own experimental community. At first this was to be a small-scale affair, but in 1942 Heard was given the money to establish a sort of monastery, which he built at Trabuco, sixty miles south of Los Angeles. The building was constructed under the direction of Isherwood's energetic cousin Felix Greene, who had given up his job with the Quaker service committee in Philadelphia to become a disciple of Heard's. He rushed round buying up materials before they were commandeered for the war, and finished the place in record time. Heard henceforward referred to the community as his college or 'club for mystics'.[23] The project had strong echoes of early Theosophy: it was intended to be non-dogmatic and non-sectarian, a gathering-place for those trying to understand their spiritual experience, or lack of it. But there were also hints of the Prieuré: inmates laboured in the garden and contributed to the communal welfare.

Trabuco was hardly a suitable venture for Isherwood, who found himself increasingly in need of more guidance than such an organisation could by its nature offer. Heard had designed the place in his own image for people of his own sort, but Isherwood felt in his spiritual life – as he had felt in his personal life – the simultaneous need to submit and to rebel. It also seems likely that he found the Swami a more congenial teacher than Heard, on the grounds that an Oriental was easier to obey than someone from his own background.

So instead of joining the loose-knit group at Trabuco he went to the other extreme, becoming an acolyte at the Ivar Avenue temple in 1943, where he shared quarters with three other men. His colleagues were George, a taciturn novice already on the path to full vows, who had paid for a private bedroom and bathroom and who spent the days making his devotions and typing up notes of everything the Swami said; and Richard and Webster, two seventeen-year-old boys from Hollywood High School whose parents were followers of Ramakrishna.

While nominally a mission, the centre did not go in for aggressive proselytising. Most of the residents were too self-aware and sardonic about their own situation. The men were more detached than the women. When Sister Sarada reported that the local pest exterminator seemed interested in their work, George summed up their attitude to unlikely conversions with the words 'From ratman to Atman'.[24] Though his attachment to the spiritual life was genuine, the novelist in Isherwood couldn't help taking a strong interest in the community's daily routine as spectacle, and his book about it is filled with piquant details of the personal habits of the residents.

Life at the centre was both domestically disciplined and personally relaxed, like a friendlier version of the Prieuré. The nuns, who had all taken Indian names, lived in another part of the complex where Sister Lalita watched over the English Amiya, the Norwegian Sarada, the American Yogini and the Irish Sudhira. All the inmates took their meals together and shared out the domestic tasks – though in Hindu fashion it was the women who did the housework. There were lectures and prayers and frequent visitors, including fellow-disciples from other Vedanta centres. And there was also a good deal of amusement. In fact, life at the centre was more amusing for everyone after Isherwood joined. The cerebral spirituality of Heard and Huxley was not for him. He told Heard that what he wanted from Swami was not moral guidance but assurance that God existed. He was as much a life-lover as he thought Heard a life-hater, joining enthusiastically in a group outing to the cinema where *The Song of Bernadette* made them all cry.

Swami took personal charge of the new acolyte, who found the guru–disciple relationship and the devotionalism deplored by Krishnamurti, Heard and Huxley ('You should hear Krishnamurti on the subject of gurus . . .!' Huxley wrote to a friend[25]) just what he wanted. Isherwood also relished the mess at Ivar Avenue, just as his kindred spirit and fellow-homosexual novelist Forster had relished it in India twenty years earlier.

Prabhavananda presided over the household as a benevolent if often despotic and erratic ruler. He was a small, jolly, friendly, emotional man, with slightly Mongolian features, a chain smoker and a passionate Indian nationalist. Quietly spoken and scrupulously polite for the most part, he was subject to occasional tantrums. He often scolded the inmates of the centre in Gurdjieffian fashion for no apparent reason, just as his master Brahmananda had scolded him, while showing favouritism to others, especially to Isherwood, whose company he enjoyed and whose fame he found flattering.

Yet while he was no recluse, the Swami managed to stay above the temptations of Hollywood, where more adeptly self-dramatising gurus were in continuous demand. People were impressed by his ability to live chastely in a notoriously corrupting world. Even Auden, who disapproved of 'all that heathen mumbo-jumbo',[26] nevertheless declared that the Swami was obviously a saint. Isherwood agreed. He found his view confirmed by the very worldliness which Heard so much disliked. When a mutual friend was caught soliciting in a men's lavatory, all the Swami said was, 'Oh Chris, if only he hadn't got caught. Why didn't he go to some bar?'[27] And though he gently pressured Isherwood to join his community and even to become a monk there, he tolerated and even approved his work in films.

Isherwood was now writing scripts for film studios, as he continued to do for the rest of his life. Soon after his arrival in California he had encountered some friends who were part of the German emigration from Hitler. Salka and Bertold Viertel had both found employment in Hollywood and they soon introduced their old friend Chris to MGM, where he was taken on at what he considered the absurdly high salary of $500 per week (though the more celebrated Huxley was getting three times that and sent most of it to Europe).

One incidental perk of working in films was meeting the stars, and there was tremendous excitement at the centre in July 1943 when Salka Viertel brought Greta Garbo to lunch. Garbo played up to the expectations of Isherwood's fellow-disciples, just as he hoped she would, comparing an actress's life unfavourably with a nun's and flirting with the Swami. The women duly found her very spiritual, the men very beautiful, and Prabhavananda commented that his only remaining worldly ambition was to meet the Duke of Windsor.

Instead he had to make do with Krishnamurti, who attended a class at the centre in 1944, sitting quietly at the back while Prabhavananda talked. At first the Swami was suspicious about his distinguished visitor. Years before, Annie Besant had pestered Brahmananda to become involved in the Theosophical Society, and the fiercely nationalistic Swami associated Krishnamurti with Theosophy and Theosophy with European colonialism. But it soon became clear that Krishnamurti no longer had anything to do with the Theosophical Society; indeed, he showed the greatest reverence for the Swami's Hindu rites and the occasion went off quietly. At the end the two men saluted one another and appeared to feel mutual respect.

Like Krishnamurti, the Swami had by this time learnt to move easily in the crazy world of California dinners, lunches and women's-club meetings so aptly caught in Huxley's novel *After Many a Summer*. In 1949 he even made indirect contact with Gurdjieff, when he visited Frank Lloyd Wright at Taliesin. Though he never became a society guru, the Swami was adept at addressing ladies' meetings, dressed in a neat grey suit and tie, and he rather enjoyed going to parties.

But the high point of his social success came when he almost found himself working for a Hollywood studio – just as Krishnamurti had briefly done twenty years before. In 1943 Somerset Maugham contacted Isherwood for advice about the epigraph to his novel *The Razor's Edge*. The epigraph was taken from the *Katha Upanishad*, and Maugham took a guarded interest in Vedanta, even writing an essay on the Ramana Maharshi, a holy man he had met in India. This essay he submitted to Isherwood for correction on points of dogma, later publishing it as 'The Saint' in his book *Points of View*. In 1945 Maugham arrived in Hollywood to script the film of *The Razor's Edge* with Cukor directing. Prabhavananda was called in as an adviser. In the end, the picture was scripted and directed by other people who ignored the Swami's offer of help, but he enjoyed his brief foray into the film world, and the occasion of it could hardly have been more suitable. Maugham's novel is about a worldly young man whose search for faith ends successfully in Vedanta, and Isherwood was often identified as a model for the hero, Larry, though he denied it.

His denials became more irritable as he realised that his own commitment to Vedanta was weakening. The pull of other lives was proving too strong. He missed his work as a novelist and sex was a constant temptation, especially whenever he visited the Viertels at Santa Monica, where the beach swarmed with attractive men. He made friends with Tennessee Williams (also writing film scripts) and they talked at length about sex, though Isherwood didn't accompany the playwright on his cruising expeditions among the cliff-tops, where a wartime horde of bored servicemen waited for pick-ups.

The trouble was that, as Denny Fouts later pointed out, Isherwood was still behaving like a tourist or a tart, sampling many worlds and settling for none. Auden was to make the same point in a different way: you had to choose one kind of life, he believed, just as you had to choose one set of beliefs and one sexual taste, understanding their advantages and accepting their drawbacks.

Like other émigrés, Isherwood was also unsettled by the distant war in Europe, though the only tangible reminders of this were the huge troop shipments out of Los Angeles and the miserable conscripts who swarmed round the bars as they waited for their berths to the Pacific islands. Stirring memories of his old life in Europe, these tokens of war brought Isherwood closer to his fellow-refugees, especially the Germans, than to his English-speaking American cousins.

For a while his enthusiasm for Vedanta was rekindled by the prospect of collaborating with the Swami on a translation of Hindu scriptures. They began with the Gita, which Isherwood rendered first into lumbering Victorian prose; and then, when that was severely criticised by Huxley, into an Audenesque Old English epic. But by the spring of 1944 he had decided not to become a monk, though he stayed in the centre for some months more, only gradually loosening his connection with it as he was drawn back into the complications of life at the film studios, where he was now working for Warner Brothers. In the summer of 1945 he moved out of the centre to live with a new boyfriend. He began to travel again, resuming his old life as a peripatetic novelist and travel writer, and though he continued to collaborate in translations with Prabhava-nanda, it was the end of their close father–son relationship.

Yet the emotional tie of this relationship remained strong, as Heard and Huxley acknowledged some years later when they appealed in desperation to the Swami to talk to their young friend about his promiscuous habits with men and drugs. By this time Heard had abandoned Trabuco in favour of a more reclusive life, and in 1949 he handed the college over to the Vedanta Society. The Swami moved in and Isherwood occasionally visited him there. These visits confirmed his view that he had been right to abandon taking monastic vows, when he saw the 'boys' who lived in the community slaving away all day at the gardening in their heavy boots and shorts as though chained to their task. Isherwood relished a spot of weeding when he felt like it, but he was no more suited to sweated labour than the spiritual life, and he knew it. He also reflected that he wouldn't be 'a good companion for the boys'.[28]

That was one way of putting it. Another was to say that Isherwood was drifting back into a life of obsessive boozing and whoring, spurred on by his quest for the perfect friend and his misery when the man of the moment turned out to be less than perfect. Though theoretically broad-minded, Huxley and Heard were distressed by this behaviour. They were also genuinely concerned for their friend. More dramatically, Heard believed that his former disciple was drifting into atheism. He even told Isher-wood that 'something' was stalking him, trying to possess him, echoing Wedgwood's dire warnings about the Black Forces in pursuit of Krishnamurti.

In the end Isherwood's problems were resolved not by religion but by the more Isherwoodian solution of meeting the eighteen-

year-old Don Bachardy in the spring of 1953. They were soon
lovers. Throughout his life Isherwood had been looking for father
figures, ranging from Auden to God. Now it was his turn to play the
parental role. In so doing he found stability in his life for the first
time.[29]

Like everything else in his life, Isherwood's drift away from
Vedanta was a personal matter, unrelated to the great shifts of
sentiment and belief in his day. Huxley and Heard, on the other
hand, liked to argue that their apostasy was a matter of principle,
though it was encouraged by their friendship with Krishnamurti,
whose disapproval of guruism and dislike of ritual chimed in with
their sentiments. After their first meeting in 1937 the three were
soon close friends – at least as close as any of them could be to
anyone – especially Krishnamurti and Huxley, who later wrote to a
friend that 'At one time I followed the somewhat mechanical
methods taught by the Swamis of the Ramakrishna Mission; but
now I find more profitable those of Krishnamurti which are much
closer to Zen methods'.[30] The admission gives a clue to what Huxley
was looking for. While Heard went in quest of divine illumination,
Huxley pursued the more mundane objective of a psychotherapy, in
both senses of the word, spiritual and mental. Huxley had a
weakness for quack remedies of every kind. He persistently thought
of human life itself as a sickness for which a cure was urgently
needed and might indeed be found, though he also had the self-
knowledge to satirise such aspirations:

> My own feeling is that, if we could combine Krishnamurti
> with old Dr Vittoz's brand of psycho-therapy and F. M.
> Alexander's method of 'creative conscious control' of
> posture and bodily function, with a bit of general semantics
> thrown in to help us steer clear of verbal and conceptual
> pitfalls, and a sensible diet, we would have solved the
> problem of preventive medicine and, along with it, at least
> half the problem of education . . .[31]

The comment on general semantics and the afterthought about 'a sensible diet' are pure Huxley: half serious, half self-mocking, part Victorian rationalist and part New Age faddist.

Equally typically, and more astutely, he concludes that 'needless to say, people will continue to go in for vaccines, popery and meprobamate . . .' As the years passed, both Heard and Huxley became less interested in religion as therapy and more preoccupied with spiritual illumination and the sense of oneness with God – or with what Heard called 'this thing'. They searched for the supreme gift of the religious consciousness, hoping to transcend their intellectual, discursive, endlessly reflective approach in favour of the immediate apprehension of unity, oneness and the godhead. Famously, they tried to achieve this state through drugs: not meprobamate (a sedative) but mescalin. In May 1953 Huxley volunteered to take part in psychological experiments conducted by the psychiatrist Dr Humphrey Osmond. The experiments involved taking 0.4 gram of mescalin. Huxley found the intensely heightened perception induced by the mescalin exciting, though he was not sure what to make of it.[32]

His friends were alarmed. Krishnamurti and Prabhavananda both regarded the use of drugs as dangerous, decadent and misleading, but Huxley continued to experiment while urging caution on others. Having satirised the use of pills to produce immediate gratification in his own utopian parody *Brave New World* (1932), he was not unaware of the perils involved and his native puritanism made him especially censorious of those who abused drugs for pleasure. He also foresaw the possible consequences of creating a drug culture with aims that were far from his own quest after spiritual enlightenment. If true knowledge is a function of being, as Huxley might have put it, false knowledge can only lead to the diminution of being. The illusion that drugs alone can be the route to enlightenment or that they can relieve the ills of the world – classic axioms of false knowledge – are both consequences and causes of mescalin misuse. Huxley insisted that mind-expanding stimulants can only serve as secondary aids to meditation and must be taken by responsible adults under carefully controlled conditions.

Despite his precautions, a drug culture did indeed come into existence as one element in the New Age mores of mid-twentieth-century California, and drug abuse in the name of spiritual illumination became widespread wherever that culture was found. The irony is that Huxley's ascetic writing about religion in these years unwittingly helped to promote the illegitimate use of drugs as 'liberated' New Age attitudes entered mainstream culture. These attitudes include the assumption that there is a direct link between enlightenment and pleasure. It is just this link that drugs were thought to provide. But Huxley well knew that the lines between the extremes of pain and pleasure and the true state of spiritual bliss are hard if not impossible to draw: mistaking one condition for another is a well-known peril of the religious life. It is one reason we are warned against hedonism in that life – and hedonism was the watchword of New Age culture in the middle years of our century.[33]

Huxley's own attitude to hedonism is well summed up in one of his best forgotten novels, *After Many a Summer*, published on the eve of the Second World War.[34] Apparently a satire in his earlier manner, it is in fact a parable. The plot concerns the quest for eternal life. Reversing Shaw's theory in *Back To Methuselah*, the book's ironic theme is that longevity is no solution to life's problems because it can only be bought at an intolerable price.

Under the patronage of a multi-millionaire terrified by death, Dr Obispo is experimenting with life-prolonging techniques. After many experiments he concludes that the secret is to be found in carp entrails. Meanwhile, working on a collection of documents else-where in the millionaire's absurd castle (based on Hearst's San Simeon), the scholar Jeremy Pordage discovers that the Earl of Gonister, an eighteenth-century libertine who wanted to prolong his life of pleasure, reached the same conclusion as Obispo two hundred years earlier. Forcing himself to eat raw carp-liver to achieve his goal, the earl died nevertheless.

The two strands of the story come together when Obispo, visiting England with his employer, takes the opportunity to investigate Lord Gonister's deserted mansion. Deep in the cellars he finds a pair of indescribably filthy, ape-like creatures who turn out to be the earl and his mistress. They have indeed survived far beyond the

natural span, concealed from curious onlookers in the cellar and
sustained by bequests in a will the earl made when he pretended to
die (in order to escape the consequences of his evil life).

Though we cannot know whether he regrets the outcome of his
experiments, the earl has paid heavily for his long years by reverting
to the condition of primitive man, the urbane aristocrat turned
chattering, copulating chimp with only the tattered ribbon of the
Garter (an order of chivalry) to indicate his human origins. This is
not the spiritual outcome of longevity envisaged by Shaw. On the
contrary, evolution has gone into reverse. For this ape-man confined to his cellar, existence has defeated its own ends, narrowed
down exclusively to the gratification of desires which were once its
luxurious embellishment. In this case, at least, knowledge has
become the enemy of being.

After Many a Summer was only the first sign of Huxley's growing
interest in the idea of regression which culminates in *Ape and
Essence*, published just ten years later in 1949. This strange little
novel is concerned with a theme which has become too painfully
familiar since 1949: the period after a nuclear holocaust. In a
fantastic parody of a Hollywood film script (which, in the way of
Hollywood, turned fantasy into reality when *The Planet of the Apes*
was made), Huxley imagines a time on the west coast of America
when:

> The Baboon [is] master,
> That monsters may be begotten.[35]

And despite an ending in which two lovers escape from the cruel
regime of the apes who now dominate the earth, this is a sombre,
even savage, book. One target is false religion – the worship of Belial
– which is lambasted as a tool of exploitation. By implication we are
to suppose that conventional 'true' religion may be put to the same
purpose. Who could guess from this novel – a very characteristic
product of a period in which the reputation of religion in general was
at a low ebb – that a vast spiritual revival was about to begin on the
west coast, powered in part by the work of Huxley himself?

EIGHTEEN

Terminations

While Krishnamurti was discovering the pleasures of private life in California, Ouspensky gave way to gloomy wartime exile in New England. The respective locations are fitting: though both Ouspensky and Krishnamurti have since been appropriated by the New Age movement associated with the west coast of America, one can imagine what Ouspensky would have had to say about *that*. For all his interest in the dottier reaches of occultism, he remained by temperament an east coast intellectual: credulous where he believed but fiercely sceptical where he did not. In his last years the inner battle between credulity and scepticism was to reach a tragic and unexpected climax.

The move to America was a matter of prudence. It was less than twenty years since the Ouspenskys had been caught out by the horrors of the Russian Revolution and Civil War: this time they were prepared. Madame Ouspensky decamped from Lyne in January 1941 and Ouspensky soon followed. He left with reluctance – although he had never warmed to the people, he liked his English life, he was attached to his cats, and he was growing old and fond of the bottle – but there was no alternative.

It was not only the immediate danger of blitz and invasion that concerned Ouspensky. Despite his disengagement from politics, he was an interested observer of the political scene and a man of strong opinions who detested the Bolsheviks. A natural reaction after his suffering and exile at their hands, this detestation was intensified by general pessimism about the European outlook. For twenty-five years, apart from a brief period of hope in the 1920s, he had watched the world sinking into brutality with a gloomy relish at the accuracy of his own prophecies. In the unlikely event of a German defeat, he predicted the triumph of Bolshevism throughout Europe.[1]

Madame Ouspensky arrived in America in January 1941, and yet another community was established, at Franklin Farms, Mendham, near New York. The farm was populated by English emigrants and by some of Orage's former American pupils, though others remained aloof, suspicious either of Gurdjieff's rejection of Orage or Ouspensky's split with the Master, or both. When Ouspensky began a course of lectures in New York, he found himself in the curious position of expounding much of Gurdjieff's doctrine, as also taught separately by his wife, while refusing to have anything to do with Gurdjieff the man and banning all reference to the Gurdjieff writings which had provided the basis of Orage's American teaching. Not surprisingly, many of Ouspensky's new pupils were confused.

Ouspensky and Sophia Grigorievna as usual went their own ways, she cleaving to pure Gurdjieffian doctrine, he preferring to teach his own synthesis of the Master's work. At the same time, he reacted furiously when anyone else attempted to synthesise elements of *his* ideas on their own account, enforcing his copyright by banning all teaching of, or writing about, the System without his explicit permission. When his disciple J. G. Bennett flouted this commandment, three thousand miles away in England, Bennett was promptly excommunicated and other pupils were forbidden to contact him. As usual, some of them interpreted the quarrel as a ploy to force Bennett to stand on his own feet, a response typical of the byzantine politics and tragicomic psychodramas which beset Gurdjieff's legacy.

Such petty outbursts apart, Ouspensky's life in America was largely a blank, the endless recycling of old ways in a new landscape. He continued to teach and drink. By the time he returned to Britain in January 1947 he was a sick and disappointed man, whose alcoholic gloom could only be compounded by the drabness of food-rationing and a post-war English winter. He had long since forgotten his own advice to a pupil who asked him how to cope with negative feelings:

Think about something cheerful. There are many things in
the system. You can take any subject and compare your
own individual questions, how you thought before and how
you think now, and you will see that you gain one thing
and another thing and a third thing.[2]

Ouspensky had always been fascinated by time travel, but it
hardly mattered how many 'things' he thought of now: neither the
past nor the present gave him any satisfaction. As for the future, it
was not even clear what he was returning *to*. Perhaps, now that
Russia was apparently closed for ever, England offered him the only
freely available part of his past and to that he was retreating: if he
had not become an Englishman, England was at least the place he
knew as home. Or perhaps he was merely escaping *from* America – a
country even less congenial than England.

For despite his eastward journeys in search of spiritual illumination, Ouspensky remained a European, a westernised Russian
steeped in the German philosophical traditions which in their time
epitomised the loftiest heights of European culture. However
heavily it leant on European religious teaching, his System was
couched in Western terms. But now there was a serious question-
mark over whether the region which had made him what he was
could any longer be regarded as civilised, let alone a suitable
location for the spiritual evolution of the planet. After two catastrophic wars, Europe was bleeding to death from self-inflicted
wounds. Ouspensky's return there, when he could easily have
stayed in America, was therefore both a homecoming and an
admission of defeat.

He was not alone in his pessimism. By the time Ouspensky
returned, J. G. Bennett was seriously investigating the possibility of
moving his own religious community from south London to South
Africa. Bennett saw the post-war period in terms of his cyclical
theory of crises.[3] He believed that Europe was approaching the end
of a life-cycle. The world wars were signs of an era in its death-
spasm.[4] Yet all was not lost. However pessimistic in theory, Bennett
was a temperamental optimist. There was a chance for survival, he
thought – but only if Europeans could turn away decisively from the

materialism of recent years to a truly spiritual path. Then there was a chance not only for Europe to save itself but also to save mankind, now threatened with extermination by man-made means. If this could be done, human beings might even prove to have acquired through recent suffering the wisdom to develop further along the evolutionary path to spiritual enlightenment. The Age of Aquarius would then be at hand.

The problem with this process of change was that it required not only the preservation of the world from destruction but the appearance of spiritual leaders of the highest calibre. Such leaders, Bennett knew, were not to be found among ordinary men. Ouspensky and Gurdjieff had both alerted him to the existence of a hidden brotherhood who directed human affairs, and Gurdjieff had hinted that he himself was either a member of that brotherhood or at least in touch with it. The objective of the Work and the System was to render oneself worthy of communion with the Brothers and even – who knows? – to become one of their number. Bennett now wondered whether he himself might not be on the way to such a destiny.

In *Back To Methuselah* Shaw had expounded not only the possibility of human immortality (or something very like it) but its absolute necessity if mankind was to fulfil its evolutionary purpose. This was the doctrine Bennett now began to expound as his writings took on an increasingly millenarian note, the note that was to be heard more and more among alternative spiritual teachers as the twentieth century approached its end. Belief in the imminence of a major upheaval in cosmic affairs – whether by nuclear war or ecological catastrophe – gave a new twist to the impetus to found self-sustaining communities. Not only would such communities serve to produce a new kind of human being: in the event of world cataclysm they might well prove to be humanity's only chance for continuing existence, and necessary refuges for the few hidden brothers who would have to regenerate the race or preside over the emergence of a new one. Either way, it seemed as though the evolution of Madame Blavatsky's baboon might be about to accelerate. But would it be forwards – or backwards, as Huxley had surmised in *After Many a Summer*? Though the prophet in Bennett expected the worst, the practical man of affairs could not believe there was nothing to be done, and the self-appointed saviour saw a starring role in Doomsday for himself.

Ouspensky did not share his former pupil's optimism. It was not that he saw no future for humanity: he simply couldn't care about it any more.[5] He had never had much time for human beings. Now that he was old, ill and tired his main pleasure consisted of long car journeys to places associated with his past, usually at night and accompanied by several cats. He clearly preferred the cats to his human companions, and indeed his own nature had always been feline: aloof, suspicious, fierce and quick. Arriving at his destination, he rarely left the car, preferring to stare out of the window while cuddling his pets on the back seat. Given the human company available to him (his wife had remained in America), one can see why. Returning home from one journey, he spent the rest of the night in the car while a female pupil stood over him at the window, her arm raised as if in benediction. A cat would never have done anything so stupid.

Ouspensky was now too ill and tired even to point this out. He was also alarmingly vague and indecisive. Having decided, after a short while coping with the drabness of the post-war regime in Britain, to return to American luxury after all, he arrived at Southampton docks to board his ship, only to change his mind at the last moment. But indecisiveness was only the outward sign of something more serious. For involved with his personal despair, his political gloom and his practical distaste for the realities of post-war rationing was a constitutional tendency to doubt which fed disastrously on the growing suspicion that his whole life had been founded on a mistake. If that were the case, perhaps it was all the same whether he stayed in London or moved to New York.

Although estranged from Gurdjieff personally (he had rejected a post-war invitation to visit Paris),[6] Ouspensky had continued to trust in the teaching for thirty years, sure that his master was – or had once been – in touch with some deep spiritual source. Now he was not so certain. While his pupils continued to believe in the existence of such a source, Ouspensky himself did not. No one can say how or why this happened: whether he underwent a late change of heart, or whether lifelong doubts reasserted themselves as his body treacherously weakened with age and years of bingeing on Château Yquem. Whatever the cause, he now lost his faith in both Gurdjieff and the System as completely as he had found it in St Petersburg three decades before.

Painful for the teacher, such a development is catastrophic for his pupils, especially when they have been subjected to the iron rule of an Ouspensky. At a final series of six meetings held in London and attended by over three hundred people – the full membership of the Historico-Psychological Society, as Ouspensky had christened his group before the war[7] – he answered questions through an intermediary. The meetings otherwise followed the usual pattern, the audience falling into a total hush for many minutes before the master painfully ascended the dais with the help of a walking-stick, and then putting a series of respectful questions to the clearly hostile Ouspensky.

The intermediary rejected most of these questions as 'incomprehensible' – a piquant reversal of the usual situation at such meetings when banal questions were met with puzzling replies. Ouspensky then declined to respond positively to most of the enquiries she did let through, and when goaded beyond endurance by questions about the School, the Source and the System, finally announced that there was no system, that the language he had been using for decades was meaningless, that no school or source existed, and that the only way forward was for each person to look into themselves and decide what it was they really wanted. Searching for the origins of wisdom, he implied, had been an illusion fostered by Gurdjieff. If they wanted to save anything from the wreckage of the past twenty years his pupils should abandon the strenuous life of the System in favour of self-knowledge. There was nothing else.[8]

The unavoidable comparison with Krishnamurti's public defection from Theosophy only underlines the sadness of the occasion. For Krishnamurti the change had meant freedom, for Ouspensky bitter acceptance of defeat. He had invested his whole life in a quest that should never have begun. Or should one say that he had forgotten his own origins? For Ouspensky himself had stated years before that the spiritual quest is its own justification. In the words of

Eliot's *Four Quartets*, published only four years before Ouspensky's death and influenced by the System, 'In my end is my beginning.'[9]

Yet some of Ouspensky's followers – and they invoked his authority for the claim – believed that their teacher was preparing himself in these days for a final tremendous test, putting all his energy into self-remembering so that he could die with full consciousness. On this account, abandoning the System in public was an example of self-mortification. What Ouspensky was rejecting, they claimed, was only the System as *they* had so inadequately understood it. Neither Ouspensky nor the System had failed, only the disciples.

Others more mundanely put Ouspensky's car trips and eccentric behaviour down to the unfortunate influence of Rodney Collin.[10] Born in Brighton in 1909, where he spent a bookish childhood reading and writing, Collin remained throughout his life the typical idealistic autodidact, full of stray facts and good intentions, with a tenuous grip on the everyday world. His marriage in 1934 to a rich woman eight years older than himself didn't strengthen his hold on practical realities. Typically, he met his wife Janet on a visit to Switzerland to see the Oberammergau Passion Play – a drama whose full significance for Collin was only to become horribly clear at the very end of his life.

In early manhood he took up the usual early-1930s range of causes, successively joining Toc H,[11] the Youth Hostel Association (for which he worked as Secretary) and the Peace Pledge Union. He also wrote for the *Toc H Journal*, *Peace News* and the YHA's evocatively named magazine *The Rucksack*. The PPU had a strong theosophical membership, dedicated to the practical implementation of pacifist principles, and it is clear from his later writing that Collin was directly influenced by theosophical cosmology, though he never joined the Society.

The turning point came when he and his wife Janet attended Ouspensky's 1936 lectures. Almost at once the pair gave their entire attention to the Work. They bought a house near Lyne Place and within a short space of time Collin was one of Ouspensky's principal lieutenants – though he remained in awe of his teacher until the end. Given the language Collin was to use about Ouspensky – equating him with the sun and the sun with God – it is easy to see why. He had no contact with Gurdjieff and showed little interest in his work, regarding Ouspensky not only as his sole teacher but as *the* teacher (though he acknowledged Gurdjieff's importance in typically extravagant language).

Collin's wife, who worked as a sort of ADC to Madame Ouspensky at Lyne Place and Franklin Farms, later suggested that her husband had virtually become Ouspensky's adoptive son; and Collin himself gives the most romantic account of the master's last days, in which the younger man features as spiritual heir apparent. Yet his relationship with his teacher remained uneasy. As Ouspensky's drinking hardened and his temper shortened he found Collin's cow-eyed devotion ever more trying. The more he depended on the younger man the tetchier he became. Sometimes the teacher would shout and rage at his disciple, and on at least one occasion slapped his face. Collin, who was already developing a strong sense of his own mission, interpreted this not as a plain rebuke but as a sort of Zen lesson, to which he responded by slapping the face of the person next to him so hard that he burst the poor's man eardrum.

Collin was passive, muddled and highly strung, spiritually ambitious and easily influenced. Though apparently gregarious and always surrounded by followers in later life, he was essentially a loner. A charming man who made friends with surprising ease, he did so like many basically solitary people precisely because he never gave much of himself away. His response to Ouspensky's death hints at the madness some observers later detected in his behaviour.

By the time Ouspensky died on 2 October 1947, the atmosphere at Lyne was already highly charged.[12] Once the body had been removed from the house for burial, Collin locked himself into the now empty bedroom where Ouspensky had died and lain in state, refusing to come out for six days and pushing away the ladders other inmates put up to the windows. At the end of the six days (without food or drink, it is said) he emerged a changed man, having assumed the mantle of his teacher. As if to underline this, his normally brisk manner was replaced by a gentle saintliness, which may have been the result of the stupor induced by fasting. Whatever the causes, it soon became clear that while Ouspensky had only gone 'in search of the miraculous', Collin thought he had now found it, in the form of his mystic inheritance from Ouspensky.

Like many of Ouspensky's pupils and colleagues, including Madame Ouspensky, Collin flatly refused to believe that his teacher had really rejected the System. Some saw in the supposed rejection a Gurdjieffian test in which Ouspensky was trying the faith of his followers by seeming to abandon his teaching. Collin even more mysteriously claimed that Ouspensky's last weeks were part of a mystical psychodrama performed for the benefit of the pupils. According to this interpretation of events, by renouncing his own teaching and thus subjecting himself to humiliation and despair Ouspensky was repeating the passion of Jesus Christ and enacting before their eyes his own doctrines of intentional suffering and objective consciousness. Thus he stripped away from himself every support in order to achieve the supreme spiritual experience of absolute sacrifice.

Only a few relatively level-headed followers seem to have accepted the obvious explanation: that Ouspensky was ill and tired and disillusioned, that his temper was soured by drink, and that pain, boredom, the fear of death, and a residual if bitter and sometimes self-destructive honesty drove him to face up to the futility of his life's work. Kenneth Walker, who had worked at the Prieuré with Gurdjieff, until he rejected the Master for Ouspensky's more congenial approach, articulated this view. Yet even Walker puzzled over the outcome of Ouspensky's career and felt somehow personally responsible for it, as though he and the others had let their teacher down through laziness or stupidity. Rodney Collin preferred the stained-glass version of events in which Ouspensky appeared as the Christ. But when assessing all these interpretations we must take account of the interpreter's character and situation – and Collin himself was well on the way to a melodramatic end which far outstripped Ouspensky's in strangeness.

Ouspensky's death left his pupils in a painful limbo. With Bennett estranged and leading a group elsewhere, and Maurice Nicholl, another major pupil of both Ouspensky and Gurdjieff, well-established in his own community in rural Hertfordshire,[13] those who had remained at Lyne now either went their own way or divided into two factions under the leadership of Rodney Collin and Dr Francis Roles (whose eardrum Collin had earlier destroyed). Collin and Roles were unstable figures, involved in their own spiritual quests, mutually hostile and ill-equipped to lead. Three of the other senior pupils, at a loss to know what to do, therefore decided to visit Madame Ouspensky, still living at Mendham. Sophia Grigorievna had never quite lost touch with Gurdjieff. After her husband's death she reopened full communications with him, dispatching to Paris a roll of silk and a cheque for $3,000 in earnest of her good will. For her the solution to the problems of Ouspensky's old pupils was a simple one. She told them in no uncertain terms to close down Lyne Place and to transfer their allegiance to Gurdjieff in France.[14]

During the war Gurdjieff had virtually disappeared from view, seen only by René Daumal, Jeanne de Salzmann and their followers. Yet by the time he died in 1949, he was once again esteemed and prosperous. It seemed that he was quite literally a survivor, outliving not only Ouspensky but many of his own followers who had perished or gone mad or fallen by the wayside. He had also survived the catastrophic decline of his own reputation in alternative religious circles in the 1930s and – most remarkably of all – brushed off serious suspicions of collaboration with the Germans during the war, when both he and his Parisian kitchen seemed to thrive despite the severe rationing. No doubt he got some of his luxuries from the small circle of devotees who remained, and others on the black market, and yet more from the American troops who flocked into Paris after the Liberation in 1944 – but that left the question of how he had access to that market, where he found the money to pay for his supplies and what his contacts were with the guardians of the occupying forces' stores?

Gurdjieff himself liked to joke that the goodies in his pantry came from the planet Karatas.[15] Hardly less fantastic is the notion that he got credit from local shopkeepers – including the prestigious Hédiard *épicerie* – by claiming to be the owner of an American oil-well from which the profits would only flow again when the war was ended. Yet this story is confirmed by several post-war pupils; and when the time came to settle accounts, his American disciples were fortunately on hand to pay up.[16]

By the time Ouspensky's former pupils contacted him things had already begun to improve, and once again it was America that came to the rescue, in the form of Kathryn Hulme and Fritz Peters. Hulme was in Europe working for UNRAA.[17] Finding herself in Paris in June 1946, she turned up at Gurdjieff's flat with packets of cigarettes, a bottle of vodka and her new girlfriend, a woman whose background Gurdjieff mysteriously guessed. Peters, who was still in the American Army, arrived in a state of mental and emotional collapse which Gurdjieff soon remedied by quite literally infusing him with energy. Stunned by flashes of blue lightning round his teacher, the young soldier immediately felt better – though the now elderly Gurdjieff had to lie down to recover his own energy after the transference.[18]

Saved from financial catastrophe by his own ingenuity, the providential end of the war and the American benefactors who paid his bills at Hédiard and elsewhere, Gurdjieff was soon restored to popular favour as a teacher, largely through the enthusiasm of Hulme, Peters, Orage's old American pupils who were free to visit Europe once more, and Jane Heap, now running a craft shop in St John's Wood. Margaret Anderson brought in her new companion, Dorothy Caruso, widow of the singer Enrico.[19] When Gurdjieff heard from Ouspensky's pupils who rushed to obey Madame Ouspensky's instruction, he told them, 'You are sheep without a shepherd. Come to me.' Led by Walker, most obeyed, which suggests that Gurdjieff's estimate was quite correct; apparently they had forgotten that his usual course of action with sheep was to shear them. Nicoll, Collin, Roles and their pupils held aloof: they shared Ouspensky's suspicion that Gurdjieff was not so much a shepherd as a wolf.[20]

The most interesting and significant figure in this post-war revival of Gurdjieff's English following was J. G. Bennett. When war broke out in 1939 the Bennetts had been planning an expedition to Syria. They decided to take a short holiday on the south coast before going to the Middle East, but Chamberlain interrupted their trip to Bognor with the bad news about Hitler and the trip was cancelled. This minor detail in the cataclysm of war has its own significance. Bennett was drawn to Syria by his increasing obsession with the Source of Wisdom and the Sarmoung Brotherhood by whom, according to Gurdjieff, it was transmitted.

Though it interrupted his search, the war turned out to be an opportunity for Bennett to bring together the two sides of his life. Bombed out of their flat in Tite Street, Chelsea, he and Winifred began looking for somewhere to live. They also wanted a place that would provide a base for Bennett's work with pupils. What they found was a house with seven acres on the outskirts of London, at Kingston in Surrey.

Coombe Springs was the property of Mrs Hwfa Williams. Once a great society beauty, she and her husband had been close friends of Edward VII and, like many of his circle, they had gambled away most of their large fortune, which included Claridge's Hotel. Now an elderly recluse, she lived in the stinking, semi-derelict house at Coombe in the company of an Italian maid, seven chows and twenty-two cats. Her almost total deafness made negotiation difficult, but in the end the Bennetts were given a lease 'for the duration' and set to work on the house. Or rather, they set their pupils to work on it, for they already envisaged a community at Coombe along the lines of Lyne and the Prieuré, in which spiritual teaching would be combined with and promoted by companionship and hard physical labour. In order to finance the operation, Bennett persuaded BCURA to relocate from Fulham to Coombe.

In return for their labour, Bennett took his pupils on the spiritual equivalent of summer reading-parties to Wales and the Lake District in vehicles fuelled by coke gas produced in a converter – a BCURA invention – towed behind. In the days of petrol-rationing and difficult travel this was a considerable luxury. On the first of these trips Bennett had a vision in which he saw in a blinding flash 'the Universal Order, and . . . how Love and Freedom redeem everything',[21] a prospect which seems worthy of its capitalised nouns. Eager to translate this vague spectacle into something more precise, Bennett was stirred to become a writer, scribbling with such energy and at such length that he wore himself out and fell ill with impetigo. But the moment was a decisive one. Over the next thirty years he poured out a vast quantity of books, pamphlets, lectures and essays, all expounding his account of the System. The major product of his great vision was *The Dramatic Universe*, a complete account of the cosmos in four volumes.

Despite the satisfactory move to Coombe Springs and his new career as a writer, Bennett had problems. Until Coombe was ready for occupation his pupils worked at weekends on an extraordinary site in the middle of London where one of their number, Primrose Codrington, had a small house hidden away behind Onslow Square with almost an acre of grounds. Here the group grew vegetables and kept chickens in the bombed gardens, and Bennett began to publicise his spirtual teaching and his writings, which were used as a basis for discussion in the group. He also began to publish, issuing a short book, *Values*, in 1942.

This was all quite unacceptable to Ouspensky, who had expressly forbidden publication or public teaching of the System in any form other than his. Bennett had also committed the even greater crime of flouting his teacher's authority by adapting elements of the System to his own ideas, and it was not long before news of Bennett's activities reached America via the small band of followers still working at Lyne – several of whom bitterly resented Bennett's pretensions to Ouspensky's favour. Ouspensky's response was to excommunicate Bennett (again). Through his solicitors he demanded the return from Bennett of any papers connected with his (Ouspensky's) work, including lecture notes, and forbade his pupils to have anything to do with the new tenant of Coombe Springs.

After the split with Ouspensky a few of the older pupils obediently boycotted Bennett, but the majority stayed with him. At weekends they met either in Onslow Sqaure or, once Bennett had taken possession, in the gardens at Coombe. Each day he gave a topic for meditation while they were working in the gardens. The usual talks and discussions took place – and the usual vagueness about their content prevailed. Many found this disconcerting, feeling that they needed a clearer sense of purpose, and one pupil offered to help by summing up their discussions over a weekend. As a result he produced a manuscript of two hundred pages which – perhaps fortunately – he promptly lost. Bennett himself described their life as a female Being visited by a cosmic Male Power.

At the same time that he was alienating Ouspensky, Bennett had been getting himself into trouble with the Mining Association (on curiously similar grounds) by giving public lectures in which he said that the age of cheap coal was over and speculated on the possibility of new forms of energy. Not surprisingly the association objected to this, pointing out that pricing policy was not Bennett's business, whereas selling coal (and not other fuels) was. He was also caught between the public demand to find ways of producing cheaper coal and the owners' insistence that the price must be maintained while simultaneously ensuring that coal held its place in the market against oil.

It is clear that even his backers were irritated by Bennett's increasing preoccupation with spiritual life and his habit of using Coombe Springs (which they paid for) as a religious retreat. They accused him of pressuring employees in the research laboratories to join his group, and complained about the embarrassment his activities caused. One episode is typical. Accustomed to take an early-morning swim in the springs at Coombe, Bennett had a vision there one day, in which every leaf seemed to be filled with the presence of Jesus. (It is hardly surprising that he had visions. Since 1939 he had been repeating the Lord's Prayer one thousand times per day, adding the phrase *'Fiat voluntas tua'*.) He remained in a state of ecstasy for three days after encountering Jesus – which was awkward, because he had to give a lecture on 'Coal and the Chemical Industry' at the Institute of Chemical Engineers on the second day. Although Bennett sensed the hostility of the audience, he claims that a feeling of warmth came over them as he proceeded to talk, and the hall filled with divine love. Sadly, the infusion did not extend to his employers, and a few weeks after his lecture, in June 1944, he was invited to resign from BCURA. The association moved its offices to Leatherhead and Bennett took over Coombe for his own projects.

His manic career continued apace. His passion for organisations found expression in a new private research laboratory, the Coal Plastics Company, and an Institute for the Comparative Study of History, Philosophy and the Sciences. The Laboratory worked on the production of plastic carbons from disaggregated coal, while the institute pursued psycho-kinetic research. The work on coal plastics was funded by a major industrial firm, Powell Duffryn, and that arrangement indirectly supported other projects at Coombe, where the resident and visiting community now numbered upwards of two hundred members. During this period Bennett also wrote a play about the burning of Chartres Cathedral, embarked on a treatise in fifth-dimension geometry and produced a report on how to increase scientific manpower in the universities.

When foreign travel became possible again after 1945, Bennett decided to explore the possibilities of setting up a community outside England. Visiting South Africa, he was granted an audience with General Smuts, who told him not to be so pessimistic about the future. Smuts evidently thought his guest somewhat out of touch with reality – an opinion confirmed by Bennett's own testimony that the rich white bosses had nothing but warm and friendly feelings for their African workers. He eventually bought a farm in South Africa, but his group stayed in England.

It was a visit to Madame Ouspensky during the summer of 1948 that set him back on the path. In America on coal-research business, he took a trip to Franklin Farms, where the stern Sophia Grigorievna, now suffering from Parkinson's disease, bluntly told him to go to Gurdjieff in Paris if he wanted further spiritual instruction. The command struck him with the force of inevitability. Returning to England, Bennett found his now elderly wife in agony with a mystery disease, but the call of spiritual wisdom was so strong that they immediately set out for Paris to meet Jeanne de Salzmann, who was to be their intermediary with the Master.

The comedy began in the summer of 1948. Gurdjieff was living at 6 rue des Colonels Rénard in considerably reduced circumstances. The château and the smart suits were gone, and he wore a red fez and open-necked shirt. But he still presided over a large court of

French and American pupils. He was also attended by a number of obedient young girls, known as his 'calves'. This group included Iovanna Lloyd Wright (daughter of Frank and Olga), and Bennett's future wife, Elizabeth Mayall.

When introduced to Bennett Gurdjieff claimed not to remember him, saying only, 'You are number 18. Not big Number 18 but small number 18,' about which Bennett reasonably comments, 'I had no idea what he meant.'[22] Despite the unpropitious beginning, Gurdjieff asked Bennett what he wanted, Bennett asked Gurdjieff to show him how to work for his Being, and Gurdjieff agreed, noting drily that while Bennett had much knowledge, in Being he was 'a nullity', a judgement Bennett accepted with proper humility.[23]

Pausing only to cure Winifred Bennett of her excruciating pain and to suggest reading and exercises for his new pupil, Gurdjieff then left for Cannes the next day, crashing his car into a lorry at Montargis and injuring himself severely. (The lorry driver was killed.) But it seems that the Master still had some of his old resilience where car crashes were concerned.[24] Despite serious injuries, including broken ribs and internal bleeding, he was brought back to Paris and insisted on dining with the Bennetts and others the following night, horrifying those present with his bruised face, bleeding ear and bandaged throat. Yet as with his first crash, the apparently devastating injuries were soon healed and his tiny apartment, crudely decorated with mirrors, dolls and glittering pseudo-orientalia, was soon bursting with people once more.

After his quarrels with Ouspensky and that master's disillusioned rejection of the System, Bennett was only too glad to rediscover Gurdjieff, whose close disciple he now became for the first time. Gurdjieff summoned all Bennett's Coombe Springs pupils to attend him in Paris. About sixty made the trip, most of them returning subsequently for weekends – quite a business given the condition of Europe in the years after the war. Kenneth Walker also visited Paris and persuaded many English Ouspensky pupils to do the same. The feasts and the toasts began again, and all the old schemes were revived. A mansion was to be bought (this time the Château de Voisins near Rambouillet), an institute started and the sacred dances performed again. Gurdjieff also proposed another visit to

New York, where he would stage a new spectacle to finance the publication of his magnum opus, *Beelzebub's Tales to His Grandson*, the book he had been writing since the late 1920s.

With the return of these visionary schemes came all the old troubles and animosities. Even Bennett himself comments that some of the pupils could not take the fierce regime of alternate praise and abuse, ritual humiliation and public dramas, to which Gurdjieff subjected them. Several newcomers were said to have broken down after their encounter with the Master, a few even requiring hospital treatment (though for what ailment is not specified).[25] All the sinister stories about suicide and madness at the Prieuré began to be heard again, the Master's supporters responding with the reasonable riposte that many who visited Gurdjieff for help went precisely because they were so far advanced in sickness, mental or physical, that no one else could help them. Was it surprising if some gave way under the strain of their difficulties?

Whatever the truth or falsehood of the rumours, their effect on the Coombe Springs contingent was certainly devastating. The Master's old talent for stirring up strife was as strong as ever and pupils rapidly divided into two parties, pro- and anti-Gurdjieff. Even the enthusiasts experienced torn loyalties, pulled between two masters, for Gurdjieff was ruthless with Bennett and his pretensions, praising him one day, hinting that he regarded the younger man as his heir on another, subjecting him to a public dressing-down on the third. Yet such was his authority that he managed to persuade the Bennetts of the necessity for this treatment, if only because, as so often before – with Jeanne de Salzmann and Sophia Ouspensky among others – Gurdjieff had conquered the wife even more effectively than the husband.

Bennett comments on something they all observed: that, however much attention they paid, no two pupils could ever agree on exactly what Gurdjieff had said. The same remark was often made about Krishnamurti. At the Prieuré Gurdjieff had strictly forbidden the taking of notes in talks, though many of the students rushed off afterwards to record his words and subsequently published them. This only helped to promote confusion, though Bennett and others saw such misunderstandings as evidence of their teacher's power:

never being the same to any two people must mean, they thought, that he spoke to each individually.

Elizabeth Mayall described an occasion when she took a friend with a problem to see the Master.[27] They sat through a long lunch during which Gurdjieff addressed not a word to the friend. Only at the end did he fix her with a piercing stare and murmur some words in an incomprehensible language. Walking away from the flat, Mayall began apologising to her friend, until she noticed that the woman was radiant. Gurdjieff, she said, had solved her unspoken problem – even though she had not understood the language he was speaking.

In October 1948 Gurdjieff set out on his final trip to America. It is hard not to feel that by this time he simply enjoyed acting the fool for the hell of it. Seen off from the railway station in Paris by a group of devout pupils, his parting words to them as he leant out of the carriage window were: 'Before I return I hope with all my being that everyone here will have learned the difference between sensation and feeling'[28] – an absurd request over which they nevertheless puzzled. In New York there were the usual crazy meals, cooked on a spirit stove in the Master's bedroom at the Wellington Hotel (where cooking was strictly forbidden). The American pupils rehearsing the sacred dances were told that they moved 'like worms in shit',[29] and Frank Lloyd Wright, now seriously ill, was ordered to take peppered armagnac for his gall bladder.[30]

More seriously, Gurdjieff affronted Ouspensky's American pupils, dismissing their former teacher as a barren intellectual and traitor who had died like a dog in a ditch for want of submission to him.[31] But this did not prevent him from visiting Madame Ouspensky at Mendham, where she showed him the manuscript of Ouspensky's account of their early years together, *Fragments of an Unknown Teaching*. Ironically enough, Ouspensky's scrupulous objectivity, just dismissed by his teacher in New York as sterile academicism, was finally vindicated at Mendham a few weeks later: Gurdjieff approved the book for publication as an accurate record of his teaching in the decade after 1915.

At the same time he pressed ahead with *Beelzebub's Tales to His Grandson*, instructing Bennett, who had followed him to America, to compose a letter inviting pupils to buy a first-edition copy for £100.[32] This letter was read out over lunch, and on the same occasion Bennett was appointed literary executor for England, the French author René Zuber for France and the Scottish journalist Lord Pentland for America. Similar promises had already been made to Fritz Peters and others. Gurdjieff clearly relished changing his will to tease the heirs.

Returning to Paris in April 1949, he embarked on the old round of café lunches, country drives and long dinners, while Bennett in London gave a series of public lectures about his master. Gurdjieff began negotiating for yet another Prieuré, this time the station hotel at La Grande Paroisse on the Seine; planned a second trip to America; contemplated acquiring pupils in 'Dutch India'; and visited the caves at Lascaux with Bennett; but his health was visibly declining.

On 14 October he collapsed at a dance class, and though he struggled back to some sort of health for a few days, Elizabeth Mayall, who met him in a fruit shop buying huge quantities of bananas, for the first time saw in Gurdjieff an old man. The pupils had watched his slow decline and knew what to expect, yet they were stunned by his rapid deterioration. Gurdjieff himself had once insisted (perhaps only half humorously) that he would never leave them; but two weeks later, on 29 October, he died in the American Hospital at Neuilly.

The days following his death were rife with contradictory rumours: that the Master's inner organs were wasted to nothing; that the body had been heard breathing after death; that it would never decompose; that he had not really died but gone elsewhere, leaving a substitute corpse in his place. Nevertheless, the funeral took place in the Russian Orthodox church in Paris, attended by a large congregation, and it became clear that Gurdjieff had played the practical joke of his career. The story was over.

Yet in another sense it was only just beginning. A few days before his death, Gurdjieff had received the proofs of *Beelzebub*. His pupils were growing in numbers as never before and his reputation was rising. Always a creature of illusion, Gurdjieff the man was now ready to give way entirely to Gurdjieff the myth.[33]

NINETEEN

Returning

Gurdjieff lived long enough to preside over an impressive revival in his fortunes. Krishnamurti lived still longer and prospered even more remarkably. A saint to his own circle and a bit of a joke to the world at large in the inter-war years, by the late 1960s he had become *the* western guru. In the process he also shook off the absurdities of Theosophy to emerge as an acknowledged and respected star in that curious firmament of New Age celebrities where the Dalai Lama and Yehudi Menuhin rub shoulders with mystical duchesses and pop singers searching for truth.

The metamorphosis involved him in two apparent paradoxes: first, he resolutely maintained his image as a solitary in pursuit of spiritual enlightenment while perceived by outsiders as part of a glamorous social élite; and second, he continued to preach the doctrines of the world's unreality and the necessity of achieving freedom from all its ties, though living very much in that world.

Neither is quite the contradiction it seems. Many holy men have taught that reclusiveness is not the best route to salvation, that the most profound solitude is to be found in human society, and that the effective way to remind ourselves of the world's unreality is to engage with life, not to retreat from it. But Krishnamurti's critics – and they were soon to include the Rajagopal family – put the worst construction on his later career. Suggesting that he had always been essentially an escapist, a conformist and a parasite, they argued that Krishnamurti merely cultivated the *appearance* of solitude and detachment in order to support his image of himself, and that this appearance had been paid for at emotional cost to those closest to him and spiritual cost to his deluded followers.

What is certainly true is that Krishnamurti began to move out of the tightly knit Ojai orbit when Allied victory put an end to his enforced isolation in California. Outwardly there was little apparent difference in his circumstances. From 1945 to his death at the age of ninety-one in 1986, he travelled the world as a spiritual teacher. The public talks and private interviews continued as they had since the early 1920s, punctuated by an endless round of luxurious holidays. Krishnamurti continued to commute between India, Europe and America, often staying with wealthy friends. There are times when his list of engagements reads more like *Jennifer's Diary* than a guru's. He also continued to rely for support on strong, rich women.

Mass meetings were resumed throughout the world. By 1982 Krishnamurti was addressing capacity audiences of three thousand people in the Carnegie Hall, New York. Regular gatherings took place in Europe on the pattern of the Star camps. Though he could not bear to revisit Ommen after its use as a concentration camp during the war, a trust was set up in 1961 to finance conferences at Saanen in Switzerland. He also spent more time with the powerful in finance and politics, regularly conferring with Nehru and his daughter Indira Gandhi, who succeeded her father as Prime Minister of India in 1966. The Krishnamurti foundations received substantial backing from tycoons: Gerard Blitz, founder of Club Mediterranée, was his financial adviser for a while. The sums involved increased dramatically in the post-war period as idealists profiting from the post-war boom looked for charitable foundations into which they could put their money. Though impossible to compute without access to accounts, donations to KWINC certainly involved millions – possibly tens of millions – of dollars. Quite why this happened it is hard to say. Many spiritual teachers amass huge endowments, though rarely on this scale and with such continuity – for there was hardly a pause in the flow of cash, from Krishnamurti's first appearance on the public scene before World War One to his death in 1986. Perhaps a lifetime's association with the rich and famous had generated the intangible aura of social acceptibility which made him a magnet for ever larger donations: he was pleasingly unworldly but reassuringly sophisticated and refined.

Besides, he never asked awkward questions about where the money for his enterprises came from, or how it was handled, claiming to be indifferent to such matters. Yet he continued to inaugurate expensive building-projects at the Krishnamurti schools and camps, and though he technically owned little property he lived the life of a rich man. His critics – who included former close friends such as Emily Lutyens – worried that he was becoming dependent on the luxury this life provided and – even worse – that it was cutting him off from all but the rich and privileged.

Krishna himself claimed that such luxury was incidental, that he could just as easily do without it, that for much of the time he lived like anyone else, and that only those who confused outward appearances with inner realities would make the mistake of assuming that he relished affluence for its own sake. To live amidst wealth, he argued, is not necessarily to be wealthy. What matters about property is one's attitude towards it, not its presence or absence. Eating and drinking very little, sleeping only a few hours and meditating and teaching for many, he lived like an ascetic in a palace, unmoved by the surroundings – or so he said. A sunset or a dawn was more important to him than a beautiful drawing-room. The cynic might argue that the enjoyment of sunsets is a sophisticated luxury. But Krishnamurti insisted, like Gurdjieff, that one must lead the life that comes to hand while remaining detached: mortifying the flesh can become as addictive as pampering it.

It is hard to believe that luxury made *no* difference to Krishnamurti. He certainly enjoyed what there was, taking it for granted that devotees would look after him, providing houses, cars and holidays of the highest standard, and they did. At the same time, he clung to simple activities. When the Saanen trustees bought him a large Mercedes he cleaned and polished it every time he came back from a drive, however short. Faithful to Baillie-Weaver's training, he bought his suits at Huntsman in Savile Row, where there were endless fittings, and his hair was cut in Bond Street. Yet he also continued to relish household chores, just as he had at Arya Vihara. Staying in Malibu with his friend Mary Zimbalist, and then at the new house she built for him at Ojai, he could be found polishing the kettle and the kitchen work-tops, stacking the dishwasher, watering the garden.

But if the outward pattern of his life remained much the same, albeit more luxurious, in private there were major upheavals. The triangular relationship with Rosalind and Rajagopal which had dominated his Californian life was drawing to a close amid bitter recriminations; he found himself drawn more and more to India and even to a rapprochement with Theosophy; and most important of all, he began to take a different view about what should happen to his work when he died.

These three changes were connected by complex links which have been interpreted in very different ways by those close to him. His surrogate daughter Radha Rajagopal has suggested that Krishna's drift away from her parents was a personal betrayal foreshadowed by the whole of their life together, in which he had played the part of the spoilt child, using the others to satisfy his need for sex, security and money.[2] Whatever his qualities, she believes he was a congenital liar and hypocrite whose *folies de grandeur* accelerated with age as he became the prisoner of his own myth. Rosalind and Raja had catered to his whims, behaving like loving parents and loyal servants; but they also told him truths he did not wish to hear and faced him with the ordinary obligations of life – obligations he was too weak, devious or lazy to meet. Having abandoned them, he surrounded himself with devotees and sycophants who widened the tragic gap between Krishnamurti's perception of himself as an unworldly saint and the reality of his selfish, jet-setting life, filled with luxuries and adoring women. Krishna's fate, as Radha presents it, is the common lot of celebrities, alienated from the real world and obsessed by fears of their own creating.

In 1946, for example, when the Happy Valley School was established on the Ojai land Mrs Besant had bought twenty years before, with Huxley and Krishnamurti among the trustees, it was left to Rosalind to work an eighteen-hour day running it, while her rich and elderly friends Robert Logan and Louis Zalk dealt with the finances – for despite the endowment there was a heavy mortgage on the property which had to be serviced by someone. Although the school was organised according to his own principles, Krishna's only contribution was to chat with the students when he felt like it. Even that fell by the way when he developed acute nephritis and Rosalind – typically – had to nurse him herself, in addition to her new duties. Once recovered, he abandoned the simple life at Ojai and took to floating about the world in the company of the rich, lying to Rosalind about his affairs with other women and treating Raja as a mere secretary. Yet later still, in 1961 when he was at loggerheads with his old friends, he began to interfere in the school's affairs, telling Zalk that it had strayed from his teaching and insisting that he be involved in the administration.[3] Was this genuine concern? A way of persecuting the Rajagopals? Megalomania? Or just insensitivity?

Krishnamurti's official biographer, Mary Lutyens, argues that the Rajagopals needed Krishna, and were not above bullying him in ways which made their eventual separation inevitable. Part of the problem was that their own personal, professional and financial connections ran very deep. Raja had come to regard KWINC, the foundation of their business empire, as his own property. Yet without Krishna it would not have existed. Raja's resentment at playing second fiddle to Krishna all his life was now also coming to the boil, aggravated by the relationship between his friend and his wife (though Radha claims that he did not know the full truth about this until 1961, nearly thirty years after it had begun). After all, Raja might argue, Leadbeater had once implied that Raja had just as much right to the Theosophical succession as Krishna – perhaps more, given Krishna's repudiation of Theosophy.

Less tangible difficulties arose from the Rajagopals' view of themselves – no doubt with the best of intentions – as Krishna's guardians. They were unable, in Lutyens's view, to see that his refusal to be possessed or dominated by anyone was not a personal betrayal but part of his spiritual mission as a unique figure whom Aldous Huxley (and Krishna himself) readily compared to the Buddha. Free spirits cannot be held to trivial responsibilities; bearing such heavy burdens, world teachers are entitled to all the help they can get from others, and especially to tolerance for their frailties, or alleged frailties. Perhaps Krishna did take a childlike pleasure in the ritzy life, but this was a sign of purity, not corruption.

One might also add, however vulgarly, that the Rajagopals had done very well out of Krishna's celebrity, one way and another. Nor can their own characters withstand criticism. Raja was solitary, secretive and often melancholy, not to say depressed. He ran his businesses autocratically, and when things went wrong between them complained loud, long and bitterly about Krishna to anyone who would listen. If we arc to believe he really knew nothing of his wife's adultery for more than two decades, that can only suggest indifference or wilful blindness; while Rosalind, according to her daughter's own testimony, though always ready to cope with practical problems, preferred to ignore emotional difficulties in the hope they would go away.

It is certainly true, however, that Krishna's ultimate aloofness led to many misunderstandings. Raja and Rosalind were not the only people in Krishnamurti's life to feel used and abandoned by him. It was not that Krishna didn't want intimacy, they felt: only that he wanted it on his own terms. On the other hand, he had preached the theory of non-attachment for many years: moving away from his California life he was putting this theory into practice, proving into the bargain the aptness of his claim that few people understood its real meaning. We might compare Krishna's alleged disloyalty with Gurdjieff's aggressive rudeness as mechanisms for distancing themselves from ensnarement by the rich, all too often inclined to look upon those they patronise as their creatures.

Clearly this argument cannot apply to personal relationships, and there is also a flat contradiction between Krishna's liaison with Rosalind as described by her daughter, and the public perception of his chastity which he tacitly encouraged. Sexual love need not exclude spirituality or even sanctity, though one might argue that the betrayal of trust involved in adultery and hypocrisy inevitably must do so. But even there we are on uncertain ground. Those who revere Gurdjieff, for example, do not see his manifest cruelty and dishonesty as failings in the usual sense, but as aspects of a character too large to be adequately accounted for in normal terms. A guru is a natural force, they argue: like a volcano or an iceberg, he (or she) may do incidental damage in the course of filling his appointed role – but we can hardly blame him for that.

One problem with such claims is that they are, by nature, beyond adjudication. If a guru is a natural force, perhaps the most sensible thing is to get out of his way? On the more mundane level, perhaps what matters here is, first, the issue of Krishna's good faith with his followers; second, his behaviour to his friends; and third, the bearing of his conduct on his teaching. Given Krishnamurti's own insistence on the individual's responsibility for himself, his emphasis on the vital importance of honesty, and the close identification of his public and private selves in his public mission, the three issues are almost impossible to disentangle. All one can say is that Krishnamurti himself promulgated the moral values by which we can judge his behaviour. If Radha Rajagopal is right, the judgement must go against him on all three counts.

In October 1947 Krishnamurti made his first trip to India in almost a decade, calling on Lady Emily in London *en route*. His visit fortuitously coincided with the granting of Indian independence, which forced former imperial subjects to choose between British nationality and loyalty to their new country. Krishnamurti chose India and the choice was fateful. Although he was to spend much time travelling in Europe and America (not to mention the rest of the world), his orientation from now on was decisively Indian, and perhaps even anti-western. He was indeed returning to his roots.

He stayed in the country for eighteen months, making several new friends, including Nandini Mehta and her sister Pupul Jayakar, an intimate of the Nehru family.[4] Krishna soon became dependent on the beautiful Nandini to help him through recurrences of the Process, which made her application to the courts for a separation from her husband in 1950 a gift to the press, who naturally speculated on Krishnamurti's role in the affair. The presiding judge in the case had no doubt about the rights and wrongs of it. Though he did not accept Mr Mehta's suggestion that Krishna was pursuing Nandini, he did agree that the former's anarchistic teachings had caused the wife to revolt against the husband, and he denied Mrs

Mehta's petition, despite her allegations of mental and physical cruelty in the marriage.[5]

However indifferent he may have been to the Happy Valley School at first, Krishnamurti also began to take a close interest in his own Indian schools at Rajghat and Rishi Valley, where his nephew eventually became Headmaster. Although these institutions were conducted according to his own principles of non-violence, free development, the avoidance of rote learning and tolerance for other points of view, such principles were by now in no way exclusive and could be regarded as forms of the progressive educational ideas that were to dominate the post-war period until the 1980s. But Rishi and Rajghat were also more than schools. There were community medical centres, farms and (at Rajghat) an agricultural institute and women's college. The schools existed to transform pupils by teaching them to think for themselves. They were emphatically not for the acquisition of knowledge. While conventional disciplines were in some sense necessary, Krishnamurti insisted that education had no other purposes.[6]

Once again, he was involved in a paradox. His interest in the schools signalled a deeper preoccupation with the future of his teaching; yet the doctrine he taught involved the rejection of dogma, the mistrust of ideas and a disdain for education as the transmission of information. If by 'ideas' – 'brutal things', as he liked to call them[7] – Krishnamurti meant the reduction of complex realities to simple formulae, learning by rote, and the substitution of mere words for experience, he was right to protest that there must be more to education than that. But if he meant to replace ideas altogether, that was a different matter. What did he propose to put in their place? Wordless communion? It was all very well, one might argue, for Krishna to reject 'ideas'; but didn't he just mean by that *other people's* ideas? And what about his own dogma? Was that not articulated through ideas? Did he not have certain formulae of his own? He was being impractical and contradictory.

There was also another difficulty. Previously, Krishnamurti had insisted that his teaching could not be reproduced by others or codified into a set of rules; that he was himself unique; that there could therefore be no straightforward transmission of doctrines;

and that he would have no disciples or pupils as such, only audiences who chanced, as it were, to overhear his words. These views went with his rejection of 'ideas'. Other teachers in the past had overcome these difficulties by resorting to esoteric methods: communicating their teaching through symbols, rituals, allegories or ceremonies. But Krishnamurti's rejection of Theosophy was in part the rejection of such an esoteric approach. Yet the very fact of his dislike for reducing what he had to communicate to a set of rules or conventional methods meant that he continued to espouse in his own pedagogic practice a subtle form of the esotericism he spurned in theory. Nevertheless, he came round to the view that his practice – if not the codified doctrines that practice embodied – was worth saving. But how was this to be done?

One way was through schools, which might hope to establish traditions of teaching that did not degenerate into mere rote. New schools were opened in England and California, and just before Krishnamurti died, a rich German friend financed the building of a luxurious study centre near the English Krishnamurti School at Brockwood in Hampshire.[8] The purpose of these institutions – whether for children, adults or both – was to promote spiritual rather than intellectual education. The schools are deliberately organised in the loosest manner: students are not taught, but 'put in a context where they can learn'. They do not follow a curriculum (though they may take traditional subjects if they wish): instead, they evolve as human beings in a community, each finding his or her own way and learning to come to terms with others.

Yet, though he refused to take any formal role in these schools, Krishnamurti visited all of them regularly, leading discussions with the students and teachers and talking privately with individuals. And even as he was insisting on the vital importance of individual discovery, the transcripts of his conversations with pupils reveal a man who mercilessly bullied his interlocutors into accepting his point of view.[9]

It was not only in his own schools that Krishnamurti became a revered teacher. He was popular throughout the world, and nowhere more so than in the California university campuses of the 1960s, where he became a star of the New Age synthesis, which encompassed every alternative cause from drugs to astrology. The combination of narcissism, idealism and libertarianism which characterised the youth movements of the 1960s appeared to chime in exactly with Krishnamurti's views. In fact, this was an illusion. Self-examination is not the same as narcissism, nor is detachment identical with libertarianism. Far from being in conflict with the established order, Krishnamurti was now very much a part of it: the licensed guru of the wealthy classes who expressed his ascetic disapproval of all the self-indulgences that went with flower power.

He did however take part in public conversations with physicists,[10] biologists and psychologists sympathetic to the New Age synthesis – which suggests an intriguing return to the spirit of Theosophy; but of other New Age figures, especially the new generation of Indian gurus, he was deeply suspicious. Travelling to Delhi by air in 1974, he found himself leaving a plane with the Maharishi, who rushed to greet the older man, clutching a flower. Krishnamurti rapidly made his apologies and left.[11] He disliked the sentimentality of those who claim that 'Love is all you need.' He was also disdainful of those who walked in his own footsteps. Some time after this encounter he told friends that he would like to see the Maharishi's balance sheet. The Maharishi might well have said the same of him.

At the end of his life Krishnamurti also managed the rapprochement with Theosophy. For nearly fifty years he had continued to visit Adyar, not venturing into the Theosophical compound, where Raja often went to see old friends, but staying at Vasanta Vihar, on the other side of the river. The Society, meanwhile, had changed. George Arundale had purged Theosophy of its links with organisations such as Co-Masonry and the Liberal Catholic Church in the years after World War Two, and the old guard hostile to Krishna had died. The Society remained something of a family affair: after Arundale's death, he was succeeded first by Jinarajadasa; then by his brother-in-law, Sri Ram; and then (after a brief interval) by his niece, Radha Burnier, who became President in 1980. For Radha Burnier the old quarrels were history: wisely, she was determined to return the Society to its non-sectarian, ecumenical roots. A longstanding friend of Krishna's, she also recognised his importance to the theosophical movement. After her election she invited him to the compound at Adyar, which he visited for the first time in forty-seven years. The Society once more began to distribute his books and advertise talks by and about him, as they still do. Krishnamurti is now once again a member – albeit honorary – of the theosophical pantheon.

The rapprochement with Theosophy makes it all the more piquant that Krishnamurti's post-war discussions were so obsessively concerned with the nature of time. In all his public lectures and private talks he insisted again and again on the vital importance of living in the present; not in the sense that we should savour only the passing moment, but so that we shall not become the prisoners of the past. The great objective of life for Krishnamurti was spiritual freedom, and that can only be achieved by learning to discard all possesive attachments, whether to things, people or our own experience and desires. There is a sense, he believed, in which the past does not exist, except as illusion, but the illusion is a very potent one. Unless we can escape from it there is no possibility of developing spiritual insight, for that depends upon the clear perception of things as they are, not as they have been or as we would like them to be.

He had long since begun to claim that he could barely remember his own past. Now he developed that negative reaction into a positive doctrine, preaching the need for psychological and spiritual liberation through the determined attempt to grasp the nowness of the moment, which can begin to free the individual from the bondage of history and desire. In terms reminiscent of both Christian and Hindu mysticism he spoke of entering the House of Death – the death of the past – which is also the House of Freedom.

That Krishnamurti himself had struggled – was perhaps *still* struggling – with desire is, with hindsight, clear from the later talks in which he frequently dilates on the topic of sex. In 'The Urgency of Change',[12] for example, he comments on how:

> Sex plays an extraordinary important part in our lives
> because it is perhaps the only deep, first-hand experience

we have . . . This act being so beautiful, we become
addicted to it, so it in turn becomes a bondage. The
bondage is the demand for its continuation . . . One is so
hedged about – intellectually, in the family, in the
community, through social morality, through religious
sanctions – so hedged about that there is only this one
relationship left in which there is freedom and intensity.
Therefore we give tremendous importance to it . . . In
freeing the mind from the bondage of imitation, authority,
conformity and religious prescriptions, sex has its own
place but it won't be all-consuming. From this one can see
that freedom is essential for love.

The equivocation here between 'one' and 'we' hints at the awkward
discrepancy between the public image of celibacy and the private
reality of love. It is as though Krishnamurti needed to speak the
truth, but had to do so in coded, impersonal terms.

No doubt the urgency of this need was underlined by the painful
predicament in which he found himself: very much a prisoner of
history in the crudest possible form. For the row with Raja and
Rosalind which affected the rest of their lives increasingly focused
on money. In 1958, in India, Krishna had signed a crucial document
assigning all his copyrights to KWINC, with Raja as President
holding effective power of attorney over all his publications. These
now amounted to very substantial assets. The reasons for this move
are uncertain. The fact that the international copyright agreement
was about to come into force that year, plus Krishna's prolonged
absence from Ojai, may have been the immediate causes, as Mary
Lutyens suggests, but whatever prompted it, the power of attorney
he had given Raja was to become the focal point for almost thirty
years of bitter litigation.

Personal antagonism apart, the problem arose from Krishna's
refusal to have anything to do with the financial affairs of his trusts,
which had been left entirely in Raja's hands. Some years earlier,
though he could not remember doing so, Krishna had even resigned
from the board. Understandably, over the thirty years of his
administration with an acquiescent board of trustees, Raja had

grown accustomed to absolute authority over KWINC. However much Krishna might put him in the shade elsewhere, in this domain he was sovereign.

Years of irritation over what Raja considered to be Krishna's irresponsibility and selfishness, exacerbated by the collapse of his relationship with Rosalind, now came to the boil, and Krishna was denied readmission to the board when he applied for it. Raja, who claimed to be sick of nannying his friend, also refused to make any more travelling arrangements for him outside America, and began to question his expenses. Krishna, on the other hand, told friends that Raja had cut off his American funds altogether, making him dependent on friends and the income from his English trusts.

The position was confused by the fact that not all the funds in the trusts associated with KWINC were income from copyrights – they also included large donations from Krishnamurti's rich supporters, some of whom were concerned about Raja's growing power and the friction with Krishna. A complicated network of companies and accounts had grown up, and only Raja was privy to all the information about them. Nevertheless, despite their worsening relations, Krishna continued to return regularly to Ojai until 1961, when Raja and Rosalind were divorced.

From 1961 to 1965, under pressure from Rosalind, Krishnamurti stayed away from Ojai, in India and Europe, and in 1968 he formally dissociated himself from KWINC, setting up the first independent Krishnamurti Foundation, with the writer Mary Cadogan as Secretary. Lawsuits between KWINC and the Krishnamurti Foundation concerning their assets soon followed – suits that echoed the property disputes between Krishnamurti and the Theosophical Society forty years before. These were settled out of court in 1974, when Raja secured a pension, lifetime occupancy of his house and control of Krishnamurti's copyrights prior to 1968; but other legal proceedings, fuelled by charges and counter-charges, dragged on for twenty years. They were only concluded after Krishna's death in 1986. Rosalind and Raja both survived him.

The last twenty years were otherwise tranquil. The fragile Krishnamurti proved to be surprisingly resilient. He continued to travel the world giving talks. Much of his life was inevitably repetition, much contradiction. Shortly before he died, the building of a luxurious Krishnamurti Centre began at Brockwood. It was to be devoted to the study of his work. Yet he also inserted into the rules of the Krishnamurti Foundation the instruction that no one should set themselves up as an authority on his 'teaching'. He had still not decided what, if anything, could be transmitted.

His uncertainty was thrown into sharp relief by the decision to commission an official biography from his old friend Mary Lutyens. While her main task was to establish an accurate record of Krishna's life, Lutyens was naturally concerned to interpret the facts in the light of her long talks with Krishnamurti himself – a concern which was all the more pressing given Lutyens's puzzlement about the nature of spiritual experience. While she had every faith that her friend was describing realities, she found both his descriptions and what they pointed to hard to grasp. The task was made no easier by the fact that she was recording a drama in which she and her family had played central roles.

As they wrestled over the very problem that had brought the Masters of Wisdom into prominence in the first place – the need for a source of authority and authenticity – her probing made Krishna nervous. Where does spiritual wisdom come from? What is its purpose? Krishnamurti had often taught that there *is* no source, that the Masters are an illusion, that each consciousness is alone in the universe with its own reflections; yet in his notebooks and conversations he referred again and again to a power which possessed him, a power which he had recognised in youth, experienced repeatedly at the height of his theosophical fame in the form of magisterial visits, and ever since in less tangible ways.

Lutyens had an insight into what he meant by 'the power' one day at Brockwood, when she passed the open drawing-room door and felt an extraordinary throbbing presence emanating from the place in which she had just been talking to her subject.[12] Others testified to similar experiences. It was this power that seemed to be the source not only of Krishnamurti's teaching but of his very being, though distinct from both. Faced with such a power, he held that his mind was a classic vacancy – a vessel through which the power passed[13] – and that the centuries had been preparing for his unique being, which he habitually referred to on such occasions in the third person.

But the way of resolving these contradictions – and the way in which Krishnamurti himself resolved them – is to locate the spiritual source within the self. This has been the solution of mystics in all ages, from ancient Buddhists and medieval Christians to Krishnamurti's friend Aldous Huxley. More significantly, it also appears among the Hindu doctrines of Advaita Vedanta, which identifies the soul as an aspect of that absolute reality to which it aspires. Krishnamurti had always insisted that individuals must work out their own destiny. But in so doing, he had simply revived an ancient doctrine – just as Theosophy said he should. By listening to the voice of his deepest self, Krishnamurti was perhaps returning to the ascetic ways of his Hindu ancestors.

TWENTY

From System to Source

The deaths of Gurdjieff and Ouspensky left their pupils bereft. At long last it seemed that they would have to face the challenge their teachers had been issuing for so many years and take responsibility for their own lives in the outside world. But since most had become pupils precisely because they found this difficult to do, and were used to taking direction from above for twenty or even thirty years, independence was out of the question. Besides, the Work typically operated in closed and hierarchically organised groups: for devotees, there *was* no outside world to speak of. Such meaning as their lives contained derived from membership of a group and obedience to a leader. The problem, therefore, was not how to live on one's own, but how to re-form the group and find a new leader.

First, they had to contend with the fact of death itself – and this many of them simply refused to do, evading it by the expedient of describing their former teachers as Ascended Masters in the theosophical manner. Having achieved the necessary perfection on earth, Gurdjieff and Ouspensky had now joined Blavatsky and Leadbeater in the Secret Brotherhood. This formula had the merit of preserving the existence of the two teachers and thus the theoretical possibility of access to them, albeit in another form. Its drawback was that the Secret Brotherhood is secret: if pupils had not been able to make contact with it during Gurdjieff's lifetime, why should they expect to do so after his death?

Their problems were compounded by confusion about the status of the teaching here below. On one point, at least, Ouspensky had been quite clear until his last-minute volte-face: that it was possible to extract a coherent and transmissible doctrine from what Gurdjieff had taught – even though this doctrine was only the *Fragment of an Unknown Teaching*, to quote the title of one of Ouspensky's works. Gurdjieff himself, on the other hand, frequently changed his mind on these matters, sometimes implying that the teaching was greater than the teacher and could be transmitted by others; and sometimes that only he, Gurdjieff, was qualified to do what he did.

Despite his personal rejection of Gurdjieff, even Ouspensky had admitted that there was a question-mark over the value of the teaching without the teacher. Was there not something essential in the pedagogic process – the living contact of master and pupil – that must be lost when the teacher has gone? Was each teacher therefore unique? But if that were the case, what was now to become of Gurdjieff's pupils? And how was the world to be served in future by his work? The Master himself had provided no easy answers to these questions. Though he left an informal organisational structure in place, he founded no church or society to embody his ideas. Though he appointed heirs to protect his work, he determined no apostolic succession and implied that his heirs had very limited powers. Though he formulated general principles in a fearsomely complex cosmology based on the arithmetic formulae of three and seven, he insisted on the uniqueness of each pupil. And although he told followers that he had learnt his lore in the hidden monasteries of Central Asia, he continued to proclaim himself supreme and *sui generis*. As usual, his pupils were faced with puzzles by the very man to whom they had looked for answers.

Their difficulties were aggravated yet further by personal and national antagonisms. Gurdjieff's last years had seemed to bring most of the diverse groups together in a common purpose, though the Master took pleasure in setting one against another. His death revealed their unity to be illusory: within weeks of his funeral, factions were squabbling over their inheritance. Having virtually ignored Gurdjieff's presence in their midst for the first twenty years, the Paris intelligentsia had belatedly begun to take an interest in him. Now the French pupils, led by Jeanne de Salzmann, claimed leadership of the Gurdjieff movement (whatever it amounted to), much to the annoyance of the English and the Americans. Jane

Heap, Madame Ouspensky and Olga de Hartmann all associated themselves with de Salzmann. Thus the main branch of the hitherto predominantly Anglo-Saxon and male chauvinist Work was run from Paris and directed by women.[1]

Gurdjieff's groups in America gradually fragmented. Ouspensky and Orage both had their own supporters there, and new heirs – men who had never even met these legendary figures – now came foward to dispute the succession. At loggerheads with the French, the English also fought amongst themselves. Though most paid lip-service to Madame de Salzmann in Paris, largely on grounds of her seniority as Gurdjieff's longest-surviving pupil, there was bitter rivalry between them at home. J. G. Bennett's pretensions to leadership caused particular offence among old habitués of the Prieuré, who saw him as an upstart and an outsider, and resented his long allegiance to Ouspensky. Perhaps Bennett aroused stronger passions because he not only claimed to be Gurdjieff's heir: in the fashion of his master, he was also inclined to hint at inspiration by still higher powers. This was presumably one solution to problems of legitimacy and authority: in Gurdjieff's absence there could always be an appeal to that Hidden Source of which he and Ouspensky had so often spoken, the Secret Brotherhood of Masters to which they now belonged – *if* one could find it.

It was not only in Gurdjieffian circles that Bennett stirred up rivalry. At home in England there were pupils still loyal to Ouspensky who resented both Bennett's appropriation of their teacher in the years between the wars and his subsequent defection to Gurdjieff. These included Rodney Collin, Francis Roles and Maurice Nicoll, who were now leading the main Ouspenskyite factions. Nicoll, formerly a Harley Street specialist and an early inmate of the Prieuré, had established a flourishing community before the war at Great Amwell in Hertfordshire, elaborating his teaching in a series of books which reinterpreted Gurdjieffian doctrine in the light of psychoanalysis. When Gurdjieff reappeared after the war, Nicoll kept aloof. Nicoll's death in 1953, however, prompted many of his pupils to transfer their allegiance to Madame de Salzmann in Paris. The others faded away.

Francis Roles – another Harley Street consultant – founded the

Society for the Study of Normal Psychology, usually known as the Study Society, to perpetuate Ouspensky's teaching. Roles was an indecisive man, and during the 1950s the Study Society was gradually taken over by one of his pupils, Leon MacLaren. Trained as a barrister, MacLaren was the son of the Scottish Labour MP Andrew MacLaren, who had founded the School of Economic Science (SES) in the mid-1930s to spread the socialist theories of the American economist Henry George.

There was at first no connection between the School of Economic Science and the Society for the Study of Normal Psychology, until Leon MacLaren decided that economic problems could only be solved by changes in the spiritual outlook of mankind. Taking over leadership of the SES from his father in 1947, he began to import into it the Ouspenskyite teachings of the Study Society, despite Andrew MacLaren's objections.[2] Leon was a powerful personality who easily dominated Roles: as the two societies developed closer links, the economic theories of the SES were gradually subordinated to spiritual teaching. The SES became a religious organisation and the dominant partner in the relationship. Though the school regularly advertises[3] a curriculum of 'practical philosophy' to be taught in evening classes – leading most people to expect conventional tuition in the history of ethics and politics – it actually teaches its own variety of Work cosmology.

The School of Economic Science took a further step into the alternative spiritual synthesis when MacLaren and Roles encountered the Maharishi Mahesh Yogi on his first visit to England in 1960. Impressed by the Maharishi, in the following year Roles led a group from the Study Society on a trip to India where they met the Maharishi's fellow-guru the Shankaracharya, a follower of the eighth-century Indian mystic and teacher Shankara. Shankara expounded the doctrine of Advaita Vedanta, which teaches that God is Absolute, and that men are potentially one with God, could they but know it. Because the manifestation of the Absolute in matter obscures this fundamental truth, humanity's task is therefore to rediscover the Absolute and thus achieve unity with it.

Roles was immediately convinced that in the Shankaracharya he had at last found the Source of Gurdjieff's and Ouspensky's teaching. Returning to London he told school members: 'All your worries are over. I am only four days old. I was only born last Thursday.'[4] Together with the Maharishi, Roles and MacLaren then established another school to teach Transcendental Meditation. It seemed as though the Sufi traditions of Gurdjieff and the Hindu traditions which had helped to shape Theosophy were about to be united in a grand synthesis; but the relationship between the three men was soon fraught with arguments about money, which was arriving in large quantities. Nor could they agree how to synthesise the Maharishi's approach and the Gurdjieff/Ouspensky teaching favoured by the SES and the Study Society. Philosophical disputes became the focus of a power struggle. By the late 1960s the three men had gone their different ways and each led a quite distinct organisation.

The Study Society gradually returned to its Ouspenskyite origins and continued to operate in a modest way in West Kensington. The School of Transcendental Meditation, led by the Maharishi, became internationally known, acquiring in the process many rich pupils and some celebrated enthusiasts – including (for a while) the pop stars George Harrison, Bob Dylan and John Lennon. Most of those who take up what is known for short as TM appear to be uninterested in its religious aspect: they are simply in search of techniques to develop their powers of concentration and relaxation. The Maharishi's school flourishes at Mentmore, its ornate stately home in Buckinghamshire, and there are branches throughout the world. Its members are mainly celebrated for their claim that sustained and intense meditation produces the ability to fly.

After its disagreements with the Maharishi and the Study Society, the SES went its own way and did indeed produce a synthesis of Hindu theology and Gurdjieffian practice. On that foundation it has prospered considerably over the past two decades. Its funds now run into millions, and the school owns substantial properties in England and abroad, bought with a continuing stream of donations, bequests and convenants. The subscriptions of ordinary members play a relatively small role in the organisation's finances, and fees are kept low to encourage recruitment.[5] Links with Shankaracharya are maintained in northern India, but the school has its main bases in central London and at MacLaren's mansion in Oxfordshire. There are flourishing branches in the United States, Australia and several European countries and the SES also runs children's schools and intensive training-courses for adults.

Economic Science now has all the features of a cult. This became clear in 1983, when scandal erupted over the management of the children's schools. At first, most parents were impressed by the standards of order and politeness, their emphasis on hard work and obedience, and their comparatively low fees. Attitudes began to change when it transpired that what they had taken to be ordinary independent schools were, in fact, instructing children in the tenets of Economic Science according to MacLaren's rule of Measure. This entails interpreting all subjects – including physics and chemistry – in terms of Gurdjieffian cosmology; teaching even the youngest children Indian philosophy and Sanskrit; conducting an exceptionally rigorous regime of attendance, costume and home-work, enforced by frequent corporal punishment; and effectively indoctrinating every child in the principles of the SES.

The scandal was prompted by a series of articles published in the London *Evening Standard* during 1982, reported in turn by other papers, which quoted parents complaining of savage punishments and bizarre homework assignments which seemed to consist largely of ideas from 'oriental' philosophy to be learnt by rote.[6] They also remarked on the vegetarian meals served to pupils, in which the ingredients were strictly controlled by Hindu dietary law. Outraged Anglican clergymen weighed into the row, suggesting that the SES was a wicked Hindu cult plotting against Christianity. The Bishop of Woolwich called it evil and corrupt. Though many parents were agnostic or Jewish, some took the hint and withdrew their children. Others stayed on. The schools, which were not technically in breach of Department of Education and Science guidelines, have survived with substantial donations by SES members. Their supporters insist that they are simply returning to old-fashioned values of discipline and hard work. Opponents accuse the SES of combining brainwashing, cruelty and the enforcement of conformity with the teaching of preposterous nonsense in place of the ordinary school curriculum.

At the heart of the row is the argument over Measure, the central feature of all SES teaching for children and adults alike. Measure is adapted from Ouspensky's systematic interpretation of Gurdjieff's doctrine, and consists of a complex, rigid and demanding set of rules governing every aspect of an SES member's life, from his diet and musical taste to his sexual behaviour. According to MacLaren, these rules correspond to the natural laws governing the universe: by observing them we thereby promote the good of the cosmos. In practice they are fiercely repressive, and at the same time conservative and eccentric, stressing the traditional roles of the sexes (down to the wearing of long skirts for women), insisting on the central role of Sanskrit chanting in education, and rejecting contemporary culture *in toto* (especially television, dancing and 'modern', i.e. post-Shakespearian, literature).

The rules are administered by 'personal tutors' to whom members report and owe absolute obedience.[7] The tutors are in turn organised by group leaders who have the authority to demand more or less anything from their charges. Group leaders take their instruction from MacLaren's assistants. Like the Work, the SES is obsessively hierarchical: the ruling elders submit absolutely to MacLaren, who supposedly submits himself to the teaching of the Shankaracharya. And like Gurdjieff, MacLaren alternates between the roles of stern teacher, mysterious power, loving father, charismatic leader and remote autocrat.

The need for Measure is founded on MacLaren's belief that men are put on earth to serve the Absolute, though they generally prove incapable of doing so. The Absolute is manifested throughout the cosmos by the natural laws identified by the SES, but it is all too often obscured by human ignorance and indifference, which are thus responsible for the evil which mars both our own lives and the evolution of creation. The function of the SES is to illuminate ignorance and dispel indifference. Observing the rules of Measure clarifies the role of natural laws in the universe and thus promotes the well-being of the Absolute – which in turn sustains the life of the righteous. Those who follow Measure hope to become part of the Inner Circle of Mankind – a group which clearly derives from the Theosophical Brotherhood of Masters. It includes familiar figures from the theosophical pantheon such as Buddha, Moses, Jesus, Socrates and Lao Tzu, and less familiar deities such as Leon MacLaren and Francis Roles.

In order to gain admission to the Inner Circle one must acknowledge first the crucial Gurdjieffian distinction between the essential self and personality; second that the essential self reflects the Absolute, unless prevented from doing so by personality; third that the aim of life is direct communion between the essential self and the Absolute; and fourth that the essential self must therefore be cultivated at the expense of the personality. MacLaren also agrees with Gurdjieff that most human activity – indeed, most human existence, as manifested in 'personality' – is futile: mere 'fertiliser for the moon' as Gurdjieff called it. If we wish to achieve a higher level of being by serving the Absolute we must do so through meditation, self-observation and intentional suffering. These techniques are taught in evening classes, weekend conferences and country-house summer schools, where the order of the day is intensive hard labour and group exercises _à la_ Prieuré. At the summer schools the sexes are strictly segregated, the food rationed and the long day (beginning at four-thirty) carefully divided into supervised activities.

Behind all this it is easy to see familiar Christian terms and values. The Absolute is God, the personal tutor a spiritual director, essence the soul, personality our human weaknesses, meditation prayer, intentional suffering the mortification of the flesh, and MacLaren himself an infallible pope. The resemblance to bleaker forms of Christianity is made even clearer by the school's dour moralism. This is Gurdjieff's teaching, with the vitality and the anarchic humour left out. Living according to MacLaren's rule of Measure involves sexual abstinence, confession, public penance, obedience and social conformity to a degree that would have made Calvin himself hesitate. Observance of orthodoxy can take strange forms. Because MacLaren admires Leonardo da Vinci and Mozart, these are the official artists of the SES. Because he enjoys claret, members take trouble to find out about vintages. Destroying personality in favour of 'essence' can look suspiciously like conditioning.

Members straying from the path are subjected to enormous

pressure from peers and tutors, who summon them to explain themselves, and then impose punishments. One woman was made to wash dishes all night – to calm her nerves.[8] Pupils are all the more vulnerable to peer-group pressure because commitment to the school tends to isolate them from other relationships with family and friends. In serious cases, MacLaren himself has been known to give rebels a talking-to – something considered to be far more alarming than any punishment. The SES is not a cult in the sense of Scientology or the Moonies: no one is kept in it against their will; but black sheep, once expelled, are totally rejected, in the Gurdjieff manner.

The order and asceticism of the SES are all the more surprising given MacLaren's own style of life, which conforms exactly to what the man in the street expects from a western guru. He lives in luxury with a staff of chauffeurs and secretaries to attend to every need. Grovelling respect is exacted from every SES pupil, and when MacLaren receives, he gives audience as a supreme potentate. He chain-smokes and drinks the best claret. Living in mansions in Oxfordshire and Hampstead, he dresses in silk shirts and fine suits, though these do not obscure the figure of a stooping, elderly man (he was born in 1911) with a paunch and what have been described as wolfish features. He is, however, a powerful and persuasive speaker with a fine voice.

But perhaps the most peculiar aspect of the SES concerns its relationship with the British Liberal Party. Leon MacLaren and his father Andrew were both socialists until 1943, when Andrew MacLaren decided that there was no hope of Labour taking up Henry George's reforming ideas and left. His son followed him out and joined the Liberals.

Once a major political force in Britain, the party of Gladstone and Lloyd George was by then a rump consisting of a handful of MPs. But although MacLaren stood without success as a Liberal candidate in two elections, he made many friends in the party. By the late 1970s, a dozen SES members were standing as Liberals, including the former chairman of the party, Roger Pincham.

What amounted to infiltration of a major political organisation inevitably became news, not least because the Liberal Party had

been involved in a series of sensational scandals throughout the
1980s, culminating in the trial of its leader, Jeremy Thorpe, for
conspiracy to murder. The press were therefore interested in any
hint of other skeletons in the cupboard – and the SES rattled many
bones. Mr Pincham eventually had to make a public denial that
there was anything sinister about the Liberal–SES connection, and
this seemed to calm the situation. When journalists interviewed Mr
Pincham in the presence of Wyn Hugh-Jones, the General Secretary
of the Liberal Party, Mr Hugh-Jones was quite relaxed about their
meeting. His only moment of alarm came when Pincham admitted
to his interviewers that he believed in levitation.[9]

Rodney Collin's search for the source of Ouspensky's teaching took
a rather different form. Unhappy in England after his teacher's
death, which seriously disturbed his mental equilibrium, he
decided to move to Mexico.[10] He knew something about the
country from visits made while looking after Ouspensky in America
during the war, and he was especially attracted to it as the home of
Evans Wentz, the leading western student of Tibetan religion,
whose scholarly work on *The Book of the Dead* was to play a part in
forming Collin's spiritual syncretism.

Collin and his wife Janet established a religious community in a
hacienda at Tlalpam on the outskirts of Mexico City, bought with
Janet's money. At first life at Tlalpam was no more than a re-
creation of Lyne, but it soon turned into something more spectacular – and ironically much closer to Gurdjieff than to Ouspensky –
when Collin bought a field in the mountains beyond Mexico City
and proceeded to build on it the Planetarium of Tetecala.

The Tetecala (a Mexican word meaning 'the stone house of God')
consisted of two semi-underground rooms, the Chambers of the Sun
and Moon, linked by a container positioned to receive the sun's full
rays at the summer solstice. There were also to be further rooms
above ground – including a library and a ballroom, and a house to
accommodate the community from Tlalpam – but these were never
built. Nor was the central building, meant to represent the laws
governing universal harmony. Collin, who interpreted Ouspensky's

death as one stage in a great Cosmic Mystery, was himself becoming increasingly histrionic. The Planetarium provided a superb stage for the beginning of his own drama.

The sun plays an important role in Gurdjieff's cosmology, where the 'Most Holy Sun Absolute' is the dwelling of 'Our Common Father Endlessness', i.e. God, and therefore the source of all creation's power and energy. Collin made it the focal point of his new religion. It was also celebrated in the name of the publishing house and bookshop he founded in Mexico City, Ediciones Sol. These institutions soon became the centre of esoteric interest throughout South America.

In a pamphlet whose very title, *The Herald of Harmony*, echoes Gurdjieff's *Herald of Coming Good*, Collin describes Gurdjieff and Ouspensky in Blavatskian language as messengers sent out by the 'Hierarchy' of the 'Great School' destined to exert a decisive influence on the next epoch of world history. Like a character out of Borges (who took an interest in Collin), he believed that a true esoteric school creates a new cosmos with its teacher for a sun. The tone is millenarian, the doctrine described as 'new' Christianity. The next epoch, according to Collin, will be the epoch of transcendental harmony, in which all differences are resolved – a suitable ambition if an unlikely hope for a follower of the Work. The change of emphasis from creative discord to universal harmony is a mark of how rapidly – if unknowingly – Collin was moving away from Gurdjieff.

In 1954 Collin dissolved the community at Tlalpam. It no longer served his purpose. Increasingly preoccupied with his own mystical role, he had little time now for pupils and communities. Instead he embarked on a search for *the* esoteric school. In the same year he also published his major work, *The Theory of Celestial Influence*, which applies the notion of transcendental harmony to the scheme of cosmic history. Collin himself is said to have sensed the otherworldly presence of its dedicatee, Ouspensky, while writing the book, but if there is a ghostly voice speaking here it is surely the mischievous Leadbeater's. Collin regurgitates the old theosophical hotchpotch of planetary cycles, the rise and fall of peoples and civilisations, cosmic aeons, reincarnations and astrological signs.

The material is barely held together by the author's obsession with harmony and Ouspensky's theory of esoteric schools, reinterpreted by Collin in terms of the 165-year cycles of the planet Neptune which govern their reappearance. Collin concluded from his complicated astrological sums that one such cycle was about to reach its climax, in coincidence with the climacteric of his own life.

The ideas in *The Theory of Celestial Influence* were not the only things about it that looked back to Leadbeater. Clearly apparent is the increasing influence of spiritualism. This owes a good deal to Collin's relationship with a Mexican spirit medium who not only 'brought through' the voices of Gurdjieff and Ouspensky for him, but even simulated their manners and appearance – without, of course, ever having met them. When the Collins visited Europe and the Near East in 1954, travelling through Iran, Syria and Turkey on the way (and meeting J. G. Bennett, engaged there on his own occult mission), they took their medium with them, and followed the guidance of her spirit voices in their search for esoteric schools.

The woman was a devout Mexican Catholic, and the esoteric school the voices led them to turned out to be the Catholic Church.[11] Collin did nothing by halves. Once persuaded that the Church had been what he was looking for all the time, Collin returned to Mexico, where he began to prepare for sainthood or martyrdom: making pilgrimages, mortifying the flesh and predicting the imminence of some great but unspecified event. He was also overworking: despite the dillusionment of many European pupils with his conversion to mystical Catholicism, this was just the turn of events needed to interest his South American audience, and new groups were springing up all over the continent.

In May 1956, Collin travelled to Lima to visit one of these groups. While there, he made a pilgrimage to Cuzco. Already in bad health, he suffered from the unpressurised cabin in the aeroplane and complained of sickness on his arrival in Cuzco. Nevertheless, he went out into the city and that afternoon came across a crippled beggar boy in the streets. He took to this boy, called Modesto, who must have been surprised when Collin volunteered to wash him. Modesto was then given shoes and clothes by Collin, who crassly told the poverty-stricken crowd which soon gathered round the rich foreigner that it was their duty to look after one another. In return for Collin's generosity, the boy showed his benefactor his home high in the cathedral bell-tower.

Collin was clearly unhinged by this time: that night he woke his wife to tell her that he had offered his body to God in exchange for Modesto's so that the boy might be made whole. He now regretted the offer because his own work wasn't complete. How was he to retract a promise made to God? His wife assured him that all would be well.

The next day he went to mass in the cathedral, then climbed the bell-tower once more, in order to tell Modesto that instead of doing a deal with God he had decided to arrange and pay for an operation to cure the boy's crippled leg. Knowledge of what happened next depends upon the testimonies of the confused Modesto and of an old woman standing in the square far below the tower. The old woman claimed that Collin simply lost his footing. According to Modesto, his patron was sitting on a ledge under the parapet and staring at the distant statue of Christ, when he suddenly lunged forward, struck his head on a beam and fell from the tower to the ground. When Collin landed his arms were stretched out like Christ on the cross, his leg drawn up like Modesto's. There was a smile on his face.

Rodney Collin was buried in Cuzco. A tablet in the square where he fell is inscribed with the words HERE RODNEY COLLIN GAVE HIS LIFE TO PROJECT HARMONY.[12] But there was no concord among his followers, and the ambiguity of the phrase 'gave his life' is typical. While Collin may have devoted his lifetime to working for harmony, there is no evidence that his fall from the tower was anything other than an unfortunate accident, and the harmony he tried to project was the naïve ideal of a muddled adolescent. Gradually the groups disintegrated, the spirit medium who had inherited their direction turned her attentions to founding a lay religious order, and the Chamber of the Moon at Tetecala was transformed into a Catholic chapel. Rodney Collin and all his works were received into the capacious bosom of Mother Church.

TWENTY-ONE

Climacteric

Nineteen fifty-six was a momentous year in Western politics. The Suez crisis and the invasion of Hungary both threatened world stability, intensifying the Cold War. The population at large, terrified by the prospect of nuclear holocaust, wondered whether these events were the beginning of the end. Occultists interpreted them as portents of an approaching climacteric, though they argued over its nature. It seemed that a decisive moment in spiritual history was about to arrive. But what form would this moment take? Was it to be the end of dialectical materialism in the Soviet bloc and consumer materialism in the capitalist world? The appearance of a teacher from the East? The annihilation of the human race and the emergence of a new order?

Certainly, there were great things happening in the spiritual realm. Rodney Collin died in 1956, predicting prodigious but unspecified events; Krishnamurti held an ecumenical meeting with the Dalai Lama within a stone's throw of the Theosophical compound at Adyar; and J. G. Bennett discovered yet another new religion. It was also the year when the Aetherius Church was founded by His Eminence the Metropolitan Archbishop Sir George King, D.Sc., Th.D., Grand Master of the Order of Saint Peter and President of the College of Spiritual Sciences in England.[1]

Two years earlier, the thirty-five-year-old Mr King (as he then was) had been quietly practising yoga in his Fulham flat one sunny May morning when he suddenly heard the Cosmic Master Aetherius saying, 'Prepare Yourself! You Are To become The Voice Of Interplanetary Parliament.'[2] Aetherius, who was speaking from Venus, went on to instruct Mr King in the manufacture of Spiritual Energy Radiators. These machines are used by giant spacecraft floating through the universe to infuse spirituality into human beings, and their power is stored in Spiritual Energy Batteries, invented by Mr King himself.

The doctrines of the Aetherius Church, which have been described by one of its bishops as a 'brilliant concept . . . too advanced for some religious minds',[3] draw on many faiths, stressing the unity of Religion and Science, East and West. In particular, they rewrite the theosophical notion of Hidden Masters in terms of advanced space technology. Mr King sees the Masters as six adepts or Warriors of Light. Travelling through space to battle with Dark Powers, these Warriors have paid two major visits to earth in recent years: on what Mr King calls Alien Mission in 1965, and Operation Karmalight in 1967–69. UFOs, popular in the 1950s, were also signs of their presence.

In order to stimulate further visits from outer space and to reinforce their effect, the Aetherius Church promotes Spiritual Pushes: days when believers gather in sacred spots on magical dates to concentrate their prayers. Mr King, who is also a spiritual healer, now lives in California, but his church is still organised from 757 Fulham Road, London SW6. In 1980 he was knighted by the Byzantine Royal House – an honour described by his assistant as 'recognised in the Italian Courts'.[4]

The equation of space travel with divine intervention also produced the Raëlian Movement. Now claiming fifty thousand members world-wide, the group began when a French journalist called Claude Vorilhon, aka Raël, was visited by an extra-terrestrial on 13 December 1973. This being described himself as a member of the Elohim and a 'father from space', and was clearly yet another avatar of the Hidden Masters. Bearing Raël off to his own planet, he explained to his guest that human beings had first been created there, adding that he and his fellows wished to establish an embassy on the earth, from which base they would eventually form a world government, world currency and world language. In the mean time, he imparted to Raël the techniques for 'Awakening the Mind by Awakening the Body', and encouraged him to pass them on. Raël duly established centres of 'Sensual Meditation' throughout the world, where members can wear their six-pointed medallions and learn to become sensually aware. For that privilege they are expected to contribute ten per cent of their income.

As this farrago suggests, what the portents of 1956 foreshadowed was not the end of the world or the advent of a new era, but the less cataclysmic appearance of the full-blown New Age. It was not one teacher who appeared from the East, but dozens. For it was in the mid-1950s that the children of Theosophy began to multiply in huge numbers, to intermarry with new cults and to create new vehicles for themselves. The Church of Aetherius and the Raëlian Movement are just two among scores of well-supported groups, and the multiplication continues apace, especially on the west coast of America.

Curiously, the Theosophical Society itself has experienced only a modest revival despite the huge increase of interest in all things occult over the last forty years. Perhaps it has become too respectable – living proof that scandal is a necessary ingredient for success. The Society still functions throughout the world from its headquarters at Adyar but its membership is elderly, its activities respectable, its profile low. The thrilling, scandalous days of Blavatsky, Besant and Leadbeater are long since gone, and members now combine the study of esoteric wisdom with humanitarian enterprises in a thoroughly dignified and worthwhile way. With dignity has come domesticity and perhaps a certain lassitude. Its ambitions tamed, the Society is now closer to the Women's Institute than to the United Nations or the Catholic Church.

If Theosophy can be described as subdued, the Work must be said to operate with a discretion that is positively obsessive. The scandals of Gurdjieff's years are long since forgotten, the upper-middle-class guardians of the tradition increasingly replaced by the anorak-and-sandals brigade. Though the Gurdjieff Society exists in England and the Gurdjieff Institute in France, they are not easy to find. They never advertise and never recruit. Classes continue and the sacred dances are passed on, but I have been told by several members that it will not matter if the Work dies out for lack of new pupils. Gurdjieff was sent to this planet on a spiritual mission which he fulfilled. It is up to others to interpret that mission. If they cannot do so, that is their problem, and it will not be solved by prostituting the teaching in some deluded drive to achieve popularity.

If Theosophy and its stepchild the Work gently decline, their offspring flourish. Most depend on the Brotherhood of Masters in some shape or form. They range in ambition from the modest to the megalomaniac, though few go so far as the Eternal Flame, a London-based, American-inspired group which promises members physical immortality in return for a small fee.[6]

Two organisations are very characteristic. At one end of the spectrum there is the Universal White Brotherhood of the French-Bulgarian sage Omraam Mikhael Aivanhov (1900–86). At their headquarters in a listed manor house in East Sussex, the brothers and sisters of the brotherhood live the simple life in order to attune themselves with Cosmic Intelligence and Creative Force as personified by the sun. They believe that men can become Masters by cultivating a blend of spiritualism and yoga. A benevolent figure who beams out of his photographs through a long white beard, the Omraam's many books teach the desirability of Universal Harmony and the possibility of transforming all through love. The brotherhood is especially dedicated to harnessing cosmic energy to higher purposes. Much of this energy comes to us in the form of sexual desire. According to the Omraam:

> Sexual energy can be compared to petrol. If you don't know how to handle it, it can burn you: it burns your quintessence. But those who know how to handle it can use it to fuel their inner motors and fly off into space.[7]

Though it has branches in America and Australia, the Brotherhood is a small, unpretentious organisation devoted to promoting plain living and high thinking. The Summit Lighthouse is more characteristic of Theosophy's major offspring and it deploys all the razzmatazz of American retailing techniques to sell its glamorous leader, the aptly named Elizabeth Clare Prophet.[8] The Lighthouse was founded in Washington, D.C., by the Rev. Mark L. Prophet (1918–73). As a child in the remoter corners of Wisconsin, Mr Prophet had visions of angels and spirits and built a private altar in the attic of his family home. In manhood he was visited by an Ascended Master called El Morya – a member of the Great White Brotherhood (not to be confused with the *Universal* White Brotherhood)[9] and a figure clearly inspired by (if not identical with) Madame Blavatsky's patron. El Morya dictated to Prophet a series of weekly notes known as the *Pearls of Wisdom* and eventually directed him to open the Lighthouse in 1957; twelve months after the inauguration of the Aetherius Church.

Four years later the much younger Elizabeth Wulf (1939–   ) of New Jersey was inspired to seek out Mr Prophet at the direction of her own Ascended Master, Saint Germain – another crib from Theosophy. Like her husband, Elizabeth Prophet had been a spiritually precocious child who communicated with Jesus and criticised the errors she heard from New Jersey pulpits. According to the official biography, her early heroes were Gandhi, Albert Schweitzer and Norman Vincent Peale, but these were all superseded after her encounter with the Master Saint Germain, who anointed young Elizabeth as a messenger of the Great White Brotherhood.

In 1963 Mark and Elizabeth were married, and shortly afterwards they moved their headquarters to Colorado Springs, where they produced four children. In 1973 Mark Prophet died and became an Ascended Master himself, while his widow carried on the good work of the Summit Lighthouse under the direct guidance of Saint Germain. In 1981 Mrs Prophet married Edward L. Francis, a much younger follower, and he soon became 'business manager' of the Lighthouse in its new incarnation as the Church Universal and Triumphant.

The Church established itself on a thirty-three-thousand-acre ranch in Montana, where it founded a working community for those who want to escape from the evils of city life and return to the simplicity of working on the land. Also based in Montana, and with some affiliation with the Church, is the Summit University Press.

The press publishes the Lighthouse's many books and charming lithographs of its Masters. The Masters include figures familiar from the theosophical pantheon, but there are also others: Sanat Kumara, Portia, Jesus In The Clouds, the Buddha of the Ruby Ray and Lady Master (*sic*) Venus. Mrs Prophet herself appears in this pantheon as Guru Ma, the Universal Mother who will one day join her first husband as an Ascended Master. Publications cover everything from cancer cures to alchemy and invariably present a rosy *Reader's Digest* picture of existence.

The reality of Lighthouse communal life is rather different.[10] The ranch is run on very strict lines, recalling Thomas Lake Harris's Brotherhood of the New Life. The day begins at five a.m. (seven days per week) with two hours of prayer and meditation, followed by breakfast and hard labour and concluding with an improving activity at which Mrs Prophet may graciously preside. Inmates are fed on a low-protein diet and all stimulants are banned, as is extra-marital sex. Sexual intercourse between married couples is limited to not more than thirty minutes, twice a week.

In return for these privileges, probationers on Guru Ma's ranch pay up to $400 per month for board and lodging. Once the probation is over, they sign away all their property irrevocably to the Church. Not that they need spare cash: followers dress plainly, join in group activities and share sleeping quarters. Mrs Prophet, on the other hand, does need the money. She occupies luxurious quarters with her young husband and varies her clothes of spotless white satin with the occasional pink and gold sari and many diamonds. She looks and behaves like a queen and her followers treat her as a goddess.

No doubt she has their welfare at heart. There is tight security at the ranch, the guards who patrol it are well-armed, and in the late 1980s Guru Ma built a huge nuclear shelter for believers to take refuge from the 1989 world holocaust predicted by Saint Germain. Observers questioning the need for these precautions in a spiritual community whose members join of their own free will are told that the guards are under orders to keep intruders out, not members in. Others wonder why Mrs Prophet needs a bunker if her followers are, as she insists, saved whatever happens, but she says that she puts her faith in Saint Germain, who ordered the building. Unfortunately, the huge oil-tanks constructed to service the shelter leaked into the Yellowstone River before the holocaust could occur, exposing Mrs Prophet, and not Saint Germain, to prosecution for pollution.

At about the same time, one of her three daughters left the ranch accusing her mother of brainwashing, while other community members spoke to reporters about bullying and exploitation. Guru Ma's troubles were compounded when a faithful follower was caught at the ranch with a huge cache of illegal arms and it became clear that the Church Universal and Triumphant was preparing to become a war zone. Among local people the discovery evoked painful memories of the nearby Rajneeshi community, which only a few years earlier had turned into a heavily armed camp before collapsing amid financial scandal when its leaders, including Rajneesh himself, fled the country in a private jet with large quantities of loose change.

But perhaps the most interesting thing about the Church Universal is that oil spillage into the Yellowstone River. Like so many founders of communities, Guru Ma took her followers away from the corruptions of civilisation to the open spaces of Montana where they could lead a 'natural' life and attune themselves through hard manual labour with the spiritual rhythms of the universe. Yet in the middle of this paradise she built herself what might stand as an emblem of all the modern world's deepest fears: a nuclear bunker fuelled by oil.

The spillage is especially ironic in view of the fact that the most powerful new force to shape the alternative spiritual synthesis in recent years has been the ecological movement: its marks are visible on both the Church Universal and the Great White Brotherhood. Ecology is to contemporary western gurus what vegetarianism, animal welfare, homoeopathy and the simple life were to their nineteenth-century predecessors. Ecological pressure groups claim to have both a coherent philosophy and urgent necessity on their side. They have also adopted the millenarian tone characteristic of so many independent teachers. The return to nature is now more than a romantic indulgence or a private spiritual practice, they insist: it has become the major political issue of our time. The row about evolution, which prompted Blavatsky's anti-Darwinian tirade in the first place, is therefore on the agenda again, but this time what is at stake is nothing less than the future of the planet. Many teachers and spiritual groups have gone Green in the last decade, identifying preservation of the planet as the chief spiritual task of mankind – in marked contrast to the unworldliness of older mystical traditions.

One consequence of this shift in opinion has been the reappearance of Anthroposophy, which has emerged as the unexpected victor in those long-ago guru wars between Besant, Tingley and Steiner. For although the Anthroposophical Society itself grows only slowly and has like Theosophy a largely elderly membership, its influence has increased out of all proportion. This owes something to the spiritual revival of the later twentieth century; and something to the carefully structured organisation established by the founder; but most of all to Steiner's interest in Green issues and the central place taken in his philosophy by the relationship between ecology and religion.

The major strength of Steiner's teaching – notably lacking from Theosophy – is its practicality. If Steiner has a theory for everything, he also has a way of putting that theory into practice. Relating grand cosmology and psychology to ecology, he situates mankind at the heart of a complex universal eco-system in which spiritual and biological forces have equally important roles to play; but he also takes account of physical existence at the mundane level: eating, sleeping, farming, making. Encouraged by the successes of the Green movement, the Anthroposophical Society has recently set up its own bank to lend at low rates of interest to ecologically sound projects: organic farms, small light industries, crafts and heritage projects.[11] The movement has also invested heavily in Steiner's educational, therapeutic and medical enterprises, all of which sit well with contemporary attitudes to ecology, relying as they do on natural systems and materials.

Where Anthroposophy leads, other groups have followed. The Emissary Foundation International, for example, has branches in Canada, Australia, Britain, America, South Africa and France, where its members live in communes and teach holistic doctrines very like Steiner's. The history of the foundation, which is a serious organisation, illustrates the changes that have taken place in many alternative religious groups over the last three decades. Founded in 1932 by Lloyd Meeker, an American Indian who taught under the name Uranda, its members were originally known as the Emissaries of Divine Light. As their name suggests, the Emissaries were a mystical order. They believed in the reality of higher beings – their version of Hidden Masters – who could impart wisdom to initiates if rightly approached.

While still emphasising spiritual life as the key to world reform, the renamed Emissary Foundation now minimises its mystical aspects, preferring to emphasise the importance of ecology and psychology.[12] No occult beliefs are required of members, whose objective is to improve both themselves and the world environment by means of 'attunement' between the individual, other people and the earth's natural rhythms. Attunement involves prayer, meditation and reflection, but practical activities play an equally important role. The foundation manages many educational projects and encourages alternative medical and financial ventures. It is in no sense a cult. Outsiders are encouraged to attend seminars in 'The Art of Living' and the group welcomes guests into its farms and ranches.

This is the acceptable face of alternative religion, and perhaps the only surprising thing about the foundation is its leadership. After Meeker's death in 1954, control passed to a follower who happened to be the head of one of England's grandest aristocratic families. Martin Cecil, later Seventh Marquess of Exeter, had left England for North America many years before, in the well-established tradition of aristocratic younger sons sent abroad to seek their fortunes. It was only when his cousin the Sixth Marquess died without male issue that he inherited the title, although the great house and estate at Burghley went to his cousin's daughters. Lord Exeter's son Michael, who married Lloyd Meeker's daughter, succeeded his father as leader of the Emissaries and Eighth Marquess in 1988, establishing a strong precedent for the application of the hereditary principle to religious movements.

*

No one responded more enthusiastically to the late-twentieth-century blend of ecology, esotericism, science and eschatology than J. G. Bennett. Indeed, one might say that Bennett was a typical New Age figure before the New Age was thought of, exploring every possible avenue of spiritual enlightenment and ready to unify his discoveries in a personal syncretism. The final decades of his life saw him on a rapidly accelerating trip through all the available alternatives as he rushed from guru to guru in search of the elusive Source – only to find it at last within himself.

After Gurdjieff's death Bennett's activities were further disrupted, by Winifred's serious heart attack in the autumn of 1950.[13] An even more devastating blow was to follow three weeks later, when he arrived at work one morning to find the laboratories sealed and himself suspended from his post. That evening's papers carried sensational headlines about Communist spying in institutions connected with atomic research. Bennett's political sympathies, his work in military intelligence, his Foreign Office record, his activities as a spiritual teacher and Gurdjieff's reputation as a spy proved a potent mixture in the Cold War atmosphere of the early '50s. Though his name did not appear in the newspapers, Bennett resigned from his post.

Driven out of employment, he dedicated himself to Coombe Springs, where he built a large new hall on the model of Gurdjieff's Study House. Then in 1953 a voice told him to search in the East, so naturally he went, despite the vagueness of the instruction. The question was, where exactly? One obvious answer was to replicate Gurdjieff's journeys in Central Asia and the Near East. On the recommendation of a princely descendant of Muhammad, he began by visiting a Damascene Sufi sheikh, Ermin Chikhou. *En route* he returned to Constantinople, now Istanbul; toured Konya, home of Djellaluddin Rumi, founder of the Mevlevi Dervishes; and had a vision in which he was told not to accept the offer of a job at the United Nations. Quite enough for one vacation.

Ermin Chikhou – himself a Nakshibendi dervish – discoursed rather puzzlingly (given his faith) on the imminent Second Coming of Christ, assuring Bennett that he had a vital role to play in this event as a sort of John the Baptist to the new Messiah. For once Bennett was sceptical; but when he returned to Syria in the following year the prophecy was repeated. Winifred Bennett, who had recently suffered a severe cerebral haemorrhage which left her more or less crazed, stayed behind at Coombe, and Bennett travelled round Syria and Iraq with his close friend and future wife Elizabeth Mayall, visiting holy men as they went. One sheikh at Damascus endorsed Ermin Chikhou's prophecy of a Second Coming, while another at Kerind told him the same thing, obligingly adding that Bennett and his fellow-traveller were destined by God to be companions. At least the second prophecy was correct. But though Bennett travelled extensively in the wilds of Turkey and northern Persia, visiting Gurdjieff's old stamping-grounds in Central Asia, the Source obstinately refused to appear.

Disappointed by his travels and wrestling with the many volumes of *The Dramatic Universe*, his epic work on the history and nature of the cosmos, Bennett was then attracted by a new idea from a very different source, when he heard from Work friends about Pak Subuh (1901–87), the Indonesian founder of Subud.[14] Instructed by his inner voices, Bennett was introduced to the new spiritual practice in the *annus mirabilis* of 1956 by Husain Rofe, a north London Jewish convert to Islam. Bennett was shocked by Rofe's vulgar claims that Subud cured the dying, virilised the impotent and made astral flying possible, but he persevered.

Subud is a form of Islamic mysticism whose name derives from three words: *susila*, *budhi* and *dharma*. Susila is a man's true character, which emerges when he acts in accordance with God's will. Budhi is the divine life force within human beings. Dharma means surrender to God's will. Subud is thus that absolute submission to God which allows the growth of the individual's true, i.e. spiritual, nature, usually overlaid by worldly concerns. Such growth can be initiated by means of the *latihan*, a Javanese word meaning 'training' – which in this case begins with a kind of meditative communal submission to God's presence. The submission is referred to as 'opening' because it involves emptying the mind of all ordinary associations, thus preparing it to receive God. A latihan session, supervised by a Subud ordinand, may last up to half an hour, during which the participants do anything from meditating in silence to screaming and talking in tongues.

The similarity between Subud, the Work and the SES is clear: the accretions of what Gurdjieff called 'personality' are being stripped away to allow 'essence' to appear. Pak Subuh also agreed with Gurdjieff, Bennett and MacLaren that withdrawal from the world is not the way to spiritual growth: Subud is a method, not a hermetic religion. But Subud differs radically from the Work in that its method involves surrender, not struggle. In this respect it is closer to Krishnamurti than to Gurdjieff. Nor does Subud have the sinister cult mannerisms of the SES. There is no tutorial discipline, no re-education.

Bennett was opened on Christmas Day 1956, and most of his pupils at Coombe immediately followed suit. Many Gurdjieffites, including former pupils of Maurice Nicoll, also received the latihan. In the following year Pak Subuh visited Britain, where he made many conversions. Even the by now demented Mrs Bennett experienced some relief from her mania – though it should also be said that many otherwise equable pupils went into paroxysms of horror and self-loathing under the effect of the latihan, which seems to have the same consequences as certain drugs, emphasising tendencies already present in the subject.

Never one to do things by halves, Bennett wrote a book about Subud and began to spread the faith throughout the world. In Sydney he held a Subud meeting in the Theosophical Society hall and journalists asked of Pak Subuh, as they had asked of Krishnamurti fifty years earlier, whether he was the new Messiah. But as Bennett himself writes: 'To enter the Adyar Hall was to be warned of the folly of a too facile belief in signs, portents and wonders.'[15]

Arriving in Mexico a few months after Rodney Collin's death, they met Aldous Huxley, who was staying there. Huxley questioned Bennett and Pak Subuh closely. Though he agreed to be opened, on the grounds that one should explore every avenue to spiritual enlightenment, he remained sceptical about Subud. Despite his enthusiastic attempts to convert Huxley, whom he had known since they both attended Ouspensky's classes before the war, Bennett gradually came to share his scepticism. The cause of his doubts was the very thing that had attracted him to Subud in the first place. It gradually dawned on Bennett that one only had to have the slightest wish for this or that answer to be given to a prayer in the latihan, to produce the desired result. Whereas if there was no wish one got no answer. QED, the latihan was an unsubtle form of self-deception. He also began to wonder about his inner voices.

It isn't clear why Bennett didn't draw from this insight any of four possible conclusions: that he had misunderstood Subud; that all such practices can become forms of self-deception; that his 'voices' had always come from within; and that perhaps all such voices always come from within. Instead he resumed his search for a new teacher, at the same time turning back to the exercises of the Work, in which he found more enduring power than the latihan. This infuriated what he now called 'the Subud Brotherhood' – formerly his colleagues – who immediately began writing tell-tale letters to Pak Subuh in the good old fashion of the Work. Nothing in the style of Bennett's life was changed. He was condemned to repeat the same pattern of behaviour time and again: finding a new guru, becoming devoted to his novel ideas, and then losing confidence in them. Only Gurdjieff lasted the pace.

At least Bennett had learnt one thing from his experience with Subud. He was beginning to realise – and not before time – that it was just too easy to discover the answer to life's problems in every passing spiritual fad. As he ruefully remarked to Elizabeth Mayall (whom he married in the autumn of 1958, three months after Winifred's death): 'All my geese are the Archangel Gabriel.'[16] However, this insight did not put an end to the search for newer and plumper birds.

One obvious place to find them was in Gabriel's own kitchen, the Christian Church. Bennett was led in this direction by Father Bescond, a monk at the monastery of St Wandrille near Rouen in France. His progress towards Christianity was briefly interrupted by a visit to yet another new discovery, Shivapuri Baba, a Hindu guru in Kathmandu, but Shivapuri encouraged his visitor to persevere in Christianity – loath, perhaps, to take responsibility for such an erratic pupil.

Father Bescond had read the book on Subud and wrote to

Bennett about it. The result was a visit to St Wandrille, which proved to be the first of many. Bennett saw in the latihan a bridge between Islam and Christianity, making comparisons between Subud and Christian contemplative practices – encouraged no doubt by yet another voice (this time no less than God's own) which told him that 'It is My Will that My Church and Islam should be united.'[17] In the monastery he sensed a God who was the fount of all love and reconciliation. Feeling 'truly at home' in the devotions of the monks at matins, lauds and compline, Bennett wondered, exactly as Collin had, whether Christianity was not after all 'the one true religion'. From that time on he began to move away from the Gurdjieffian encouragement of productive conflict to a Collinesque pursuit of harmony. Alas, he was to find only war.

CONCLUSION

The Baboon Triumphant

In June 1962 Bennett received a letter from an old friend. Reggie Hoare had been a colleague in Military Intelligence and a pupil of Ouspensky's. After the war he had followed Bennett from Ouspensky to Gurdjieff, and then from Gurdjieff to Subud. In his letter Hoare explained that he had recently met a man who claimed to have been sent to the West by an esoteric school in Afghanistan. Believing the claim, he invited Bennett to dinner to meet his new discovery.

The visitor, called Idries Shah, described himself as a messenger from 'the Guardians of the Tradition'. Later producing a document entitled *Declaration of the People of the Tradition*,[1] Shah explained that the Guardians belonged to an invisible hierarchy which had chosen him to transmit their wisdom to suitable individuals. He was now looking for European pupils and helpers, and for introductions to the rich and powerful whose help he needed to transform the world. To this end he had founded SUFI: the Society for Understanding Fundamental Ideas.

To begin with, Bennett disliked and mistrusted his new acquaintance, who chain-smoked and tried too hard to please. But half-way through their first meeting he suddenly realised for reasons he could not explain that Shah was the real thing: a genuine emissary from the Hidden Brotherhood described by Gurdjieff. Later, he sought confirmation of this feeling in prayer. The answer was equivocal; and, though Bennett decided to help Shah, he thought it wise to institute enquiries into his background.

Shah's later account of his origins paints a brilliant picture of this background, claiming kinship with the Sasanid kings, Abraham, Muhammad *and* the Duke of Hamilton.[2] The duke comes into the story because of a legend concerning the marriage of Shah's father to a scion of the Douglas-Hamilton family, though Shah's mother was in fact a Miss Mackenzie, whom his father met while an (unsuccessful) medical student in Edinburgh. Miss Mackenzie may, of course, have been the duke's illegitimate daughter: if so, we have not been told.

The descent from Muhammad is more likely, the Prophet's family being less exclusive and more fertile than the average Scottish duke's. But even here things are not quite what they seem. If indeed descended from Muhammad, it is not through the senior male line, as Shah's supporters have claimed, because there isn't one. Muhammad's three sons died young and the family was continued through his daughter Fatima, her husband Ali and their two sons Hasan and Husain. Even if we accept the grandsons as 'direct male lines', Shah's claim to be a Sayyid marks him out as the offspring of Husain, the younger son, whose progeny may now number more than a million.

In fact these manifestations of the Leadbeater syndrome obscure the really interesting facts about Idries Shah's background. His family were Afghan tribesmen from Paghman, fifty miles west of Kabul, rewarded with land and a title for their pro-British sympathies in the years before the First Afghan War. When the British were defeated by the Afghans in 1841 and the family property expropriated, their head, Jan Fishan Khan, moved to a small estate at Sardhana, near Delhi, where his descendants still live.

Presumably hoping to perpetuate the family's profitable relationship with the imperial government, Jan Fishan Khan's grandson – Shah's father Ikbal Ali (1894–1969) – settled in Britain before the First World War. Although Idries was born (in 1924) at Simla, in the shadow of the Himalayan foothills which had meant so much to early Theosophists, he grew up in the less prepossessing landscape of Sutton, a south London suburb to which his father had migrated in search of good fortune.

He migrated in vain. Though Ikbal dabbled in business, literature and politics, he had little success. During the war Idries and his brother Omar were evacuated to Oxford. After 1945, Idries served briefly as his father's representative in Uruguay, where he was involved in a scandal over the importing of halal meat which caused the British Ambassador in Buenos Aires to describe Ikbal bluntly as a swindler. It was not a promising start to his career as a spiritual teacher.

After that he disappears from public view, emerging again in the mid-1950s to work for a while as secretary-companion to the Director of the Museum of Magic and Witchcraft in the Isle of Man and to produce his first book, *Oriental Magic*, published in 1956. In the tradition of Blavatsky and Gurdjieff, Shah claims that the missing years were devoted to studying Sufism in remote but unspecified corners of Central Asia – though it is unclear why this should have been necessary, in the light of his later claim that he and his family themselves represented the most venerable Sufic tradition in the world.

Meeting Bennett was Shah's greatest stroke of good fortune. The events that followed their first encounter are obscure and there are no accounts available apart from Bennett's own memoirs. Idries Shah has never given his own side of the story.[4] On the other hand, he has never contradicted Bennett's carefully phrased account in *Witness*. And, however the negotiations were conducted, the astonishing upshot of their dealings was that, three years after their first meeting, in the winter of 1965/6 Shah persuaded Bennett to present him with the valuable property at Coombe Springs, lock, stock and barrel.

How did he bring off this coup? Showing considerable psychological insight, Shah did not confine his campaign to flattery. Sensing Bennett's respect for proclaimed authority and his extreme susceptibility to any possibility that the latest goose might just be the real thing, Shah alternately cajoled and bullied him. He also displayed considerable business sense. Coombe belonged not to Bennett himself but to trustees. Though they were largely under Bennett's control, they had to be convinced. Several were unhappy about Bennett's involvement with Shah; besides, no one at Coombe wanted to give up work there.

When the trustees tried to persuade Bennett to lease or lend the property, Shah was adamant: there must be an outright gift or nothing at all. Bennett tried to negotiate, but the more conciliatory his behaviour the more outrageous Shah's demands became. The new teacher wanted to know how Bennett could have the nerve to negotiate with the Absolute.[5] Either he had faith or he didn't. The whole affair was skilfully turned into a personal test of Bennett's commitment to spiritual growth.

As if to prepare Shah's way with Bennett, a book by 'Rafael Lefort' had appeared earlier in the same year, purporting to be an account of the author's recent meetings with Gurdjieff's teachers, who hinted that Gurdjieff had been an unsatisfactory pupil and was about to be superseded by none other than Idries Shah himself. 'Rafael Lefort' was almost certainly Shah,[6] and the book a crude attempt to hijack the Work for Shah's own purposes. If so, it was an attempt that worked; though by now, according to his own account, Bennett had begun to suspect the likely consequences of handing Coombe Springs over to the new Messiah.

The truth is probably that Bennett was tired of Coombe – and tired, perhaps, of the old people and the old ways. It was time to move on. Everything about his career proclaims his need for novelty and excitement. Here was a wonderfully Gurdjieffian risk. When Madame de Salzmann asked him what he got from his dealings with Shah, Bennett replied, 'Freedom!',[7] and the minute the deal went through an enormous weight lifted off his shoulders. It is also clear that Bennett, torn between his desire to play the role of Jesus and his instinct to be John the Baptist, believed that at last his chance to be a true prophet might just have come. This could be the moment predicted all those years before in the cemetery overlooking the Bosporus. And perhaps he recalled another prophecy, made by Madame Blavatsky almost eighty years earlier, that no Master of Wisdom would come out of the East until the year 1975. With only ten years to go and Shah preparing for his mission, this prediction might have been approaching fulfilment.

We must therefore assume either that Bennett genuinely believed in Shah – or, as seems more likely (and more interesting), that he knew perfectly well what was involved and welcomed the adventure. Like so many of the characters in this story, Bennett found the thirst for spiritual insight and the itch for worldly excitement impossible to distinguish. The figure who comes unavoidably to mind here is Laurence Oliphant, whose career Bennett's so curiously echoes. For both men the one thing to be avoided was dullness. Scandal, fraud and dishonour paled into insignificance beside the absolute imperative of religious salvation, which was to be found in strenuous effort. Scandal, fraud and dishonour might, indeed, even be the means to such salvation. Gurdjieff had insisted on the link between the disturbing and the spiritually nurturing. If human beings need shock therapy to awaken them from their sleep, what is the superior man but one who can administer the treatment himself?

Once Bennett was convinced of Shah's good will, the trustees were soon persuaded and the new owner took possession of Coombe. The consequences were all that Gurdjieff himself might have wished. Shah's first act was to eject Bennett and the old pupils from their own house, banning them from the place except by his specific permission. His second act was to sell the property to developers for £100,000 in the following year, buying a manor house at Langton Green near Tunbridge Wells in Kent with the proceeds.[8]

The handing-over of Coombe is perhaps the single most bizarre episode in the bizarre story told in this book. This property transaction reveals more about the appeal of alternative spiritual movements than any amount of metaphysics. With no solid evidence to back him up (how could there be any?), Shah's claims to be the representative of the 'People of the Tradition', and his insistence that he had come direct from the Sarmoung Monastery described in Gurdjieff's writing (but never located), netted him a handsome profit.[9] Yet even now, Bennett would not give up. Expelled from Coombe and doubtful about the genuineness of Shah's claims, he resumed his search once more. Though he had long understood his own weakness for confusing plausible geese with spiritual swans, he still could not accept that there *was* no swan. On the contrary: he cherished the even more ambitious hope that he himself might be the bird in question.

But Bennett's career had effectively spent itself with Shah. Everything from now on was repetition, expansion, development. He continued to make long visits to the monastery at St Wandrille, and he and his wife were received into the Catholic Church. The impressively named Integral Science Education Research Group was founded, and the Centre for Structural Communication. These gave rise to a teaching machine – an elementary computer called the Systemaster – and a journal, *Systematics*. A company called Structural Communications Ltd also appeared. Bennett was soon involved in negotiations with IBM and GEC for the right to develop Systematics. But this involvement in *knowledge* was a tacit admission that the goal of *wisdom* remained as inaccessible as ever.

Yet another new school was established at the prompting of an inner voice, this time the Institute for Continuous Education, at Sherborne House in the Cotswolds. It was Lyne, Coombe and the Prieuré all over again, even down to the work necessary to prepare the house for its new inhabitants. Bennett had plenty of time to prepare a curriculum when he ruptured himself trying to teach pupils how to dig properly.

But it seems that for once the voice was wrong. That Bennett was not cut out for teaching was pointed out to him by his final guru, Hasan Shushud, an Itlaki Sufi whom he discovered in these years. Shushud gave Bennett new meditation exercises but told him – like all those sheikhs in Damascus – that 'You have been chosen to be one of the rare ones who are destined to go all the way to final liberation from the conditions of existence. Your only home is the Absolute Void.'[10] At last Bennett could give up the search for the Source, for he now embodied that source himself. According to Shushud, he no longer required a teacher because he was himself a Master: the prophet of a new epoch in which men would learn to co-operate with higher powers. These higher powers have so far only been able to work through men who have chosen the right path to enlightenment, but according to Shushud we are entering a new age in which such men will become demiurgic intelligences themselves, though Bennett's pupils sadly showed no sign of it. He was still reflecting on this puzzle when he died, a good Catholic, in 1976.

★

But death was not to be quite the end of J. G. Bennett's story. The last words were to be written by Gary Chicoine, a charismatic personality in the mould of Idries Shah.[11] A native of Wyoming, Chicoine spent his early twenties in England, where he met Bennett and became his disciple in that Master's last decade. Attracting several senior pupils to his cause after Bennett's death, Chicoine took over the Coombe Springs Press; moved it to Yorkshire, together with the straggling remains of the Coombe community; and rechristened himself the Sadguru Swami Narayan Avadhoot. He also set up the Alexandria Foundation and announced his appointment as the western representative of the Adiguru Dattatreya, the 'supreme spiritual teacher on our planet', who resides in Maharashtra in northern India.

Drawing on the long tradition of Secret Brotherhoods and Inner Circles (all of which he loftily dismisses in his own writings as crude approximations to the truth), Chicoine describes Dattatreya as head of the Central Spiritual School: a being above even the theosophical Lord of the World who lives at Shamballa. Dattatreya is an avatar of Melchizedek, the guru of Jesus Christ. He is the guiding spirit of all world religions – though the leaders of these religions seem not to know it. He is the superior of Buddha and the master of Shankaracharya, patron of the SES. He is an incarnation of the sacred banyan tree and the whole world is his ashram. In short, as Chicoine puts it: 'He is the Guru of Shirdi Sai Baba (not to be confused with Sathya Sai Baba, who is *not* Shirdi Sai Baba reincarnated).'[12] Chicoine persuaded Bennett's wealthy supporters to swallow this nonsense for a while, and one even published a book on the subject of his teaching. But evidently he soon tired of acting as the Dattatreya's representative in Yorkshire. In the mid-1980s the Coombe community finally dissolved and Chicoine retreated to Wyoming, eventually disappearing entirely from public view.

Before his departure, however, he left one final message for the planet. A circular letter was sent out to former pupils and interested observers telling them that their master had abandoned his mission because they had all proved too stupid to understand it. Chicoine added that the whole affair had been by way of a huge practical joke, and that the inability of his followers to take this on board was proof

– if proof were needed – that they were beyond even his spiritual ministry.

How many of those who received this letter, I wonder, heard as they read it the distant laughter of Madame Blavatsky's baboon?

NOTES

Abbreviations

BL	*The Letters of H. P. Blavatsky to A. P. Sinnett*
CITS	*Candles in the Sun*
ISOTM	*In Search of the Miraculous*
KTYOA	*Krishnamurti: The Years of Awakening*
MWRM	*Meetings With Remarkable Men*
ODL	*Old Diary Leaves*
OLWMG	*Our Life with Mr Gurdjieff*
TBY	*To Be Young*
TLADOK	*The Life and Death of Krishnamurti*
TPH	Theosophical Publishing House
TPS	Theosophical Publishing Society

Introduction: The Colour Turquoise

1. D. Icke, *The Truth Vibrations*, Aquarian Press, 1991.
2. *Sun*, 29 Mar 1991.
3. Arianna Huffington, *The Fourth Instinct*, Simon & Schuster, 1994.

Chapter 1: The Source and the Key

1. Prince's early career is recorded in his 1842 book, *The Charlinch Revival*. But see also A. Huxley, *The Olive Tree*, Chatto & Windus, 1936; and J. Montgomery, *Abodes of Love*, Putnam & Co., 1962.
2. There is a huge literature on Victorian religion and dissent.

Especially relevant to the present discussion are W. S. Smith, *The London Heretics*, Dodd, Mead, 1968; and O. Chadwick, *The Secularization of the European Mind in the Nineteenth Century*, Cambridge University Press, 1975.

3. The most readable accounts of the Fox sisters are to be found in R. Pearsall, *The Table Rappers*, Michael Joseph, 1972, and E. W. Fornell, *The Happy Medium: Spiritualism and the Life of Margaret Fox*, University of Texas Press, 1964.

4. Home was a professional. Most mediums were amateurs, operating on a small scale in the suburbs, catering for a middle- and lower-middle-class clientele emancipated from the conventional forms of religion, but not from the emotional sustenance they provided. There was enormous scope for trickery, often of the crudest kind, and fake mediums were regularly – and sometimes literally – stripped and discredited. Yet many seem to have been genuinely convinced of their power, and succeeded in convincing their audiences. Most were highly strung and vulnerable. Like actors and singers, they lived on their nerves, and were only as good as their last performance. Unlike actors and singers, there was no way they could practise and perfect their gifts – unless, paradoxically, they were cheats, in which case they could work on their fraud. Mediums, even sincere ones, were also unusually vulnerable to unscrupulous minders and managers. The simplicity or vacancy which suited them so well to the job made them equally susceptible, one might say, to human and spirit manipulation.

Boredom was another problem, among mediums and their clients alike. While it was easy to become addicted to seances, visitors looked impatiently for novelty and mediums tried to provide it. Given the impossibility of practising, there was little for the medium to do between seances but calm his or her nerves with drink. Alcoholism was another common problem, perhaps inevitable among a community whose members lived in a blaze of publicity and scrutiny while relying for success on unreliable gifts no one understood and many denied. Mary Rosina Showers, the well-known English medium, conducted seances while drunk, and the Fox sisters both drank themselves to death. There was also the puzzle for 'genuine' mediums about what was happening to them in seances; for even if one is entirely sceptical about the reality of spirits and their messages, the line between conscious frauds and sincere believers is impossible to draw. Practitioners were as baffled as anyone else by their own gifts. 'Mental exhaustion' was a common diagnosis when mediums fell ill, as they frequently did, and many of them collapsed or burnt out early. It was not an easy life.

For histories of spiritualism see J. Oppenheim, *The Other World, Spiritualism and Psychical Research in England, 1850–1914*, Cambridge University Press, 1985; T. H. Hall, *The Spiritualists: The Story of Florence Cook and William Crookes*, Helix Press, 1962; and R. Brandon, *The Spiritualists*, Alfred A. Knopf, 1983. There is a life of Home by E. Jenkins: *The Shadow and the Light: a Defence of Daniel Dunglas Home, the medium*, Hamish Hamilton, 1982. For the rapidly increasing literature on the links between feminism and spiritualism see A. Owen, *The Darkened Room: Women, Power and Spritualism in Late Victorian England*, Virago, 1989.

5. R. D. Owen, *The Debatable Land Between This World And The Next*, n.p., 1872, p. 46.

6. Summaries of Swedenborg's life and work can be found in all the texts listed in note 4 above. But see also S. Toksvig, *Emmanuel Swedenborg, Scientist and Mystic*, Yale University Press, 1948, and I. Jonsson, *Emmanuel Swedenborg*, New York, 1971. Most of Swedenborg's major religious works have been translated into English and there is a collection of letters in A. Acton, *The Letters and Memorials of Emmanuel Swedenborg*, Pennsylvania, Bryn Athyn, 1948.

7. On mesmerism see R. Darnton, *Mesmerism and the End of the Enlightenment in France*, Harvard University Press, 1968. Mesmerists were by no means the only group who believed in the existence of a force-field that could be moulded by the will. The followers of Baron Reichenbach (d. 1869) experimented with a magnetic fluid they called Odyle or Od.

8. For Christian Science see S. Gottschalk, *The Emergence of Christian Science in American Life*, University of California Press, 1973.

9. The major source for Harris is still H. Schneider and G. Lawton, *A Prophet and a Pilgrim, Being the Incredible History of Thomas Lake Harris and Laurence Oliphant: Their Sexual Mysticisms and Utopian Communities Amply Documented to Confound the Skeptic*, Columbia University Press, 1942.

10. Laurence Oliphant, quoted in Rosamund D. Owen, *My Perilous Life in Palestine*, Allen & Unwin, 1928, p. 28.

11. See A. Taylor, *Laurence Oliphant*, Oxford University Press, 1982, and M. Oliphant, *Memoir of Laurence Oliphant and of Alice Oliphant, his wife*, William Blackwood & Son, 1891.

12. Oliphant's ventures included acting as aide to the Earl of Elgin when that peer was Governor General of Canada; accompanying the

first British mission to the heart of Japan (during which several of the party were hacked to death by fanatical anti-Westerners); taking part in the 1857 expedition against the Chinese (again led by Elgin) during which the Summer Palace was burnt as retribution for the Chinese refusal to kowtow to the British government's scandalous trade in opium; interfering with Napoleon III's plans to unify Italy; reporting the Franco-Prussian War from the German HQ; dabbling in a dozen minor financial and diplomatic intrigues in the Balkans and Central Europe; building railways in the Middle East; financing a transatlantic telegraph cable; plotting against the Ottoman Empire; attempting to settle the Spanish succession; and, most ambitiously of all, campaigning with some success to establish a Jewish homeland in Palestine. Outside the closed circle of high society Oliphant extended his reputation with journalism and a score of travel books and novels.

Chapter 2: Maloney and Jack

1. The main source for Olcott is the colonel's own meandering autobiography, *Old Diary Leaves*, 4 vols., TPH Adyar, 1895–1935. H. Murphet, *Hammer on the Mountain: The Life of Henry Steele Olcott*, TPH Adyar, 1972, repeats, supplements and sometimes corrects the colonel's factual narrative, though short on interpretation.
2. For a detailed account of events at the Eddy farmhouse see R. Pearsall, op. cit.
3. The main source of Blavatsky's early life is Blavatsky herself, especially in her correspondence with A. P. Sinnett. Another often cited source for information about her first three decades is the posthumous volume of memoirs by her cousin, Count Witte. The book is generally thought to be a forgery, though Endersby (see below) suggests that Witte actually wrote some memoirs which were subsequently altered by Tsarist agents.

Among biographies, J. Symonds, *Madame Blavatsky*, Odhams, 1959, is by far the most vivid and amusing, though it tails off towards the end. However, a better guide to what is known about the mundane facts is probably Victor Endersby's tendentious volume, *The Hall of Magic Mirrors*, Carlton Press, 1969. Endersby's book is partly based on the extensive research of HPB's great-nephew, Boris de Zirko. But see also R. S. Hutch, 'Helena Blavatsky Unveiled', *The Journal of Religious History*, 11, no. 2 (1980).
4. *The Letters of H. P. Blavatsky to A. P. Sinnett*, T. Fisher Unwin, 1925 (*BL*), p. 149.

5. V. Jelihovsky, *The Truth About Madame Blavatsky.*

6. HPB's gynaecological history is as perplexing as everything else about her. In 1885, under attack by enemies of the Theosophical Society who accused her of – among other things – promiscuity, she was examined by a Dr Leon Oppenheim, who diagnosed *anteflexio uteri.* As proof of her virginity, she sent Dr Oppenheim's report to Olcott with a characteristic comment: 'Here's your stupid new certificate with your dreams of virgo intacta in a woman who had all her guts out, womb and all, by a fall from horseback . . . And yet the doctor looked, examined *three* times, and says what the professors Bodkin and Pirogoff said at Pskoff in 1862. I could never have had connection with *any* man, because I am lacking in something and the place is filled up with some crooked cucumber . . .' (quoted in Symonds, op. cit., p. xx).

At the same time she wrote to Sinnett, to whom a copy of the certificate was sent, that the doctor had discovered '*congenital* [her emphasis] crookedness of the uterus', remarking by the way that 'I had always had a dim conception that "uterus" was the same thing as "bladder".' *BL*, p. 177.

Endersby declares that Blavatsky was a hermaphrodite. Others have suggested that she was a lesbian or a transvestite. The matter is complicated by the spectral existence of her 'ward' Youry, with whom she was granted a passport to travel through Russia in 1862. Youry, who died young, was the child of a friend.

7. The two officers are mentioned in a pamphlet by W. A. Carrithers, *An Open Letter to the Author of 'Priestess of the Occult'*, n.d. According to Carrithers, Major Cross, who was land agent to the Dalai Lama, reported that natives described a white woman travelling to the north of Tibet in 1867. Murray testified (after her death) that he had actually detained Blavatsky as she attempted to enter Tibet in 1867.

8. On 12 December 1903 Colonel (later Sir) Francis Younghusband crossed the Tibetan border with a party of British soldiers and an escort of Gurkhas and Sikhs. They were accompanied by ten thousand coolies, seven thousand mules and four thousand yaks. On 3 August 1904 Younghusband entered the city of Lhasa on a diplomatic mission to the Dalai Lama. For the British authorities – and especially for Younghusband's patron, the Viceroy Lord Curzon – this was an important moment in a long struggle between the Russian and British Empires for mastery in Central Asia. The story is well told in P. Hopkirk, *The Great Game, On Service in Central Asia*, Oxford University Press, 1991.

9. This notion was by no means new. See J. Webb, *The Harmonious Circle*, Thames & Hudson, 1980, pp. 526–27.

10. C. Wachtmeister, *Reminiscences of Madame Blavatsky and the Secret Doctrine*, London, privately printed, 1893.

11. On Shamballa see R. Guenon, *The Lord of the World*, trans. C. Shaffer, Olga de Nottbeck, Anthony Cheke and Anthony Blake, Coombe Springs Press, 1983. Guenon's book was first published in 1927.

Marco Pallis describes the kingdom of Shamballa (or Shambala) as a 'legend, current in all Lamaist countries'. Pallis also discusses the possible identity of Shamballa with Agarttha, a place which seems to have been invented by the French occultist St Yves d'Alveydre. See M. Pallis, 'Ossendowski's Sources', in *Studies in Comparative Religion*, vol. 15, nos. 1 and 2, winter/spring 1983, pp. 30–41.

12. E. B. Lytton, *Zanoni*.

13. There is no satisfactory modern biography of Bulwer Lytton. The standard life is still V. Lytton, *The Life of Edward Bulwer, first Lord Lytton, by His Grandson*, 2 vols., Macmillan, 1913.

14. Alphonse-Louis Constant (1810–75) was educated for the priesthood, which he abandoned to become a disciple of the Mapah (aka Louis Ganneau, who appointed himself a divinity on 15 August 1838. Ganneau preached – among other things – Communism and the gospel of androgyny (hence his new name 'Mapah', which derives from the first syllables of *maman* and *papa*)). Also a socialist and a Swedenborgian, Lévi became a practising magician and occultist after the failure of the 1848 revolution, which he supported. Unappreciated in France, he visited London, where he became a friend of Bulwer Lytton; the two men corresponded on occult matters and Lévi summoned up spirits on the roof of a shop in Regent Street in Lord Lytton's presence. The standard – and very partisan – biography is P. Chacornac, *Eliphas Lévi: Rénovateur de l'Occultisme en France*, Chacornac Frères, 1926. But see the excellent sketch in R. Lee Wolff, *Strange Stories*, Boston, Gambit, pp. 260–64, and F. King, *Ritual Magic*, Neville Spearman, 1970, passim.

Blavatsky, who considered Lévi a theoretical occultist, not a practical adept (see *BL*, p. 62), knew both his main pupils: Baron Spedalieri, whom she met in Marseilles in 1884, and Frau Gephardt, an early enthusiast for the Theosophical Society in Germany.

15. On Rosicrucianism see F. Yates, *The Rosicrucian Enlightenment*, Arkana, 1986. An excellent brief statement of Rosicrucian doctrine can be found in R. Lee Wolff, op. cit., pp. 163–66.

16. Symonds, op. cit., pp. 32–37.

17. Quoted in Symonds, op. cit., p. 36.

18. Unless otherwise indicated, the rest of this chapter is based on Olcott's detailed account of events in *ODL*, vol. i, and *People from The Other World*, American Publishing Company, 1875.

19. Robert Dale Owen was the son of Robert Owen and himself a radical of some standing who had published a scandalous bestseller about birth control, advocating sexual equality and free love. In a distinguished public career he had served in Congress and as American Minister to Naples. It was in Naples, after the death of a son, that he developed an interest in spiritualism and became a friend of Daniel Dunglas Home. Returning to the United States, he wrote *Footfalls on the Boundary of Another World*, which still takes a cautious line on spiritualism, but by the time he met the Holmeses, Owen was ready to become infatuated. See further Rosamund Dale Owen, op. cit.

Chapter 3: News from Nowhere

1. Symonds, op. cit., p. 67.

2. Symonds, op. cit., p. 84.

3. *ODL*, vol. i, p. 286.

4. On Smith and the Mormons see M. Ruthven, *The Divine Supermarket*, Chatto & Windus, 1989, pp. 55–91.

5. The Silesian cobbler Jacob Boehme or Böhme (1575–1624) evolved an elaborate philosophy to account for the presence of evil in a world created by a benevolent and all-powerful God. Drawing on the language of alchemy, he thought of his work as a 'theosophy': a study of divine wisdom. Boehme exerted a profound influence on both mainstream and mystical philosophy. See further S. Hobhouse, *Jacob Böhme, His Life and Teaching*, London, 1950.

6. In a letter of 5 December 1878 quoted in H. Murphet, op. cit.

7. Olcott records in *ODL* that 'an impressive Hindu' deposited the money before vanishing.

8. *BL*, p. 305.

9. *BL*, p. 33.

10. *BL*, p. 160.

11. *BL*, p. 28.

12. *BL*, p. 305.

13. These superscriptions are carefully transcribed in A. T. Barker's edition of the letters, which makes gripping reading – not least because of Blavatsky's vivid English. Her penchant for schoolboy slang litters the letters with 'fibs', 'noodles', 'bosh' and 'spooks', and General

Blavatsky is curtly dismissed as 'the old whistle-breeches'. Her favourite colloquialisms include 'in hot water', 'blew me up', 'ye gods', 'what a life', 'stick her nose into', 'science be hanged', 'Holy shadow!', 'many salaams', 'one of these fine days', 'does not care a fig for', 'you will catch it', 'flapdoodle', 'that old ass', 'who in the name of Dickens?', 'beastly', 'a fine row', 'pitch into', 'left in the lurch', 'cooked' and 'nailed'. This language occasionally colours even the Master's messages, with hilarious effect. See *Blavatsky Letters* and *Mahatma Letters*, passim.

14. *BL*, p. 6.
15. *BL*, p. 306.
16. *BL*, p. 45.
17. Quoted in Murphet, op. cit.

Chapter 4: Troubles

1. On the early days of the TS see J. Ransom, *A Short History of the Theosophical Society*, TPH Adyar, 1938. A summary of the Society's history can be found in B. F. Campbell, *Ancient Wisdom Revived*, University of California Press, 1980. Unless otherwise stated, the membership figures given here and elsewhere in this volume are taken from Ransom, who is also the source for the statement of theosophical objectives.
2. There is – surprisingly – no biography of Anna Kingsford to replace E. Maitland's two-volume *Anna Kingsford: Her Life, Letters, Diary and Work*, George Redway, 1896.
3. Maitland, op. cit., vol. 2, p. 229.
4. Maitland, op. cit., vol. 2, p. 125.
5. Maitland, op. cit., vol. 2, p. 291.
6. Marie de Pomar, daughter of the Conde de Pomar, married the Fourteenth Earl of Caithness as his second wife in 1872. She was created Duchesse de Pomar in her own right by Pope Leo XIII in 1879. Her house in Nice was the Palais Tirenty.
7. *BL*, p. 66.
8. 'Christocentric' and 'christological' are both familiar terms in esoteric circles, referring to the distinction between Jesus as a historical personage and his transformation by the Christ spirit.
9. *BL*, p. 45.
10. *BL*, p. 80.
11. *BL*, p. 66.
12. *BL*, p. 89.

13. F. Hartmann, 'Report of Observations Made During a Nine-Months Stay at the Headquarters of the Theosophical Society at Adyar, India, 1884'.

14. Idem.

15. On the SPR see A. Gauld, *The Founders of Psychical Research*, Routledge & Kegan Paul, 1968.

16. Quoted in Symonds, op. cit., p. 221.

17. *BL*, p. 95.

18. R. Hodgson, 'Report of Committee appointed to investigate Phenomena in connection with the Theosophical Society', Society for Psychical Research, Dec 1885.

19. Blavatsky's letters are full of indignant denials that she had ever criticised the British government in India. The accusations of spying were commonplace in India, rarer in England. However, on 3 January 1889 the *Pall Mall Gazette* bluntly asserted that HPB and her friend Olga Novikoff were both Russian spies.

20. Hodgson, op. cit.

21. *BL*, p. 37.

22. *BL*, p. 135.

23. *BL*, p. 77.

24. *ODL*, vol. ii, p. 214.
A brahmin born to moderately well-off parents in 1857 (his nephew later became Speaker in the lower house of the Indian Parliament), Damodar was an intense young man, subject to visions and, according to Olcott, physically as 'frail as a girl' (*ODL*, vol ii, p. 212). Having been converted to Theosophy by reading *Isis Unveiled*, he renounced both his wife and his share of the family fortune to join the Society. Damodar was a highly strung man who seems to have been involved in the forging of letters from KH. He also stirred up trouble in the Theosophical compound during the absences of Blavatsky and Olcott, so perhaps it is not surprising that, in June 1886, Koot Hoomi wrote to Olcott that Damodar had to suffer for his indiscretions (*ODL*, vol. ii, p. 213). All the same, the punishment of death for his sincere if misguided meddling seems a little excessive, and Olcott's response unduly sanguine. For more on this episode see S. Eek, *Damodar and the Pioneers of the Theosophical Society*, TPH Madras, 1965.

Chapter 5: Apostolic Succession

1. It was not the first time she had been so threatened. Shortly before she left India, a would-be theosophical chela, Mohammed Murad Ali

Beg, formerly chief cavalry officer to a minor maharaja, went mad and attacked Blavatsky with a sword. Fortunately, there was no damage done.

2. All the quotations in this paragraph are taken from Olcott's letter to Blavatsky reprinted in *BL*, p. 333.

3. *BL*, p. 123.

4. *BL*, p. 182.

5. *BL*, p. 328.

6. Idem.

7. Constance Wachtmeister's fervently partisan account of her years with HPB can be found in *HPB and the Present Crisis in the Theosophical Society*, London, 1895, and *Reminiscences of Madame Blavatsky and the Secret Doctrine*, London, 1893, from which this episode is taken.

8. These episodes – and many others – are vividly narrated in Solovieff's *A Priestess of Isis*, trans. W. Leaf, Longman's Green, 1895.

9. *BL*, p. 103. She calls him Judas in the same letter.

10. *BL*, p. 77.

11. *BL*, p. 78.

12. *BL*, p. 200.

13. W. B. Yeats, *Collected Works*, Stratford on Avon, 1908, vol. vii, p. 192.

14. This society, which first met on 16 June 1885, appears to have been independent from the Kingsford Hermetic Society, established on 22 April in the previous year.

15. Yeats, op. cit. The full text of Yeats's quotation from Mohini reads: 'We Easterners are taught to state a principle carefully, but we are not taught to observe and to remember and to describe a fact. Our sense of what truthfulness is is quite different from yours.'

16. Yeats thought there were four possible ways of explaining the Masters: '1) They are probably living occultists, as HPB says, 2) They are possibly unconscious dramatizations of HPB's own trance nature, 3) they are also possibly but not likely, as the mediums assert, spirits, 4) They may be the trance principle of nature expressing itself symbolically.' (*Memoirs*, ed. D. Donoghue, Macmillan, 1972, p. 281.) Readers may wonder whether these explanations are any less mystifying than Blavatsky's own. Nevertheless, Yeats remarks in *The Trembling of the Veil* that he found the vagueness of most esoteric writing irritating and he was clearly impressed by Blavatsky's decisiveness and the incredible detail of her texts, especially *The Secret Doctrine*.

17. W. B. Yeats, *Memoirs*, p. 281.

18. Apart from Yeats, the members of the Golden Dawn included the black magician Aleister Crowley; the founder of Watkins occult bookshop in London; Annie Horniman of the Old Vic, who subsidised many of the proceedings; and the philosopher Bergson's sister, who married the Dawn's leader, McGregor Mathers. The organisation bore a certain resemblance to the Theosophical Society. It had Inner and Outer Orders, Adepts and Secret Chiefs, advancements on the Path and Egyptian Brothers (encountered by one of the members in the British Museum). It was Mathers's ambition to restore the Egyptian mysteries and, like Blavatsky, he claimed exclusive access to the Secret Chiefs. This claim rebounded in the late 1890s when Mathers became embroiled in a row about forged correspondence between chiefs and members, and the Golden Dawn was torn apart. Mathers himself later drew the obvious parallels between HPB's fate and his own.

But fraternities of the Rosicrucian/Golden Dawn variety were different from Theosophy in one vital respect: Rosicrucianism is secret, exclusive, mystical and intensely hierarchical, where Theosophy is (theoretically) open, rational and democratic. Yeats, who equated magic with imagination and saw poetry as a means of embodying the hidden cosmic order, soon came to understand this.

19. The standard biography is F. Whyte, *The Life of W. T. Stead*, Jonathan Cape, 1925. More recent accounts can be found in A. Taylor, *Annie Besant*, Oxford University Press, 1992, and W. S. Smith, op. cit.

20. This account of Annie Besant's early years draws mainly on her own *Autobiography*, TPH Madras, 1908. The most recent life is by Ann Taylor (see note 19 above). Mrs Taylor, who draws extensively on Besant's unpublished correspondence, devotes a substantial part of this excellent book to her subject's theosophical years.

21. On Bradlaugh see H. B. Bonner, *Charles Bradlaugh: A Record of His Life and Work by His Daughter*, T. Fisher Unwin, 1895. There is a more recent biography by D. Tribe: *President Charles Bradlaugh MP*, Elek, 1971. But see also the Taylor and Smith works cited in noted 19 above.

22. See Taylor, op. cit., pp. 261–62.

23. G. B. Shaw, *Back to Methuselah*. Believing in evolution, Shaw rejects Darwin's theory – though he respected its inventor – because it takes mind and purpose out of the universe, rendering existence meaningless. Though a self-proclaimed rationalist, Shaw does not pause to consider the possibility that life might indeed be without meaning. Instead, he prefers Lamarck's notion of purposeful develop-

ment, which he combines with a Nietzschean notion of will to produce what he calls 'the religion of metaphysical Vitalism'.

This theory is expounded in the Don Juan act of *Man And Superman*, a parody of romantic comedy, in which Shaw presents the life force in the form of sexual desire. The idea is presented from a different point of view in the series of five plays constituting the *Back To Methuselah* sequence, first published in 1921. Perpetuating the species here gives place to personal longevity. In a curious backward compliment to the Brotherhood of Masters, Shaw suggests that the average span of three score years and ten is too short for the world's statesmen and thinkers to take the long-term decisions necessary to the survival of the species. These will only come about when human beings begin to live for at least three hundred years. At present they die when they are merely children: in consequence they behave like children. But eventually some will live for thousands of years, and in the last play of the sequence Shaw envisages what the world will be like when this happens.

Longevity was a common theme at the time, perhaps because popular belief in the soul's immortality was eroding fast and the population was beginning to live longer (though few lived as long as Shaw himself).

24. Symonds, op. cit., p. 247.
25. Annie Besant, *Autobiography*, p. 311.
26. For Bradlaugh's hostile attitude to HPB and Theosophy – and therefore to Annie's conversion – see his paper, the *National Reformer*, 2 November 1884.
27. See M. D. Conway, *Autobiography, Memories and Experiences*, Cassell, 1904, vol. ii, p. 264. This memoir by a leading non-conformist who was not a Theosophist but knew Besant and Blavatsky well throws fascinating light on their circle. See also his *My Pilgrimage to the Wise Men of the East*, Constable, 1906.
28. For a favourable account of Judge see S. Eek and B. de Zirkoff, *William Quan Judge, Theosophical Pioneer*, TPH Wheaton, 1969.
29. *Westminster Gazette*, 29 Oct 1894.
30. A. Besant, *The Neutrality of the Theosophical Society*, privately printed, 1894, p. 13.

Chapter 6: Second Generation

1. On this see A. Taylor, op. cit., pp. 270–72.
2. Stead thought that Chakravarti had hypnotised Mrs Besant (see his *Borderland*, vol. ii, p. 170). American journalists covering the World

Parliament of Religions perhaps came nearer to a version of the truth when they claimed that Chakravarti slept at the threshold of her bedroom.

3. See B. Das, *The Central Hindu College and Mrs Besant*, Divine Life Press, 1913.

4. After World War One the wealthy Alice Cleather travelled in India and China in search of wisdom. She was a ruthless intriguer and a prolific writer of indignant pamphlets, including *H. P. Blavatsky: Her Life and Work for Humanity*, Calcutta, 1922: *H. P. Blavatsky: The Great Betrayal*, Calcutta, 1922; *Buddhism: The Science of Life*, Peking, 1928; and *The Pseudo-Occultation of Mrs A. Bailey*, Manila, 1929.

5. Tingley's life story has been ably told by E. A. Greenwalt, who also documents the rise and fall of Point Loma in *California Utopia: Point Loma 1897–1942*, Point Loma Publications, 1978.

6. Quoted in C. Ryan, *H. P. Blavatsky and the Theosophical Movement*, Point Loma Press, 1937, p. 343.

7. On Gottfried de Purucker (1874–1942) see Greenwalt, op. cit., pp. 194–96. H. N. Stokes wittily dismissed Purucker's extensive writings as 'Theosophical Jabberwock'.

8. *New York Herald*, 5 April 1897.

9. Jerome Anderson in the *San Francisco Chronicle*, 25 Mar 1902. I owe this reference to Greenwalt.

10. There is an excellent life of Leadbeater – *The Elder Brother: A Biography of Charles Webster Leadbeater*, Routledge & Kegan Paul, 1982 – by Gregory Tillett.

11. Leadbeater's fantasy-autobiography is scattered through memoirs and conversations recorded by pupils. But see especially *Saved by a Ghost. A True Record of Adventure in Brazil . . .*, Bombay, office of *The Theosophist*, 1911.

12. The belief that Christ is actually present when the bread and wine change to flesh and blood.

13. C. W. Leadbeater, *How Theosophy Came to Me*, TPH Adyar, 1930, p. 62.

14. See C. Jinarajadasa, *The 'K.H.' Letters to C.W. Leadbeater*, TPH Adyar, 1941, passim.

15. Leadbeater later explained that he had recognised in the boy the spirit of his dead brother Gerald. Jinarajadasa (1875–1953) graduated from St John's College, Cambridge, married an Englishwoman in 1916 and eventually became President of the TS in 1945.

16. Or so Leadbeater himself claimed, as reported by Jinarajadasa in his preface to later editions of *The Astral Plane*.

17. The letter is extensively quoted in Tillett, op. cit., and in *The Evolution of Mrs Besant* by the Editors of *Justice*, Madras, 1918.
18. Idem.
19. I owe this point to Taylor, op. cit., p. 283.
20. Quoted in A. Nethercot, *The Last Four Lives of Annie Besant*, Hart-Davis, 1963, p. 96.
21. Quoted in Tillett, op. cit., p. 93. Sinnett also denied that the spectral visitors to the colonel's sickbed could have been Masters, insinuating Annie's undue influence over Olcott's forgiving letter to Leadbeater.

Chapter 7: Boys and Gods

1. See C. W. Leadbeater, *The Masters and the Path*, TPH Adyar, 1925.
2. H. P. Blavatsky, *Preliminary Memorandum*, quoted in Tillett, op. cit.
3. See A. Besant, *The Coming of the World Teacher*, TPH Adyar, 1925, and C. W. Leadbeater, *Why a Great World Teacher?*, Sydney, OSE, 1915. Both writers use the terms Messiah and World Teacher interchangeably.
4. Leadbeater's letters to Annie Besant on this subject were published in *The Theosophist* for June 1932, from which this quotation is taken.
5. See E. Wood, *Clairvoyant Investigations by C. W. Leadbeater and the Lives of Alcyone*, privately printed, 1947. See also the *Theosophical Journal*, Jan–Feb 1965, where the matter is discussed.
6. See E. Wood, op. cit.
7. Leadbeater to Besant, 1909, quoted in M. Lutyens, *Krishnamurti: The Years of Awakening (KTYOA)*, John Murray, 1975, p. 33.
8. The episode is vividly described in *KTYOA*.
9. E. Lutyens, *Candles in the Sun*, Hart-Davis, 1957, p. 78.
10. According to Mary Lutyens, in the summer of 1913 Miss Dodge settled £500 p.a. for life on Krishnamurti and £300 p.a. on Nitya. This was in addition to the £125 per month Mrs Besant allowed Krishnamurti for his living expenses in England. See M. Lutyens, *The Life and Death of Krishnamurti*, John Murray, 1990.
11. *KTYOA*, p. 100.
12. *CITS*, p. 39.
13. *CITS*, p. 43. Leadbeater had told Annie that this was the particular shade of Lord Maitreya's aura.
14. Idem. Sir Edwin hated Theosophy. He wrote to his wife, 'I don't want to lose you, darling, in those vasty mists . . .' (*CITS*, p. 38).

15. Leadbeater to Besant, quote in *Extracts from letters from C. W. Leadbeater to Annie Besant 1916–1923*, ed. C. Jinarajadasa, TPH Adyar, 1952.

16. *Isis Unveiled*, vol. ii. p. 544.

17. C. W. Leadbeater, *Australia and New Zealand: The Home of a New Sub-Race*, Sydney, Theosophical Society, 1915.

18. H. N. Stokes, *O.E. Library Critic*, 25 Jun 1919.

19. Das, op. cit.

20. A. Cleather, *H. P. Blavatsky: The Great Betrayal*.

21. Stokes, op. cit.

Chapter 8: Ahriman and Lucifer

1. See R. Steiner, *The Ahrimanic Deception*, trans. M. Cotterell, pp. 3–15; *Three Streams In Human Evolution*, trans. C. Davy; and *The Influence of Lucifer and Ahriman*, trans. D. S. Osmond. There are hundreds and possibly thousands of references to the powers of Ahriman and Lucifer scattered through Steiner's other hugely voluminous works.

All texts by Rudolf Steiner are quoted in the Rudolf Steiner Press editions, unless otherwise indicated.

2. All the biographies of Steiner are equally dreary. The best is probably S. C. Easton, *Rudolf Steiner: Herald of a New Epoch*, The Anthroposophic Press, 1980. Unless otherwise indicated, the following pages are based on Steiner's autobiography, *Mein Lebensgang*, translated by R. Stebbing as *Rudolf Steiner, An Autobiography*, The Anthroposophic Press, 1977. This book traces the author's life up to the early years of this century. For a personal reminiscence by someone who worked with Steiner see F. Rittelmayer, *Rudolf Steiner Enters My Life*, Christian Community Press, 1954. On the relationship between Steiner's life and work see also A. P. Shepherd, *A Scientist of the Invisible*, Hodder & Stoughton, 1954.

There is a huge German literature on Steiner, too extensive to list here, almost all of it by followers or by Steiner himself. English-speaking readers may wish to consult the catalogues of the Rudolf Steiner Press in the UK and the Anthroposophic Press in the US, and the excellent Anthroposophical libraries in London and New York.

3. Ernst Haeckel (1834–1919) expounded in particular the theory of sexual selection.

4. See R. Steiner, *A Theory of Knowledge Implicit in Goethe's World Conception*, trans. O. D. Wannamaker.

5. See R. Steiner, *Aspects of Human Evolution*, trans. R. Stebbing, and *The Karma of Materialism*, trans. R. Everett.

6. There are many affectionate portraits by admirers, including A. Steffen, *Meetings With Rudolf Steiner*, Verlag für Schone Wissenschaft, 1961; F. Rittelmayer, op. cit.; and Gunter Wachsmuth, *The Life and Work of Rudolf Steiner*, Whittier Press, 1955 (an otherwise intolerably tedious book by Steiner's main lieutenant).

7. On von Sievers see the uninspiring M. Savitsch, *Marie Steiner von Sievers: Fellow Worker with Rudolf Steiner*, trans. J. Compton-Burnett, Rudolf Steiner Press.

8. Edmond Schuré, the enormously prolific and influential author of *The Great Initiates*, Rider, 1912.

9. Unless otherwise indicated, the following pages are based on Ouspensky's own *In Search of the Miraculous (ISOTM)*, Arkana, 1987; the 'Autobiographical Fragment' appended to his *A Further Record*, Routledge & Kegan Paul, 1986, pp. 299–303; *The Strange Life of Ivan Osokin*, Stourton Press, 1947; and *A New Model of the Universe*, Alfred A. Knopf, 1934. For the history of Anthroposophy in Russia see N. Berdyaev, *Dream and Reality*, Greenwood Press, 1950. On Russian Theosophy see N. Zernov, *The Russian Religious Renaissance of the Twentieth Century*, London, 1963. The best discussion of Ouspensky's relationship with Gurdjieff is to be found in J. Webb, op. cit.

10. *An Episode of Flatland*, Swan Sonnenschein & Co., 1911.

11. Ouspensky's own account of the development of his ideas in *In Search of the Miraculous*, *A New Model of the Universe* and *A Further Record* is probably still the best. But see also Webb, op. cit., pp. 109–17.

12. On this view of Nietzsche see A. R. Orage, *Frederick Nietzsche, the Dionysian Spirit of the Age*, London and Edinburgh, 1906, and *Consciousness, Animal, Human and Superhuman*, TPH Benares, 1907.

13. On Russian occultism see J. Webb, *The Occult Establishment*, Open Court Publishing, 1976.

14. On Keyserling, see below Chapter 12.

Chapter 9: War Games

1. For Leadbeater's views on war see *The Great War*, TPH Adyar, n.d., and *The Theosophist*, January 1915.

2. R. Steiner, *The Karma of Untruthfulness*, vol. i, trans. J. Collis.

3. R. Steiner, *Destinies of Individuals and of Nations*, trans. A. R. Meuss.

4. These lectures include 'The Evolution of the German Soul', 'The Enduring and Creative Power of the German Spirit', 'The Rejuvenating Power of the German Folk-Soul', etc., etc.

5. My source for the events of Steiner's last twenty years is S. C. Easton, *Rudolf Steiner: Herald of a New Epoch*, The Anthroposophic Press, 1980. But see Chapter 8 note 2.

6. See R. Steiner, *The Tension between East and West*, trans. B. A. Rowley.

7. On the Aryan controversy and its ramifications see M. Olender, *The Languages of Paradise*, Harvard University Press, 1992.

8. In H. S. Chamberlain, *The Foundations of the Nineteenth Century*, John Lane, 1911.

9. The idea of spirit patrols seems to have surfaced in modern times among mesmerists, who claimed during the Crimean War that their founder was too busy shepherding the souls of dead soldiers to pay attention to other things. Leadbeater had written about Invisible Helpers as early as 1896. See his *Invisible Helpers*, TPH London, and Steiner's *Between Death and Rebirth*, trans. E. H. Goddard and D. S. Osmond. One incidental advantage of being killed in the war was that your soul could be reborn as a Theosophist.

10. *CITS*, p. 86.

11. Quoted in G. Painter, *Marcel Proust: A Biography*, vol. ii, Chatto & Windus, p. 223.

12. See the essay on war in the *Pelican Freud Library*, vol. xxii, Penguin, 1983, p. 48.

13. On Diaghilev see Richard Buckle's excellent biography.

14. Others have taken the possibility of a direct relationship between Blavatsky and Gurdjieff much further. See especially two articles in the *American Theosophist* by Seymour Ginsburg: 'Gurdjieff's Contribution to Theosophy', *AT 75*, no. 11, December 1987, pp. 406–10, and 'HPB, Gurdjieff and the Secret Doctrine' in the previous issue. I am grateful to Mr Ginsburg for corresponding with me on this topic, and for letting me see a copy of 'Gupta-Vidya: Foreshadowed by Blavatsky, Brought by Gurdjieff', a paper he delivered to the Theosophical History Centre in July 1989. I am also grateful to Mr Ginsburg for pointing out to me the passage in *A Study of Gurdjieff's Teaching*, 1957, by Gurdjieff's long-time pupil Kenneth Walker. Walker refers to a letter by HPB which predicts that 'the next great teacher of Eastern ideas in Europe will be an instructor in Oriental dancing' (Walker, p. 152). Neither I nor Mr Ginsburg have been able to trace this letter.

15. The historian of Gurdjieff's early life faces exactly the same

problem as the historian of Blavatsky's first forty years: the only source is the subject himself. Unless otherwise stated, therefore, the following pages are based on Gurdjieff's own *Meetings With Remarkable Men* (*MWRM*), trans. A. R. Orage, Arkana, 1985.

As to lives of Gurdjieff, J. G. Bennett, *Gurdjieff: Making a New World*, London, 1973, is a vivid, touching memoir by a controversial pupil; but incomparably the best biography is the most recent: J. Moore, *Gurdjieff, The Anatomy of a Myth*, Element, 1991, to which the present book is much indebted. Also useful are J. and E. Bennett, *Idiots in Paris: Diaries of J. G. Bennett and Elizabeth Bennett 1949*, Coombe Springs Press, 1980, and C. S. Nott's appallingly titled *Teachings of Gurdjieff: Journal of a Pupil. An Account of Some Years with G. I. Gurdjieff and A. R. Orage in New York and at Fontainebleau-Avon*, Routledge & Kegan Paul, 1961.

16. Quoted in J. G. Bennett, *Gurdjieff: Making a New World*.

17. For a detailed account of this period see P. Hopkirk, op. cit. On the question of Gurdjieff's identity with a Tibetan agent see J. Webb, *The Harmonious Circle*, op. cit., pp. 52–73. Webb explores the evidence exhaustively.

18. Abdullah (1881–1945) was (probably) half Russian and half Afghan. An adventurer and a fantasist, he published his autobiography, *My Nine Lives* (Hurst & Blackett), in 1934.

19. P. Dukes, *The Unending Quest*, Cassell, 1950.

20. Reprinted in G. I. Gurdjieff, *Views from the Real World*, Arkana, 1984.

21. A monumental sculptor, Mercourov (1881–1952) prospered under the Communist regime. Both Gurdjieff (*MWRM*, p. 71), and Thomas and Olga de Hartmann (*Our Life with Mr Gurdjieff*, Arkana, 1992, p. ix), appear to refer to this relationship.

22. *ISOTM*, p. 7.

23. *ISOTM*, p. 7.

24. *ISOTM*, p. 11.

25. *ISOTM*, p. 15.

26. *ISOTM*, p. 24.

27. *ISOTM*, p. 21.

Chapter 10: Travels

1. The account of Gurdjieff's life between the outbreak of the Revolution in March 1917 and his departure from Constantinople in August 1921 is based on three memoirs: Ouspensky, *ISOTM*; T. and

O. de Hartmann, *OLWMG*; and C. B. Roberts, *In Denikin's Russia*. Given the complexity of the narrative, I have not annotated particular references unless taken from other sources.

2. This prospectus is quoted in *ISOTM*, pp. 380–81.

3. On the Fourth Way see P. D. Ouspensky, *The Fourth Way*, Routledge & Kegan Paul, 1957, and *ISOTM*, pp. 48–51, 312–13.

4. On Jaques-Dalcroze and Eurythmics see below, pp. 200–1.

5. P. D. Ouspensky, *Letters From Russia*, Arkana, 1992.

6. I owe this detail to James Moore's reading of the Nott papers. See Moore, op. cit., p. 382.

7. Moore conjectures that Gurdjieff visited the city in 1885 and 1889. Given intense Turkish–Armenian antagonism, the Greek-Armenian Gurdjieff would have found himself in a delicate situation.

8. Sabeheddin was the grandson of one sultan and the nephew of three others, including the last, Mehmet VI Vahdettin (whose reign came to an end in 1922), and the notorious Abdul Hamid II (reigned 1876–1909), whose repressive policies hastened the demise of the Ottoman Empire.

9. J. G. Bennett, *Witness*, Omen Press, Tucson, 1974. The following pages are based on Bennett's own account. This paints a rather different view of events to the Foreign Office files on Bennett (especially PRO files in the FO 371 series) which make surprising reading. They cover the decade from 1921 to 1931. In them Bennett is variously accused of smuggling hashish, salting a gold mine, fomenting rebellion and compromising the Comptroller of the Royal Mint. British records are not the only ones in which he figures. The Turkish and Greek governments both had extensive files on Bennett during the 1920s. On 3 March 1928 he was charged with attempting to bribe the land registry in the Greek port of Kavalla.

10. Mary Lilian, Lady Rothermere (1875–1937), was the estranged wife of the first Viscount Rothermere, co-founder of the Harmsworth newspaper empire. She was to be a generous patron of both Ouspensky and Gurdjieff.

11. Sinclair gives a vivid description of Hellerau and its regime in his novel *World's End*. He took an interest in all the independent spiritual teachers of the day, including Gurdjieff.

12. A. S. Neill was an educational reformer who ran a series of progressive schools throughout the first half of the century. But see also E. Muir, *An Autobiography*, London, 1954.

13. There is a biography of Orage by P. Mairet. But see also P. Selver,

Orage and the New Age Circle, Allen & Unwin, 1959, and W. Martin, *The New Age under Orage*, Manchester University Press, 1967.

14. H. Jackson, 'A. R. Orage: personal recollections', in *The Windmill*, 1948, vol. 3, no. 11.

15. Born in Liverpool and largely self-educated, Holbrook Jackson published his most celebrated work, *The Eighteen Nineties*, in 1913. It is still a useful guide to many aspects of that period's literature. He also produced biographies of Edward FitzGerald, George Bernard Shaw and William Morris.

16. Holbrook Jackson in *The Windmill*, op. cit.

17. Orage, op. cit.

18. The South African Beatrice Hastings was born Emily Alice Haight in 1879. She became a passionate defender of Madame Blavatsky and wrote several angry pamphlets denouncing Hodgson, the SPR and Emma Coulomb. See J. Carswell, *Lives and Letters*, London, 1978.

19. For Mitrinovic see Selver, op. cit., and J. Webb, op. cit.

Chapter 11: Affairs

1. Elizabeth Lutyens, *The Goldfish Bowl*, Cassell, 1972, p. 35. The young Betty Lutyens tried to swallow Theosophy out of love for her mother, but found it unpalatable. Determined to break away from her family, she decided to become a professional musician and took composition lessons from a theosophical teacher called Foulds, whose own *World Requiem* had been dictated to him by St Michael. This man involved her in occult practices with such damaging results that she had a nervous breakdown at seventeen.

2. Mary Lutyens gives her own account of this love in her touching *To Be Young*, Hart-Davis, 1959.

3. *CITS*, p. 157.

4. *TBY*, p. 141.

5. *TBY*, p. 12.

6. On Rajagopal's early life and background see the memoir by his daughter R. R. Sloss: *Lives in the Shadow with J. Krishnamurti*, Bloomsbury, 1991, pp. 40–45.

7. Reported by his daughter to be 'even larger' than the £500 p.a. settled on Krishnamurti. See Sloss, op. cit., p. 47. Miss Dodge also found herself paying salaries to the officials at the London TS headquarters – a disaster, according to Emily Lutyens, because it encouraged people to scramble for lucrative jobs rather than working

for the good of the cause, especially when a trade union representative joined the Society and insisted on union rates of pay (*CITS*, p. 34).

8. The letter is quoted in *TLADOK*, pp. 19–20.

9. Arundale to Emily Lutyens, 18 Jan 1915. Quoted in *CITS*, p. 74.

10. Frank Buchman founded the Oxford Group, later relaunched as Moral Rearmament. Asserting the reality of divine guidance, he taught the Four Principles: honesty, purity, unselfishness and love. Amy Semple MacPherson was an American evangelist whose career ended in adultery and scandal.

11. I. Smith, *Truth is a Pathless Land*, TPH Madras, 1989, p. 15.

12. *TBY*, passim. According to Mary Lutyens, Krishnamurti was especially attracted to a certain Helen Knothe – a passion made acceptable by the belief that Helen was the reincarnation of HPB.

13. Memoranda reprinted in *KTYOA*. See also Sloss, op. cit., pp. 58–60, and Tillett, op. cit., pp. 205–7.

14. Quoted in *Letter from Mr T. H. Martyn to Mrs Besant*, edited and published by H. N. Stokes, 1921, p. 2.

15. Idem.

16. Quoted in *KTYOA*, p. 140.

17. See note 14 above.

18. *Australian Star News*, 11 Jan 1927, p. 67.

19. *TBY*, p. 180.

20. *TBY*, p. 158.

21. E. Lutyens, op. cit.

22. *TBY*, p. 117; Leadbeater himself expounded the theory in an article entitled 'Rock Consciousness', later published in the *Liberal Catholic*, October 1947.

23. *CITS*, p. 157.

Chapter 12: Life Classes

1. For Ouspensky and Gurdjieff on the notion of 'school' (without the definite article) see *ISOTM*, pp. 222–31, 240–54, 285–86. See also Ouspensky, *A Further Record*, passim.

2. There is no good life of Keyserling and little of interest on his work. The following biographical facts are taken from M. Gallagher Parks, *Introduction to Keyserling*, Jonathan Cape, 1934. There is a long commentary on Theosophy in Keyserling's *Reisetagebuch eines Philosophien*, trans. J. H. Reece, as *Travel Diary of a Philosopher*, Cape, 1919. On the philosophy see Keyserling, *Schopferische Erkenntnis*, trans. T. Duerr as *Creative Understanding*, Cape, 1929. Gallagher

Parks, op. cit., also offers a useful commentary on the development of Keyserling's ideas. And see also R. Landau, *God is My Adventure*, Unwin, 1964.

3. Almost unknown in English-speaking countries, the German-speaking philosopher Rudolph Kassner (1873–1959) developed, like Keyserling, a semi-mystical theory of wholeness. Preferring myths to concepts, things to ideas, poems to theorems, Kassner believed that reality can only be effectively apprehended through the concrete. He influenced Rilke, Valéry and Yeats among others.

4. On the Goetheanum see R. Steiner, *The Arts and Their Mission*, trans. L. Monges and V. Moore. Also H. Biesantz, A. Klingborg et al., *The Goetheanum: Rudolf Steiner's Architectural Impulse*.

5. R. Steiner, *The Cycle of the Year as Breathing Process of the Earth*, trans. B. D. Betteridge and F. E. Dawson.

6. See R. Steiner, *An Introduction to Eurythmy*, trans. G. Hahn.

7. *MWRM*, p. 285.

8. Quoted in *THC*, pp. 234–35. 'Duliotherapy' was 'slave therapy'.

9. The following account of life at the Prieuré is based on the description in F. Peters, *Boyhood With Gurdjieff*, Wildwood House, 1976; and *OLWMG*.

10. The followers of Thomas Lake Harris used the same term to describe their spiritual labours. It probably derives from the 'Great Work' by means of alchemy, in which base metals are supposedly transmuted into gold.

11. Webb, op. cit., p. 231.

12. Not everyone agreed. Denis Saurat, who visited Orage at the Prieuré, was horrified by his condition. See D. Saurat, *La Nouvelle Revue Francaise*, xli, 242, Nov 1933.

13. C. Bechofer Roberts, 'The Forest Philosophers', *Century Magazine*, cviii (1), May 1924, p. 73.

14. J. G. Bennett several times hints at such rumours without giving evidence, e.g. *Witness*, p. 121. But see Webb, op. cit., pp. 333–35.

15. See *Daily Mirror*, 19 Feb 1923; *Daily News*, 15–20 Feb 1923; and *New Statesman*, xx (516), 3 Mar 1923.

16. M. D. Luhan, *Lorenzo in Taos*, Secker & Warburg, 1933, p. 128.

17. In a letter to Violet Schiff, 20 Sept 1922, British Library. I owe this reference to J. Moore, op. cit., p. 188.

18. Roberts, op. cit., p. 76.

19. Webb, op. cit., p. 246.

20. I. Baker, *Katherine Mansfield: The Memories of LM*, Michael Joseph, 1971, p. 218.

21. Idem, p. 223.
22. Idem, p. 226.
23. A. R. Orage, 'Talks with Katherine Mansfield', reprinted in *Selected Essays and Critical Writings*, ed. Read and Saurat, London, 1935.
24. *Letters to John Middleton Murry*, ed. J. Middleton Murry, Constable, 1951, p. 700.

Chapter 13: Calamities

1. For details of this campaign see Easton, op. cit., pp. 270–309.
2. See S. Prokofieff, *Rudolf Steiner and the Founding of the New Mysteries*, trans. P. King, Rudolf Steiner Press.
3. On the Threefold Social Order see R. Steiner, *The Renewal of the Social Organism*, trans. E. Bowen Wedgwood and R. Marriott.
4. R. Steiner, *Deeper Insights into Education*, trans. R. Querido. See also Francis Edmunds, *Rudolf Steiner Education*, Rudolf Steiner Press, 1985.
5. See F. Huseman, *The Anthroposophical Approach to Medicine*, 3 vols., trans. P. Luborsky and B. Kelly.
6. R. Steiner, *Karmic Relationships in Esoteric Studies*, 8 vols., trans. G. Adams, C. Davey and D. S. Osmond, 1972–83.
7. These episodes are described in Peters, op. cit., p. 64 (bicycles) and pp. 59–60 (pocket money).
8. On Orage's relationship with Gurdjieff, see especially Moore, op. cit., and A. Alpers, *Life with Katherine Mansfield*, Cape, 1980.
9. For the influence of Gurdjieff and Orage on American writers see Z. Gale, *Preface to a Life* (1926); G. Munson, *The Dilemma of the Liberated* (1930); J. Toomer, *Essentials* (1931) and E. Wilson, 'The Literary Consequences of the Crash', reprinted in *The Shores of Light* (1953).
10. See G. Leblanc, *La Machine à Courage*, 1947; and M. Anderson, *The Unknowable Gurdjieff*, Routledge & Kegan Paul, 1962.
11. This is the scheme which Orage's pupil Charles Daly King describes in *The Oragean Version* (1951).
12. See e.g. Peters, op. cit., pp. 126–30.
13. See E. Merston, *Talks With Sri Ramana Maharshi*, Tirvannamalai, 1963. See also Moore, op. cit., pp. 357–58.
14. Peters, op. cit., pp. 8–12, and *OLWMG*.
15. J. G. Bennett, *Gurdjieff*, p. 41.
16. Peters, op. cit., pp. 6–8, 11–13.
17. Toomer and Ouspensky, who both believed that Gurdjieff was

above 'accident', thought there must be some other reason for the crash. See Webb, op. cit., pp. 293–98.

18. Peters, op. cit., p. 95.

19. Webb, op. cit., p. 346.

20. Moore, op. cit., p. 232.

21. *OLWMG*, p. 155.

22. Peters, op. cit., pp. 28–29.

23. Gurdjieff, *Life Is Real Only Then: When 'I Am'*, Arkana, 1989, p. 121.

24. An economic theory proposed by Major C. H. Douglas (1879–1952) and based on the need for price control.

25. Webb, op. cit., p. 372.

Chapter 14: The End of the Path

1. See G. S. Arundale, *A Fragment of Autobiography*, Adyar, Kalakshetra, 1940. Also *Personal Memories of G. S. Arundale*, TPH London, 1967.

2. *CITS*, p. 132.

3. Mrs Besant was to be Rector of the World University, and Arundale Principal. That Annie envisaged Wedgwood as Director of Studies shows the quality of her judgement. See *KTYOA*, p. 214.

4. *CITS*, p. 135.

5. *KTYOA*, p. 236.

6. *CITS*, p. 137.

7. Mrs Besant described this moment in *The Theosophist*, January 1926.

8. Quoted in Tillett, op. cit., p. 220.

9. *KTYOA*, pp. 236 and 266.

10. *KTYOA*, p. 245.

11. A point frequently made by Krishnamurti himself. See also I. Smith, op. cit., passim.

12. See Sloss, op. cit., pp. 200, 249, 303, 317. This author devotes an index entry to the topic.

13. The image of the flame recurred. Emily Lutyens quotes him as saying in 1927, 'I am the flame, I have united the source and the goal' (*CITS*, p. 161).

14. 'The World Teacher is here' was also the title of a talk Mrs Besant gave at the 1927 Ommen camp. There is some confusion over whether the World Teacher was always 'here' in the sense that he had used Krishna as a vehicle throughout his life, or whether he had arrived at a particular moment. There is also doubt about what 'here' actually

means: merely in possession of Krishna's consciousness, or publicly manifested as such? Mrs Besant confused the issue even further by announcing the World Teacher's appearance in several ways and on several occasions.

15. Jinarajadasa was forgetting that only a few months earlier he had accepted the claim that the whole point of the Society and the Liberal Catholic Church was to prepare for the World Teacher's coming.

16. See Tillett, op. cit., p. 311. But see also Nethercot, op. cit., passim.

17. *CITS*, pp. 135–36.

18. On Annie's extraordinary burst of energy in old age see A. Taylor, op. cit., pp. 322–25.

19. On Krishnamurti's finances see *KTYOA* and Sloss, op. cit., passim. Information concerning the complex financial organisation of KWINC is available in the Los Angeles County Court records and in the archives of the Krishnamurti Foundation of America.

20. Most of the speech is reprinted in *CITS*, pp. 172–74 and *KTYOA*, pp. 272–75.

21. *CITS*, p. 175.

22. *CITS*, pp. 186–88.

Chapter 15: Private Lives

1. See Chapter 11, note 10.

2. On the Peace Pledge Union see Chapter 17 below.

3. This is not to say, of course, that Hitler had no time for spiritual matters. On the contrary, he is famous for dabbling in the occult, consulting court astrologers in the later years of his reign before taking important decisions. Other leading Nazis were involved with occult schools of various kinds, Hess at one time cultivating Steinerism, while Rosenberg took an interest in Gurdjieff. More generally, Nazi myth-making made explicit the Aryan connotations of recent Europe occultism. Wagner provided a useful focal point for both parties. Hitler's passion for *Parsifal* rivalled Steiner's, though he drew rather different conclusions from it, finding in the opera not the symbolic representation of Christian mysticism but the celebration of sacrifice in a higher racial cause.

4. See Webb, op. cit., p. 389.

5. Moore, op. cit., p. 249.

6. Peters, *Gurdjieff Remembered*, Wildwood House, 1976, p. 228.

7. Peters, op. cit., pp. 202–6.

8. Peters, op. cit., pp. 207–10.

9. Peters, op. cit., pp. 186–91.

10. Frank Lloyd Wright, *Wisconsin State Journal*, 3 Nov 1951, section 2. See also R. C. Twombly, 'Organic Living . . .', *Wisconsin Magazine of History*, Winter 1974/5.

11. Peters, op. cit., pp. 219–28.

12. Moore, op. cit., p. 229.

13. Later a Marxist and the author of at least one first-rate novel, *The Law*, trans. P. Wiles, Eland Books, 1985.

14. The American novelist Djuna Barnes (1892–1982) published her one celebrated book, *Nightwood*, in 1936. Janet Flanner (1892–1978) contributed her 'Letter from Paris' to the *New Yorker* for fifty years from 1925, under the pen-name Gênet.

15. The American novelist Kathryn Hulme.

16. K. Hulme, *Undiscovered Country*, Muller, 1967, p. 74.

17. M. Anderson, op. cit. All quotations in this paragraph are taken from that short book.

18. For vivid descriptions of Gurdjieff's life at this time, and especially his celebration of Christmas, see Hulme, op. cit., pp. 85–133.

19. Hulme, op. cit., p. 162.

Chapter 16: Sinners

1. There are suggestions that Ouspensky's exile was not quite what it seemed. Some pupils fantasised that he and Gurdjieff were in league to give the *impression* of a split in order to provoke creative tension among their pupils. This argument is supported by the fact that Ouspensky continued to visit the Prieuré until the final absolute break with Gurdjieff in 1931.

2. Bennett, op. cit., p. 173.

3. *Witness*, pp. 85–170, is the main source of the following pages. This outline of Bennett's career was confirmed as accurate by the late Mrs Elizabeth Bennett in conversation with the author. Foreign Office records, however, paint a rather different picture. See PRO FO 370, passim.

4. William Jennings Bryan (1860–1925) fought three presidential campaigns as Democratic candidate in 1896, 1900 and 1908. Bennett refers to one: I have not been able to establish which.

5. FO files 371, piece 12179.

6. Bennett, op. cit., pp. 173–74, 189.

7. Frieda Lawrence to Rosalind Rajagopal, quoted in Sloss, op. cit., p. 182.

Chapter 17: Gurus in the War

1. M. Random, *Les puissances du dedans, Luc Dietrich, Lanza del Vasto, René Daumal, Gurdjieff*, Denoël, 1966.
2. Both men expressed these views consistently from the early 1920s until their deaths.
3. I have been unable to trace the origins of this phrase. It describes a doctrine taught by Krishnamurti in different forms from about the time he left the Theosophical Society.
4. On negative emotions see P. D. Ouspensky, op. cit., pp. 19–48.
5. On this point see *TLADOK*, pp. 92–93, where Miss Lutyens quotes several unpublished letters on the subject.
6. Idem, p. 94.
7. On Huxley see the marvellous life by Sybille Bedford: *Aldous Huxley: A Biography*, Alfred A. Knopf/Harper & Row, 1974.
8. A network of relationships which made him a remote and unlikely cousin of Bishop Wedgwood.
9. N. Annan, *Leslie Stephen, The Godless Victorian*, University of Chicago Press, 1984, pp. 232–33.
10. Aldous Huxley to Leonard Huxley, 12 Nov 1917. Reprinted in D. Grover-Smith, *The Letters of Aldous Huxley*, Chatto & Windus, 1969, pp. 136–37.
11. See Huxley's pamphlet, *What Are You Going To Do About It? The Case For Constructive Peace*, Chatto & Windus, 1936, and his *An Encyclopaedia of Pacifism*, Chatto & Windus, 1937.
12. On Dick Shepherd and the PPU see S. Morrison, *I Renounce War: The Story of the Peace Pledge Union*, Shepherd Press Ltd, 1962. The Pledge is reprinted in Bedford, op. cit., pp. 317–18.
13. G. Heard, 'The Poignant Prophet', in *The Kenyon Review*, 1965.
14. See the final chapter of *Those Barren Leaves*, Chatto & Windus, 1925.
15. *Do What You Will*, Chatto & Windus, 1929, p. 3.
16. Sloss, op. cit., p. 170.
17. Grover-Smith, op. cit., p. 719.
18. For a vivid portrait of Gerald Heard see the character of Augustus Parr in Christopher Isherwood's novel *Down There on a Visit*, Methuen, 1962. See also Bedford, op. cit., passim.
19. A holy man, regarded by many devout Hindus as an avatar,

Ramakrishna spent his life in a temple near Calcutta. After his death in 1886 his chief disciples founded the Ramakrishna Order of monks, to which Prabhavananda belonged.

20. The following description of life at Ivar Avenue is based on C. Isherwood, *My Guru and his Disciple*, Eyre Methuen, 1980.

21. Idem, p. 74.

22. Quoted in Bedford, op. cit., p. 453.

23. Isherwood, op. cit., p. 96.

24. Idem, p. 122.

25. Grover-Smith, op. cit., p. 963.

26. Isherwood, op. cit., p. 204.

27. Idem, p. 222.

28. Idem, p. 202.

29. Isherwood continued to see the Swami regularly at Trabuco and in Los Angeles, and his old master kept up the pressure for him to rejoin the monastery and to bring Don with him. Isherwood refused, but he did write two books about his experiences which were a way of keeping the faith: *Ramakrishna and his Disciples* (1965) and the delightful *My Guru and his Disciple*.

30. Grover-Smith, op. cit., p. 608.

31. Idem, p. 818.

32. On these experiments see Bedford, op. cit., pp. 602–3, 618–19, 726–34, 754–55; and L. A. Huxley, *This Timeless Moment: A Personal View of Aldous Huxley*, Farrar, Straus & Giroux, 1968.

33. Huxley embarked on the direct exploration of the spiritual life in three books produced during the 1940s. The novel *Time Must Have a Stop* (1944) is not a success. Huxley's attempt to portray, in Bruno Rontini, the character of a man whose goodness grows out of his religious enlightenment, has convinced few readers, though the author enjoyed writing this book more than most of his others.

The more successful *Grey Eminence* (1941) is about what happens to a man who aspires to sainthood and ends up in politics. The story's moral is that the highest purposes are worthless without charity and a personal sense of the divine.

Drawing on the eastern texts favoured by Theosophists, *The Perennial Philosophy* (1946) examines the nature of reality, the individual's experience of God, and ways of relating that experience to everyday life. Well aware that he might be described as 'another Mrs Eddy', Huxley insisted that *The Perennial Philosophy* is not an attempt to found a new religion, but a record of the best that has been thought and written about it.

34. A. Huxley, *After Many a Summer*, Chatto & Windus, 1939.
35. A. Huxley, *Ape and Essence*, Chatto & Windus, 1948, p. 33.

Chapter 18: Terminations

1. P. D. Ouspensky, *A New Model of the Universe*, pp. xv–xx.
2. Ouspensky, *A Further Record*, p. 69.
3. Published by Hodder & Stoughton in four volumes as *The Foundation of Natural Philosophy*, 1956; *The Foundation of Moral Philosophy*, 1961; *Man and his Nature*, 1966; and *History*, 1968.
4. Bennett, op. cit., pp. iii–vi.
5. On Ouspensky's last months see R. Collin, *The Mirror of Light*, London, 1959, passim; and Webb, op. cit., pp. 439–60.
6. Moore, op. cit., pp. 290–91.
7. The membership of this society was fixed at three hundred. Its objectives were:
   (i) the study of problems in the evolution of man and particularly the idea of *psycho-transformation*;
   (ii) the study of psychological schools in different historical periods and in different countries, and the study of their influence on the moral and intellectual development of humanity;
   (iii) practical investigation of methods of self-study and self-development according to the principles of psychological schools;
   (iv) research work in the history of religions, of philosophy, of science and of art with the object of establishing their common origin where it can be found and different psychological levels in each of them.
   Number iv is pure Theosophy. Indeed, when one remembers that Ouspensky's approach had always been to look within for esoteric truth by psychologising it, this whole programme is little more than an elaboration of Theosophy.
8. See Webb, op. cit., pp. 447–49.
9. Eliot's poem sequence is coloured by Ouspenskian notions of time and recurrence. See T. S. Eliot, *Collected Poems*, Faber & Faber, 1965, pp. 189–223.
10. On Collin see J. Collin-Smith, 'Beloved Icarus', in the *Astrological Journal*, vol. xiii, no. 4, autumn 1971; and A. Logan (the pseudonym of Joyce Collin-Smith), *Answering Gods*, Tlalpam, Ediciones Sol, 1951.
11. Toc H: a society formed to preserve the spirit of comradeship formed in World War One, called after signallers' names for the initial letters of the first meeting-place, Talbot House.

12. On the final days see J. Collin-Smith, op. cit., passim; and Webb, op. cit., pp. 454–60.

13. For Maurice Nicoll see B. Pogson, *Maurice Nicoll, A Portrait*, London, 1961.

14. K. Walker, *Venture With Ideas*, Jonathan Cape, 1951, pp. 134 ff.

15. Hulme, op. cit., p. 256.

16. Webb, op. cit., p. 470.

17. United Nations Relief and Rehabilitation Agency.

18. Peters, op. cit., pp. 247–252.

19. Madame Caruso became a devoted pupil of Gurdjieff, whose last months she describes in *A Personal History by Dorothy Caruso*, Hermitage House, 1952.

20. Webb, op. cit., p. 461.

21. Bennett, op. cit., p. 187.

22. Bennett, op. cit., p. 238.

23. Idem.

24. See Caruso, op. cit., pp. 291 ff.

25. The late Elizabeth Bennett confirmed this observation in conversation with the author, but declined to name examples.

26. Bennett, op. cit., p. 240.

27. In conversation with the author.

28. Bennett, op. cit., p. 249.

29. R. de Ropp, *Warrior's Way*, George Allen & Unwin, 1980, p. 199.

30. Moore, op. cit., p. 303.

31. Bennett, op. cit., pp. 251–54.

32. The text of this letter is reprinted in *Witness*, pp. 253–54.

33. I owe this point to James Moore.

Chapter 19: Returning

1. *TLADOK*, p. 156. The widow of a film producer, Mrs Zimbalist was Krishnamurti's mainstay from 1964 until his death.

2. A major theme of Mrs Sloss's book, *Lives in the Shadow with J. Krishnamurti*. The following pages contrast her account with Mary Lutyens's in her two-volume biography of Krishnamurti (*The Years of Awakening* and *The Years of Fulfilment*) and in her abbreviated biography *The Life and Death of Krishnamurti*.

3. Sloss, op. cit., pp. 203–9 and 275–78.

4. According to Mrs Sloss, Rosalind was jealous of Nandini and attacked Krishnamurti for having an affair with her. Their friendship is described by Nandini's sister Pupul Jayakar in her *Krishnamurti*,

Harper & Row, 1986. This volume adds a third perspective to Sloss and Lutyens by emphasising the Indian aspects of its hero's life.

5. See *Time*, 16 Jan 1950. Mrs Sloss quotes parts of this article in op. cit., p. 218.

6. On Krishnamurti's educational theory see especially 'For The Young' in *The Krishnamurti Reader*, ed. M. Lutyens, Penguin, 1970; *Education and the Significance of Life*, Victor Gollancz, 1955, passim; and *The Beginnings of Learning*, Victor Gollancz, 1975.

7. I have been unable to trace the first use of this phrase, which occurs frequently in the later talks.

8. Friedrich Grohe, a retired manufacturer of bathroom and kitchen taps and a generous patron of Krishnamurti causes.

9. See for example the conversations gathered together in *The Impossible Question*, Victor Gollancz, 1972, and *The Beginnings of Learning*, where Krishnamurti's determination to impose his views under the guise of 'dialogue' is impossible to ignore. This is not, of course, to deny the interest of what he has to say.

There are many moments in these conversations when Krishnamurti sounds surprisingly like Ouspensky in both tone and doctrine. Readers wishing to pursue the comparison should consult *The Krishnamurti Reader*, and P. D. Ouspensky, *A Further Record*.

10. These conversations bore fruit in the influential work of David Bohm, Professor of Theoretical Physics in the University of London and a friend of Albert Einstein. Bohm's *Wholeness and the Implicate Order*, Routledge & Kegan Paul, 1980, makes frequent reference to Krishnamurti's view.

11. The story is told by M. Lutyens in the second volume of her biography, *The Years of Fulfilment*.

12. The episode and others like it are described in *The Years of Fulfilment*.

13. For a detailed account of what this means in practice see *TLADOK*, pp. 159–168.

Chapter 20: From System to Source

1. I owe this point to a conversation with James Moore.

2. For a more detailed account of the school's recent history see the excellent if somewhat over-sensational *Secret Cult*, Lion Publishing, 1984, by P. Hounam and A. Hogg.

3. Large posters regularly appear at London tube stations.

4. Hounam and Hogg, op. cit., p. 42.

5. On the school's finances see Hounam and Hogg, op. cit., pp. 47–49.

6. These articles form the basis of *Secret Cult*.

7. The following six paragraphs are based on conversations with two former members of the SES who have asked not to be named. Readers will find a fuller discussion of similar experiences in Hounam and Hogg, op. cit., passim.

8. Hounam and Hogg, op. cit., p. 16.

9. Hounam and Hogg, op. cit., pp. 218–32.

10. This account of Collin's activities in Mexico is based on G. Zodec, *Lessons in Religion for a Sceptical World*, Mexico, 1956, and J. Collin-Smith, op. cit. But see also A. Logan, op. cit.

11. Webb, op. cit., pp. 490–91.

12. Quoted in Webb, op. cit., p. 496.

Chapter 21: Climacteric

1. A fuller account of Dr King's biographical details may be found in 'The Aetherius Society: A Brief Introduction', The Aetherius Society, 1984. 'The Theology of Aetherius' by the Rt Rev. Dr R. Lawrence, BA, The Aetherius Society, 1980, gives a summary of aetherial doctrine and history. This document specifically acknowledges Madame Blavatsky as the woman who made modern occult history possible.

I would like to take this opportunity to thank Dr Lawrence for his courteous response to my enquiries.

2. R. Lawrence, op. cit., p. 19.

3. Idem, p. 20.

4. Idem, p. 20.

5. On the Raëlians see E. Barker, *New Religious Movements*, HMSO, 1989, pp. 200 ff.

6. See Barker, op. cit., pp. 179 ff. The group hold regular meetings in London, Manchester and Bristol. My thanks to Paul Massey, their director, for answering questions about the Eternal Flame.

7. Omraam M. Aivanhof, *Sexual Force and the Winged Dragon*, Editions Prosveta, 1987. Prosveta publish dozens of titles by the Omraam in several languages.

8. The brief official biographies of Mr and Mrs Prophet and a summary of their doctrines can be found in E. C. Prophet: *Teachings of the Ascended Masters*, Summit University Press, Montana, 1989. For a

complete listing of their scores of publications, lithographs, cassettes etc., readers should apply for the lavishly illustrated Summit University Press catalogue, Box A, Livingston, MT 59047-1390.

9. Another theosophical offshoot, also known as the Supreme Order of Aquarius and the Pre-Initiatic School of Half-Gegnian and based in St Louis, Missouri.

10. See 'Mother Knows Best and It's the Worst' by A. Pielou, in *You* magazine, 1 Oct 1989, pp. 16–20.

11. This bank is included in a whole group of financial institutions registered under the name Mercury Provident plc. The British Anthroposophical Society has moved in from the social and political fringes. It recently began negotiating with the Department of Education and Science to register its own technical institute, Michael Faraday College at Brighton, as the first 'Green' City Technology College, under a new government initiative to promote scientific and technological education. The Prince of Wales has also taken a keen interest, visiting farms funded by the society and championing their forms of alternative medicine.

12. The shift in emphasis can be judged by comparing the biography of Martin Exeter – *One Heart, One Way* by C. Foster, Foundation House Publications – with writings by his son, e.g. *My World, My Responsibility*, Emissary Foundation International, n.d. Martin Exeter espouses an existentialist mysticism which emphasises the importance of communication with the source of being. Michael Exeter concentrates on ecological responsibility.

13. The remainder of this chapter is based on Bennett's own account in *Witness*, pp. 273–319, supplemented by my conversations with the late Elizabeth Bennett.

14. On Subud and Pak Subuh see Bennett, op. cit., pp. 320–34, and A. B. Paul, *Stairway to Subud*, Coombe Springs Press, 1965.

15. Bennett, op. cit., p. 331.

16. Bennett, op. cit., p. 349.

17. Bennett, op. cit., p. 347.

Conclusion: The Baboon Triumphant

1. This manifesto – *Declaration of the People of the Tradition*, Octagon Press, 1966 and 1974 – is reprinted in Bennett, op. cit., pp. 356–58.

2. Shah's career has been documented by Professor Elwell-Sutton, whose account I follow here. See L. P. Elwell-Sutton, 'Sufism and Pseudo-Sufism', *Encounter*, vol. xliv, no. 5, May 1975, pp. 9–17. But

see also J. Moore, 'Neo-Sufism: The Case of Idries Shah', *Religion Today*, which is careful to distance Gurdjieff from Shah. Both writers dismiss out of hand Shah's claim to represent Sufi teaching in the West.
3. PRO, FO 371, 1946, AS/4439/46. See also Moore, op. cit., p. 7, where the charge is further documented.
4. Mr Shah has been unable to answer my letters.
5. Bennett, op. cit., p. 360.
6. On this point see N. Saunders, *Alternative London*, Nicholas Saunders, 1970, p. 109.
7. Bennett, op. cit., p. 362.
8. On the sale of Coombe see Bennett, op. cit., pp. 359–63 and Elwell-Sutton, op. cit., pp. 14–15.
9. After his triumph at Coombe it might be expected that Shah would relax. Far from it. He maintained a high profile in the press and Bennett was not the only distinguished figure he convinced of his genius. His glamorous international life is described in L. Courtland, *The Diffusion of Sufi Ideas in the West*, Boulder, Colorado, 1972.

From the 1960s on, Shah built up a powerful network of supporters influential in literature and the media, of whom the most celebrated were the poets Robert Graves and Ted Hughes and the novelist Doris Lessing.

Shah even persuaded Graves to lend his name to publication of a new version of Omar Khayyam's *Rubáiyát* in collaboration with his brother, General Omar Ali Shah. This translation was supposedly based on a manuscript never before seen in the West. Shah never produced the manuscript and, as Moore puts it, Graves's book was soon exposed by scholars as 'a nullity cubed; a "translation" (which was not a translation but a copy of a Victorian commentary); of the twelfth century "Jan Fishan Khan MS" (which did not exist): of a composite stanzaic poem by Khayyam (which he did not write)'. Moore, op. cit., p. 6.

Miss Doris Lessing not only refused my invitation to comment on Shah's teaching: her reply to my letter specifically forbade me to mention in my book that she had even refused. But see Doris Lessing, 'An Elephant in the Dark', *Spectator*, 18 Sept 1964.
10. Bennett, op. cit., p. 376.
11. My thanks to Andrew Rawlinson of the Department of Religious Studies at Lancaster University for drawing my attention to Gary Chicoine and for providing me with information about him and a rare copy of his pamphlet.
12. Sadguru Swami Narayan Avadhoot, *Adiguru Dattatreya and the*

Non-Sectarian Central Spiritual School, Coombe Springs Press, n.d., p. 13. Sadguru Swami Narayan Avadhoot is, of course, Gary Chicoine. He is also witheringly dismissive of Idries Shah.

BIBLIOGRAPHY

Abdullah, A., *My Nine Lives*, London, Hurst & Blackett, 1934

Anderson, M., *The Unknowable Gurdjieff*, London, Routledge & Kegan Paul, 1962

Annan, N., *Leslie Stephen, The Godless Victorian*, University of Chicago Press, 1984

Arundale, G. S., *Conversations with Dr Besant*, Adyar, TPH, 1941
A Fragment of Autobiography, Adyar, Kalakshetra, 1940
Personal Memories of G. S. Arundale, London, TPH, 1967

Barker, A. T. ed., *The Mahatma Letters to A. P. Sinnett from the Mahatmas M. and K.H.*, London, T. Fisher Unwin, 1924
The Letters of H. P. Blavatsky to A. P. Sinnett, London, T. Fisher Unwin, 1925

Barker, E., *New Religious Movements*, Norwich, HMSO, 1989

Bedford, S., *Aldous Huxley: A Biography*, New York, Alfred A. Knopf/Harper & Row, 1974

Bennett, J. G., *The Crisis in Human Affairs*, London, Hodder & Stoughton, 1948
What Are We Living For, London, Hodder & Stoughton, 1950
Dramatic Universe, 4 vols., London, Hodder & Stoughton, 1956–68
Concerning Subud, London, Hodder & Stoughton, 1958
Gurdjieff: A Very Great Enigma, London, Coombe Springs Press, 1966
Gurdjieff: Making a New World, London, Coombe Springs Press, 1973
Witness: The Story of a Search, Tucson, Omen, 1974

Berdyaev, N., *Dream and Reality*, London, Greenwood, 1950

Besant, A., *Why I Became a Theosophist*, London, Freethought Publishing Co., 1819

The Coming of the World Teacher, Adyar, TPH, 1925
The Neutrality of the Theosophical Society, privately printed, 1894
The Case Against Judge, n.p., 1895.
An Autobiography, Madras, TPH, 1908
A Letter to Members of the TS, Adyar, privately printed, 1908
Autobiographical Sketches, London, Freethought Publishing Co.,
    1885
The Theosophical Society and the Occult Hierarchy, London, TPH,
    1925
Blake, A. G. E., *A History of the Institute for Comparative Study of
    History, Philosophy and the Sciences*, Daglingworth, privately
    printed, 1981
Blavatsky, H. P., *Is Theosophy a Religion*, Adyar, TPH, 1947
Isis Unveiled, 2 vols., London, W. J. Bouton, 1877
The Secret Doctrine, 2 vols., London, Theosophical Publishing
    Co., 1888
The Voice of the Silence, London, TPH, 1889
The Secret Doctrine, vol. iii, London, TPS, 1897
Practical Occultism, London, TPH, 1923
Bohm, D., *Wholeness and the Implicate Order*, London, Routledge &
    Kegan Paul, 1980
Bonner, H. B., *Charles Bradlaugh: A Record of His Life and Work by
    His Daughter*, London, T. Fisher Unwin, 1895
Bragdon, C., *The Secret Springs*, 1939
Brandon, R., *The Spiritualists: The Passion for the Occult in the
    Nineteenth and Twentieth Centuries*, New York, Alfred A.
    Knopf, 1983
Bright, E., *Old Letters and Memories of Annie Besant*, Adyar, TPH,
    1936
Brooks, F. T., *Neotheosophy Exposed*, Madras, Vyasashrama
    Bookshop, n.d.
The Theosophical Society and its Esoteric Bogeydom, Madras,
    Vyasashrama Bookshop, 1914
Buckle, R., *Diaghilev*, London, Weidenfeld & Nicolson, 1979
Burrows, H., and Mead, G. R. S., *The Leadbeater Case*, London,
    privately printed, 1908
Butkovsky-Hewitt, A., *With Gurdjieff in St. Petersburg and Paris*,
    London, 1978
Campbell, B. F., *Ancient Wisdom Revived: A History of the
    Theosophical Movement*, Berkeley, University of California
    Press, 1980

Caruso, D., *A Personal History by Dorothy Caruso*, New York, Hermitage House, 1952

Chacornac, P., *Eliphas Lévi: Rénovateur de l'occultisme en France*, Paris, Chacornac Frères, 1926

Chadwick, O., *The Secularization of the European Mind in the Nineteenth Century*, Cambridge University Press, 1975

Clarke, R. B., *The Boyhood of J. Krishnamurti*, Bombay, Chetana, 1977

Cleather, A., *H. P. Blavatsky: Her Life and Work for Humanity*, Calcutta, 1922

  H. P. Blavatsky: The Great Betrayal, Calcutta, 1922

  Buddhism: The Science of Life, Peking, 1928

  The Pseudo-Occultation of Mrs A. Bailey, Manila, 1929

Collin, R., *The Theory of Eternal Life*, London, 1950

  The Theory of Celestial Influence, Tlalpam, Ediciones Sol, 1952

  The Christian Mystery, Tlalpam, Ediciones Sol, 1953

  The Herald of Harmony, Tlalpam, Ediciones Sol, 1954

  The Mirror of Light, London, 1959

Collin-Smith, J., 'Beloved Icarus', *Astrological Journal*, vol. xiii, no. 4, Autumn 1971

Conway, M. D., *Autobiography, Memories and Experiences*, 2 vols., London, Cassell, 1904

  My Pilgrimage to the Wise Men of the East, London, Constable, 1906

Cooper, I. S., *The Ceremonies of the Liberal Catholic Rite*, London, St Alban Press, 1964

Corson, E. R. ed., *Some Unpublished Letters of Helena Blavatsky*, London, Rider & Co., n.d.

Darnton, R., *Mesmerism and the End of the Enlightenment in France*, Cambridge, Mass., Harvard University Press, 1968

Das, B., *The Central Hindu College and Mrs Besant*, Madras, Divine Life Press, 1914

Daumal, R., *Mount Analogue*, trans. R. Shattuck, London, Penguin, 1959

Dukes, P., *The Unending Quest*, London, Cassell, 1950

Easton, S. C., *Rudolf Steiner: Herald of a New Epoch*, New York, Anthroposophic Press, 1980

Edmunds, F., *Rudolf Steiner Education*, London, Rudolf Steiner Press, 1973

Eek, S., and de Zirkoff, B., *William Quan Judge, Theosophical Pioneer*, Wheaton, Ill., TPH, 1969

Eliot, T. S., *Collected Poems*, London, Faber & Faber, 1965

Elwell-Sutton, L. P., 'Sufism and Pseudo-Sufism', *Encounter*, xliv, no. 5, May 1975, pp. 9–17

Endersby, V., *The Hall of Magic Mirrors*, New York, Carlton Press, 1969

Fornell, E. W., *The Unhappy Medium: Spiritualism and the Life of Margaret Fox*, Austin, University of Texas Press, 1964

Fussell, J., *Mrs Annie Besant and the Leadbeater Advice*, Point Loma, privately printed, 1913
  Mrs Annie Besant and the Moral Code, Point Loma, privately printed, 1909

Gauld, A., *The Founders of Pyschical Research*, London, Routledge & Kegan Paul, 1968

Gottschalk, S., *The Emergence of Christian Science in American Religious Life*, Berkeley, University of California Press, 1973

Greenwalt, E. A., *California Utopia: Point Loma 1897–1942*, San Diego, Point Loma Publications, 1978

Gurdjieff, G. I., *Views from the Real World*, London, Arkana, 1984
  Beelzebub's Tales to His Grandson, London, Arkana, 1985
  Meetings With Remarkable Men, trans. A. R. Orage, London, Arkana, 1985
  Life Is Real Only Then: When 'I Am', London, Arkana, 1989

Hall, T. H., *The Spiritualists: The Story of Florence Cook and William Crookes*, New York, Helix Press, 1962

Harris, T. L., *The Arcana of Christianity*, New York, 1858
  The Wisdom of the Adepts, Santa Rosa, 1884

Hartmann, T. and O. de, *Our Life with Mr Gurdjieff*, London, Arkana, 1992

Hastings, B., *The Old New Age: Orage and Others*, 1936

Hodgson, R., 'Report of Committee appointed to investigate Phenomena in connection with the Theosophical Society', Society for Psychical Research, Proceedings, iii, part 9, Dec 1885, pp. 201–400

Hounam, P., and Hogg, A., *Secret Cult*, Tring, Lion Publishing, 1984

Hulme, K., *Undiscovered Country*, London, Frederick Muller, 1967

Huxley, A., *Those Barren Leaves*, London, Chatto & Windus, 1925
  Do What You Will, London, Chatto & Windus, 1929
  What Are You Going to do About it? The Case for Constructive Peace, London, Chatto & Windus, 1936
  Ends and Means, London, Chatto & Windus, 1937

An Encyclopaedia of Pacifism, London, Chatto & Windus, 1937
After Many a Summer, London, Chatto & Windus, 1939
Grey Eminence, London, Chatto & Windus, 1941
Time Must Have a Stop, London, Chatto & Windus, 1944
Ape and Essence, London, Chatto & Windus, 1948
Letters, ed. D. Grover-Smith, London, Chatto & Windus, 1969
Huxley, L. A., *This Timeless Moment: A Personal View of Aldous Huxley*, New York, Farrar, Straus & Giroux, 1968
Icke, D., *The Truth Vibrations*, London, Aquarian Press, 1991
Isherwood, C., *Down There on a Visit*, London, Methuen, 1962
Ramakrishna and his Disciples, London, Methuen, 1969
My Guru and His Disciple, London, Eyre Methuen, 1980
Jayakar, P., *Krishnamurti: A Biography*, New York, Harper & Row, 1986
Jenkins, E., *The Shadow and the Light: a defence of Daniel Dunglas Home, the medium*, London, Hamish Hamilton, 1982
Jinarajadasa, C. ed., *C. W. Leadbeater*, Adyar, TPH, 1938
The 'K.H.' Letters to C. W. Leadbeater, Adyar, TPH, 1941
The Astral Plane, Extracts from letter from C. W. Leadbeater to Annie Besant 1916–1923, Adyar, TPH, 1952
Eds. of *Justice*, *The Evolution of Mrs Besant*, Madras, privately printed, 1918
Keyserling, H., *The Travel Diary of a Philosopher*, trans. J. H. Reece, 2 vols., London, Jonathan Cape, 1926
Creative Understanding, trans. T. Duerr, London, Jonathan Cape, 1929
King, C. D., *The Oragean Version*, 1951
King, F., *Ritual Magic*, London, Neville Spearman, 1970
Krishnamurti, J., *The First and Last Freedom*, London, Victor Gollancz, 1954
Commentaries on Living, London, Victor Gollancz, 1956, 1959, 1960
The Krishnamurti Reader, London, Penguin, 1970
The Urgency of Change, London, Victor Gollancz, 1971
Krishnamurti's Notebook, London, Victor Gollancz, 1976
The Beginnings of Learning, London, Penguin, 1978
The Impossible Question, London, Penguin, 1978
Krishnamurti's Journal, London, Victor Gollancz, 1982
Landau, R., *God is My Adventure*, London, Unwin Books, 1964
Leadbeater, C. W., *Invisible Helpers*, London, TPS, 1896
Saved by a Ghost, Bombay, Office of *The Theosophist*, 1911

Australia and New Zealand: the Home of a New Sub-Race, Sydney,
Theosophical Society, 1915
Why a Great World Teacher?, Sydney, OSE, 1915
An Occult View of the War, London, TPH, 1918
The Lives of Alcyone, 2 vols., Adyar, TPH, 1924
The Masters and the Path, Adyar, TPH, 1925
The World Mother as Symbol and Fact, Adyar, TPH, 1928
How Theosophy Came to Me, Adyar, TPH, 1930
The Band of Servers, Adyar, TPH, 1941
The Astral Plane, London, TPH, n.d.
The Great War, Adyar, TPH, n.d.
The Masters of Wisdom, Adyar, TPH, n.d.
Leopold, R. W., *Robert Dale Owen: A Biography*, Cambridge,
Mass., Harvard University Press, 1940
Lessing, D., 'An Elephant in the Dark', *The Spectator*, 18.9.64
'If You Knew Sufi . . .', *Guardian*, 8.1.75
Lewin, L. ed., *The Diffusion of Sufi Ideas in the West*, Colorado,
Keysign Press, 1971
Logan, A., *Answering Gods*, Tlalpam, Ediciones Sol, 1951
Luhan, M. D., *Lorenzo in Taos*, London, Secker & Warburg, 1933
Lutyens, Edwin, *The Letters of Sir E. Lutyens to his Wife*, ed. J.
Ridley and C. Percy, London, Collins, 1985
Lutyens, Elizabeth, *The Goldfish Bowl*, London, Cassell, 1972
Lutyens, Emily, *Candles in the Sun*, London, Hart-Davis, 1957
Lutyens, M., *Krishnamurti: The Years of Awakening*, London, John
Murray, 1975
Krishnamurti: The Years of Fulfilment, London, John Murray
The Life and Death of Krishnamurti, London, John Murray, 1990
To Be Young, London, Hart-Davis, 1959
Lutyens, M. ed., *Education and the Significance of Life*, London,
Victor Gollancz, 1955
The Krishnamurti Reader, London, Penguin, 1970
The Second Krishnamurti Reader, London, Penguin, 1973
The Beginnings of Learning, London, Victor Gollancz, 1975
The Impossible Question, London, Victor Gollancz, 1975
Lytton, E. B., *Zanoni*, 2 vols., London, Saunders & Otley, 1842
A Strange Story, 2 vols., London, Sampson, Lowe, 1862
Lytton, V., *The Life of Edward Bulwer, First Lord Lytton, by His
Grandson*, 2 vols., London, Macmillan, 1913
Maitland, E., *Anna Kingsford: Her Life, Letters, Diary and Work*, 2
vols., London, George Redway, 1896

Mansfield, K., *Letters to John Middleton Murry*, ed. John Middleton Murry, London, Constable, 1951

Martin, W., *The New Age under Orage*, Manchester University Press, 1967

Meade, M., *Madame Blavatsky: The Woman behind the Myth*, New York, Putnam's, 1980

Montgomery, J., *Abodes of Love*, New York, Putnam's, 1962

Moore, J., *Gurdjieff: The Anatomy of a Myth*, Shaftesbury, Element, 1991

   Gurdjieff and Mansfield, London, Routledge & Kegan Paul, 1980

Murphet, H., *Hammer on the Mountain: The Life of Henry Steele Olcott*, Wheaton, Illinois, TPH, 1972

Nethercot, A., *The First Five Lives of Annie Besant*, London, Hart-Davis, 1961

   The Last Four Lives of Annie Besant, London, Hart-Davis, 1963

Nott, C. S., *The Teachings of Gurdjieff*, London, Routledge & Kegan Paul, 1961

   Journey Through This World, London, Routledge & Kegan Paul, 1969

Olcott, H. S., *People from the Other World*, American Publishing Co., 1875

   Buddhist Catechism, Adyar, TPH, 1947

   Old Diary Leaves, 6 vols., Adyar, TPH, 1972–75

Oliphant, L., *Piccadilly*, London, William Blackwood, 1853

   Sympneumata, London, William Blackwood, 1885

   Masollam, London, William Blackwood, 1886

   Episodes in a Life of Adventure, London, William Blackwood, 1887

Oliphant, M., *Memoir of Laurence Oliphant and of Alice Oliphant, his wife*, 2 vols., London, William Blackwood, 1891

Oppenheim, J., *The Other World, Spiritualism and Psychical Research in England, 1850–1914*, Cambridge University Press, 1985

O'Prey, P. ed., *Between Moon and Moon*, London, Hutchinson, 1984

Orage, A. R., *Frederick Nietzsche, the Dionysian Spirit of the Age*, London and Edinburgh, 1906

   Consciousness, Animal, Human and Superhuman, London and Benares, TPH, 1907

   Psychological Exercises, 1930

Ouspensky, P. D., *The Fourth Way*, London, Routledge & Kegan Paul, 1957

   A New Model of the Universe, London, Arkana, 1984

A Further Record, London, Arkana, 1986
In Search of the Miraculous, London, Arkana, 1987
The Strange Life of Ivan Osokin, London, Arkana, 1987
Tertium Organum, London, Arkana, 1990
Letters from Russia, London, Arkana, 1992
Owen, A., *The Darkened Room: Women, Power and Spiritualism in Late Victorian England*, London, Virago, 1989
Owen, R. D., *The Debatable Land Between this World and the Next*, London, n.p., 1872
Owen, Rosamund D., *My Perilous Life in Palestine*, London, Allen & Unwin, 1928
Parry, B., and Rivett, R., *An Introduction to the Liberal Catholic Church*, Sydney, St Alban Press, 1973
Paul, A. B., *Stairway to Subud*, London, Coombe Springs Press, 1965
Pearsall, R., *The Table Rappers*, London, Michael Joseph, 1972
Peters, F., *Boyhood with Gurdjieff*, London, Wildwood House, 1976
Gurdjieff Remembered, London, Wildwood House, 1976
Pigott, F. W., *The Parting of the Ways*, London, TPH, 1927
Price, L., *Madame Blavatsky Unveiled?*, London, Theosophical History Centre,
Prokofieff, S., *Rudolf Steiner and the Founding of the New Mysteries*, trans P. King, London, Rudolf Steiner Press, 1988
Prophet, E. C., *Teachings of the Ascended Masters*, Livingston, Montana, Summit University Press, 1989
Ransom, J., *A Short History of the Theosophical Society, 1875–1937*, Adyar, TPH, 1938
Reyner, J. H., *Ouspensky: The Unsung Genius*, London, Allen & Unwin, 1981
Rittelmeyer, F., *Rudolf Steiner Enters My Life*, London, Christian Community Press, 1954
Roberts, C. B., *In Denikin's Russia*, London, 1921
A Wanderer's Log, London, 1922
Let's Begin Again, London, Jarrolds, 1940
Ryan, C., *H. P. Blavatsky and the Theosophical Movement*, Point Loma Press, 1937
Schuré, Edmond, *The Great Initiates*, London, Rider, 1912
Schneider, H., and Lawton, G., *A Prophet and a Pilgrim, Being the Incredible History of Thomas Lake Harris and Laurence Oliphant: Their Sexual Mysticism and Utopian Communities*

Amply Documented to Confound the Skeptic, New York, Columbia University Press, 1942

Scott, E., *The People of the Secret*, London, Octagon, 1983

Selver, P., *Orage and the New Age Circle*, London, Allen & Unwin, 1959

Shah, I., *Destination Mecca*, London, Rider, 1957
The Sufis, New York, Doubleday, 1964
The Exploits of the Incomparable Mullah Nasruddin, London, Jonathan Cape, 1966

Shepherd, A. P., *A Scientist of the Invisible*, London, Hodder & Stoughton, 1954

Sinnett, A. P., *The Occult World*, London, L. Trubner, 1881.
Esoteric Buddhism, London, Chapman & Hall, 1888
Incidents in the Life of Madame Blavatsky, London, TPS, 1913
The Early Days of Theosophy in Europe, London, TPH, 1922

Sloss, R. R., *Lives in the Shadow with J. Krishnamurti*, London, Bloomsbury, 1991

Smith, I., *Truth is a Pathless Land*, Madras, TPH, 1989

Smith, W. S., *The London Heretics, 1870–1914*, London, Dodd, Mead, 1968

Solovieff, V. S., *A Modern Priestess of Isis*, trans. W. Leaf, London, Longman's Green, 1895

Steffen, A., *Meetings With Rudolf Steiner*, Dornach, Verlag für Schone Wissenschaft, 1961

Steiner, R., *Rudolf Steiner, An Autobiography*, trans. R. Stebbing, New York, Anthroposophic Press, 1977
The Influence of Lucifer and Ahriman, trans. D. S. Osmond, London, Rudolf Steiner Publishing Co., 1954
The Tension between East and West, trans. B. A. Rowley, London, Hodder & Stoughton, 1963
The Arts and Their Mission, trans. L. Monges and V. Moore, New York, Anthroposophic Press, 1964
Three Streams in Human Evolution, trans. C. Davy, London, Rudolf Steiner Press, 1965
A Theory of Knowledge Implicit in Goethe's World Conception, trans. O. D. Wannamaker, New York, Anthroposophic Press, 1968
Karmic Relationships in Esoteric Studies, trans. G. Adams, C. Davey and D. S. Osmond, 8 vols., London, Rudolf Steiner Press, 1972–83
Between Death and Rebirth, trans. E. H. Goddard and D. S. Osmond, London, Rudolf Steiner Press, 1975

Deeper Insights into Education, trans. R. Querido, New York, Anthroposophic Press, 1983

The Cycle of the Year as Breathing Process of the Earth, trans. B. Betteridge and F. E. Dawson, New York, Anthroposophic Press, 1984

An Introduction to Eurythmy, trans. G. Hahn, New York, Anthroposophic Press, 1984

The Ahrimanic Deception, trans. M. Cotterell, New York, Anthroposophic Press, 1985

The Karma of Materialism, trans. R. Everett, London, Rudolf Steiner Press, 1985

The Renewal of the Social Organism, trans. E. Bowen Wedgwood and R. Marriott, London, Rudolf Steiner Press, 1985

Destinies of Individuals and of Nations, trans. A. R. Meuss, London, Rudolf Steiner Press, 1986

Aspects of Human Evolution, trans. R. Stebbing, Hudson, NY, Anthroposophic Press, 1987

The Karma of Untruthfulness, trans. J. Collis, 2 vols., London, Rudolf Steiner Press, 1988–92

Stokes, H. N. ed., *Letter from Mr T. H. Martyn to Mrs Besant*, Washington DC, H. N. Stokes, 1921

Symonds, J., *Madame Blavatsky*, London, Odhams, 1959

Taylor, A., *Laurence Oliphant*, Oxford University Press, 1982
Annie Besant, Oxford University Press, 1992

Taylor, M. E., *Remembering P. D. Ouspensky*, Yale University Library, 1978

Tillett, G., *The Elder Brother: A Biography of Charles Webster Leadbeater*, London, Routledge & Kegan Paul, 1982

Tribe, D., *President Charles Bradlaugh MP*, London, Elek, 1971

van Manen, J., *A Mysterious Manuscript*, Adyar, Office of *The Theosophist*, 1911

Wachsmuth, G., *The Life and Work of Rudolf Steiner*, New York, Whittier Press, 1955

Wachtmeister, C., *Reminiscences of Madame Blavatsky and the Secret Doctrine*, London, privately printed, 1893
HPB and the Present Crisis in the Theosophical Society, London, privately printed, 1895

Walker, K., *Venture With Ideas*, London, Jonathan Cape, 1951
A Study of Gurdjieff's Teaching, London, Jonathan Cape, 1957

Webb, J., *The Occult Establishment*, La Salle, Ill., Open Court Publishing, 1976

The Harmonious Circle, London, Thames & Hudson, 1980

Wolff, R. L., *Strange Stories and Other Explorations in Victorian Fiction*, Boston, Gambit, 1971

Whyte, F., *The Life of W. T. Stead*, London, Jonathan Cape, 1925

Whyte, H., *H. P. Blavatsky*, Adyar, TPH, 1920

Wood, E., *Clairvoyant Investigations by C. W. Leadbeater*, Adyar, TPH, 1947

Wright, F. L. *An Autobiography*, London, Faber & Faber, 1945

Yates, F., *The Rosicrucian Enlightenment*, London, Arkana, 1986

Yeats, W. B., *Collected Works*, 8 vols., Stratford on Avon, 1908

Yeats, W. B., *Memoirs*, ed. D. Donoghue, London, Macmillan, 1972

INDEX

Abbott, E. A.: *Flatland*, 159
Abdul Hamid Estates Inc., 298–300
Abdullah, Achmed, 175
Adare, Edwin Richard Wyndham
  Wyndham-Quin, 3rd Earl of
  Dunraven and Mount-Earl, 12
Adyar (Madras): as Theosophical
  Society HQ, 66, 107, 267; and
  Society conflicts, 68; Emma
  Coulomb scandals at, 78, 80, 82;
  and Tingley's Point Loma,
  112–13; Leadbeater at, 117;
  hierarchical arrangement, 162;
  Krishna attends 1925
  Convention, 270–1
Aetherius Church, 380–2
Agapemone (Abode of Love),
  Spaxton, Somerset, 6–7
Agastya, Master Rishi, 144, 211
Ahriman (spirit), 145, 249, 253
Aivanhof, Omraam Mikhael, 383
Akashic Record, 120, 130
Alexander, F. M., 329
Alexandria Foundation, 399
Ali, Ikbal, 395
Ames, Julia, 93
Anderson, Margaret, 257, 289–90,
  343; *The Unknowable Gurdjieff*,
  290
Andreae, Johann Valentin, 38

Anthroposophical Society (and
  Anthroposophy): Steiner founds,
  155–7; and Great War, 165–6,
  170; attracts Theosophists, 205;
  and education, 227; and Dornach
  school, 233–4; and dance, 237;
  decline, 248, 249; Steiner on
  Movement, 251; persecuted in
  Germany, 284; revival and
  influence, 387
Arnold, Matthew and Thomas, 312
Arundale, Francesca, 90, 118, 129,
  137, 208
Arundale, George: and Leadbeater,
  118, 209; teaches Krishnamurti,
  132, 210–12; on Temple of Rosy
  Cross, 139; marriage, 208, 217,
  266; with Krishnamurti in
  England, 210; and control of
  Liberal Catholic Church, 267;
  Krishnamurti's hostility to, 226;
  dispute with Krishnamurti, 266,
  269; in Holland, 267; projects,
  ambitions and directives, 267–8,
  273; 1925 visit to Adyar, 270;
  disbelieves Krishnamurti's status,
  271, 274; Leadbeater opposes,
  273; and Krishnamurti's assets on
  leaving Theosophical Society,
  279; succeeds Besant as President